UNIVERSITY OF
WINCHESTER

RETHINKING THE GREAT WHITE NORTH
Race, Nature, and the Historical Geographies of Whiteness in Canada

Edited by Andrew Baldwin, Laura Cameron, and Audrey Kobayashi

UBCPress·Vancouver·Toronto

20 19 18 17 16 15 14 13 12 11   5 4 3 2 1

Printed in Canada on FSC-certified ancient-forest-free paper
(100% post-consumer recycled) that is processed chlorine- and acid-free.

Library and Archives Canada Cataloguing in Publication

Rethinking the Great White North : race, nature, and the historical geographies of whiteness in Canada / edited by Andrew Baldwin, Laura Cameron, and Audrey Kobayashi.

Includes bibliographical references and index.
Also issued in electronic format.
ISBN 978-0-7748-2013-4 (bound); ISBN 978-0-7748-2014-1 (pbk.)

1. Canada, Northern – Social conditions. 2. Canada, Northern – Historical geography. 3. Whites – Race identity – Canada. 4. Native peoples – Canada, Northern – Social conditions. 5. Canada – Race relations. 6. Racism – Canada. I. Kobayashi, Audrey, 1951- II. Cameron, Laura, 1966- III. Baldwin, Andrew, 1970-

FC104.R468 2011   305.800971   C2011-903657-6

---

e-book ISBNs: 978-0-7748-2015-8 (pdf); 978-0-7748-2016-5 (epub)

Canadä

UBC Press gratefully acknowledges the financial support for our publishing program of the Government of Canada (through the Canada Book Fund), the Canada Council for the Arts, and the British Columbia Arts Council.

This book has been published with the help of a grant from the Canadian Federation for the Humanities and Social Sciences, through the Aid to Scholarly Publications Program, using funds provided by the Social Sciences and Humanities Research Council of Canada.

UBC Press
The University of British Columbia
2029 West Mall
Vancouver, BC V6T 1Z2
www.ubcpress.ca

Contents

Acknowledgments / ix

Introduction: Where Is the Great White North?
Spatializing History, Historicizing Whiteness / 1
ANDREW BALDWIN, LAURA CAMERON, AND AUDREY KOBAYASHI

Part 1: Identity and Knowledge

1 "A Phantasy in White in a World That Is Dead":
Grey Owl and the Whiteness of Surrogacy / 19
BRUCE ERICKSON

2 Indigenous Knowledge and the History of Science, Race,
and Colonial Authority in Northern Canada / 39
STEPHEN BOCKING

3 Cap Rouge Remembered? Whiteness, Scenery, and
Memory in Cape Breton Highlands National Park / 62
CATRIONA SANDILANDS

Part 2: City Spaces

4 The "Occult Relation between Man and the Vegetable": Transcendentalism, Immigrants, and Park Planning in Toronto, c. 1900 / 85

PHILLIP GORDON MACKINTOSH

5 SARS and Service Work: Infectious Disease and Racialization in Toronto / 107

CLAIRE MAJOR AND ROGER KEIL

6 Shimmering White Kelowna and the Examination of Painless White Privilege in the Hinterland of British Columbia / 127

LUIS L.M. AGUIAR AND TINA I.L. MARTEN

Part 3: Arctic Journeys

7 Inscription, Innocence, and Invisibility: Early Contributions to the Discursive Formation of the North in Samuel Hearne's *A Journey to the Northern Ocean* / 147

RICHARD MILLIGAN AND TYLER MCCREARY

8 Copper Stories: Imaginative Geographies and Material Orderings of the Central Canadian Arctic / 169

EMILIE CAMERON

Part 4: Native Land

9 Temagami's Tangled Wild: The Making of Race, Nature, and Nation in Early-Twentieth-Century Ontario / 193

JOCELYN THORPE

10 Resolving "the Indian Land Question"? Racial Rule and Reconciliation in British Columbia / 211

BRIAN EGAN

11 Changing Land Tenure, Defining Subjects: Neo-Liberalism and Property Regimes on Native Reserves / 233
JESSICA DEMPSEY, KEVIN GOULD, AND JUANITA SUNDBERG

Interlocations

Extremity: Theorizing from the Margins / 259
KAY ANDERSON

Colonization: The Good, the Bad, and the Ugly / 264
SHERENE H. RAZACK

Notes / 272

References / 285

List of Contributors / 318

Index / 322

Acknowledgments

Compiling this collection of essays has been an immensely rewarding experience. Considerable time and energy have gone into the publication of this text, much of it in the form of assistance and commitment from numerous people. We wish to acknowledge those without whose labour this collection would not have been possible: Loren Becker, Priya Sinha, and Martha Moon. Those who assisted with the workshop include Joan Knox, Sheila MacDonald and Kathy Hoover, Matt Rogalsky, Josh Lyon, Kym Nacita, and Paul Treitz. We owe each of you an enormous debt of thanks. We offer a special thanks to Cheryl Sutherland for her work coordinating the Kingston workshop and to Victoria Henderson and Lily Hoang for compiling the text for UBC Press. At UBC Press, we acknowledge the efforts of Randy Schmidt, Megan Brand, Ann Macklem, and Deborah Kerr.

In February 2008, we hosted a workshop in Kingston, Ontario, where most of the essays in this book were presented. The dialogue was a robust one, and we wish to thank all those who participated. After each author presented his or her paper, an invited discussant commented on it. The chapters in this text owe much to this process. We wish to thank the discussants for their generous intellectual contributions: (in alphabetical order) Kay Anderson, Claire Campbell, Richard Day, Caroline Desbiens, Terry Goldie, Renée Hulan, Alan MacEachern, Minelle Mahtani, Jill Scott, and Peter Van Wyck. Special thanks also are due to Kay Anderson and Sherene

Razack, who were given the daunting task of commenting on the entire collection of papers as a final exercise. Both offered incisive essays, which appear as a closing section called Interlocations. We also thank Renisa Mawani, Lauren Vedal, Amina Mire, and Leela Viswanathan for their important contributions, and Paul Carl from the Four Directions Aboriginal Students Centre at Queen's University for welcoming participants to Kingston. Michael Kerr and Duberlis Ramos from the Colour of Poverty Campaign gave a presentation on the racialization of poverty in Canada, which provided an important political economic context and for which we are most grateful.

We want to thank the Social Sciences and Humanities Research Council of Canada for providing us with generous funding through the Aid to Research Workshops conduit. Thanks also to the Network in Canadian History and Environment, the Department of Geography at Queen's University, the Canada Research Chair in the Historical Geography of Nature, the Queen's University Office for Research Services, the Queen's University Faculty of Arts and Sciences Dean's Conference Fund, and the Queen's University Vice-President Academic for their generous support.

Andrew Baldwin wishes to thank Anne Godlewska and Fiona Mackenzie and all the participants in the "Nature, Environment, Whiteness" paper sessions at the 2007 annual meeting of the Association of American Geographers. Most of all, he thanks Tara, Quinn, and Adele.

Laura Cameron would like to thank the Queen's Coalition of Anti-Racist Faculty and her inspiring students, particularly Drew Bednasek, Emilie Cameron, Matt Cavers, Sophie Edwards, Kirsten Greer, and Martha Moon. Special thanks to Matt and Arden Rogalsky for their support given in so many ways.

Audrey Kobayashi wishes to extend heartfelt thanks to Emilie Cameron, Kym Nacita, and Cheryl Sutherland for their multifaceted support, and special thanks to Mark Rosenberg for everything he does to make things both possible and enjoyable.

Finally, Laura and Audrey wish to acknowledge Andrew Baldwin's vision and dedication, which have been key to the success of this project from the start.

RETHINKING THE GREAT WHITE NORTH

Introduction
Where Is the Great White North?
Spatializing History, Historicizing Whiteness

ANDREW BALDWIN, LAURA CAMERON,
AND AUDREY KOBAYASHI

Myth is constituted by the loss of the historical quality of things.

– Roland Barthes, *Mythologies*

Racisms also dehistoricize – translating historically specific structures into the timeless language of nature.

– Stuart Hall, *Race, Articulation and Societies Structured in Dominance*

The Great White North is an enduring Canadian myth. It weaves history, geography, aesthetics, science, and even comedy into a national imaginary that invokes a metaphor of nature's purity to reinforce norms of racial purity. The double meaning of the word "white" parallels a double movement in our social and cultural history both to assert the dominance of whiteness as a cultural norm and to build a sense of national identity linked closely to nature and wilderness. Non-whites and Indigenous peoples have been excluded from that norm to one degree or another since the nation's inception. But whiteness also suggests innocence. According to Sherene Razack (2002b, 2), "a quintessential feature of white settler mythologies is, therefore, the disavowal of conquest, genocide, slavery, and the exploitation of the labour of peoples of colour."

The physical North establishes a point of reference, meliorates carto-graphic anxiety, and founds Canada's spatial imaginary as both location and expanse. In both cartographic and mythical terms, the "North" is a mutating landscape whose horizons seem forever in retreat. Its meaning has shifted significantly over time. For much of our history, it was the locus of the long-sought Northwest Passage. During the Cold War, it was a hovering zone of danger that sent us scurrying to build the Distant Early Warning (DEW) Line as a fortification against communism (Farish 2006). From the Canada First movement to John Diefenbaker's northern development rhetoric to the politics of diamond mining (Grace 2002), the North is invoked as an im-portant source of economic value. In late modernity, melting polar ice has set off a cascade of environmental and geopolitical anxieties. Sometimes the "Great White North" refers in stolid and timeless terms to the snowy terri-tory north of the Arctic Circle, spatially remote, ahistorical, pre-human; but at others, it is synonymous with the country as a whole, its people, and the values upon which the nation was built, a creation of a population forging a common destiny. But transcending its meaning as an economic and political frontier, the North draws together cultural value and identity to produce a metaphor of imperial grandeur, innocence, and sovereignty.

The late pianist Glenn Gould, surely an icon of Canadian arts and cul-ture, is one example of a culture broker who has helped construct the myth of the Great White North. He addressed the link between the ideas of the North and Canadian identity in a 1968 one-hour Canadian Broadcasting Corporation (CBC) radio program titled "The Idea of North."[1] He interviews a nurse, a geographer, an anthropologist, a bureaucrat, and a surveyor – all inhabitants of the South who travelled to the North – about their personal experiences, setting their words together in a fugue-like discourse to achieve a social construction that he calls "contrapuntal." According to biographer B.W. Powe (1987, 164), "Typically, when he refers to Canada, it is his ground, mere space. 'The Idea of North' was for Gould an emptiness waiting for re-creation: the North was a landscape of leaves, wind, water, elements to be managed by his (limitless?) electronic imagination."

Experimental and avant-garde as Gould's music and radio documentar-ies were, they capture what he believed to be the multiple threads that con-stitute a whole fabric. Gould believed that contrapuntal music, or any form of discourse including the radio interview, could be the basis for creating, or imagining, a state of existence by giving rhythm, a kind of life force or ani-mation, to ideas that, although different in rhythm or voice, blend harmoni-ously when played together. Contrapuntal music, like social mythology and like landscape, gains meaning and strength through simultaneous expression. Gould's rendition therefore displays the immense power of cultural iconography to construct meanings that run deeply through the national identity.

We seek to tell a different story in this collection, however, about both the mythical and physical qualities of the Great White North and its meaning for Canadian racialized identity. The shuddering absence of Inuit or First Nations voice in Gould's contrapuntalism baldly illustrates a point now well established in cultural analysis: meaning is generated as much through presence as absence, as much through what is said as through what remains unsaid and silenced. The resonant contrapuntalism that consolidates the North as a textured presence in Gould and in Canadian iconography is simultaneously sliced apart by effacement. The effect, though, is not to produce a discordant image that recuperates the aesthetic through asymmetric sound, but to leave the North open as a route into our vulnerability, as a route for thinking precariousness as a universal human condition whose power-geometries never fully come to rest.

We foreground the racial legacy that infuses northern narrative and aesthetic, practice and science, history and geography (Hulan 2002), not by recounting explicit acts of racial violence perpetrated against people of colour, nor by retelling the history of colonial violence, the forced settlement of the Inuit, or the routine denial of First Nations treaty rights, now such an entrenched element of Canadian political economy, although all these things are part of our national heritage. We focus, rather, on conceptualizing the Great White North through the category of whiteness, now a standard feature of contemporary race and racism analysis. Posing whiteness as a fundamental category in the northern imaginary instigates debate among the contributors on the myriad ways that the North articulates with, diverges from, abets, and intermingles with the related categories of race and nature as they conjugate across the Canadian landscape. In so doing, we draw inspiration from what has been called the "cultural politics of race and nature" (Moore, Kosek, and Pandian 2003, 6), an analytical mode that traces the genealogical, recursive, and performative ties that bind categories of "nature" and "race" in the exercise of white normativity and power. In short, we press theoretical advances in debates about race and racism into dialogue with a concurrent rethinking of nature now under way across the social sciences (see Cronon 1996b; Braun and Castree 1998; Whatmore 2002).

Notwithstanding the fact that since the adoption of a multiculturalism policy in 1971 there is at least nominal official recognition of Canada as a diverse society, the normative vision of Canada as a white man's country is still pervasive. We believe that the power of collective imagination to give life to metaphors such as that of the Great White North provides one of the reasons that racialized norms are so difficult to shake free of their social moorings. We offer this volume, therefore, as a collection of critical analyses of this enduring metaphor.

Situating Whiteness Scholarship

By placing these essays together in a single volume, we make several assumptions about race, nature, and whiteness. First, and perhaps most important, race is a social construction. We do not wish to "re-ontologize race" in any biophysical sense (Saldanha 2006). Instead, we insist, emphatically so, that race and the meaning of race are constructed within broader social discourses that touch upon so many aspects of our lives – politics, economics, culture, education – in powerful ways. This means that specific kinds of skin carry all sorts of interrelated, contradictory meanings, some derogatory (black as dangerous) and some far more ambivalent ("Asian" as intelligent). It also means rejecting the deeply troubling assumption that the meanings of skin are rooted in biology, genetics, or culture. The ontology of race may be floating, its meanings contingent, but it remains fungible, and its effects are no less felt, embodied, and material. Meanings of skin are produced in relation and as integral to all manner of epistemologies (knowledge systems), including those of science, biology, genetics, and culture, and their attendant modes of power and social control. Moreover, race thinking is not simply a product of racial knowledge or outmoded racial hierarchy; it grounds the very production of knowledge, whether scientific (see Bocking, Chapter 2, this volume), geographical (Kobayashi 2003), literary (Coleman 2006), historical (Razack 2002b), legal (Mawani 2007; Razack 2008), or what have you. In spite of its constructedness, race remains an important analytical device for thinking about social relations both historically and in the present. Unlike liberal proponents of "post-racism" (Gordon and Newfield 1994), who espouse a rejection of the term "race" on the basis that race has no place in rational thought and practice, we believe that the persistence of racialized social relations – including the racialization of poverty (Galabuzi 2008), environmental racism (Pulido 2000), "white" neighbourhoods (Dwyer and Jones 2000), racist law (Razack 2008) and immigration policy, and racialized discourses (Goldberg 1993) – demands that the idea be retained. We say this because as an essentialism (which we do not espouse) it represents the historical product of social construction.

A second assumption at work in this text is that "whiteness" is a corollary to race. This is one of the formative insights of what has come to be called whiteness studies in Anglo-American social science (see, for example, Ignatiev and Garvey 1996; Saldanha 2007). The category "race," at least in the so-called West, has historically been used to characterize difference. Early representations of race, current in the eighteenth century and persisting to the present, tended to associate race with putative biological difference. According to this mode of thinking, outward signs of biological differences, such as skin colour and hair texture, were signs of an inner or innate difference shared by all those with similar physical attributes. In the post–Second World War era, many argue that biological racism has been supplanted by cultural racism, in which one's culture comes to signify one's race (Henry and Tator 2010). One of the operative assumptions in whiteness studies is that both forms of race thinking – race as biological *difference* or race as cultural *difference* – are conceptualized against some assumed white norm. Moreover, both logics either explicitly or implicitly organize difference into a racialized hierarchy at the top of which sits white normativity. The more a so-called race of people was believed to differ – in morality, industry, or capacity for rational thought – from the presupposed superiority of the white person, the farther down it would be placed on the racial hierarchy. If we take these insights together, within the logic of race, whiteness is the standard against which all other races are measured or valued. Or, to put it in slightly different terms, whiteness is the norm against which constructed racial differences become meaningful. Race thinking is a system of power whose violence lies in its capacity to normalize whiteness (Kobayashi and Peake 2000).

A good many whiteness studies in the Anglo-American tradition of social sciences trace the genealogy of whiteness as a category of social identification (Du Bois 1966). Much of this work is found in American labour history, perhaps not surprisingly given how profoundly the history and abolition of slavery have shaped all manner of American identifications. (We note that pre-Confederation Canada is similarly marked by a history of slavery, although one all too often erased from official accounts.) Of these historical accounts, several stand out. In 1935, W.E.B. Du Bois wrote one of the most comprehensive histories of black America's contribution to post–Civil War reconstruction. Du Bois presented what is now a formative idea in contemporary whiteness studies: whiteness is a designation granted to the American working class as a form of psychological compensation for its low social status. It designates white privilege as a form of economic self-investment, or currency. The 1990s saw a profusion of texts that traced the historical origins of such privilege. Perhaps most notable is David Roediger's *Wages of Whiteness* (1991). Roediger's principal argument is that from the early nineteenth century, the white American working class struggled to differentiate itself from black slavery for fear of lapsing into conditions of white slavery. This was a fear of attenuated freedom and autonomy resulting in the diminished capacity of white workers to identify with the principles of the American Revolution: freedom from indirect taxation (or rule) and individual liberty. At stake in the whiteness of nineteenth-century America was access to American identity, specifically workers' capacity to represent the revolutionary republican ideal. Of course, the paradox of this psychological wage is that the primary beneficiary of the American Revolution was the bourgeoisie, not the working class, which would by definition remain in the thrall of the American bourgeoisie and capital. Another account of the historicity of whiteness is Noel Ignatiev's *How the Irish Became White* (1995), in which he argues that American working-class Irish were not always thought of as white; the English, for instance, commonly associated Irishness with negritude well into the twentieth century. Ignatiev suggests that the Irish were accepted into the fold of white privilege through their denigration of and active dissociation from blackness. Helen Marrow (2009) has suggested that a similar political distancing is repeated in contemporary America where newly arrived Latino immigrants in North Carolina distance themselves from the experience of African Americans.

To frame whiteness as just a historical artifact tethered to class politics, however, forecloses geography and geographical imaginaries as integral to the consolidation and circulation of white normativity. Following the French philosopher of space Henri Lefebvre (1991, 44), we contend that if whiteness is above all else a complex system of contradictory and converging values, then the stability of such values is not pre-given, but is instead guaranteed through some corresponding "discourse upon social space." Moreover, if white normativity is integral to the formulation of historical and contemporary forms of racism, its power lies in its unequal capacity to naturalize its geography. This is not to suggest that white normativity has a singular geography or history. We have no interest in privileging a white meta-narrative. It is, however, to argue that whiteness in all its historical-geographic variability is fundamentally concerned with spatializing racial difference in ways that allow for its spatial practices to pass unquestioned. This observation leads us back to Stuart Hall's (1980) germinal insight that racisms are historically situated phenomena whose contours shift and change in response to specific social histories. We would like to renovate Hall's insight by suggesting that racisms are not simply historical, but historical-geographic.

If the capacity to naturalize one's geography is integral to the exercise of white normativity and the maintenance of white privilege, our argument points to the idea that nature is an important resource in the articulation of whiteness. Such a view parallels a series of related social sciences interventions, not least in geography, about the naturalness – or rather the unnaturalness – of nature (Braun and Castree 1998, 2001). Common across these interventions is the idea that "nature," though conjuring up notions of innocence, aesthetic beauty, and the absence of human folly, is actually a deeply fraught term instrumental in maintaining all manner of oppressive social relations. There is not scope to develop this idea in any detail here, but the gist of these debates is that nature is a social construct used to maintain hegemonic social relations across a number of epistemological sites, from colonialism (Braun 2002) to capitalism (N. Smith 1984) to racism (Kobayashi 2003). Our motive in compiling these essays into a single collection stems from an interest in historicizing nature in the Canadian context and teasing out how white normativity in Canada is contingent upon historical geographies of nature. In this sense, we consider this collection an opening, a point of departure for subsequent debate and theorizing on the historical-geographic relations between nature, whiteness, and the discipline of geography in Canada.

Such an interest is in keeping with what Donald Moore, Jake Kosek, and Anand Pandian (2003, 3) insist is "the historical specificity of particular racisms and naturalisms." For them, "the political stakes of race and nature lie in the ways they become *articulated* together in particular historical moments" (ibid., emphasis in original). And as Hall (1980) reminds us, the nation provides perhaps the most important site for considering the historical situatedness of racisms. Racism and naturalism emerge out of specific national historical contexts and discourses. Given that such narrations are spatialized (they always are), we are most interested in exploring a historical geography of race, nature, and whiteness in this text. Nonetheless, by interrogating race, nature, and whiteness through the site of the nation, we do not mean to privilege the nation-state as the exclusive formation through which race, nature, and whiteness articulate; national discourses find spatial expression in a host of other historical geographies – the urban, the rural, landscape, place. This book therefore addresses national discourses in these sites, too.

Only in recent years, with the rise of awareness that the Canadian nation, past and present, is thoroughly racialized, have scholars been in a position to question the complicated process through which metaphors of national identity circulate. This growing area of research has only just scratched the surface of Canadian experience, and scant attention has been paid to how it might usefully inform our understanding of Canada, Canadian identity, and Canadian geography. This is a significant oversight for a number of reasons.

Canada is routinely constructed in liberal democratic discourse as a tolerant multicultural state, lending Canadians a degree of innocence when compared to more overtly intolerant national cultures; however, as a number of critical scholars now argue (Brown 2006; Thobani 2007), multiculturalism, along with the principle of tolerance that underwrites it, can be a profoundly depoliticizing ideal. On the one hand, tolerance poses as a discourse of justice, especially when used in conjunction with political liberalism (Brown 2006). For instance, in the aftermath of the Second World War's eugenic atrocities, tolerance talk emerged as one of the post-war principles that would modernize international relations as a means of bringing justice to an otherwise genocidal twentieth century (United Nations 1948; UNESCO 1956). Such a discourse was recapitulated in Canadian nationalist multiculturalism, perhaps most closely associated with Pierre Elliott Trudeau (Thobani 2007). Multiculturalism would mark a new beginning in so-called race relations, replacing denigration with toleration as the dominant value deployed to manage difference in the public domain. And yet, on the other hand, it is precisely the use of tolerance as a political tactic that calls attention to its depoliticizing effects (Kobayashi 1993; Brown 2006). While tolerance appears to correct historical injustices by offering the marginalized an entry into the dominant social order, it simultaneously depoliticizes by denying that the marginalized are constituted by history and power. The marginalized are simply objects to be tolerated, but their marginality never requires explanation.

The limits of tolerance are confirmed, however, when one confronts Canada's colonial legacy and the historical geographies of dispossession and displacement that continue to mark the experience of non-white and Aboriginal people in Canada. So, despite liberal assurances to the contrary, Canada is a polity whose juridical-political structure, history, spatial arrangements, and social relations are thoroughly racialized and marked by racist ideology. This may come as a bold, even shocking, statement to some readers, so let us clarify our position here. We are not saying that Canada is full of neo-Nazi groups and routinely the site of physical violence that targets people of colour, although we need to be clear that extreme forms of xenophobia are alive and well in Canada, as they are in all polities. Rather, racism is about much more than simply overt forms of hatred; it is an elemental part of all systems of representation, whether academic, scientific, aesthetic, or national. What this means is that the struggle to challenge and undermine "race thinking" (Arendt 1973, as used by Razack 2008) extends beyond merely identifying and prosecuting acts of racial hatred or even marginalization, as important as these are. It also extends beyond the cozy edification afforded by multiculturalism and tolerance talk. Such a politics means taking stock of the ways that race thinking infuses systems of representation, permeates the symbolic register, organizes the production of knowledge, and provides a foundation for conceptualizing difference or sameness; in other words, it thoroughly conditions the always discursive relations between citizens. In the Canadian context, this means that in order to gain a fulsome appreciation for how race thinking organizes both iconic and mundane forms of life, we must interrogate the spatial production of national symbolism and knowledge, and the sites in which race is foundational as opposed to merely peripheral, accidental, or irrational. Such a project necessarily means attending to all manner of natures that symbolize Canada, "wilderness" and "North" being perhaps two of the most obvious. It is perhaps the contrapuntal quality of these expressions of race thinking, the simultaneous recitation of ideas and images that in themselves are banal but speaking together create a symphonic harmony, that gives the movement of race thinking its animation and strength. The essays in this book trace this relation across several sites, not only the Arctic, but other landscapes both "wild" and cultivated, including urban landscapes and tourist parkland.

The cultural politics of nature, race, and whiteness bear importantly on Canada in another way: Canada is often recognized both for its stunning natural beauty and its expansive reserves of natural resources. Official Canadian national culture celebrates both facets, often in very contradictory ways. Yet rarely do we ask whose histories are called upon to understand Canada as a "natural" space or a storehouse of natural resources. Nor do we ask whose histories are elided when Canada is imagined in such idealized, naturalized terms. Two examples illustrate what we mean in this respect. The first comes from *Globe and Mail* columnist Margaret Wente, a conservative feminist with a reputation for seizing on the racial angle of issues current in the mainstream media. In a recent polemic over Canadianness, wilderness, and sexuality, Wente recounts her own efforts to connect with Canadianness via wilderness canoe trips. It's a pointless anecdote until, in closing, she remarks that she's had sex in a canoe and worries over whether the children of Pakistani and Chinese immigrants will think to do the same. The implication is that somehow Canada might become less Canadian unless measures are taken to ensure that immigrants are taught the j-stroke. This is citational history at its most insidious. Wente's intervention was inspired by Pierre Berton, like Gould a Canadian cultural icon, whose alleged comment linking Canadianness and making love in a canoe has had far-reaching implications.[2] Against a backdrop of imagined wilderness, it privileges the universality of Canadian canoe culture, marginalizes dark-skinned bodies as peripheral to national origins, and positions white heterosexual procreation in a canoe as the highest achievement of national identity. Tongue-in-cheek or not, it resonates deeply with the constructed meaning of the nation.

Historian Ian McKay (2008, 350, 351, 354) recounts an equally stark positioning of whiteness at the core of early-twentieth-century Canadian identity possessed by white settlers:

> Their Canada was in essence a White settler society, and the nationalism of the majority of its population was a British nationalism. This Canada was, if the term is taken in its fullest cultural sense, a grand experiment in 'whiteness,' an imagined community founded upon the British occupation of the northern section of North America ... To be a true Canadian was to be White, English-speaking, and Protestant – with some allowance made for French-Canadian Catholics, provided they were deferential to the Empire ... Whiteness in Canada was an expression of confidence in British geopolitical might and cultural pre-eminence – and haunted by an ambient dread that both might be lost in the twinkling of an eye. It was both anti-modern, based upon notions of blood, soil and military valour, and ultra-modern, mobilizing up to date technology and drawing, so it was thought, upon the latest word in evolutionary theory. It gloried in the steel rails and steamships that bound the Empire together, and visualized a future in which the backward and benighted peoples of the world would be redeemed and reordered through their exposure to their racial and cultural superiors.

McKay's point is that the standard "railroads and wheat" story of Canada is better understood as a white imperial project authored by the British and carried out by their white territorial minions. This observation reinforces the contention that both nature and whiteness are social constructions, the result of specific human actions, taken both by choice and without reflection as part of an assumed normative identity.

Why This Text?

The essays gathered here are intended as resources to help understand and frame complex issues that are deeply rooted in specific past geographies but that frequently burst through in everyday instances of incomprehension and violence. *Rethinking the Great White North* is organized in four parts, each of which explores an important historical geography of race, nature, and whiteness in Canada. These four geographies – identity and knowledge, city spaces, Arctic journeys, and Native land – represent both commonplace and critical entry points to urgently needed discussions in society today. The organization reflects our desire to make this volume accessible to the wider public and teachers of, for example, urban geography, Indigenous studies, Canada's North, and tourism studies, who seek to engage students in these vital issues.

Part 1, "Identity and Knowledge," begins by confronting the spatial logic of race head-on, exploring how whiteness in Canada works as the standard against which all other "races" are valued. In Chapter 1, Bruce Erickson examines the life and legacy of early-twentieth-century conservationist Archibald Belaney, who adopted the First Nations identity of Grey Owl to authorize his concerns for the vanishing Canadian wilderness. Erickson argues that Grey Owl's popularity allows us insight into how whiteness as a master signifier is produced through the visual coding of bodies and space, here via the codification of "wilderness as a national white space" (22). Science, a mélange of relatively well-respected and funded practices in the North, is often (mis)understood to be a producer of neutral and objective knowledge of nature, floating free in universal space. In Chapter 2, drawing upon situated histories of northern science, Stephen Bocking charts the changing status of Indigenous knowledge for scientific endeavour. He reveals how whiteness "maintains an analogical relationship with science": both whiteness and science "assert their status as unmarked or as objective," and both enjoy and exercise the power that this status allows (42-43). Bocking's argument throws in stark geographical relief a key distinction between science and Indigenous knowledge: science, "in asserting an absence of racial identity, tacitly affirms its whiteness," whereas Indigenous knowledge "asserts an identity defined in terms of both race and place" (43). In

Chapter 3, Catriona Sandilands critically examines Cape Breton Highlands National Park and highlights the permanent removal of the Acadian community of Cap Rouge in the making of this national domain. She underscores the ways in which increasing *ecologization* of parks has facilitated erasures of human presence and activity: excising the social to create natural sites of nature's functioning renders places timeless and outside of history. She argues that the whiteness of parks is "so universal that it appears to be written in nature itself" (81).

How have politics of nature and whiteness shaped Canadian cities and the lives of southerners? In Part 2, "City Spaces," Phillip Mackintosh begins Chapter 4, his study of transcendentalism and the park-planning impulse in turn-of-the-twentieth-century Toronto, by asking, "Did 'white' haute bourgeois reformers use 'transcendentalized' parks to transform immigrants into 'higher forms' of citizens?" (86). In answering this question, Mackintosh investigates the ways that nature, in the form of parks and playgrounds, was positioned by Toronto's city planners not only to beautify the city but also as a method to erase immigrant identity and to racially sanitize immigrant neighbourhoods. In Chapter 5, figuring nature not as "cleanser" but as "contagion," Claire Major and Roger Keil explore a different nexus of nature-race politics in twenty-first-century Toronto. The 2003 outbreak of severe acute respiratory syndrome (SARS) was a harrowing crisis for the city as a whole. It also exposed "the fault lines of racialization" (107). As Major and Keil argue, workers of colour, including nurses, hotel housekeepers, and live-in caregivers, were affected disproportionately by the outbreak of the disease and the subsequent racialization of community relations. Chapter 6, the final essay in this section, by Luis Aguiar and Tina Marten, moves west to the smaller urban centre of Kelowna, British Columbia, to examine how white privilege was secured in the hinterland and how it continues to play out in recruitment policies and settlement campaigns today. Registering alarm at how racialization continues to manifest in Kelowna, the authors urge a close examination and discussion not only of racist labour practices but of the history and geography of the white privilege that sustains inequality.

In Part 3, "Arctic Journeys," we present a complementary pair of essays that address an archetypal Canadian journey to the North but work to different critical ends. The journey is that of Hudson's Bay Company (HBC) explorer Samuel Hearne, who in 1771 travelled more than two thousand miles with his Chipewyan Dene guides, from Prince of Wales's Fort to the Coppermine River, near present-day Kugluktuk, Nunavut. The story has been retold countless times since, but its first appearance in written form was as Hearne's own narration, *A Journey to the Northern Ocean*. The Canadian Museum of Civilization frames this iconic Arctic story as one of benign intention and mutuality with the Arctic's inhabitants, but in Chapter 7, Richard Milligan and Tyler McCreary interrogate Hearne's text and the racial motivations that justified and ennobled the ensuing violent dispossession of land and power. Their discursive analysis highlights *A Journey*'s "stabilizing posture of innocence that was a necessary precedent for white dominance to attain the status of powerful invisibility" (148). Milligan and McCreary argue that any retelling of the story must aim "not to erase the violent intrusion of whiteness in the semiotics of space, but to expose the toxicity of its grammar and rhetoric" (165). Chapter 8, Emilie Cameron's engagement with Hearne, proceeds with a similar sense of gravity and responsibility. Tackling the material geography of story itself, Cameron posits that stories that anchor geographies of the Arctic are important "not only because of their imaginative force, but also because of their influence over the material conditions of life in the region" (170). She invokes actor-network theory as she approaches one of the key episodes in *A Journey*, the Bloody Falls massacre story, as a "material ordering practice" (172) and begins to follow a particular "natural" (183) material central to the narrative: copper. Finding that actor-network theory works best in tension with critical whiteness studies, Cameron suggests that alternative stories help us to "remember otherwise" (190) but adds that more work must be done to make these other stories matter.

The final section, Part 4, addresses the theme of "Native Land," a phrase boldly emblematic of white Canadian identity, with three chapters that focus on the implications of colonial injustice for Canada today. In Chapter 9, Jocelyn Thorpe interrogates the wilderness tourist destination of Ontario's Temagami, showing how travel writing, racialization, and the social construction of nature combined "to make Temagami appear 'naturally' as a wilderness space for white men to visit" (208-9). In creating this pre-eminent site of wild "national" nature, travel writers simultaneously expunged the Teme-Augama Anishnabai and their claim to land. Next, in Chapter 10's careful contextualization of the "Indian land question," Brian Egan contends that recent attempts to reconcile Indigenous peoples' claims to the territory of British Columbia with those of the state and private landowners are seeking to *stabilize* the normative view of BC as a white province governed by white sovereignty. In Chapter 11, Jessica Dempsey, Kevin Gould, and Juanita Sundberg approach the question of race, rights, and land by identifying the reproduction of racialized subjectivity in the insidious rhetoric of neo-liberal private property rights. For Dempsey, Gould, and Sundberg, this rhetoric reconstitutes Aboriginal subjectivity through a language of economic citizenship akin to the ideal typical values of Canadian white subjectivity: autonomous, landowning, self-sufficient, and industrious.

The collection ends with contributions from two prominent feminist anti-racist scholars: Kay Anderson and Sherene Razack. Considering our project from different places and positionalities, their pieces re-emphasize particular threads of the book's arguments and provide openings for further discussion. Together they call attention to an emergent methodological tension in the study of race and racism in the social sciences, between, on the one hand, a representational approach to the study of race and racism (Razack) and, on the other, post-humanism (Anderson).

Why Now?

These essays and closing interlocations draw out the historical geographical dimensions of white normativity in Canada by recounting genealogies of nature and whiteness. Yet as essential as historical context is to our analytical approach, we recognize the importance of reflecting on just what this project entails. Although nature is a key resource in the articulation of whiteness and white identity, it is often elevated by white people as a national universal, and with it the exalted white subjectivity by which it is constituted. Paradoxically, however, we note, following Robyn Wiegman (1999), that disaffiliation from universal signifiers that connote whiteness and promote white hegemony, such as some sacrosanct form of ahistorical or pre-historical nature, is also a common feature of white discourse. Disaffiliation is the practice by which white people distance themselves from the economy of signs that frame white hegemony. Its effect is profound: it allows the liberal majority to assert that racialization is something that *used* to occur but that no longer does, while the everyday embodiment of whiteness is simply absorbed into normative discourse, a part of nature. The discourse of white disaffiliation effectively places "white anti-racism" in a minority position, while giving white anti-racists the appearance of having transcended their whiteness, and indeed, having transcended race. In Canadian national discourse, multiculturalism is an important technology through which white disaffiliation is sustained because it allows white Canadians to believe that racism is no longer a structural feature of their political culture.

Perhaps more controversially, however, we note that the social construction of nature – now a standard feature of academic geography – provides a broad methodology through which white disaffiliation might be said to occur. This body of scholarship is important because it situates discourses of nature centrally within broader questions about hegemony; however, in quite another sense, it is a potentially dangerous intellectual project because it can treat questions about race as merely peripheral, not central. Indeed, as increasing numbers of white scholars distance themselves from the universals of nature in the interest of social, gender, or racial justice, we might begin to see more clearly how white hegemony operates through recourse to a new particularity. The danger here lies in the belief that newly forged particular solidarities between, say, white academics and individuals and groups racialized as non-white have somehow overcome colonialism or racism, when in fact they are contingent on the mobility of white subjectivity, the ability of white subjects to disavow prior claims to universality. This mobility is a defining feature of contemporary white privilege. Failure to recognize it risks reproducing white supremacy under the guise of a socially just particularism. There is no direct line of flight out of this troubling paradox.

Rethinking the Great White North provides a vocabulary for thinking about whiteness, nature, and Canada. To be white in Canada signifies all manner of values, some consistent with Canadian myth, some that directly contradict hegemonic Canadian values. On one level, this text helps navigate what it means to be white in Canada. It reminds us that being white is as much about innocence as it is about violent domination, as much about purity as about the imposition of order, as much about guilt and obsession with "goodness" (Ahmed 2004) as about absolution. It also draws our attention to the anxious desire to recuperate the meaning of whiteness – to find some way of being white in Canada that allows "white" Canadians to sit comfortably with the psychic scars that mark the skin of white identity. But perhaps above all, it reminds us of the fluidity of whiteness, its irreducibility, its shifting terms, and its extraordinary capacity to endure.

PART 1

IDENTITY AND KNOWLEDGE

1

"A Phantasy in White in a World That Is Dead"
Grey Owl and the Whiteness of Surrogacy

BRUCE ERICKSON

It is not hard to see that racial discourses affect, and are constructed through, bodies. How we make sense of racialized bodies, however, depends upon a variety of features, including the spaces those bodies inhabit. By looking at the discourse of wilderness in the writing and life of the popular naturalist Grey Owl, this chapter examines how wilderness has become enmeshed in the racial coding of bodies in Canada. Grey Owl's wilderness shows an investment in whiteness as a foundational category of being. His story, and the celebration of wilderness that follows it, is made legible by accepting whiteness as the privileged modern (Canadian) subject position. This suggestion pushes analyses of whiteness that focus on merely the unequal social relations that are a consequence of racial discourse.

Take George Lipsitz's (1998, 233) claim that "the problem with white people is not our whiteness, but our possessive investment in it." This notion indicates a common sentiment across whiteness studies – that it is not the physical properties of race that are problematic but the social relationships that have made those physical characteristics meaningful.[1] For Lipsitz, such relationships are clearly a matter of economics. His book documents various ways in which whiteness names a specific economic relationship, from property rates to employment opportunities. By documenting what he calls the "possessive investment in whiteness," Lipsitz (ibid.) details the profits received through strategies of racial differentiation and concludes that whiteness "has more to do with property than with pigment."

Lipsitz's argument is effective, especially through his empirical examples from the past fifty years. Yet throughout his analysis, he assumes that whiteness, or simply "white," is a pre-existing racial category at work within the framework of property capitalism. This assumption needs careful investigation, for despite the fact that the economic function of race is readily exposed with a little careful thought, race continues to be naturalized outside of the economic sphere. Thus, one consequence of an analytical focus on the economic investment in whiteness is that it can lead to a short-sighted counter-politics (McWhorter 2005). A privileged reading of the economic sphere of whiteness ignores the question of the subject's relationship to race and whiteness. When this occurs, whiteness studies run the risk of merely finding "ways of being white, (or of ceasing to be white) that purify individuals of racial complicity or guilt" (ibid., 551). The question then emerges: How does skin pigmentation eclipse its function in accumulating property?

Ladelle McWhorter (2005) states that the danger here stems from an analytical approach that characterizes the power of whiteness as a "power over" others. This view of power as juridical-political not only leaves whiteness studies in the precarious position of desiring its own innocence through, for instance, a divestiture of power, it also curtails the possibility of serious political action in relation to whiteness by non-white subjects. This is a fault not only of looking at race as an economic relationship but of any theory of whiteness as a set of privileges possessed, exercised, or enjoyed by individuals. To avoid this dangerous path, McWhorter suggests we illustrate the ways in which whiteness works through relations of power to create the subject of race itself. The economic analysis of whiteness illustrates how whiteness has been mobilized for economic gain, but McWhorter asks us to go further by considering how we come to recognize whiteness as a category. How is it, she asks, that we have been conditioned to accept race as part of a subject's being? This line of questioning views whiteness as a classifying logic that enables the larger system of racial differentiation in which whiteness is thought of as the founding principle of race rather than just a privileged actor within it.[2] I argue that this perspective works in tandem with the economic analysis of race by showing how capitalism is embedded within conceptions of what it means to be a subject. Borrowing from Kalpana Seshadri-Crooks (2000), I argue that whiteness is the master signifier of race, to use a term from Lacanian psychoanalysis, which "quilts" together various racial practices that, in turn, come to structure social organization (see also Winnubst 2006). Whiteness does so by establishing a specific visual field, most commonly understood as the marks of the body, as significant to social relations, attempting to assert a pre-discursive origin for race in anatomy. As a master signifier that guides our way of looking and our processes of assigning value, whiteness affects more than just our understanding of white people and their "others"; it also helps us understand property capitalism. I want to extend this claim by arguing that whiteness also helps us understand the concept of wilderness in Canada.

The relationship between capital and whiteness has long been a part of race relations in Canada, as Kristin Lozanski (2007, 224) points out: "In Canada, whiteness is synonymous with colonialism insomuch as the liberal, bourgeois, propertied self is literally founded upon Indigeneity. Any memorializing of colonial legacies in Canada is deeply embedded in a capitalist economic system wherein ownership of property and resources is mapped onto the annexation of land from Indigenous peoples, who continue to seek to carve out self-determination from a federalist system of government." Lozanski argues that, in Canada, the necessary connection between whiteness and indigeneity comes from the juridical classification of bodies. But she also states that this connection is formed out of a psychic investment in the idea that race is a necessary marker of one's being. European colonialism relied upon the logic of whiteness to establish the difference between self and other, a feat that inevitably tied the ontology of white subjects to the ability to materially control First Nations bodies.[3] Yet it is not merely control *over* bodies that is fundamental to the colonial production of whiteness in Canada, as Lozanski clearly shows, but also the production and control of *space.* Such control over space is abundantly evident in Canada in the memorializing of specific wilderness legacies, such as the idea of North (Shields 1991; Grace 2002; Hulan 2002) or the Group of Seven (MacHardy 1999; Jessup 2002). Although much has been written on these legacies, I want to examine the production of wilderness through the life of Archibald Belaney, better known as Grey Owl, an early-twentieth-century Canadian writer who achieved national notoriety in the 1930s as a proponent of wilderness conservation. Grey Owl is an important, yet paradoxical, figure in this respect. He provides a vivid example of how wilderness is coded through the figure of the Imaginary Indian (Francis 1992), yet we know his portrayal to be fraudulent. The use and acceptance of Indian surrogacy in Belaney's life and legacy to help us understand and preserve wilderness connects the discourse of whiteness, and the field of visibility that race relies upon, to the iconic wilderness of Canada. This image of wilderness is not only a matter of preserving "nature"; it is also complicit in preserving the whiteness of the nation.

My argument is built upon two central claims. First, Belaney's perform-ance as Grey Owl reflects the dominant use of "playing Indian" (Deloria 1998) as a prosthetic to the desires of the European nation. That is, it at-tempts to heal the wounds of colonialism without admitting responsibility. Second, the use of surrogacy to promote wilderness conservation estab-lished a connection between the visual codes of "Indian" (as exemplified by Grey Owl) and the generic vision of wilderness that Belaney portrays in his writing. For example, though knowing the danger of his masquerade, Margaret Atwood (1995, 60) asserts an important place for Grey Owl pre-cisely because of his care for wilderness (which is necessarily mobilized through his masquerade): "If White Canadians would adopt a more trad-itionally Native attitude towards the natural world, a less exploitative and more respectful attitude, they might be able to reverse the galloping en-vironmental carnage of the late twentieth century and salvage for them-selves some of that wilderness they keep saying they identify with and need. Perhaps we should not become less like Grey Owl, but more like [him]." Grey Owl's direct connection to conservation discourses, in distinction to other wilderness legacies in Canada, makes his production of wilderness important to interrogate; the authority offered to conservation by Grey Owl rests upon the investment in whiteness manifest in the performance of sur-rogacy. This argument leads me to conclude that Grey Owl's popularity pro-vides an example of how the logic of whiteness as a master signifier is established through the visual codification of both bodies and space, includ-ing the coding of wilderness as a national white space.

A Phantasy in White

The obsession with incorporation, assimilation, and death that has accom-panied much writing on the Indian in North America is played out in a passage of Grey Owl's first book, *The Men of the Last Frontier* (Grey Owl 1931).[4] Originally published in 1931, the book was an ode to Grey Owl's life as a trapper and a guide before he became a conservation figure in the Canadian public. He describes the eerie beauty of the forest in winter, where the diffused light plays tricks on the eyes and reveals the witchery of the wilderness: "Athwart the shafts of moonlight, from out the shadows, move soundless forms with baleful gleaming eyes, wraiths that flicker before the vision for a moment and are gone. The Canada lynx, great grey ghost of the northland; the huge white Labrador wolf; white rabbits, white weasels, the silvery ptarmigan: pale phantoms of the white silence. A phantasy in white in a world that is dead" (ibid., 39).

Earle Birney (1990) once described Canada as haunted by its *lack* of ghosts. In contrast, Grey Owl's image of Canadian wilderness holds ghosts almost everywhere he looks, as the past dominates his view of life in the woods. The wilderness is a vanishing frontier; trappers, guides, and fire rangers are men of days long forgotten; and characters are often seen disappearing into the wild. Yet, as a British Canadian representing a fictional way of life that he saw as already almost dead, surely Grey Owl himself, whose fantasy of living as an Indian anchored his concern for the dying Canadian wilderness, is the "phantasy in white in a world that is dead."

Grey Owl became a national success not only because he presented a bygone life but also because he was keenly aware of what the public was looking for in the "dead world" of the Canadian wilderness. Before taking on the moniker "Grey Owl," he began life as Archie Belaney. He spent his early years living with his two aunts in Hastings, England, where he dreamed of leaving the confines of Victorian life for a life in the woods of North America (D. Smith 1990).[5] The stories of North American Indians, which he picked up by reading Ernest Thompson Seton and James Fenimore Cooper, played a formative role in his boyhood imagination. A friend would recall that "[Archie] absolutely worshipped the outlook and behavior of the North American Indians" (George McCormick, quoted in ibid., 20). After convincing his aunts to let him leave Hastings for North America, Belaney made his way to Toronto and by autumn 1906 found himself, at the age of eighteen, in Temagami, a district of central Ontario, where he started living out his childhood dream (D. Smith 1990).[6]

The pattern of his life over the next twenty years consisted of escaping to the wilderness and away from multiple failed relationships. During this time, he lived in Temagami, where his earnings from winter trapping (a skill learned from his close association with an Ojibway family from the Teme-Augama Anishnabai, including his first wife, Angele Egwuna) were supplemented by a monthly pension from his aunts back in England. His first job, however, was as a member of the cleaning staff at the Temagami Inn, and it was here that Belaney began to obscure his family history, claiming to be from the American southwest, part of an Apache family that had travelled with the Buffalo Bill Show (ibid.). Leaving Angele and their daughter after two years of trapping with them, Belaney made his way west to Bicotasing,

Ontario, where he worked as a fire ranger and a trapper. He left Bicotasing (and a second pregnant girlfriend) in 1915, enlisted in the Canadian Army, and fought as a sniper in the First World War. His return to Canada in 1918 (after being injured in the war and married a second time) found him back in Bicotasing, alienated from his first two wives and his two children. He returned to his life as a trapper and fire ranger, gained a reputation for drinking (he distilled his own moonshine during Ontario's Prohibition), and befriended Alex Espaniel, the son of an Ojibway Hudson's Bay Company manager (ibid.). Clearly, like that of many celebrities, Belaney's life was complicated and contained its share of less honourable moments, and though remarking on them may seem a little trite, they are important because despite a very public record of these failings, he is still celebrated as a conservationist. Much like his Indian surrogacy, his drinking and failed relationships are overlooked or forgiven in modern tales of his success (see Atwood 1995; Attenborough 1999; Jackson 2000).[7]

Despite being immersed for much of this time in the lives of Ojibway, Cree, and Métis, Belaney was reluctant to abandon the images he had formed as a child, including that of First Nations dancing. As Donald Smith (1990, 73) writes, "Archie gave special attention to his 'Indian war dance' which he introduced at Bisco. His war dance surprised the local Ojibway and Cree, for, as fur buyer Jack Level put it, 'the Bisco Indians didn't know his brand of Indian lore.' Archie's inspiration came, of course, from his boyhood reading of Fenimore Cooper and Longfellow. His boyhood acquaintance at the Hastings Grammar School, Con Foster, recalled an earlier version of it." Belaney claimed authenticity for these performances via his creation of fictional parents, a Scottish trapping father and an Apache mother. His biographer notes that he altered his appearance to bolster his claim to genuineness, growing his hair long, dyeing it black, hennaing his skin, and practising "Indian-looking expressions" in the mirror (ibid.).

It was during his time, while living with his third wife, Gertrude Bernard (better known in Grey Owl's writing as Anahareo), that Belaney gave up beaver trapping, which hitherto had been his primary occupation and identity. Influenced by Bernard, he rescued two orphaned beaver kits and raised them in their trapping cabin. These beavers were the start of a dream for Belaney, which he describes in *Pilgrims of the Wild* (Grey Owl 1934, 256): "Instead of persecuting [beavers] further I would study them, see just what there really was to them. I could perhaps start a colony of my own; these animals could not be permitted to pass completely from the face of this wilderness ... There was nothing simple about it. I had first to discover a family of beaver not already claimed by some other hunter, tame them; so far an unheard of proceeding, but I had faith in the crazy scheme, and was convinced by what I knew of our little fellows that this was possible."

Not knowing how to support himself while populating the country with beavers, Belaney made a series of moves across Ontario and Quebec, and finally chose to devote himself to beaver conservation through writing and public speaking. After writing several articles for *Country Life* and *Forest and Outdoors* (the Canadian Forestry Association magazine) he accepted a job with the National Parks Branch as a spokesman and moved west to Riding Mountain National Park in Manitoba in 1931 and Prince Albert National Park in Saskatchewan in 1932.

It is important to note that Belaney's public life justified and furthered his Indian surrogacy.[8] His first articles focused on the non-Indian trappers with whom he identified, distinguishing them from "Indians." His pen name, Grey Owl, emerged only after his articles were enthusiastically received, and interestingly he initially toyed with the name White Owl (D. Smith 1990). It seems plausible that changing his name from Belaney to Grey Owl was consciously intended to promote his conservation message; he could have believed that, without being an "authentic Indian," he might not be as successful in presenting his message (ibid.; Francis 1992; Loo 2006). Certainly, this is one narrative of his transformation, as demonstrated in Anahareo's (1972) story of his preparation for a lecture tour of England. He asked her to make a fancy hunting shirt, with beadwork and tassels, to which she replied that there was no time, "and besides, all that fancy stuff would make him look sissified" (ibid., 173).[9] Their difference in opinion came about because Belaney strived to appear as "the Indian they expect me to be," not the bushman Anahareo knew him to be. Grey Owl had to be dressed up for his audience because, as he explained, he would "do anything, and I mean *anything*, if I thought it would make people listen to what I've got to say" (Belaney, quoted in ibid., emphasis in original).

It becomes clear, then, that Belaney's Indian masquerade intensified the more he spoke on behalf of the land and the beaver. It has consequences not just for the racial ideas held within the identity and writings of Grey Owl but also for the *space* that he was trying to save.[10] Atwood's (1995) celebration of Grey Owl follows this line, privileging Belaney's moral message about space over his racial transformation. Yet, just as the image of the Indian that Grey Owl came to represent was itself a fantasy, so too was the space that Belaney sought to produce. It was, in effect, a white space. To clarify this dynamic, let me explain the role of whiteness in performances of Native masquerade *and* in the production of wilderness in Canada.

Indian Surrogacy

In her genealogy of the adoption of "Indian practices" into American culture, Shari Huhndorf (2001, 14) argues, "Going Native in its modern manifestations originates in the relations between two simultaneous late-nineteenth-century events: the rise of industrial capitalism, with its associated notions of linear historical progress; and the completion of the military conquest of Native America." Americans have often turned to constructed images of the Indian as a means of creating a specific American identity (Deloria 1998; Huhndorf 2001; Smith-Rosenberg 2004), such as Frederick Jackson Turner's reliance on encounters with savages in his frontier thesis, or the Boy Scouts' image of the ecological Indian. Through their use of an evolutionary model of history, in which contemporary Western civilization is seen as the end point of history, these performances situate the white North American subject as the legitimate heir to the legacy of a dying Indian race.

Grey Owl, writing in Canada, depended upon a similar set of historical and intellectual conditions for his popularity. Drawing on a form of savagery heavily influenced by Ernest Thompson Seton, another English immigrant to Canada, Grey Owl's message signalled a need to incorporate the past, symbolized by the Indian way of life, into a modern life that has forgotten what the world was once made of. Exemplifying the linear model of history, *The Men of the Last Frontier* (Grey Owl 1931, 7-8) romantically describes the disappearing way of life of the trapper, associating Grey Owl's own life with the "urge that drove Champlain, Raleigh, Livingstone, and Cook into the four corners of the earth; the unquenchable ambition to conquer new territory, to pass where never yet tromp the foot of man." The trapper, being pushed "further and further towards the North into the far flung reaches where are only desolation and bareness, must, like the forest that evolved him, bow his head to the inevitable and perish with it ... And with him will go his friend the Indian to a memory of days and a life that are past beyond recall" (ibid., 26). This path mimicked the disappearance of the frontier in Frederick Jackson Turner's (1975) discourse. The inevitable disappearance is heralded by modern capitalism, and the phantasy in white in a dead world – the creatures of wilderness and the night – were ghosts created by the advance of capitalism. Grey Owl's literature invites his audience to ingest those ghosts and adopt them as their own, and thus begin to feel better about the changing nature of the world around them (along with their role in benefiting from that change). The popularity of Grey Owl's symbolism, and the elevation of a primitive way of life, draws on the anti-modernist movement. Most noticeable as a "a recoil from an 'over-civilized' modern existence" (Lears 1981, xv), anti-modernism developed in the face of the changing economic and social structures, including increased consumerism, immigration and racial diversification in urban environments, and the rationalization of the workforce. Nostalgically looking to the past, Indian masquerade imagines the possibilities of life for the white subject outside these constraints.

The second aspect of Huhndorf's (2001) argument – the idea that practise of Native masquerade was shaped fundamentally by the military conquest of North America – suggests that white audiences desired a form of savagery without having to encounter the perceived danger of that savagery. Indeed, "the living performance of 'playing Indian' by non-Indian peoples depends upon the physical and psychological removal, even the death, of real Indians" (Green 1988, 31). This palliative effect enables such performances to act as a form of surrogacy, as Carroll Smith-Rosenberg (2004) argues, for surrogacy requires the replacement of a loss. In this case, it is possible to see the loss and surrogacy as mutually constitutive; white North American subjects acted in place of the disappearing Indian (both symbolically and geographically, as Aboriginal people were moved onto reserve land) and helped legitimize that disappearance. The act of surrogacy acknowledges the wounds of loss with the hope of establishing something that can replace the item that was lost: "In this way, surrogacy works to suture the wounds [that] change gashes open" (ibid., 1329). The relationship between First Nations and Europeans in North America was one of both accommodation and annihilation, in which the latter, in various forms, took precedence (White 1991). For a newly developing country, once the physical threat to the "European" nation was minimized, it was possible for that nation to dictate the modes of both annihilation and accommodation. Indian surrogacy was one form in which the European nation saw room for accommodation, but it was not necessarily the only place. Yet, partially because of the primacy of images of the Indian promoted by surrogate practices, the political agency of Aboriginal people, or even their actual presence, was muted, as illustrated by some of Grey Owl's interactions with them.

For instance, in 1936, Belaney met Johnny Tootoosis by chance in an Ottawa breakfast café (D. Smith 1990). Tootoosis, a representative of the

League of Indians of Western Canada, whose grandfather stood alongside Louis Riel in the second North West Rebellion, was in town arguing for greater religious and cultural freedoms on reserves and in residential schools. Belaney was in town seeking support for his film about the old-time trappers and river men of the Missisaugi River. As Donald Smith (ibid., 161) points out, whereas Tootoosis and the League of Indians of Western Canada spoke about the contemporary political landscape of First Nations within the Canadian government, "in contrast, Grey Owl championed their old way of life and their beliefs." The two men represented two different approaches to the incorporation of First Nations communities into Canada's nascent political culture. Tootoosis saw the potential for accommodation by the government for Aboriginal political agency, but Grey Owl saw Native culture as a life in the past at odds with modern Canadian life. Grey Owl's form of surrogacy acts to legitimize a colonial relationship by objectifying the other and removing its subjective agency. In surrogacy, "the colonized other, denied the basic characteristics of subjectivity, not only gives up its essence to the colonizer; it is transformed into a mirror that reflects and confirms the colonizer's power" (Smith-Rosenberg 2004, 1331). Grey Owl, as a performer of an imagined past, rather than a political figure for the future, was reflecting the desire of the European nation to suture the gash of colonial change.

In contrast, some may argue that given Grey Owl's identification with First Nations communities, his work *was* asserting a place for Native peoples in Canadian life. For example, he sometimes used his mastery of language to argue in court for Native hunting rights in the face of white trappers' interference (D. Smith 1990). In addition, his children's book *The Adventures of Sajo and the Beaver People* (1935) hinges on the undeserved mistrust a new outpost clerk has for Native people; refusing to give an advance to Sajo's father, as was the custom of many outposts, he leaves the main protagonist's family without any provisions for the winter. These and other aspects of Grey Owl's writings inspire Joe Sheridan (2001, 422, 423) to argue that "Grey Owl abandoned colonial paradigms in favour of an Indigenous cultural perspective, learning the narrative qualities of his adopted landscape," and that he "grew to understand the epistemological rootedness of ecological interconnection." Accordingly, this learning allowed Belaney to counter the imperial project of "manufacturing homogenized space through agriculture and development at the expense of cultural and natural diversity" (ibid., 434).

Yet, despite his personal actions, Grey Owl's masquerade was integral to the construction and popularity of a new regime of white space that inevitably envisioned the Canadian wilderness without a First Nations presence. Grey Owl's story in the production of Canadian wilderness is important because his was among the most popular conservation messages in the early twentieth century. In opposition to Sheridan's (2001) understanding of Grey Owl's wilderness as essentially place-based, I see Grey Owl's conservation efforts as key to establishing a monolithic and homogeneous wilderness, and as part and parcel of an homogenizing imperial geography. Alongside his generic brand of Indian imagery, Grey Owl's narrative of disappearing wilderness life flattened the diversity of both natural and cultural life in Canada's North by attaching itself to a state-sponsored discourse of wilderness preservation. Important historical events prior to his entry into public life, including the hanging of Louis Riel for treason and the legal ban on significant Native cultural and religious practices such as the potlatch and the sun dance, reflected a European confidence in the military conquest over Native land. To cite Huhndorf (2001), this suggests that Archie Belaney's performance as Grey Owl depended upon the conquest and disappearance of actual Native people, and the conservation ethic he left in his wake mimics this evacuation and acts as a continuation of a colonial spatial conquest. The production of wilderness in Grey Owl's texts and the popular representations of his life and work are drawn from the myth of the vanishing Indian, and it was his performance of this trope that ensured that wilderness remained enmeshed in the visible codes of whiteness. As the colonial other, Grey Owl embodied a perspective that English Canadians could easily recognize, adopt, and protect while at the same time deferring concern for any contemporary First Nations issues. Wilderness became a backdrop to understanding the space of Canada as a white space.

To understand how the relationship between surrogacy and preservation works in the production of white wilderness space, it is important to consider the role surrogacy played (and continues to play) in the production of difference and whiteness. Smith-Rosenberg (2004) describes the imitation of Native practices as surrogacy to show that the identification made by the subjects in the performances depends for its meaning upon absolute difference between cultures. In the modern enactment of playing Indian, whether it be Grey Owl, the use of Indian names at summer camps (Wall 2005), or in professional sport cultures (Black 2002), the surrogate Indian, rather than illustrating a common bond between cultures, works to provide a distinction between white and Native. For example, Ernest Thompson Seton, a key figure in the development of the Boy Scouts of America and the summer youth camp movement in North America, encouraged young boys and girls to play "primitive" as part of the construction of a balanced modern identity (Huhndorf 2001). While playing Indian, white youth would learn skills that they could take away and fold into their modern lives. Importantly, however, not just anyone could transfer these skills from camp to city life. Rather, this transferral had to be carefully guided by self-declared Indian experts such as Seton himself (ibid.). The fact that, in a modern world, the white surrogates could utilize the strength attributed to Native resilience was what elevated them above their invented Indians. Drawn from a linear history, this practice of Indian masquerade in Canada was built upon the implied belief that Indigenous people were not able to adapt to modern life; thus, it was up to men like Seton to draw these lessons out. Key to understanding the signifier "Indian" in these cases was the difference it articulated between white and Indian, modern and primitive.

Had the articulation of an absolute difference between Native and European not anchored Grey Owl's performance, his creation of a fraudulent identity would have been unnecessary: he was not merely someone who had learned to live like an Indian; he *was* an Indian (Francis 1992). Even after his fraud was exposed, he "evoked a capitulation to an idealized image of Native difference. He rewarded an audience desirous of a peaceable kingdom by offering them an image of themselves as the benevolent subjects of a beneficent nation-state" (Dawson 1998, 123). In Belaney's success as "the first Indian that really looked like an Indian" (Lloyd Roberts, quoted in Francis 1992, 131), wilderness was central to his costume, and a primitive life, the forest, the lakes, and the beaver (whom he often called "little Indians") were understood as the necessary authentic aspects of Native life that could not have been adopted by a white man. Opposed to the reality of modern First Nations life that articulated itself in, against, and beyond the imposition of European society on its land, Grey Owl performed a clear demarcation of the difference between Indian and white by remaining in the past. This distinction came through in his writing, but it was most visceral when he brought the visible markers of difference of his wilderness life to the public; his cabins, his canoe, and his costumes helped him remain as a ghost in the land. This ghost, though, was a fantasy of the white imaginary, whose function was to construct a difference predicated on the perceived baseline of life, the white subject.

Surrogacy and the Production of Wilderness

Central to Grey Owl's performance was the image of wilderness that comes from his writing. *The Men of the Last Frontier* describes this wilderness: "Side by side with the modern Canada there lies the last battle-ground in the long-drawn-out, bitter struggle between the primeval and civilization" (Grey Owl 1931, 29). This battleground exists in "uncharted" territories "where civilization has left no mark and opened no trails," beyond the "picturesque territories" of tourist wilderness (ibid.). More specifically, "this 'Backbone of Canada' so called, sometimes known as the Haute Terre, stretches across the full breadth of the continent, East and West, dividing the waters that run south from those that run north to the Arctic Sea. In like manner it forms a line of demarcation between the prosaic realities of a land of everyday affairs, and the enchantment of a realm of high adventure, unconquered, almost unknown, and unpeopled except by a few scattered bands of Indians and wandering trappers" (ibid., 30).

This image of the "virgin wilderness" sets the scene for the description of life that Grey Owl has observed. Until he began writing, his travels were limited to the areas in Ontario surrounding Temagami and Bicotasing, and to the Ontario-Quebec border. Although he had spent two years with his first two pet beavers in the Gaspé region of Quebec, his knowledge of "uncharted" wilderness was confined to his experience of these areas. And yet his writing and desire for conservation speak of a more wide-ranging wilderness, extending from the Gaspé to the lower reaches of the Northwest Territories and west to the Rockies. We know from his life that the image of a "dark, forbidding panorama of continuous forest" (ibid.) is based on second-hand knowledge, not what he had personally experienced to that point. Given the first-person perspective in his writing and the intimacy with which he portrays the landscape, this reliance upon second-hand information is perhaps a little surprising; it suggests that the landscape he writes about, and perhaps even his experience of that space, is produced in conversation with already existing myths about the forests of Canada. These myths of nature in Canada, as the Canada First movement and the formation of the Group of Seven demonstrate, have a genealogy with close connections to nationalist and imperialist sentiments (Mackey 2002). Grey Owl's (1931, 29) assumption of a continual unbroken land, "a veritable sportsman's paradise, untouched except by the passing hunter, or explorer," builds upon the national imagination of the northern forest as Canada's strength.

It is important to recognize how the Canadian boreal forest, as Grey Owl's virgin wilderness is now known, became an object within the Canadian political and social field. In 1908, writing as the first dean of forestry at the University of Toronto, Bernhard Eduard Fernow championed forest conservation as a strategy to maintain Canada's growing international clout in the years to come (A. Baldwin 2003, 2004). Fernow's "rhetoric gathered up the forest on a national scale and pressed this national forest into the service of Canada ... assigning to it a moral duty" (A. Baldwin 2004, 190). His intention was to rationalize the Canadian forest, a project that ultimately resulted in a forest classification system in 1937, which was the first scientific classification of the forest area that Grey Owl spoke about. It is true, as Sheridan (2001) asserts, that Grey Owl's writing argued for a view of nature that stood outside the regime of rational scientific discourse; indeed, his stories of beavers and trees exceeded the language of scientific forestry. For Grey Owl, however, just as for Fernow and the rationalized discourse of conservation, wilderness existed not simply as a space outside the civilized nation, but as the foundation upon which the nation itself was created. Thus, conservation is not just about the provision of wilderness space, but is also to some extent about maintaining the "real" of the nation, which means that wilderness space is at once both material and symbolic.[11]

The wilderness in Belaney's narratives exists abstracted from the histories of colonial and economic production, and is redefined in terms of its relation to the growing nation. In this redefinition, Grey Owl disavows the specificity of the land by establishing it as an idea rather than a place. Despite his warnings against the development of the North, his texts present the North as commodity, something to be desired by the sportsman for vacations and by the nation for its economic possibilities. He explains that, "as a woman's hair is – or was – her chief adornment, so Canada's crowning glory is her forests, or what remains of them. With her timber gone, the potential wealth of the dominion would be halved, and her industries cut down by one-third" (Grey Owl 1931, 165). Although eloquent descriptions of moose, bears, beaver, and Indian life thread through Grey Owl's stories, what hooks us into them is the concern for a specific image of the nation, one laced with a racial, gendered, and sexual identity. The wilderness Belaney describes fulfils the desires of the ideal white national subject. Citizens of this developing nation are encouraged to practise their identification with the nation by consuming an abstract wilderness. Through his cabins in Prince Albert and Riding Mountain National Parks, still open to the public, the federal government created an incentive for citizens and visitors to inhabit this national subject position. We can also note that Pierre Elliott Trudeau's iconic image canoeing in a buckskin jacket owes much to Grey Owl's popularity and national message.

It is relevant here to consider how this regime of wilderness production through conservation discourse was a part of the ever-expanding reach of economic relationships of capitalism. In *The Production of Space,* Henri Lefebvre (1991) argues that capitalist relationships require us to conceive of space in the model of the commodity form. Where Marx proposed that a commodity be reconsidered as a fetish whose abstract value replaces the social relations required for its production, Lefebvre (ibid., 89-90) suggests that, in terms of space,

> a comparable approach is called for today, an approach which would ana-
> lyze not things in space but space itself, with a view to uncovering the social
> relationships embedded in it. The dominant tendency fragments space and
> cuts it up into pieces. It enumerates the things, the various objects, that
> space contains ... Thus, instead of uncovering the social relationships (in-
> cluding class relationships) that are latent in spaces, instead of concentrat-
> ing our attention on the production of space and the social relationships
> inherent to it ... we fall into the trap of treating space as space "in itself" as
> space as such.

Whereas the commodity fetish requires the value of the product to be determined as a thing "in itself," a spatial fetish removes the social histories
that shaped our understanding of space. The production of space as "abstract space" (ibid., 49) – that is, space that follows the logic of the commodity fetish – gives value to space through the ideological use the space
fulfils. Specifically, space reflects the values of certain actors, mirroring
their identity through the values attached to it. Lefebvre describes this in
relation to the production of twentieth-century urban space in France. His
analysis demonstrates that urban middle-class space legitimized the authority of *both* the middle class and an inherently unequal economic system. Yet this vision of space as a "mirror of [middle class] 'reality'" (ibid.,
309) conceals a history of class conflict, alienation, and the normalization
of middle-class desires. Rather than reflecting reality, space hides the production of social inequalities. In Canada, wilderness serves a similar function for the white English Canadian by naturalizing colonialism and the
ever-expanding reach of capital (through the production of the forest as a
commodity).

Lefebvre's analysis illustrates the expanding role of production under capitalism, showing us that urban space can no longer be simply understood as a place of residence, but must be perceived as part of a broader pattern of capital accumulation. Wilderness can no longer be seen as merely a natural part of the nation, but as a way of naturalizing and legitimizing the nation. Although Lefebvre concentrated on the production of economic relations, framing his analysis through class, we should be clear that the production of other relationships of identity, such as gender and race, work through this process and are themselves usefully understood to work hand-in-hand with the production of a capitalist state. Thus, the wilderness space that Grey Owl's conservation efforts worked to create was used to establish the model rational forest of Fernow's dreams and the reflection of a caring and compassionate colonial nation that some find in Belaney's writing (Dawson 1998).

Whiteness as a Regime of Visibility

The power of Grey Owl's production of space comes from the way in which visual codes of space mask the historical circumstances that established those same visual codes. Considering the role played by visibility in the production of wilderness through surrogacy can help us understand the place that whiteness has in the meaning of wilderness in Canada. Anchoring their authority through the discourse of wilderness and Indian masquerade, Belaney's preservation aims relied upon the visual field to ensure success. Both the Indian and the wilderness exist as visual codes within Canadian society (perhaps most easily seen in their perpetual use in advertisements from the turn of the century onward), and both are made legible by racial discourses of civilization.[12] The dominant image of Canadian wilderness at the turn of the century was "of a primitive way of life, a primordial world, doomed to disappear in the face of advancing white settlement and technology" (Jasen 1995, 81). In such narratives, wilderness and race are understood in relation to their distance from modernity; wild spaces and the Indian are placed outside of the modern, whereas the urban and the white subject are folded into modernity as *the very embodiment* of modernity. Given this, racial discourses of space depend upon making the differences between white and Indian, urban and wild, legible within the public imagination, enabling symbolic hierarchies that help to naturalize structural inequalities. These differences are articulated through a politics of looking, and as Kalpana Seshadri-Crooks (2000, 19) argues, to understand race we need to understand how we "reproduce the visibility of race as our daily common sense, the means by which we 'tell people apart.'" Shannon

Winnubst (2006, 61, emphasis in original) reminds us that the power of race comes from the fact that "political values are enacted upon the basis of *how bodies look.*" In my discussion of wilderness as a code of racial visibility, I argue that bodies are read in tandem with the spaces around them. Both Winnubst and Seshadri-Crooks draw their lessons from Jacques Lacan's explanation of the split subject, one whose bodily coherence (and the image of itself as a subject) is put in doubt by the necessary mediation through which the subject can encounter that body.[13]

Briefly, Lacan's (2002) theory of the subject suggests that individuals become aware of their own subjectivity through a misrecognition of an outside object as internal to themselves (such as their own image in the mirror). This development establishes a relationship between self and other as necessary; the self (in its initial experience of wholeness as experienced through the mirror image) sets up a fictional relationship whereby the other sustains the unity of the self. One place in which the subject negotiates its identification with the other is through the structures of language. Language provides the subject with a set of pre-existing groups through which identifications work. The most powerful of these structures, such as family, gender, sexuality, and race, are presented as natural and ahistorical forms of community, and the misrecognition of the mirror stage, the fundamentally flawed perception of self, embeds a strong unconscious need for subjects to make these identifications.[14]

Race exists within this transformation as an ahistorical structure of signification. Exhibited and naturalized on the visible marks of the body, race offers subjects a position within the social body, mimicking the misrecognition of the mirror stage and giving a semblance of coherence and completeness to the subject. The organizing principle of this set of identifications is the signifier of whiteness. Constructed as the pure form of being, "whiteness" is the ideal position to which all other signifiers of race are compared. What the Lacanian framework suggests is that whiteness engenders a series of cultural practices and discourses that make up our understanding of race. Perhaps this is easiest to comprehend by examining the claim that whiteness is an "invisible" race. If invisible, whiteness is not marked as race. Difference from whiteness becomes the identifying feature that gets coded as a racial marker. Whiteness then exists as the pure form of being, and all other races are tainted replicas of this origin. As an unconscious investment in being, racial being is not simply a matter of identifying with race (through the coded identifying features) but is an attempt to overcome difference from the pure being – an ideal promised by whiteness. As Seshadri-Crooks (2000,

21) explains, "this is what it means to desire whiteness: not a desire to be-come Caucasian (!) but, to put it redundantly, it is an 'insatiable desire' on the part of all raced subjects to overcome difference."[15] In this way, whiteness functions as a master signifier, the idealized point upon which the other signifiers within that discourse (in this case, racial discourse) depend for meaning, for location.[16] Whiteness, as Winnubst explains (2006, 14-15, em-phasis in original), is "the 'master' signifier around which all other [racial] signifiers and practices are oriented – it shapes the ways they do and do not interact, the blind spots they do and do not perpetuate, the entities, acts, and desires they do and do not proclaim meaningful and thereby valuable. As an effect of these cultural practices and discourses, 'whiteness' is sedi-mented by repetition into a pattern that *appears* as solid, as 'natural,' posing as a prediscursive, a-historical, ontological given." Thus, within the regime of whiteness, race becomes a necessary marker of being, with wholeness as-cribed to the mythical marker of whiteness, the solid state of non-difference. The closer a subject comes to the states of whiteness, the more authority that subject has within this regime of visibility. Thus, a subject has authority through the disavowal of difference from this imagined origin.

If the space of non-difference offers authority, one of the key factors in establishing power relationships is the production of difference. It is here that we can see Grey Owl's connection to the master signifier of whiteness. Although he was not attempting to be white, his surrogacy nonetheless em-bodied the difference necessary for the smooth functioning of racial dis-course (in Seshadri-Crooks' formula, even as he dressed Native, he was desiring whiteness as the master signifier of race). By maintaining a clear distinction between white and Indian, Grey Owl naturalized the legitimacy of white conceptions of race. Located in the visual marks of the body, these racial differences are naturalized as categories of being (again, the reason why Belaney could not just be a white man living in the wilderness). Attempts to locate empirical evidence of race outside of the visual realm, from the Comte de Buffon (DiPiero 2002) to the Human Genome Project (Haraway 1997), have failed simply because it is through the act of looking that race is identified. As Seshadri-Crooks (2000) reminds us, seeing is a skill that de-mands training, a skill that is acquired as one becomes a subject; as we learn language, we also learn the patterns of visibility and the spatial patterns that encompass language. Yet, if racial classification were viewed solely as a learned behaviour, the power of race would long ago have been diffused; if it is to maintain its status as a master signifier, whiteness must be made to ap-pear outside of its historical construction as the founding point of race.

Visible difference allows race to be naturalized in the space of the body, thereby giving race an ahistorical appearance. A Lacanian framework is essential here: whiteness works unconsciously to disavow history by presenting itself as a nodal point for all forms of racial difference.

Indian surrogacy works within this logic to promote difference as an inescapable part of the triumph of Canada as a nation. Grey Owl's ability to look his part naturalized the difference between "his people" and the white audience. By relying upon visual codes of wilderness, including a log cabin, lakes, his canoe, the beavers, and their land, he established a set of ahistorical differences. Highlighted by the ghost of a dead way of life, this regime of visibility maintained colonialism's conclusion that the real Indian needs to die off. Grey Owl, as Indian surrogate, established codes of difference by drawing upon visual markers that naturalized the identities of the Canadian nation. His legacy, then, falls within the folds of whiteness, and by considering the role of whiteness within the production of the Indian surrogate, we can also see that the legacy of wilderness that Grey Owl drew from and helped to promote is connected to the regime of whiteness. In Belaney's masquerade, dominant white Canadian codes of wilderness are drawn into the establishment of the racial order, such that wilderness as an ideal is given meaning through the master signifier of whiteness.

Perhaps the role of whiteness in his performance is most apparent, and most important to see, in the way that contemporary representations of Grey Owl view his surrogacy as incidental to the real goal of his life – the conservation of the land of the beaver. As illustrated earlier, Joe Sheridan (2001) perceives Belaney's relationship with the land as evidence of his respect for First Nations. More widely recognized representations of Grey Owl find his masquerade compelling because they believed it allowed him greater access to a disappearing way of life and more authority to speak about it. Richard Attenborough's 1999 movie *Grey Owl* uses this logic to allow the viewers' identification with a fraud. The controversy of the imposture is dealt with in the movie by the reporter Cyrus Finney, who discovers it two years before Grey Owl's death. Upon hearing Grey Owl's public performance, Finney decides not to reveal his true identity, remarking, "I knew that what he was saying was far more important than who he really was" (Attenborough 1999). Like Atwood, who suggests that we be more like Grey Owl, Attenborough, Sheridan, and many others see the space Grey Owl inhabits as part of a moral message that speaks to the heart of the nation of Canada. Indeed, this message helps justify Belaney's complete transformation into Grey Owl. In these celebrations, the wilderness he produced becomes a necessary part of Canadian life. Its meaning depends upon the same logic of race embedded within Indian surrogacy, where Canadians look to it as a palliative space against the destabilizing effects of capitalism. Like Grey Owl's cabins, wilderness exists as a vacation spot to reflect back the whiteness of the nation to itself. Given the increased use of the recreational value of wilderness in contemporary environmental activism (through groups such as Mountain Equipment Co-op, the Canadian Parks and Wilderness Society, and the David Suzuki Foundation), we should be cautious about how whiteness has come to inflect attempts to preserve Canadian wilderness.

2 Indigenous Knowledge and the History of Science, Race, and Colonial Authority in Northern Canada

STEPHEN BOCKING

A persistent theme in the history of northern Canada is the intersection of colonial and scientific authority. This intersection has been evident in the extension of administrative control over the region, the orientation of its economy toward southern markets, and the redefinition of the northern environment as an area vulnerable to southern industry. Critiques of this intersection have been implicit in other, contrasting developments, including the devolution of authority to territorial governments and land claim regions, renewed interest in local resources, and views of the northern environment that incorporate Indigenous perspectives. Together, these exemplify the relations between the extension (and transformation) of colonial authority, and the construction of geographies of nature, culture, race, and knowledge.

Until fairly recently, virtually no government agency or scientist has accorded Indigenous knowledge more than token recognition, a stance in contrast to the authority granted science. Indigenous knowledge was viewed as anecdotal and non-quantitative, more folklore than data, failing to meet standards of scientific evidence and reasoning. Now, however, it is being applied in wildlife management by territorial agencies, its use is required in assessing new developments, and it has gained a presence in northern research. Governments and other agencies are recognizing and gathering it, and scientists of many disciplines apply it in their research (Duerden and Kuhn 1998; Berkes 1999; Usher 2000). This development in perceptions of

Indigenous knowledge is essential to the history of state-Aboriginal relations, given the importance of wildlife and the land to northern communities (Dick 2009).

This chapter explores the evolution in the status of Indigenous knowledge, particularly among scientists. Previous study of this subject has often focused on a few events of special importance, such as Thomas Berger's Mackenzie Valley Pipeline Inquiry of 1974-77, which emphasized the deep experience and insights of Aboriginal peoples regarding their homeland; on demonstrations that Indigenous knowledge could be more reliable than conventional science; or on the formation of institutions applying Indigenous knowledge to wildlife and environmental management. Some accounts have also recognized the disruptions implicit in removing knowledge from its social context, coding and reifying it as "traditional ecological knowledge" (TEK), and incorporating it within bureaucratic approaches to decision making. Study of Indigenous knowledge in northern Canada must also consider the parallel global history of assertion of Indigenous knowledge, accompanied by broader recognition of the rights of Indigenous people.

Although it recognizes these dimensions of the relations between science and Indigenous knowledge, this chapter pays special attention to the history of science. This is essential if scientists' views of Indigenous knowledge are to be understood, because scientists saw themselves not solely as northern researchers, but as members of larger professional communities. At the same time, however, they subscribed to the categories of race and nature that framed southerners' perspectives of northern Canada. The history of northern science, including its relations with Indigenous knowledge, can thus be a productive site for deepening our understanding of the historical geography of race, nature, and science. It can also bring debates about colonialism and power in contact with the politics of scientific and Indigenous knowledge production.

Boundaries and Geographies of Knowledge

Scientific knowledge – as both empirical information and source of authority – has been a consistent presence in the history of imperialism. A prevalent image has been that of superiority, implying the task of "civilizing" colonized peoples, with scientists assisting in annexing territories into imperial forms of political and economic rationality. Descriptions of human and environmental differences provided the essential foundation for this assumption of superiority, pursued through efforts to classify races and places in terms of hierarchies and boundaries – as, for example, Warwick Anderson (2003) explains took place in the tropics. Yet when we examine the actual practices of knowledge production in these contexts, we see not merely expressions of superiority, but exchanges in all directions, with explorers and scientists on the periphery learning from the colonized, paying close attention to local conditions and knowledge, and instructing scientists in both the imperial centre and other colonies, often challenging imperial ideologies and scientific agendas (Grove 1995; W. Adams 2003; Hodge 2007). These diverse exchanges, which recall Richard White's (1991) account of the "middle ground" of accommodation and common meaning once formed by Natives and Europeans in the Great Lakes region, exemplify how colonialism must be understood not solely in terms of overarching themes of power and domination, but as a local phenomenon that is fractured and contested (Braun 2002).

After the 1940s, however, during the era of "high modernism" and confidence in technology, science, and rationality, Indigenous knowledge and practices were commonly rejected as wasteful or ignorant (Harvey 1989; Scott 1998). But this was accompanied by resistance: to state-led economic modernization, to global capitalism and privatization, and to science-based approaches to nature conservation (Guha 1997). Since the 1980s, a wider suspicion of modernist assumptions regarding the capacity of global theories to explain local realities has given force and credibility to these instances of resistance.

Furthermore, the status of Indigenous people and their knowledge has been radically revised. The superiority of Western knowledge and development has been questioned, the value of local knowledge, particularly in agriculture and resource management, has been recognized, and Indigenous people themselves have asserted their rights to self-determination (Brokensha, Warren, and Werner 1980). These developments were acknowledged by the World Commission on Environment and Development in *Our Common Future* (1987), and they have been furthered by institutions ranging from the United Nations Educational, Scientific and Cultural Organization (UNESCO) to the Arctic Environmental Protection Strategy. Numerous studies have dealt with related issues, including the implications of "decolonizing" knowledge – that is, of discarding the notion of science as objective, universal knowledge (Apffel-Marglin and Marglin 1996), the allocation of access and control over resources, intellectual property rights, and the challenges of communicating between science and oral knowledge (Cruikshank 1998).

Several concepts can contribute to understanding the relationship between science and Indigenous knowledge. One is "boundary work" – the practices by which scientists distinguish between science and other ways of understanding the world, and thus assert the authority of their accounts (Gieryn 1999). Those seeking to dismiss Indigenous knowledge do so by excluding it from science, often by noting its anecdotal nature, its inaccuracy (as evaluated by comparison with scientific knowledge), or its spiritual dimensions. In contrast, scientists seeking to draw on Indigenous knowledge often emphasize those aspects, such as taxonomic classifications, that can be most readily understood in scientific terms. In effect, they redraw the boundary around science to include those aspects of Indigenous knowledge that have meaning within science.

A second concept relevant to this relationship is the "situated" character of science. Scientific practices, including the assertion of universal authority, reflect their social, institutional, and environmental contexts. It is therefore necessary to understand knowledge (whether Indigenous or scientific) not in isolation, but in relation to other forms of knowledge, their institutions, and relations of power and authority. The situated nature of knowledge compels study of the sites in which it is produced and applied, how it travels between these sites, and how different forms of knowledge interact. This perspective also implies that knowledge does not compel acceptance merely because it corresponds to the "truth"; rather, acceptance must be understood in terms of the interpretation of knowledge claims within particular cognitive or institutional frameworks (Anderson and Adams 2008). The situated nature of science also draws into question the distinction between local and global knowledge. What might be considered "global" (such as scientific perspectives) reflects the influence of local circumstances, whereas the "local" (such as Indigenous knowledge) gains its meaning at least in part in relation to global factors, including the empowerment of Indigenous peoples. The distinction between scientific and Indigenous knowledge is thus rendered ambiguous, as each must be understood within distinctive contexts (Agrawal 1995).

Finally, we can draw on the concept of "whiteness" – an element of critical race theory employed to understand efforts to assert human differences – to examine the racialized nature of the distinction between scientific and Indigenous knowledge. As an identity that is racially "unmarked," and is thus defined as the normal against which other identities are evaluated, whiteness constitutes both an interpretative framework and a set of power relations (Kobayashi 2003; Garner 2007). It also maintains an analogical relationship with science: both assert their status as unmarked or as objective and thus as defined in terms of absence, whether of racial identity or of bias; both exercise, through various social relationships, the power that accompanies this status; and both do so in ways that are time- and place-specific. This concept also throws into sharp relief the distinction between science and Indigenous knowledge: in asserting an absence of racial identity, the former tacitly affirms its whiteness, whereas the latter asserts an identity defined in terms of both race and place.

Concepts of boundary work, situated science, and whiteness justify study of the relations between science and Indigenous knowledge in terms of the distinctive interactions between North and South in Canada, and also as a manifestation of a global phenomenon. Such an approach implicates the contested identity of the North, as either a distinctive place, demanding forms of knowledge unique to that region, or as a place that can be understood in terms of concepts derived from study elsewhere. As we will see, northern research and the recognition of Indigenous knowledge have been shaped by local circumstances, including the distinctive racial identity and political and institutional history of the North, and by factors not specific to the region, such as transnational academic disciplines.

Northern Identities, Southern Authority

The history of relations between science and Indigenous knowledge is embedded in the history of images of the North. The North has long occupied a privileged place in the Canadian imagination, whether as a pristine but fragile wilderness, a terrifying and forbidding landscape, a place for moral regeneration, or a land of economic opportunity (Grace 2002; Hulan 2002). Even as meanings of the "True North" have varied, so too has the space it occupies, being defined as much by its relation to elsewhere as by its "essential" features. This has been especially evident in science. The distinctive northern environment – tundra, permafrost, dark winters, brief but brilliant summers – has long inspired in scientists a sense of wonder and of the sublime, as well as debates regarding whether knowledge gained here might be relevant elsewhere, or whether the landscape might be understood in terms of broader scientific conceptions. Scientists have accordingly located the North in diverse ways, defining it as unique, hence requiring special ideas and techniques, or as a place similar to more familiar sites to the South (albeit colder or less productive). Scientists have thus both affirmed and challenged the distinctive identity of the northern environment. In doing so, they have exemplified how places do not have stable, essential identities, but are open and dynamic, with their identities constructed within wider networks of social relations and knowledge.

This history of northern science has also been influenced by the history of the region itself, including relations between governments and Aboriginal peoples, and more generally, the formation and subsequent critique of colonial authority in the North. Throughout much of the twentieth century, concerns regarding sovereignty combined with an appetite for northern resources to impel Canadians' interest in "their" North (S. Grant 1988; Zaslow 1988). This interest has been exemplified by persistent efforts to enlist the True North in representations of national identity – and thus to assert that ownership of this northern space extends beyond those who live within it (Shields 1991, 162-99). Accordingly, certain northern narratives became linked to powerful institutions and were incorporated into how Canada understood itself, even as other narratives were marginalized.

One of the more pervasive of these was the perceived obligation to manage northern resources and Aboriginal people. Post-war government policies extended a tradition of intervention in northern hunting cultures, marked by successive Game Acts, the designation of Wood Buffalo National Park (and manipulation of its bison), and the formation of a network of game reserves (McCormack 1992; Loo 2006; Sandlos 2007). Persistent efforts were also made to commercially exploit northern wildlife, through trapping, sport hunting, and domestication of caribou/reindeer and muskoxen. Conservation became a chief tool of colonialism, justifying control over Aboriginal hunting and, where possible, the incorporation of Aboriginal people into an agrarian economy. These interventions deepened in the post-war era to include not only regulations, but educational efforts (such as the notorious "comic books" warning of the dangers of wasting country food), as well as promotion of alternative resources (such as fish in place of caribou) (Kulchyski and Tester 2007; Sandlos 2007). At its most extreme, intervention encompassed relocation of communities, often to sites deemed more abundantly endowed with wildlife (Tester and Kulchyski 1994; Marcus 1995; Bussidor and Bilgen-Reinart 1997).

Colonialism through conservation gained its impetus from several sources, including a romantic desire to preserve sport hunting opportunities and the imperatives of progressive conservation and efficient resource management (Loo 2006; Sandlos 2007). Perhaps most significant, however, were concerns regarding the apparent wastefulness of Aboriginal hunters (a staple theme in natural history narratives since the early twentieth century). Reinforcing these concerns was the view that the hunters had been corrupted by exposure to modern society and so were liable to hunt to excess once they were no longer limited by primitive technology. During the 1950s, other factors, including hunting crises that resulted in famine (possibly the consequence of shifts in caribou migration, as well as the move by the Inuit to settlements, with attendant reduced mobility), a declining fur trade, and the promise of a new northern mineral economy, led federal officials to conclude that the traditional economy was no longer viable. Policies toward Aboriginal people shifted accordingly, from encouraging dispersal and reliance on the land to promoting settled communities integrated into the dominant society and economy (Dickerson 1992; Damas 2002). The consequence was social transformation – particularly among the Inuit, who moved in just a few years from a camp-based culture to settlements.

The fact that wildlife managers intervened in hunting and social life far more in the North than elsewhere in North America reflected administrators' desire to transform and modernize northern society (Usher 2004). Attitudes regarding race and space pervaded this imperative of transformation. Northern racial identities were defined not only in terms of ancestry, but, particularly for the Inuit, in terms of relationships with the land, as expressed through food gathering and other aspects of daily life (Piper 2008). The perception that these relationships (and therefore racial identities) had been ruptured by colonization and economic and technological transformation could thus justify assimilation of northern Aboriginal people into the dominant society. This process was encouraged by the close association between white identity and state objectives, and more generally, between whiteness and progress itself (ibid.).

These attitudes also implied a dismissal of Indigenous knowledge, a stance most evident in relocations, which both denied a community's local knowledge and rendered it irrelevant. Hunting crises and transformation of settlement patterns encouraged the view that whatever knowledge Indigenous peoples once possessed – their ingenuity for survival was another staple of early natural history narratives – could not have survived this rupture. Instead, hunting and knowledge of the land were seen as outdated: a vestigial remnant awaiting assimilation into the dominant culture. Consistent with this, studies of the economic basis of northern communities tended to dismiss the significance of country food.

Scientists and Indigenous Knowledge

During the post-war era, scientists flooded north in unprecedented numbers. The federal government was responsible for much of this activity, providing support for northern research through such initiatives as the Polar Continental Shelf Project, which began operations in 1959. Federal agencies, including the Canadian Wildlife Service, the Fisheries Research Board, and the Defence Research Board, also fielded large numbers of scientists. By the 1960s, many universities were establishing centres and programs for northern research. Non-governmental agencies such as the Arctic Institute of North America also played a role.

Scientists were mainly trained in the South, wrote for southern audiences, and addressed southern concerns. This framing of science in terms of southern agendas was also evident in its relations with Indigenous knowledge. Before the Second World War, scientists and explorers had commonly lived and travelled with Aboriginal people. Some of the most celebrated northern explorers, including Robert Peary and Vilhjalmur Stefansson, had considered Indigenous knowledge essential to survival (Diubaldo 1978; Dick 2001). In contrast, the new facilities of post-war northern science, including aircraft and research laboratories provided by the Polar Continental Shelf Project, meant that scientists no longer needed to live among Indigenous people, learn their techniques for travel and survival, or indeed, have any contact with them. For example, in 1955, Kenneth Hare, leader of a geographic research team at McGill University, argued that for study of large-scale patterns of vegetation, aerial survey was clearly superior to observations based on river travel assisted by Native guides (Hare 1955). The "view from above" provided by aircraft could enable scientists to extend their perspective over much larger areas, breaking with a previous reliance on ground study. Overall, scientists sought consciously to break from past approaches to the northern environment. In doing so, they were also asserting a new identity, one more attuned to southern disciplines and institutions than to the northern context (Bocking 2009). It was very much a "white" identity: seemingly objective, disengaged from local social and cultural circumstances – and one from which Native people were excluded. Evidently not perceived as contributors to the northern scientific agenda, no Natives attended the First National Northern Research Conference in October 1967 (Kupsch 1968). And thus, as scientists took to the air and to laboratories, Indigenous knowledge itself was commonly dismissed as subjective and partial.

This orientation toward southern concerns and the dismissal of Aboriginal knowledge were especially apparent in wildlife science. During the 1950s and 1960s, through studies of caribou, polar bear, muskox, and other species, the Canadian Wildlife Service became the most active research agency in the North. The service was essential to the imposition of a firmly interventionist program of wildlife management that integrated research and management (including bureaucratic priorities such as revenue generation), and employed biological and scientific rationales to justify decisions, including those with political and social implications (Kulchyski and Tester 2007; Sandlos 2007).

Most significantly, the service stressed that Native-wildlife relations required expert supervision, thereby exemplifying the legitimating role of science in federal colonial interventions. As part of their attempt to impose science-based management on northern hunters, service biologists denied the existence of Indigenous knowledge and methods of resource management (Kelsall 1968). This perspective was reinforced by scientists' view of Natives as a chief cause of wildlife depletion, a view especially evident in their efforts to publicize incidences of apparent slaughter of caribou. Throughout the 1960s and much of the 1970s, wildlife scientists argued that Native hunters had little capacity for conservation, as no restraint could evolve under conditions in which survival depended on a variable food source. Instead, faced with fluctuating wildlife populations, hunters were opportunistic, killing wildlife wherever encountered. Wastefulness toward wildlife was thus portrayed as a racial characteristic particular to northern Natives. This racialization of knowledge and attitudes regarding wildlife could then contribute to justifying authority over Native livelihoods (Kobayashi 2003). When, in the 1970s, Natives began more forcefully to assert a role in northern wildlife management, wildlife scientists responded by asserting that, though better communication and cooperation would help, science-based management must retain a primary role. Science was viewed as the only reliable source of knowledge about wildlife populations and the only rational basis for managing hunting. This argument was also framed, in part, in racial terms. Science was presented as not merely a body of technique and knowledge that could provide accurate information, but as a nonracial perspective, something that was exclusive to non-Indigenous (that is, white) people. In other words, as three wildlife managers explained, science was "not a part of the Indian or Inuit tradition" (Simmons, Heard, and Calef 1979, 20). Even as late as 1981, scientists still insisted that Native hunting had originally been limited only by primitive technology and a low population, and any more elaborate conceptions of the relations between hunters and animals were discounted (Theberge 1981).

This view was also reinforced by the practice of wildlife science. Service scientists emphasized large-scale aerial survey of wildlife populations and study of the factors influencing their dynamics – an approach consistent with accepted practices within the North American wildlife research community (Bocking 2007). Overall, these practices reinforced the boundary between scientific and Aboriginal knowledge by emphasizing methods and forms of information incommensurable with the latter.

However, other northern researchers during this period drew on aspects of Indigenous knowledge, declining to claim such a firm boundary between it and science. One example was the wildlife ecologist William Pruitt. In his research, he used Inuit terms to designate different types of snow. Describing the Inuit as the "wisest instructors" on the nature of snow, he argued that their terms enabled far more precise description than was possible with English words. His use of these terms supported his ambition to demonstrate the ecological significance of snow and, more generally, to oppose the inappropriate application in the North of concepts and techniques developed in temperate regions. His goal was a distinctive northern perspective on ecological science, known as "boreal ecology" (Pruitt 1978). Thus, for Pruitt, Indigenous knowledge, once removed from its racial and cultural context, could contribute to northern ecology and particularly to the development of boreal ecology as a distinct scientific specialty.

Other wildlife scientists also used Indigenous knowledge. For example, polar bear researchers applied it to describing bear behaviours and as an aid in locating dens. Scientists also used Inuit observations of ringed seal behaviour. Thomas Smith and Ian Stirling (1975, 1305) discussed Inuit words and ideas regarding seal lairs and behaviour, noting that this information could be corroborated by scientific observations, and they acknowledged that their Inuit assistant "still knows more about the breeding habitat of the ringed seal than we do."

These examples illustrate how Indigenous knowledge was drawn on by scientists, by supplying information or observations not available through conventional research. Understanding this in terms of boundary formation, we can see how some scientists shifted the boundary of science so as to include Indigenous knowledge, even while excluding those aspects, such as its social, cultural, and racial dimensions, that would not contribute to their scientific goals. Thus, perspectives on race and whiteness were also implicated in these shifting assertions of the boundary between science and Indigenous knowledge. Just as whiteness could be constructed as a category lacking racial identity, science could be asserted as pure and objective knowledge, as the standard against which other forms of knowledge could be evaluated, and as excluding those forms of knowledge, such as Indigenous knowledge, that had an explicit racial identity (Kobayashi 2003; Garner 2007). Thus, this boundary could be defined at least partially in terms of what science, like whiteness, was not.

These episodes also illustrate the situated nature of science. Scientists seeking to develop ideas particular to the North have been most receptive to Indigenous knowledge. In contrast, researchers within disciplinary frameworks defined outside the North (such as wildlife biology) have tended to be less receptive. Thus, where scientists located their practice influenced their conception of its relations to Indigenous knowledge. Finally, these episodes illustrate how, though the colonial regime in the North (as elsewhere) drew on universalizing discourses of progress, modernity, and rationality, it was also shaped by diverse local factors and by scientific communities that had distinctive views on the relations between Indigenous people and science. In short, this regime was not monolithic, but fractured, heterogeneous, and open to diverse influences from both within and without the scientific community – a condition implying potential instability (Braun 2002).

The Case of Anthropology

Northern Aboriginal peoples have long been of special interest to anthropologists, as "primitive" subjects, unsullied by modernity, adapting to a difficult environment, or in Harvey Feit's words, as research subjects at the "absolute zero of human culture" (quoted in D. Anderson 2004, 1). Often, their perspectives on Indigenous knowledge have been shaped by debates regarding the impacts of European contact, such as whether family hunting territories originated prior to or as a result of contact (a question contested by Frank Speck, Diamond Jenness, and other early Canadian anthropologists). More generally, evidence of these impacts, such as adoption of new technologies, responses to social pressures, pursuit of new trading opportunities, and Native territorial expansion and population displacements (which sometimes negated knowledge of and relations with specific places), has disrupted the simplistic assumption that, until recently, Aboriginal people in Canada were entirely adapted to and in harmony with the local environment (Krech 1999; Wynn 2007, 59-77). Overall, anthropological perspectives on Indigenous knowledge have continually evolved, in response to both disciplinary concerns and policy and institutional considerations specific to the Canadian context.

Anthropology in Canada is of particular relevance to the boundaries between science and Indigenous knowledge because it has been at the centre of debates regarding research and colonial authority. Between the 1940s and late 1960s, much northern anthropology, including that sponsored by the federal government through the Northern Co-ordination and Research Centre, focused on understanding the transition of Aboriginal people to a modern economy and on providing advice to administrators and policy makers to facilitate this change (Hughes 1984). It was assumed that Indigenous knowledge would be lost during the process. However, by the 1960s, some anthropologists in the North had begun to examine it on its own terms. A significant early work was Richard Nelson's *Hunters of the Northern Ice* (1969), which was based on field work in Alaska in 1964 and 1965, and since described as a seminal study of Inuit knowledge and adaptation to the Arctic environment. Eleanor Leacock (1969) also drew attention to Indigenous knowledge, noting the "prodigious knowledge" of elders.

By the late 1960s, other northern researchers were applying Indigenous concepts to anthropology. On the Belcher Islands, Milton Freeman studied the Inuit's perceptions and knowledge of the environment, and their use of this knowledge in decisions regarding settlement and hunting. Questioning whether there can be an objective basis for evaluating the relations between Natives and wildlife (an assumption central to science-based wildlife management), Freeman (1967) described how hunters' decisions reflected not only the abundance of wildlife, but their availability, as influenced by social structures, knowledge, and other aspects of culture. In other research, he emphasized the value of Indigenous knowledge as a source of information regarding, for example, eider duck wintering areas and muskoxen populations. He also demonstrated that Indigenous knowledge of the ecology of Southampton Island was superior to that provided by science. Freeman's work in the 1960s marked the beginning of a long and influential career in anthropology.

The early 1970s saw the emergence of Indigenous knowledge as an active area of northern anthropology. Henry Lewis (1977) described the importance of fire to Aboriginal strategies of adaptation in the boreal forest. Harvey Feit (1973, 1988) worked with the Quebec Cree, describing their knowledge of wildlife populations and other ecological phenomena, such as the importance of snow to moose behaviour, and situating this knowledge within their worldview, in which animals, winds, and other aspects of nature are seen as "like persons," causality is personal, and hunting success is influenced by the hunter's previous behaviour. He also explained how the Cree regulated their harvests by rotational hunting. Julie Cruikshank's (2005) studies of stories of Athapaskan women demonstrated the importance of landscape, flora, and fauna to their knowledge; she also found a remarkable persistence and conservatism in these accounts, making them more attractive to scientists and historians. In British Columbia, Robin Ridington (1982) described the technical content of oral traditions and argued that such information serves as a critical adaptive resource for hunters. Ridington also explained how hunters and gatherers view the world as imbued with human qualities of will and purpose. Thus, understandings exist between hunters and game, with each knowing the other before they meet. Hunters seek to think like animals, to predict their behaviour. They study the life cycles of plants and animals, accumulate information about topography, seasonal changes, and mineral resources, and plan their movements accordingly. They then organize and express this knowledge through dreams, songs, and stories. In the 1970s, Fikret Berkes described how sub-Arctic fishers adapt to unpredictable environmental changes, relying on both knowledge and cooperation in harvesting. In the following decades, Berkes would study many aspects of Indigenous knowledge and resource practices, in Canada and elsewhere (Berkes 1999). Finally, in northeastern BC, Hugh Brody (1981) showed how Natives had developed particular cultures and social systems that drew on environmental knowledge and skills, particularly for hunting.

Science and Indigenous Knowledge in the Global Context

By the late 1970s, therefore, diverse views regarding Indigenous knowledge were evident within the northern scientific community. Some scientists, including anthropologists, saw it as a source of information about the northern environment, or alternatively, as an entire worldview, incorporating social and spiritual as well as empirical dimensions. In contrast, wildlife biologists (with other scientists) tended to dismiss it – and indeed, any knowledge that had not been generated by the scientific community. This diversity reflected the existence of boundaries not just between science and Indigenous knowledge but also between scientific disciplines. There was no single "scientific" perspective on Indigenous knowledge.

To understand these views, it is helpful to return to the framework noted earlier, of contrasting conceptions of the North as a distinctive region requiring its own forms of knowledge, or as a region that can be understood on the basis of concepts developed elsewhere. These conceptions, in turn, provide a basis for examining how scientists understood their own identity, whether as northern scientists who approached the region on its own terms or as scientists who, though working in the North, defined their identity in terms of broader disciplinary or institutional priorities. For example, to what extent was Canadian anthropology shaped by distinctive northern circumstances, such as the Native context, land claims, and federal government support, or alternatively, in response to developments in the wider discipline of anthropology?

The evolving views of northern anthropologists regarding Indigenous knowledge can be at least partly understood in terms of broader trends in their discipline. In the 1950s, anthropologists began to develop a greater awareness and interest in how societies perceive, adapt, and relate to their environment, as well as an ambition to recast anthropology as a predictive science that could generate general principles. These tendencies were reflected in the formation of the field of cultural ecology by Julian Steward and his colleagues. They emphasized the reciprocal links between culture and environment, and placed adaptation and functional relationships with nature (analogous to those studied by ecologists in other species) at the centre of anthropological inquiry (Hardesty 1977). Since then, ethnoscience (the study of conceptions of the world held by a people or culture) and human ecology (the study of adaptive responses to the environment) have become highly active research fields. Indigenous perspectives have also been closely studied in numerous other fields, including agriculture, pharmacology, and botany. Anthropologists also drew on ecology to construct the subfield of ethno-ecology. As initiated by Harold Conklin in 1954, and since expanded upon by many anthropologists, the "ethno-ecological approach" compels attention to how people understand their local environment (Nazarea 1999). A parallel development has been the emergence of cognitive anthropology, in which, instead of fitting cultures within an ethnocentric narrative of primitive to modern, anthropologists strive to understand them on their own terms. Anthropologists and human ecologists have sought to view Indigenous knowledge as part of comprehensive holistic perspectives, embedded in complex social systems of resource use, choice, and decision making that are essential to adaptation to the environment. Their insights have been extended by related disciplines, including political ecology. These trends led many anthropologists to view Indigenous knowledge as part of the defining subject matter of their discipline (Grillo 1997; Sillitoe 1998).

In northern Canada, anthropology reflected many of these intellectual currents, including an interest in adaptation, in Indigenous perspectives on human-environment relations, and in research methods that involved listening and participating. As an active outpost of the anthropology discipline, northern Canada became a site for exploring and applying ideas developed within cultural ecology, ethnoscience, and other branches of anthropology, and for creating new roles such as that of translator between modern states and Aboriginal populations (Balikci 1989; Wenzel 1999).

As for anthropologists, so also for environmental scientists: trends elsewhere tended to encourage openness to Indigenous knowledge. In the 1970s, a small group of scientists led by C.S. Holling developed the concept of adaptive management, as a way of acknowledging the incompleteness of knowledge and the possibility of "surprises." Its principle of a close relationship between science and management has been interpreted as consistent with Indigenous knowledge because it breaks down the conventional distinction between learning about a resource and using it. Environmental scientists' attitudes toward Indigenous knowledge have also been shaped by experience in controversies, in which knowledge has been seen as something other than simply objective – as, rather, the product of negotiation between scientists, their patrons, and other interests (Bocking 2004). Historians and sociologists of science have demonstrated how science is a complex amalgam of practical skills, technical devices, theory, and social strategies intimately tied to its wider political, social, and institutional contexts – eroding the view of environmental science as a realm of knowledge somehow separate from society. Political ecologists have added their own insights to the dynamics of local knowledge (Forsyth 2003; Robbins 2004).

Interest in Indigenous knowledge has also been generated by critiques of Western science. Fritjof Capra (1983, 41), for example, has suggested that Indigenous knowledge contains an "intuitive wisdom" about the world. Critiques of science, or even of modern society, have been projected onto Indigenous knowledge, now designated as a source of new environmental attitudes for Western society, creating the phenomenon of the "ecological Indian" (Krech 1999). Such critiques often invoke Indigenous knowledge at the expense of its specific historical context. Enrolled as an alternative space outside modernity, it is given meaning, not on the basis of its own properties, but through its positioning in opposition to another perspective (Braun 2002).

Some of the dynamics shaping the work of anthropologists and environmental scientists have also been important for wildlife biologists. They too saw themselves not merely as northern scientists, but as members of a larger scientific profession. However, this cosmopolitan identity had different implications for their relations with Indigenous knowledge. Antagonism between northern wildlife managers and Aboriginal people perpetuated a theme evident in other colonial contexts, particularly Africa, of conflict between management (including designation of protected areas) and local uses of wildlife – a conflict, moreover, that, being tied to the "civilizing" mission of colonial or state authorities, has often possessed an explicitly racial dimension (Neumann 2004). Scientific considerations also shaped biologists' views of Indigenous knowledge. As scientists, they made assumptions regarding reliable knowledge, which encouraged them to see Indigenous knowledge as anecdotal, subjective, and poorly amenable to experimental test – in short, as unscientific. It was also seen as inseparable from the immediate context of hunting, and hence as contrary to the objective of developing universal theoretical generalizations. Two foundational principles of wildlife management also contradicted Indigenous perspectives: that each resource user acts as an individual, in competition with others, and that resource users could not police themselves but must be regulated by an expert authority. Neither principle was compatible with the view of harvesting as intrinsic to the life and culture of a community. More specific theoretical and practical commitments were also important. Biologists' understanding of wildlife populations emphasized demography (births, growth, and deaths), physiological factors influencing the health of populations, and range ecology. Observations of behaviour, of relative changes in the status of local populations, or of possible long-term cycles in populations were viewed as irrelevant. The theoretical commitments implied by reliance on large-scale aerial overviews of wildlife populations also tended to render place-based Indigenous knowledge irrelevant.

Overall, therefore, relations between science and Indigenous knowledge – both openness and rejection – have been influenced by perceptions of whiteness and race, and by the structure of scientific knowledge itself. This corroborates Ravi Rajan's (2006) conclusion that science in colonial contexts was shaped not just by its function as a tool of empire, but by its own institutions, networks, and disciplinary priorities. The importance of these structural factors exemplifies how, though some scientists have recognized Indigenous knowledge as important, they have done so by incorporating it within existing orders of knowledge. Through this incorporation, the concept itself of Indigenous knowledge has been brought into existence – at the expense, according to some critics, of its marginalization. Such has been its fate elsewhere, as when Indigenous people have been integrated into a critique of modernity, as part of environmentalists' views of a balanced nature (Braun 2002). This has also been, at least in part, the fate of Indigenous knowledge in the North, insofar as its formation has accompanied the extension of scientific disciplines and southern priorities into the region. Yet, as I discuss below, northern Indigenous people have also been less susceptible to this form of marginalization.

Science and Indigenous Knowledge in the Northern Context

Scientists' perceptions of Indigenous knowledge have been shaped not just by developments within their disciplines, but by events within the North itself, including Native activism and political development, affirmation in the courts of Aboriginal treaty rights, negotiation of land claims, and movement toward co-management of wildlife. Evolving views of the North have also been significant: these have ranged from an "empty" resource frontier or "pristine" wilderness to that of homeland, long occupied by humans and densely populated with species that have their own intentions and social relations with people. These political and perceptual changes have had a variety of consequences for Indigenous knowledge. Most immediately, they have encouraged efforts by communities to collect their own knowledge, and in doing so, to assert their rights to the land itself (Gwich'in Renewable Resource Board 1997; McDonald, Arragutainaq, and Novalinga 1997). These studies have shown that northern land and waters remain crucially important to Aboriginal communities, as a basis for both material well-being and cultural and social integrity. In doing so, they have challenged the strictly biological perspective on renewable resources and impacts of industrialization (and its accompanying denial, consistent with attitudes of whiteness, of the significance of racial and cultural identities) that had provided the basis for decision making. They have also shown the value of local control over documentation of Indigenous knowledge, exhibiting thereby a greater degree of agency than Indigenous people elsewhere, including those at sites of contention, such as Clayoquot Sound, where they must often respond to the ways in which others, such as environmentalists, frame the local environment (Braun 2002). This agency experienced by northern Aboriginal peoples exemplifies a relation between race, space, and the assertion of identity that would repay further study by geographers (Kobayashi 2003).

In the 1970s, another factor began to influence attitudes toward Indigenous knowledge, albeit indirectly. Growing research activity led to resentment, as scientists often failed to make any real connection with, or provide benefits to, northern communities. Science was also implicated in negative attitudes regarding federal agencies. In particular, the Department of Indian Affairs and Northern Development lost credibility because of its centralized structure, its failure to consult, and its perceived preference for resource development, regardless of impacts on communities or the environment. This affected science because it came to be seen as simply a tool of government and thus an unaccountable instrument of outside authority – a perception only strengthened by scientists' frequently dismissive attitude toward local knowledge and by their consistently perceived identity among northerners as "whites" (Berkes 1999; Piper 2008).

One consequence of these changing views was that territorial governments and communities began to assert a stronger role in influencing scientific research, through guidelines, licences, and other measures. New agencies appeared, such as the Science Institute of the Northwest Territories (now the Aurora Institute), as well as processes within land claims settlement areas for review of research. Demanding more than the fulfillment of reporting and employment requirements, communities began to insist that their own knowledge be incorporated into research. Increasingly, scientists found that to obtain permission to do research, they had to demonstrate some awareness of Indigenous knowledge. Closer working relationships within cooperative resource management institutions such as the Beverly and Qamanirjuaq Caribou Management Board also encouraged biologists to recognize the value of hunters' knowledge.

These northern developments have also influenced Canadian anthropology, joining with disciplinary changes such as the formation of cultural ecology and ethno-ecology to encourage interest in Indigenous knowledge. The combination is exemplified by the career of Fikret Berkes: a background in human ecology and an invitation from the Quebec Cree to document their approach to managing their fishery led to his extensive study of Indigenous knowledge (Berkes 1999). Many anthropologists have also defined as part of their identity the role of mediator between Indigenous people and government. This has been encouraged by changes in the institutional and social position of anthropology, including increased study of anthropology in universities (permitting greater independence from federal policies) and anthropologists' interest in asserting Native rights to self-determination. As anthropologists themselves have pointed out, anthropology in Canada has been noteworthy for its dual emphasis on Native cultures and advocacy, not least by supporting challenges to federal policy and to the presumptions regarding race and knowledge that underpin it (Harrison and Darnell 2006). Certain anthropology departments such as that of McGill University have been particularly important in providing space for this sometimes contentious interaction between disciplinary factors and the local context of

Canadian anthropology. Often reaching an audience beyond their own colleagues, anthropologists have introduced the concept of "advocacy anthropology," with scientists working for the rights of Native peoples (Wenzel 1991). However, distrust of researchers and a desire to speak directly to society have generated resistance to this role, posing new challenges and uncertainties for anthropologists (Asch 2001).

Land claim negotiations have also provided opportunities for anthropologists to construct this role of mediator. Because an effective negotiating position required establishing that certain lands had long been occupied, a demand arose for studies of land use and occupancy. In Quebec, negotiations for the James Bay Agreement necessitated documentation of Native land use and knowledge, drawing on information provided by hunters, trappers, and other land users, as well as assessment of the impact of the James Bay hydro project on Native ways of life (IRRC/AINA 1996). This research drew on anthropologists' experience, gained through McGill's Cree Developmental Change Project, which was established in 1964 (Hedican 1995). In the Northwest Territories, the Inuit Land Use and Occupancy Project, initiated in 1973 and directed by Milton Freeman, used map biographies and other techniques to document land use (Milton Freeman Research Limited 1976). Such techniques served not so much to accurately represent the cultural dimensions of Native knowledge as to translate it into a format suited to land claims negotiations. This work also introduced some anthropologists (including Hugh Brody, who participated in the Inuit study) to Indigenous knowledge, influencing their future careers.

Finally, empirical results have shaped attitudes toward Indigenous knowledge. In the 1970s, it began to be compared directly against scientific predictions. The result was often diminished confidence in science and more credibility for Indigenous knowledge. One such encounter involved the Beverly and Qamanirjuaq caribou herds. In the late 1970s, biologists claimed that the herds had been depleted and were now in "crisis." In response, the Inuit argued that the population was much larger. More extensive surveys in 1982 confirmed the Inuit position (Freeman 1989). Since then, the accumulation of Indigenous knowledge of caribou (by, for example, Michael Ferguson, who has collected Inuit knowledge on Baffin Island since 1983) has increased its credibility among wildlife biologists, helping to shift their attitude from denial to acknowledgment and acceptance (Ferguson, Williamson, and Messier 1998).

Other developments in the study of wildlife, and particularly caribou, have also influenced attitudes. For instance, Indigenous hunters had always noted the behaviour and well-being of individual animals and had viewed herds not simply as collections of individuals but as social units. In contrast, biologists tended to discount these as irrelevant to wildlife population dynamics, and in fact Indigenous knowledge was seen as less credible in part because of its attention to these "unscientific" factors. Once, however, biologists began to consider them (learning from hunters, for example, that older males, even if biologically irrelevant, play an important role in protecting the herd against predators), another impediment to acceptance of Indigenous knowledge was removed (Freeman 1979). Similarly, empirical evidence encouraged biologists to be receptive to other aspects of Indigenous knowledge, such as the possibility that caribou herds are not geographical, but biological units, lacking close ties to specific calving grounds. Overall, Indigenous knowledge provided, for scientists, an increasingly significant source of empirical information. As Fred Roots, among the most experienced Arctic experts, once noted, "It is a truism to say that one of the most underutilized sources of information ... is the accumulated practical knowledge that the Inuit possess ... Southerners who have worked or studied in the Arctic for many years and know it well are those most conscious of the soundness and depth of traditional knowledge" (quoted in Freeman 1992, 90). An essential point, however, is that recognition of the empirical value of Indigenous knowledge has not come merely through force of evidence. As in science generally, acceptance of knowledge claims also required a supportive framework, including institutions and disciplines predisposed to accept these claims, and a shift in perceptions regarding the relations between "white" science and knowledge that is tied to a racial identity.

Conclusion

The interaction between science and Indigenous knowledge provides an opportunity to examine the relations between the geographies of nature, peoples, institutions, and knowledge. These relations have been shaped by political, economic, and cultural factors specific to northern Canada and by other factors that range far beyond. This corroborates the conclusion of other scholars: that colonialism combines local and global attributes (W. Anderson 2002; W. Adams 2003; Hodge 2007). Even as it draws on universalizing discourses of modernity and reason, its operation and consequences are situated phenomena: highly local, shaped by institutions, forms of expertise, cultural and political conditions, and environmental circumstances. There is, therefore, no such thing as "the" colonial (or post-colonial) condition. Such an analysis also draws attention to the diverse and sometimes contradictory perspectives of those who act on behalf of the state. As Paul Nadasdy (2003) has argued, it is insufficient to view the state as a monolith pursuing a coordinated agenda of colonization and domination.

As this account also illustrates, knowledge – both Indigenous and scientific – has been central to the evolving relations between North and South, and to the definition of the North as a distinctive region. This identity, however, remains contested and ambiguous. Ambiguity is also evident in the diverse and sometimes contradictory roles of science in state-Aboriginal relations. Science has served, as so often in environmental affairs, to guide and legitimate state actions in the North. Yet it has also provided the basis for critiquing those actions and accompanying assumptions, including the dismissal of Indigenous knowledge. That these at times conflicting motivations within the colonial structure could eventually provide the basis for challenging that structure was illustrated most clearly by the role of anthropology in validating the notion of Indigenous knowledge – demonstrating how challenges can arise from spaces within as well as outside (Braun 2002).

The complex and ambiguous interactions between northern science and colonialism have been particularly evident in claims regarding the racial identity of knowledge. These claims, like colonialism itself, have exhibited both a global and local character. A global ideology of race and human difference authorized northern colonial structures that, in practice, were racialized as white by virtue of the local historical and geographical context of northern Canada. And just as whiteness has been globally asserted as a racially unmarked identity – the objective normal against which other identities could be evaluated – so too, in their local context, northern scientists defined their own identity as "white" by asserting that their knowledge was objective and thus disengaged from the northern social and cultural context. This was particularly evident in their assertion of a boundary between scientific and Indigenous knowledge. They defined this boundary not only in terms of methods and theory, but in terms of race, by distinguishing between the objective non-racial "white" identity of science and the racialized identity of Indigenous knowledge.

This history of science and Indigenous knowledge in northern Canada raises several research questions. Some relate to the workings of racism in the context of environmental space. This is a matter of pressing concern in Canada, particularly in places defined as politically or economically marginal, such as communities exposed to urban industrial hazards, that are situated downstream from the Athabasca tar sands or other resource projects, or that inhabit Indigenous landscapes that environmentalists persist in viewing as "pristine" wilderness (Gosine and Teelucksingh 2008). Further study could enhance our understanding of the role of knowledge in enforcing, and sometimes critiquing, these and other instances of environmental racism and injustice. This study could also contribute to our understanding of the concept of whiteness, both by indicating the value of this concept as part of a research agenda for the history of science in the North and, more generally, by suggesting a critique of reductive approaches to whiteness that neglect the specific historical contexts of racialization, including scientific institutions and disciplines. Finally, there are implications for understanding the meaning of race in the history of science, including the need to seek this meaning not just in terms of studies in the human sciences of race itself, but through attention to the practise of science across a range of disciplines and situations (see, for example, Nash 2006).

Throughout this northern history, the visibility and authority of Indigenous knowledge has increased. Refracted through racial identities, science, practical concerns, and institutional requirements, it has carried multiple meanings and has been deployed in diverse ways – exemplifying how it is not something that has been "discovered," but has been constructed through encounters with other forms of knowledge (Cruikshank 2005). Yet there is also room for debate over the significance of this trend. As we have seen, Indigenous knowledge has often been rendered visible only when it was consistent with scientific perspectives. Just as scientists tended to recognize only those aspects of Indigenous knowledge that could be understood in terms of their own disciplines, so too do environmental management agencies still prefer to draw on those aspects that can be expressed via the tools of management, such as geographic information systems (even as national and international environmental institutions apply Indigenous knowledge on scales far beyond its origins, and pharmaceutical firms recognize it only to the extent that it aids in identifying plants with commercial possibilities). These observations exemplify how the formation of new institutions can leave unrevised preferences for forms of evidence and argument, including quantitative reasoning and particular kinds of causal reasoning, that historically have been the purview of science (Nadasdy 2003). As a consequence, Indigenous knowledge has been reshaped, reified, and detached from its contexts – exemplifying its asymmetrical relationship with science, in which the boundary they share is defined by scientific, not Indigenous, criteria (Bravo 1996). Such an outcome exemplifies the ambiguity of post-colonial conditions, marked by a continuing tension between colonial pasts and present aspirations.

ACKNOWLEDGMENTS

My thanks to the editors of this volume for organizing the workshop Rethinking the Great White North (Queen's University, February 2008), which provided an opportunity to think about the history of science, nature, and race in northern Canada, and also for their extremely helpful comments on an earlier version of this chapter. Thanks as well to the anonymous reviewers for their helpful comments and to Liza Piper, for providing a copy of an unpublished paper.

Cap Rouge Remembered?
Whiteness, Scenery, and Memory in Cape Breton Highlands National Park

CATRIONA SANDILANDS

On the north side of the river, there is a fine bench which will make a first-class site for a Parks Bungalow camp. At the present time, there are about eight families along this bench who would have to be removed and their lands redeemed outright and turned over to the Dominion.

– R.W. Cautley

The beach was wide, and a reef, one hundred metres out to sea, did provide some protection. Nevertheless, with the aid of capstans, the fishermen still had to haul their boats onto the cobble beach after each day's work.

– La Bloque interpretive panel

It is a bright July afternoon on Le Buttereau trail in the southwest corner of Cape Breton Highlands National Park (CBH). The meadows through which I am hiking, on the top of a cliff overlooking the sparkling Gulf of St. Lawrence, are filled with the pink blooms of wild roses. Given where I am as well as the roses' obvious fecundity, I guess that these are common Virginia roses *(Rosa virginiana)*. Virginia roses like clearings and open woods: they are also called pasture roses. They are indigenous to eastern North America, but they are hardly the fragile poster children of protected areas management plans. They frequently grow around settlements, in vacant lots, in ditches. Michael Pollan (2001, 4) would argue that, in light of our apparently endless willingness to clear space for them, they have domesticated human beings very well indeed. They are, nonetheless, beautiful, and today the combination of roses and ocean and towering cliffs is truly the stuff of picture postcards.

The roses have enjoyed pretty much undisturbed mastery of this plateau for more than seventy years, but the open clearings that invited them to grow and thrive here are much older. Until 1936 Le Buttereau was part of the Acadian community of Cap Rouge, a group of about thirty-seven families that was permanently displaced, along with their livelihoods, to produce what Alan MacEachern (2001, 47) has called the "sublimity by the sea" that was the aesthetic raison d'être of the park. The 120-plus-year history of Canada's national parks has been marked with many examples of land expropriation, ranging from the extinguishment of Aboriginal hunting, fishing, and timber rights to the banning of resource extractive activities within parks to the expropriation of private landholdings and the removal of their owners from park properties, a policy that was actively pursued by Parks Canada until the 1970s. Although historically there has not always been a perceived contradiction between the desired aesthetics of national parks and the presence of non-tourist economic activities (Mortimer-Sandilands 2009), the act of park establishment has, especially since the 1911 Forest Reserves and Parks Act, often involved the cultivation of particular kinds of "natural" park landscape through the limitation and removal of unsightly reminders of productive life. Hence, the forced removal of the community of Cap Rouge: it was not conducive to the viewscape.

So the wild roses are actually ghosts of the Cap Rouge Acadians: at Le Buttereau, there were six small farms (Rousseau 1972, 2), and as I hike through the roses, I walk through expropriated land that was probably pasture for a good hundred years. The blooms seem to be part of the rugged beauty of the cliffs – another element in the park's carefully preserved primordial nature – though really, the mass of thorny pink-flowering bushes speaks of land laboriously cleared and forcibly vacated. But the ghosts in this place are not all as subtle. Behind me, on the part of Le Buttereau trail that leads through the forest along what was an old path of the Cabot Trail connecting Cap Rouge with nearby Chéticamp, five small stone house foundations are plainly visible. Indeed, the foundations are not only mostly cleared of undergrowth, but each is marked with an official sign indicating who used to live there. One reads, "David à Sambo et Rose Chiasson (10 enfants)." Another reads, "Séverin à Édouard et Nélée LeBlanc (10 enfants)." And a third, "Joseph à Cacoune et Marie Deveau (11 enfants)."[1] According to a larger interpretive panel along the trail, these families were the last to be removed from the park in 1936. Although the panel also notes that each house would have had a kitchen, dining room, bedrooms, and a loft, and that each family would also have had a barn for its animals, the foundations seem extremely small, particularly when juxtaposed with the number of children who would have lived there.

In this chapter, I would like to consider the ghosts of Cap Rouge in more detail. I will argue that the landscape that is now this small part of CBH has been subject to a sequence of historical erasures and reorganizations, deploying certain ideas of nature, race, and heritage in order to produce the park as a *park*. I will focus on two of these reorganizations. First and most obviously, the 1936 expropriations literally removed productive labour from view; in particular, they highlight the fact that the park was established in order to facilitate a scenic experience of nature in line with emerging practices of automobile tourism oriented, in this case, to a scenic landscape intended to be perceived and experienced while driving along the Cabot Trail. Less obviously, perhaps, these expropriations were also racialized: though the Cap Rouge Acadians were not the only landowners forced to leave the park in 1936, the community was the only one eliminated wholesale. Indeed, the farming community of Pleasant Bay, at the northwest corner of the park, was largely untouched: park boundaries were drawn around it. As planning documents of the period show, Pleasant Bay's (apparent) "settlement" was legible and significant to the park's creators in a way that Cap Rouge's "cottages" were not. In addition, as MacEachern and Ian McKay (1992) have both suggested, Pleasant Bay's Scottishness was consistent with a broader "tartanization" of Nova Scotia, of which the "Highlands" park was vanguard, in full governmental force at the time; the evictions at Cap Rouge were thus also part of a reorganization of the landscape toward a racialized, romantic, and anti-modern Gaelicism that, as McKay argues, responded to the multiethnic industrialization of Cape Breton with waves of pipers, crofters, and highland cattle.

But the expropriations themselves are only part of the story of the unfolding of whiteness in the park. After a more general discussion of the dynamics of whiteness in national parks, the second moment I would like to consider is very much in the present, and concerns the *interpretation* of the expulsions for the contemporary park visitor (like me). Through the activities of the park cooperating association Les Amis du Plein Air (Les Amis), a series of interpretive panels was created in the area around Cap Rouge, at both Le Buttereau and La Bloque, the site of the community's lobster cannery, fishing shacks, and wharf (La Bloque also includes a replica fishing shack). Although, on the one hand, these panels make the expropriations visible by marking an age that was ended at the park's creation, on the other, their focus on the Cap Rouge community as part of a "vie passée" (and a particularly hard and poor one at that) places the past firmly *in* the past, part of a narrative that affirms the park as a "step above" the era that it replaced. Hiking Le Buttereau and reading the panels along the way thus become experiences of a progress in which the present "preserved" nature of the park justifies the violences of its creation as ultimately *necessary*. This narrative is possible partly because the park claims status as a "universal" (read white) nature to which all particular interests (read Acadian) are, in the final reckoning, subordinate. As part of a history of modernity, the now acknowledged ruins of Cap Rouge confirm the privilege of the hiker, the consumer, the tourist as the subject for whom history occurs. As part of an intersecting history of whiteness, they also confirm the racialized hierarchy by which whiteness, as a master signifier, produces the Acadian as a differential subject in the signifying logic of the master-visitor-consumer, a position that "remains outside of the play of signification even as it enables the system" (Seshadri-Crooks 2000, 20) of racial logic at work in CBH.

The Expropriations at Cap Rouge

As National Parks Branch chief surveyor R.W. Cautley made clear in his 1934 report to Parks Commissioner J.B. Harkin recommending a Cape Breton site in preference to other possible locations in the province for the creation of a new national park, not only was the proposed area generally unsuitable for other forms of large-scale economic development (such as industrial logging and mining), but it also included exactly the kind of dramatic, visually appealing landscape considered necessary for park establishment: "The scenic values of the site are outstanding" (Cautley 1934, 20). The choice of this kind of landscape – "rugged coastline and mountain grandeur" (ibid., 29) – for the first Canadian national park in the Atlantic Provinces was, as MacEachern (2001) has documented, quite intentional: even if Cape Breton wasn't exactly Banff, it had to possess something of Banff's monumentality in order to be park-worthy. As a result, Cautley emphasized the site's spectacular visual qualities, MacEachern's "sublimity," throughout his report. What is important to note here is, first, that the primary aesthetic feature recommending the park was the *coastline,* not the much larger interior: as Cautley (1934, 18) explained, "the high tableland which forms the interior of northern Cape Breton is singularly devoid of scenic attraction," but "the great scenic value of the site is the rugged coast itself with its mountain background." Second, by 1932, that very coastline was already serviced by a road, the internationally publicized Cabot Trail: although sections of the trail would need to be rebuilt to rectify prohibitively steep grades, "a highway could be built along the coast which, in my opinion, would be the most spectacular marine drive that I have ever seen in any part of Canada" (ibid., 19).[2] The combination of these two factors highlights the significance of a third: that the best part of the coastline for the Cabot Trail, "from the bridge across Chéticamp to Pleasant Bay" (ibid.), was already inhabited by quite a large number of people, including established settlements in the Cap Rouge area. Cautley recognized the complexities involved in expropriation on a rather large scale – there were also properties at Pleasant Bay, Ingonish, the Clyburn Valley, and Big Intervale to consider, not to mention the Oxford Paper Company's lease for timber rights in the tablelands. Nonetheless, it was absolutely clear to him that the residents must leave in order to facilitate the *driver's* experience of the outstanding scenic values of the area, especially on the spectacular west coast of the proposed park: "It is recommended to adopt a point 100 feet south of the Chéticamp River as the south-westerly corner of the Parks [sic] boundary, and the natural scenic features of the surroundings make this entrance of the Park almost ideal" (ibid., 25).

In keeping with Cautley's recommendations, the Cape Breton site was indeed chosen, and the park was officially created on 23 June 1936. Its boundary was drawn well north of most of the population on the east coast of the island and avoided the majority of the communities comprising the settlement of Ingonish. In addition, Neil's Harbour (at the northeast corner of the park) and Pleasant Bay (northwest) were largely excluded, the latter despite Cautley's recommendation that the whole community be included due to its potential as an access point to the (also scenic) Crown lands to the north (ibid., 24). At the southwest corner, the boundaries of the park essentially followed Cautley's preference: the Chéticamp River marked the park entrance. Within these boundaries, numerous private landholdings needed to be expropriated to facilitate the park's development. According to Wilfred Creighton (1994, 2), the provincial forester sent to negotiate payment with local residents for their lands, "there were 70 homes in the park and about 300 private landowners. Most of the homes were at Cap Rouge," which included about 175 people (fifteen families) and also boasted a general store, a quay, a post office, and a school (Aucoin n.d., 4) as well as the fishing and canning operation at La Bloque.

When considering these boundaries and expropriations, one is immediately struck by the fact that Cap Rouge, which had been settled officially in 1821, was the only community that was removed entirely to make way for the park. Every last family was relocated by 1940, at which point the post office also officially closed. Cautley (1934, 22) had been clear about the rationale for not including the region of the east coast south of Cape Smokey in his plans: "The settlement along this part of the coast has been established for several generations and some of the present owners have well-developed farms." He was similarly clear about Pleasant Bay: "It is out of the question to expatriate all the inhabitants of such an old established settlement" (ibid., 24). Why, then, did the 115-year-old, 175-member, service-providing community of Cap Rouge not register in Cautley's assessment as "settled"? Although it acknowledged the post office and the school, Cautley's report (ibid., 25) ultimately trivialized the Cap Rouge settlement and rendered, in a short paragraph, a decision of isolation and underdevelopment:

> I was unable to get along the coast north from the above point, namely six miles north of Chéticamp bridge, but it is unlikely that there are any more settlers unless near the mouth of Fishing Cove River ... Altogether, there may be a dozen dwellings, exclusive of those on the bench immediately north of Chéticamp River, and I think the Nova Scotia Government should be asked to buy them out.[3]

MacEachern (2001, 55) argues that Cautley recommended expropriation at Cap Rouge because its families were fishers rather than farmers: "He neither understood nor approved of how the inhabitants of Cap Rouge lived. The fishing community did not show the material signs of permanence which Pleasant Bay, with its big farms, did."[4] Cautley (1934, 26) insisted that moving the fishing operation to Chéticamp would actually work in favour of the Cap Rougeans: Chéticamp, he rationalized, was "the only good harbour for boats on the entire west coast and is within a few miles and affords much better opportunities for fishing and farming than where they are now." Nonetheless, the expropriations were hardly made in the name of community members' economic well-being. Rather, the character of the community clashed with the aesthetic qualities that Cautley sought: he viewed the stretch of coast between Chéticamp and Pleasant Bay as the largest scenic feature of the park. Its emptiness underscored its appearance as a remote, exotic location for adventurous road travellers, and subsistence agriculture and fishing by large families were simply not congruent with uninterrupted, sweeping views of rugged coastlines. As Cautley (ibid., 18) emphasized, the key was the coast: "It is only as one approaches the coast that the original plateau has been so cut up by the erosion of many extraordinary steep mountain torrents as to become a picturesque mountain terrain, with serrated sky line and distinctive peaks."

It is also clear that Cap Rouge's identity as an *Acadian* community played a role in its downfall. At one level, as MacEachern argues, the large Scots-owned farms of Pleasant Bay were simply more comprehensible to the likes of Cautley than were the large families and smaller subsistence farming and fishing landholdings of the Cap Rougeans. Cautley probably felt that the demise of Cap Rouge was not at all equivalent to ploughing under larger properties. At another level, however, there was a particular clash between the Cap Rougeans' existence and the desire for a "picturesque" park landscape. Specifically, CBH was, in Ian McKay's (1992) now famous terms, an important subject of the tartanism that was sweeping Nova Scotia under Premier Angus Macdonald. Settlements such as Pleasant Bay were congruent with the manufactured Highland image of the park, but Cap Rouge underscored the fact that the region was ethnically diverse. Thus, although the beginnings of an Acadian "folk" industry were already under way in western Cape Breton and centred in Chéticamp (Ross and Deveau 1992, 112), the "folk" whose ethnic traditions were to be highlighted *inside* the park were Highland Scots, not Acadians.[5] To put it rather baldly, the "picturesque" of the Cape Breton Highlands was contingent on its resemblance to a romantic anti-modern view of the Scottish Highlands; Gaelic-speaking (or at least Scots-named) settlers with established farms that evoked nostalgic images of Scotland were at least somewhat congruent with this view, whereas co-existing French-speaking ones with large families, community fishing operations, and a cannery were not.

Macdonald's Celtophilia was far from subtle. As McKay documents extensively, his political and economic vision for Nova Scotia in the 1930s was intimately tied to his embrace of the idea that the province was essentially Scottish. In the first place, Macdonald displayed, even during the Depression years, a strong commitment to tourism as a form of provincial economic development. In the second place, he understood "the importance as a tourist feature of retaining the distinctive habits and customs that characterize the various races represented in our population" (Macdonald, quoted in McKay 1992, 17). Perhaps most significantly, he understood that the "distinctive" essence of Scottishness, tourist attraction or otherwise, lay in the romantic figures of Highland clans, kilts, haggises, and bagpipes, not in, say, intellectual inheritances from the Scottish Enlightenment or, more locally, in traditions of Cape Breton coal miners with more hybrid ancestries. The result of this potent combination was Macdonald's active promotion and institutionalization of a simulated Nova Scotian "Highland" culture throughout his regime as premier. Centred on rural communities and on simulations of "traditional" Scots emblems, foods, and arts, tartanism involved the cultivation of a primitivist idea of the people and landscapes of Cape Breton. Apparently untouched by (contaminating) modernity, Cape Breton "Highlanders" were portrayed as possessing the stalwart bravery of Robert the Bruce and as living authentically and naturally in romanticized family and settlement forms brought directly from the old country. Needless to say, these images resembled neither the reality of most Gaelic Cape Bretoners, many of whom had worked in mining and industry for generations, nor the mixed farming and fishing practices of the scattered communities of rural northern Cape Breton, nor really any historical or current life in the Scottish Highlands themselves.

McKay demonstrates that Cape Breton Highlands National Park played a particularly important role in the larger development of this romantic tartanism. First, there was the name: "Highlands" was a strategic choice, not one that emerged organically from the high tablelands of the park's interior.[6] Second, Macdonald set about provisioning the park with infrastructure to support the idea that a trip through it was a journey into an authentic Scottish landscape experience. As premier, Macdonald was responsible for the (expensive) construction of the provincially owned Keltic Lodge inside the park boundaries (opened in 1940) and for the development of the Highland Links Golf Course, replete with individual hole names such as Tam O'Shanter and Muckle Mouth Meg.[7] Macdonald was persistent in this park en-Scotsment. As McKay notes, he wrote to the federal minister responsible for the park in 1949 suggesting that its foresters wear kilts (and recommending the Macdonald tartan to boot). He also suggested that, "if for no other reason than a publicity stunt, [the park should] have two or three highland cattle browsing in the little pasture that now exists in full view of the dining room at Keltic Lodge" (quoted in McKay 1992, 31).

Although (thankfully) the cattle never materialized, the expropriations did, and it is important to recognize that the desire for spectacularly iconic live-stock and the banishment of actual Acadian families were related elements of the fantastic landscape that was, and is, CBH. Although it is certainly true that the promotion of the Highlands as essentially and romantically Scot-tish would simply have been rather rudely interrupted by the existence of a decidedly un-romantic, un-Scottish fishing community at Cap·Rouge, it is equally the case that the Acadians interrupted the *pristine-ness* of the rugged coastal spectacle in a way that, apparently, golf courses and Scots-owned farms did not. Thus, as MacEachern's and McKay's research suggests, the expulsions at Cap Rouge constituted a moment at which the commodifica-tion of nature as picturesque was expressed with a strongly racialized view of the "rugged" and "unspoiled" as a space for the articulation of whiteness. If it were to resemble a park, the "wilderness" of Cape Breton needed to be organized and represented in a way that conformed to existing aesthetics and expectations, and if these aesthetics and expectations were to be real-ized, any hint of ethnic "marking" on the landscape must either be romanti-cized or removed. The Scots were rendered anachronistically, part of a concerted attempt to present the population of Nova Scotia as essentially Gaelic and anti-modern as possible. The Acadians of Cap Rouge were taken out altogether. Both acts effectively "cleared" the landscape in order to con-firm a particular racial hierarchy.

One could argue that, although the Scots certainly haven't always been white, in the 1930s, the Gaelic speakers of Cape Breton came to be seen as rather *whiter* than the Acadians (and certainly more so than the Mi'kmaq, who were not mentioned at all). More precisely, as McKay reveals, several thinkers contemporary to Macdonald, including Dorothy Duncan in her book *Bluenose: A Portrait of Nova Scotia* (1942), pursued a Highland iden-tity for Nova Scotia that was not only anti-modern but quite overtly racist, based on what looks like a hysterical response to popular social anxieties about miscegenation and contamination. Duncan believed that ethnic mix-ing in the Cape Breton mining towns was responsible for the "dilution" of the hardiness of the Cape Breton Highlander. Her view was grounded in the idea that "there was an essential Highland nature, but it could rarely, if ever, surface in a world tainted by industry and racial mixing" (McKay 1992, 25).[8] In this context, I would argue that the Scots *became* white under Macdonald;

the retroactive creation of a pure pre-modern Highland Scot was a defensive position designed to rescue a *possibility* of whiteness from the murky, urban, industrial ground of racial hybridity in which the Scots settlers were as enmeshed as anyone else.[9] Understood in this light, the mere presence of the Cap Rouge Acadians inside "the Highlands," a place that was supposed to represent the very essence of an originary racial landscape threatened by industry, by cosmopolitanism, and even by ethnic co-existence, was enough to invoke the spectre of Cape Breton's ethnic plurality, its "mongrelization," a co-existent hybridity that could undermine the romantic ideal of the isolated and primitive pre-Clearance clan untainted by the modern. The link between an anti-modern wilderness politics and a thoroughly modern racism is, as other essays in this volume attest, hardly news; what is interesting here, however, is that the landscape became white through the literal removal of the racialized stain of the *modern*, the haunting presence of which was marked, rather ironically, by a small community of subsistence Acadian fishers.

As indicated by both MacEachern's and McKay's research, then, the articulation of racialization and picturesque commodification that occurred in the creation of "the Highlands" in the period around 1936 involved both a physical emptying of the landscape of Acadian hybridity and an equally physical imposition of a romanticized Scottishness.[10] A 1942 travelogue written by Clara Dennis confirms the success of this articulation. Driving the Cabot Trail from west to east, she acknowledges the existence of Chéticamp, but once she enters the park, there is only wilderness and Scottishness. At Cap Rouge, the "wild northern country" contains "the one and only collection of houses to be met on this lonely trail" but mostly mountains and sea in "glorious combination" (C. Dennis 1942, 290). With the exception of "a desolate looking log cabin" at French Mountain (ibid., 291), the landscape remains unpeopled until she reaches Pleasant Bay, where she encounters such perfect examples of Highland Scottishness that she spends several pages describing their valour and fortitude. She also draws a direct link between the landscape of the Isle of Skye and Pleasant Bay: the Scots "left their rugged wave-washed shore for the equally rugged, wave-washed shore of Cape Breton" (ibid., 296). Arthur Walworth (1948, 16) replicates both the drive and the view: en route to Pleasant Bay from Chéticamp, he "bent around the head land, dipped into Rig Wash [La Rigouèche], and came up to the only settlement that one meets in these highlands – a scattering of huts that is called Cap Rouge, after the red cape beyond. Here we moved on a

level, and flowers and crops lined the way. But only for a moment." Interestingly, he notes that his host in Pleasant Bay is "a cosmopolite: French
and Irish flowed with the Scottish blood in his veins" (ibid., 20). Still, the
landscape is Highland, not cosmopolitan: his description of the settlement
itself is, unsurprisingly, replete with references to the Auld Country, the
Presbyterian Church, Robert Burns, and, of course, Skye.

Whiteness, Parks, and Modernity

In *Desiring Whiteness,* Kalpana Seshadri-Crooks (2000, 7, 21) argues that
whiteness is not merely one category of racialized difference among others.
It is rather a "master-signifier" that "promises a totality, an overcoming of
difference itself." For the subject of race, whiteness is not just the top of the
food chain; "it represents complete mastery, self-sufficiency," and the "system of race as differences among black, brown, red, yellow, and white makes
sense only in [this] unconscious reference to Whiteness."[11] Whiteness is, to
be sure, a representational category with a history of contingent power relations and struggles attached to its specific manifestations, but it is also a
privileged term that promises to offer access to a being that escapes the
contingencies of representation, an experience of identity beyond history
and particularity. It is thus a "fraudulent signifier ... which promises everything while disavowing its symbolic origins" (ibid., 21).[12] Seshadri-Crooks
(ibid.) summarizes her argument: "Race is a regime of visibility that secures
our investment in racial identity. We make such an investment because the
unconscious signifier Whiteness, which founds the logic of racial difference,
promises wholeness ... Whiteness attempts to signify being, or that aspect of
the subject which escapes language. Obviously, such a project is impossible
because Whiteness is a historical and cultural invention."

The expropriations at Cap Rouge were not only racist in the obvious sense
of privileging recently whitened Scots over apparently less white Acadians in
the creation of a picturesque nature for purposes of visual consumption, but
were also racialized in Seshadri-Crooks' terms: they participated in the creation of CBH as a site for the fantastical experience of whiteness as wholeness. Tuned to a simulacral image of the Highlands, CBH erased its own
process of contingent racial marking by replacing a conflictual cosmopolitan past with a unitary naturalized one, as if it had always been Highlands,
and as if Scots naturally grew there because of its obvious affinities with the
Isle of Skye. With this agenda, as Seshadri-Crooks (ibid.) might put it, the
Acadians in the park threatened to expose and amplify *racial anxiety* (already named by the likes of Dorothy Duncan) because they exposed the

"historicity of Whiteness" – the fact that *any* European ethnic identification with or embodiment of the Cape Breton landscape could not help but be a product of struggle and contingency.[13] One thinks of its colonization by the Portuguese, French, and English, the dispossession of Mi'kmaq territories, and the expulsion of the Acadians from Nova Scotia in 1755 (Le Grand Dérangement) as well as Le Petit Dérangement, the expulsion of the Cap Rougeans. With the Acadians safely elsewhere (actually, in Chéticamp), the fantasy of whiteness as unity was not only sustained in the space of the park but also given added vigour by contemporary naturalizing discourses of pristine, untouched wilderness in which CBH's (originating) whiteness could now be planted.[14] In other words, at the park's creation, a white park-space was founded on the disavowal of the site's contingent racialized past and on the simultaneous production of CBH as the geographic home for and bearer of a Celtic whiteness that even actual Scots (and even the actual Isle of Skye) could not possess.

Seventy years afterward, it would be clear to even a casual observer that CBH has undergone another discursive transformation. As is apparent in both its 1987 *Management Plan* and its most recent interpretive materials, CBH has gone from being a "playground [for] the folks of eastern Canada" to being a representative of "the Maritime Acadian Highlands Natural Region" (Walworth 1948, 15; Environment Canada 1987, 1) in a network of national parks now understood as bearers of ecological meaning rather than recreational or scenic potential. In this process, alongside other Canadian national parks, CBH has become increasingly immersed in an environmentalist discourse that has subtly (and sometimes not so subtly) moved parks into new kinds of articulation of discourses of nature with those of race and nation (Mortimer-Sandilands 2009). With changes in the mandate of the national parks to focus on such ideals as "ecological integrity," involving a distinct ecologization of park landscapes away from their original functions as repositories of scenery and aesthetic experience and toward a more scientized understanding as sites for biogeographic preservation, there has been a corresponding change to the racialized dynamics of park landscapes.

In CBH, the identificatory bonds with Highland heritage have been considerably loosened. For example, although the scenic vistas from the Cabot Trail remain a primary tourist draw, generating a fair number of postcards of solitary pipers on lonely Acadian-less cliffs, recent guidebooks have increasingly emphasized the distinctiveness of CBH as an ecological entity, drawing the interior tablelands, once understood as aesthetically worthless, into a very different map of the park traced along environmental, rather than ethnic/aesthetic dimensions. The stated purpose of the park is, now, "to protect and preserve ... examples of the landforms, features, and ecosystems of the Boreal, Taiga, and Acadian Land Regions of the Park with their representative, rare, and significant plant and animal species" (Environment Canada 1987, 2). Although the protection and preservation of "cultural heritage resources" are still mandated, there is no indication whatsoever in documents such as the *Management Plan* that this heritage is to be read as primarily Scots. Thus, the Lone Shieling still exists, but it is now discursively blended into the landscape named as the Acadian Mountains; it may be "a tribute to the Scottish crofting life of many Cape Breton pioneers before they emigrated from Scotland," but its standing as a park icon now coexists with such ecologically elevated occupants as rare pygmy and Gaspé shrews and old-growth hardwood forests, all of which share equal guidebook billing with the simulacral crofters in the *Park Lover's Companion* to Cape Breton Highlands (C. Barrett 2002, 113-14). Entities that had no standing whatsoever in the original conception of the park are now portrayed as the underlying reason for its existence, and these entities are decidedly not Scottish.

But the declining emphasis on CBH as Highlands has not resulted in the emergence of any kind of genuinely unracialized landscape. In fact, I would argue that the loosening of ties between Celtic identity and park nature has involved a modern rearticulation of the universality of whiteness, specifically through the reinscription of CBH as a site that "preserves" a nature that lies outside human history and thus outside racialization, even as the act of park preservation itself carries racialized inflections. It is not that CBH denies human inhabitation or claims to be an untouched wilderness: "There is," the *Management Plan* explains, "a long history of human activities in northern Cape Breton" (Environment Canada 1987, 2), and it goes on to note archaeological evidence of Aboriginal cultures, most recently the Mi'kmaq, as well as various episodes of European immigration.[15] But this history is clearly in the past: "Most of the areas used for agriculture before the establishment of the Park have *returned to a natural state*" (ibid., emphasis added), and CBH itself is a break from that history in that nature has been allowed to "return" rather than, say, to take a new shape (including a new history) as a *park* (that is, as a historically specific organization of nature). Thus, in the midst of a shift from ethnic/aesthetic to ecological signification of the landscape, there has been a concomitant redrawing of park heritage according to geological and/or evolutionary, rather than primarily socio-historical, *time.* This shift has served to place all human activity in a different perspective; understanding itself as a site for preserving a nature that is far older than any human occupation of Cape Breton (an originary nature rather than any specific set of human relations to it), the park perceives itself as outside the history that occurred before its creation – indeed, outside history altogether.

This understanding of park-time not only takes CBH out of time but also supports the illusion that its current organization of space and meaning is given in timeless, rather than contingent, relations. More precisely, the present-nature of the park comes to appear as the evolutionary destiny of the landscape. History was the messy misguided bit that intervened between the formation of the Appalachian Mountains and the park's creation in 1936 (no mention, of course, of the history that has occurred since), and the park is simply the means through which that destiny can now, unfettered, unfold. CBH thus becomes a universal space as it takes on the aura of timelessness. It is, at least ideally, not organized by particular social desires for the landscape, and thus it transcends any stain of particularity, be it gendered, racialized, or nationalist (Mortimer-Sandilands 2009).[16] That the parks *are* organized by particular social desires for the landscape – not least the facilitation of particular tourist practices of visual consumption – and are fully part of a still conflictual history that includes, in some cases, outstanding land claims, tends to be erased in the self-congratulatory position by which they simply "preserve" what should have been there anyway. Parks thus naturalize their own particularity as universal and as *modern.*

Clearly, the naturalization of parks as embodiments of the modern is part of a process by which certain racialized relations to landscape are not only privileged but also universalized. If we consider the establishment of CBH, the conflicts over Aboriginal hunting and fishing rights in the interests of "game preservation" both historically and in the present (Sandlos 2007), the use of parks for punitive/instructional labour for "aliens" in both world wars (Waiser 1995), the ongoing association of camping and parks with European Caucasian desires for nature recreation, and both overt and more subtle uses of white nationalist rhetoric throughout the history of the parks movement in Canada (Mortimer-Sandilands 2009), it would seem that parks embody and offer quite particular sets of human relations to natural environments and that these relations are strongly tied to white-Caucasian desires.[17] That parks are now able to appear as "natural" repositories for nature is a clear indication that these white-Caucasian desires have become "white," a sort of master signifier for nature experience to which any "black, brown, red, or yellow" position must unconsciously (and sometimes consciously) refer.

If we apply Seshadri-Crooks' argument, then, the ecologization of the present-nature of parks promises to overcome racial difference in the realization of a nature "preserved." Invested as parks are, however, in the disavowal of their contingency and historicity – as they take up, for example, a stance of preserving rather than creating nature – they serve as spaces for the experience of whiteness, a set of nature-encounters already bearing, but carefully hiding, their racialized particularity. And in this case, whiteness is clearly a master signifier of racialized superiority, invisible but with systematic effects in CBH as elsewhere.

Interpretive Memory and the Ghosts of Cap Rouge

The ecologized rewriting of the history of CBH according to a geologic-evolutionary time frame, as well as the passage of human time from 1936 to the present, has allowed for a resignification of the expulsion of the Acadians from Cap Rouge. In the context of the park's claim to be beyond the history it replaced, the Acadian presence is no longer an anxiety-producing stain of the modern but rather an archaic remnant *against* which the park's modernity is established. Now that the Cap Rouge settlement has become a moment of the past in the midst of a larger unfolding of history toward the present – a present that appears to be a progression beyond history – it is now quite "safe," and indeed, its safety-in-the-past ensures that its appearance in the present can now confirm, rather than disrupt, the universality of whiteness. What was in 1936 a risky embodiment of hybridity to be repressed in favour of a mythic Gaelic wilderness can now be reconceived as an isolated moment in the progressive narrative that has brought us to the post-historical "now."

Bruce Braun (2002, 111) has argued that the act of mourning a nature lost to progress functions, paradoxically, to confirm that progress: "To the extent that modernity achieves its coherence through a temporal narrative that understands the present as that which transcends, supersedes, and ultimately destroys the past, mourning presents itself as modernity's most pervasive psychical form." In a similar vein, the memorialization of the Cap Rouge expropriations by way of the permanent interpretive displays along Le Buttereau and at La Bloque has the paradoxical effect of confirming their validity. They were, in the temporal narrative by which the park establishes itself as both the embodiment of progress and the preservation of nature, inevitable. This narrative does not mean that it is not important to mark the expulsions by making them visible in some form; it does suggest, however, that memorialization alone is not sufficient to challenge the universalist narrative by which CBH performs whiteness.

As the guidebooks tell us, Le Buttereau is a moderate 5.5-kilometre loop hike; it connects with another trail, Le Chemin de Buttereau, to form (with La Bloque) the primary permanent interpretive node marking the Acadian presence in CBH. Le Chemin de Buttereau, one guidebook tells us, is "the original Cabot Trail, first walked by the Acadians, where you can now walk through clumps of spruce trees so thick they form tunnels" (Lawley 1994, 9).[18] Le Buttereau itself, says another, "passes through mixed woods and beside old fields that are remnants of several Acadian farms that existed here before the Park was created. The farms were small and life was divided between farming and fishing. A few stone cellars can be seen but the fields are growing back in with spruce, wild rose and spirea" (C. Barrett 2002, 85). Both books are silent as to why the farms ceased to exist, preferring to highlight the wildlife that one might encounter along the trails. But Clarence Barrett (ibid., 82, 85) in particular is clear in his implication that the Acadians were a blip: not only is he about thirty years off in his estimation that "this narrow valley was the site of Acadian farms until the early 1900s," but he is supremely confident in his assertion that "eventually the forest will reclaim them."

As documents written to both respond to and organize tourist desire, these guidebooks are interesting. They describe a present experience (the hike) with little or no differentiation between, say, the ruins of a farm and the possibility of a fox sparrow nest. The description of the hike, at least, thus reduces the landscape to a series of viewable commodities, each of which is of interest only in the moment at which it appears to the reader-hiker *in the present;* they are thus exemplary fetishes, bearing neither histories nor life cycles (we also learn nothing about fox sparrow nesting practices).[19] The ruins are thus already ruins at the point where they matter to the consumer, and their meaning is the one presumed to be the hiker's; neither book indicates that the foundation stones and old well-cover, for example, might mean something else to someone else, either in the past or, crucially, in the present.

The hiker-consumer is thus the universal subject for whom the landscape exists, and (although the guidebooks do not adopt exactly the same position as Parks Canada) the act of consuming nature through this particular recreational practice is written into the landscape along the trail, as well as in choices of where to clear or not clear undergrowth, where to place benches and platforms, and where to erect interpretive signs that might cause the hiker to stop and look at specific items along the way. That same universal hiker-consumer is also written into the *content* of the landscape interpretation on the two trails and at La Bloque. Although the panels and displays organized by Les Amis are more candid that the Cap Rouge properties were expropriated, the fact that the history of the expulsions still privileges a (universal) tourist's consumption of that history ends up reaffirming the particular set of nature-relations – the park, the trails, the clearings, even the proliferation of wild roses – that enables the tourist to consume the park, including the expropriations themselves.

In 1985, the Parks Canada centenary, Les Amis erected a series of interpretive panels commemorating the Cap Rouge community.[20] At La Bloque, the community's fishing centre, the first panel reads (in both French and English), "When Cape Breton Highlands National Park was created in 1936, more than 30 Acadian families inhabited this region. Although *La Bloque* was the economic centre with its lobster cannery, fish shacks and wharf, people lived not only in the neighbourhood of the wharf but also at *Ruisseau du Canadien, Rivière à Lazare, Ruisseau des Maurice, Presqu'île, Source de la Montain, Le Chemin de Buttereau* and *La Rigouèche*. Fishing brought our pioneers here as early as 1821. Today these fishing families from Cap Rouge, their land expropriated, reside for the most part in Chéticamp." Clearly, Les Amis is making a political point here: its use of the first-person plural – *our* pioneers – is highly unusual; interpretive panels are supposed to be objective, and this one is not. Also, it both names and renders the fact of the expropriations in the present, the families *still* in Chéticamp, the effects of the expropriation *not* safely in the past. But, with the passive voice, no agent is revealed to have done the expropriating, and although a subsequent panel hints at the reason it occurred – "this coastline, north of the Chéticamp River, is today one of the most picturesque parts of Cape Breton Highlands National Park" – no real explanation is given.[21] The reader is left to wonder: why were these properties taken away, and by whom?

The answers to these questions are never directly given in any of the permanent interpretive displays.[22] Instead, what we are offered is some detail about what life was like for the people who lived there, including a number of reproductions of period photographs (all the panels are in sepia tones). At La Bloque, we are told about the hardships of fishing in the area: "Although the rocky cliffs and jagged coastline of Cap-Rouge [sic] offered very little shelter for fishing boats, cod was plentiful near these shores." As quoted in the epigraph to this chapter, life was difficult for the fishers, who "still had to haul their boats onto the cobble beach," but a wharf was built in 1900 and a cannery in 1911, meaning that La Bloque actually had at least a small community-owned industrial centre for the twenty-five years before its expropriation. Similarly, on Le Chemin de Buttereau, a panel tells us that "the nights were long and several blankets made from scraps of old material helped warm the beds" but also that "each family had a horse and wagon, cows, sheep, pigs and chickens. They grew oats, hay and a variety of vege-tables." There is thus some ambivalence in the overall interpretation of Cap Rouge: life was hard, but perhaps it wasn't entirely desperate, even if (as other panels state) "they would often go barefoot in order not to wear out the soles of their shoes," and "fishermen only received 50 cents for 100 lobsters."

But the fact that we are never told directly that the people had their land taken away in order to *make the park,* combined with the clear sense that their lives were pretty tenuous, gives the reader of the panels a strong indi-cation that, really, this way of life was on its way out anyway, park or no park. Even though the interpretive booklet *Cap-Rouge: Sur les traces des habi-tants* (Aucoin n.d., also published by Les Amis and also sepia-toned) dis-cusses the extensive community infrastructure that was in place at Cap Rouge in 1936, it is largely devoted to documenting the "vie passée" of the "pionniers au Cap Rouge," from a list of winter provisions for a nineteen-member family (that is, seventeen children) to transport on "la route très périlleuse" that was the Cabot Trail prior to its redevelopment as a road suitable for automobile travel.[23] Ultimately, then, we are left with the sense that the hard days of the *pionniers* are the stuff of heritage and are (thank-fully) over; the park exists not because it destroyed a viable community, but because it was part of the natural evolution of Cape Breton toward modern-ity, a project in which the dispossessed of Cap Rouge were beneficiaries, not victims. The break between "then" and "now" is absolute, and the "now" was, it seems, inevitable. As Réjean Aucoin (n.d., 15) writes, "Il est difficile aujourd'hui de s'imaginer la vie rudimentaire de ces gens. Il y a à peine un demi siècle, aucune route carrossable reliait Chéticamp et Cap-Rouge aux autres communautés du nord du Cap-Breton. Il n'avait pas d'électricité, pas d'eau courante et aucune installation moderne dont on ne saurait se passer aujourd'hui."[24]

Walking along Le Chemin de Buttereau past the ruined foundations of the settlers' houses, we are never asked to read the history of the place as one of struggle or dispossession. Despite their attempt to reveal the place as

having a particular past, the memorial plaques to large families in tiny houses ask us to accept that tradition has, here, long since given way to modernity in an orderly and necessary way. These plaques are truly memorials; as a
gesture to the dead (even though they are not dead but displaced), they are
ghosts that ultimately reinforce the legitimacy of the expropriation rather
than challenging it. They do not ask us to consider that the establishment of
the park might have been an act of arbitrary enclosure for particular *tourist*
purposes and certainly do not reveal that this enclosure was – and that the
position of the tourist is – racialized. The universality of the park, its simple
embodiment of benevolent nature-preservation, is, perhaps paradoxically,
reiterated at each marker. "Look at the past," say the plaques, "and bear witness to the inevitability of progress. Aren't you glad?"

But how is this modernity also about whiteness? The telos of the park
toward the present state of its post-historical achievement appears, as witnessed by this trail, to have *required* the expulsion of this impossibly excessive community. There may have been a loss, but it was a necessary one
carried out in the interests of the greater good. The "excessive other" thus
marks the privileged and universal position of the observer of the ruins, the
visitor hiking along the trail. The gaze of park visitor is not part of the represented scene so much as its judge, and it thus remains hidden from scrutiny
even as it organizes the representation and hierarchization of the landscape
and its history. In short, in their decrepitude, their indication of excess, and
their consignment to nature and the past, the ruins mark the visitor not only
as bourgeois but as white, as the unracialized position conferring differential and racialized meaning on the persons and landscapes with which it is
compared. The Cap Rouge Acadians serve as a sort of racialized *abject* to the
park; the messy ethnicized particularity of their unsustainable inhabitation
has been – and continues to be – expelled in order to create the unmarked
universal position that is the ideal park subject, the consumer, the bearer of
whiteness as the inevitable subject of modernity.

Conclusion

In many ways, the whiteness of national parks is part of their constitution.
Particularly insofar as they embody (or claim to embody) universal nature-
desires – for preservation, for healthy recreation, for education about the
natural landscapes of the nation – they erase the traces of their sometimes
violent histories of dispossession in the crafting of a spatial/temporal narrative that links originary natures directly to the present moment at which
parks simply "preserve" (or ought to preserve) them, and in the facilitation

of a tourist experience of that achievement. That preservation, recreation, and education in a designated wilderness space is a highly particular articulation of nature-desires is seldom questioned in Euro-Canadian conversations (although definitely challenged in others, particularly by Indigenous peoples who refuse the recreational understanding of park-nature as a space apart from livelihood). Whiteness is, here, so universal that it appears to be written in nature itself, other claims to nature becoming not only particular but anti-nature, polluting, or destructive. Whiteness is perpetuated in parks by abjecting racial difference, and the equation of Euro-Canadian nature-desires with park claims to a benevolent inevitable modernity renders silent most other possibilities.[25]

Given this structural quality, is there any way that national parks such as CBH might participate in a different regime of race and nature? I would suggest that they can, and that in CBH at least, the foundations are already there for a different possibility. As some of the materials produced by Les Amis already note, the descendants of the Cap Rouge families are still there, part of the thriving Acadian community of Chéticamp and, as it happens, already inclined to question the legitimacy of the expropriations. A document from the CBH archive written in English by Leo Boudreau (n.d., 3) gives voice to this questioning. The people at Cap Rouge, he states,

> were all illiterate, with nobody to fight for them. At that time, our local Municipal councilor was the contact man representing the three phases of Government, and was the only leader they could lean to. The people involved depended on this person, but to their astonishment and disappointment, they received the following two answers from their leader. "I promised the Government I would not bother them concerning this problem." Second answer. "Take that offer or you'll get nothing at all." It seems that our Municipal Councilor was so anxious to get the National Park under way, that he would take it at any price.

Boudreau departs from the park's public interpretation by making Cap Rouge an issue of *contestation* in several ways. First, he names the expropriations as a "deportation" (ibid., 2), thus linking them to a broader history of injustice against Acadians in Nova Scotia. Second, he offers an overtly political interpretation of the park's creation, questioning the removal of the Acadians and the preservation of "all the other villages"; he names these acts as interested, "criminal" (ibid., 3), and crucially, particular. And third, he places the expropriations in the middle of a story of Chéticamp that traces the community's history from the founding of Quebec in 1608 to the present, crafting a distinctly Acadian cultural imaginary in which to locate Le Petit Dérangement that is quite different from the one presumed in the park. It connects Cap Rouge to the living community of Chéticamp rather than to the ghostly "reclaiming" forest, thus rendering the ongoing resentment of the expropriations both visible and present.

The point, here, is not to assume the validity of Boudreau's claims, to assess whether the compensations were fair, or even to demand a public apology for past wrongs. Instead, I would simply like to note that CBH could quite easily insert this view into its interpretive materials and thereby encourage a more active questioning of the relationship between parks and social identities. If the park were to demonstrate the racialized character of its own origins, allow other particularities to challenge the universality of the nature-narrative via which it justifies its existence, and show that the ruins at Cap Rouge are relics of power and conflict, not commodity-testaments to the inevitability of progress, the hiker could be prompted to question the relations by which she is able to smell the wild roses at Le Buttereau and perhaps even to consider the particularity of her desires to do so.

ACKNOWLEDGMENTS
The author wishes to thank Kate Krug for her company on the trails of Cape Breton Highlands, Alan MacEachern for his comments on an earlier version of this chapter, and Andrew Baldwin, Laura Cameron, and Audrey Kobayashi for (patiently) organizing our collective rethinking of the Great White North.

PART 2

CITY SPACES

The "Occult Relation between Man and the Vegetable"
Transcendentalism, Immigrants, and Park Planning in Toronto, c. 1900

PHILLIP GORDON MACKINTOSH

> *The greatest delight the fields and woods minister is the*
> *suggestion of an occult relation between man and the vegetable.*
> *I am not alone and unacknowledged. They nod to me and I to*
> *them. The ... effect is like that of a higher thought or a better*
> *emotion coming over me.*
>
> – Ralph Waldo Emerson, *The Best of Ralph Waldo Emerson*

Had Emerson passively accepted this supposed "occult relation" between humans and nature, instead of investing nature with metaphysical properties of social uplift, would the nature-in-the-city ideal have been less influential in modern city building? Certainly, the nature-as-source-of-higher-thinking conceit has a problem (despite a liberal affinity for such an interpretation of nature): conflating nature and "higher thought" enabled transcendentalists to establish a geographical premise for social and moral revivification, a position that subsequently became the impetus for city beautification's preoccupation with parks and playgrounds, parkways, squares, gardens, boulevards, and greenswards – in a phrase, physical infrastructure. The environmental determinism embedded in this assumption, however, compels suspicion and questions: was park planning in cities such as Toronto City Beautiful's transcendentalist response to the era's acute dissatisfaction with immigrants and their neighbourhoods? Did "white" haute bourgeois reformers use "transcendentalized" parks to transform immigrants into "higher forms" of citizens?

It is not new to think of nature in the form of urban parks as having social benefit, or to connect parks to the rhetoric of social and moral reform (Schmitt 1969; Cavallo 1981; Wilson 1981; Cranz 1982; Rosenzweig and Blackmar 1992; Young 1996; Pipkin 2005). Galen Cranz (1982, 7) even notes the presence of a popular transcendentalism in turn-of-the-twentieth-century park reform. More novel, though, is the association of the urban parking (a term coined by park planners to refer to the planning and construction of parks) impulse with the social reform intimated in the transcendentalist thinking of Ralph Waldo Emerson: a nature-influenced social evolutionary perfectionism. We find this association in three of his ideas: "that within the form of every creature is a force compelling it to ascend to a higher form" (Emerson 1941, 236), that "beautiful" nature could effect this social ascendancy, and that "the soul assimilates its world" (Wood 1976, 387). These ideas are explained below.

Given Emerson's premises, Cranz's observation allows us to imagine park planning as an expression of transcendentalist environmental determinism. Thus, park planning becomes social geographic practice. A method for transforming immigrants into a "higher" form of citizen, it equates with the sanitization of racial elements in the modern city (Mahtani 2008). In the "Episcopal city of Toronto" (Goheen 1970, 54), where immigrants and their "unhygienic" geographies challenged the hegemony of old-stock, caste-prone "white" Protestant families (Baltzell 1966), park planning spatially defined race. Indeed, such transcendentalist planning initiatives as Toronto's Plan of 1909, or Toronto City Council's intervention for the Elizabeth Street playground, correspond with David Theo Goldberg's (2002b, 233-34) conclusion that the modern state is a racial state: both these examples of park planning in early Toronto demonstrate how "the apparatuses and technologies employed by modern states have served variously to fashion, modify, and reify the terms of racial expression, as well as racist exclusions and subjugation." Claims of "race suicide" (Bacchi 1982, 580; Valverde 1991, 91) and calls for white "Canadians [to] prodominate [sic] as they should" (Clark 1898, 3) echoed in Toronto. The attempt of the Plan of 1909 to wrap Toronto in parklands, or the effort of city council to put a playground on the main thoroughfare of Toronto's most impoverished immigrant neighbourhood, alludes to an uncritical faith in the transcendentalist ability of nature to produce more enlightened, beautiful, and "fairer" (Emerson 1963, 192) immigrants.

Transcendentalism

This is not the forum to engage in a protracted discussion of transcendentalism, whose historical presence in North America is documented in a vast corpus of literature (see Capper 1998). I will, nevertheless, briefly address Ralph Waldo Emerson and his ideas as they affected popular transcendentalism at the turn of the twentieth century. And though Emerson was American, Phillip Mackintosh and Richard Anderson (2009) amply illustrate Toronto's engagement with Emersonian ideas. However, let me begin with a brief discussion of City Beautiful to contextualize the nature-in-the-city transcendentalist ideal.

The success of the White City, the Beaux Arts planning and design utopia built for Chicago's 1893 Columbian Exposition, inspired many North American urban reformers to concentrate their city-shaping efforts on municipal beautification, a movement labelled City Beautiful (see Wilson 1989). Exasperated with the congestion, pollution, poverty, social heterogeneity, and general inconvenience of urban modernity, beautifiers pursued a program of reform based on the aesthetics, hygiene, technology, and crucially, the presumed social order of the White City. Planning and design lessons derived from the White City, founded on the principles of fine art and architecture, would be instrumental for "the making of a new citizen," as planning theorist Charles Zueblin (1905, 57) insisted. Particularly influential was the White City's incorporation of green space and nature as an ameliorating urban influence: Fredrick Law Olmsted built parks, waterways, and even an island garden centrepiece, and his use of trees, grass, and horticulture contrasted strikingly with the alabaster architecture and white concrete pavements designed by Daniel Burnham (and a team of architects that included Louis Sullivan and Charles McKim among others). The effect of this nature-enhanced urbanism on a society that equated industrial modernity with a "great blemish" (J.C. Adams 1896, 4) "immensely strengthened, quickened and encouraged" (Robinson 1899, 771) beautifiers' resolve over the next decade: "We are tired of polluted air and water, dirty streets, grimy buildings and disordered cities. From the White City ... the lesson has been impressed that ugliness and inconvenience for the present and the future will yield to the magic power of the comprehensive plan" (Zueblin 1905, 82). As master plans for the rejuvenation of an entire city, comprehensive plans in the first decades of the twentieth century obsessed on the type of park and parkway building found in Toronto's Plan of 1909 (Figure 4.1). And as an impetus of City Beautiful, the comprehensive placement of attractive "squares, playgrounds and parks in the midst of dense populations" (Eliot 1902, 381) created propinquity between urban nature and urban people. In short, City Beautiful put city people under the behaviour-moderating influence of Emerson's transcendent nature.

What were the intellectual and moral informants of City Beautiful's park-planning impulse? To answer this, three points regarding Emerson's transcendental influence on park planners need elaboration: transcendentalism as a priori nature, transcendental nature as a divine manifestation of moral-aesthetics, and transcendentalism as social reform. Emerson, a Harvard-trained philosopher/theologian, embraced the idea of a deity-created and deity-inspired nature. Emerson's (1963, 150) nature existed before history and expressed the creative will of God, or the "Over-soul, within which every man's particular being is contained and made one with all other."

This divine a priori ontology imbued nature with moral-aesthetic potential, the idea that beauty is necessarily moral, necessarily good (Mackintosh 2005, 690). As Emerson (1963, 206) argued, "the world is not painted or adorned, but is from the beginning beautiful; and God has not made some beautiful things, but Beauty is the creator of the universe." The corollary to divine beauty was ugliness, the result of "dislocation and detachment from the life of God" (ibid., 213). Ugliness, in people or things, presented such a contrast to the beauty of nature that Emerson (ibid., 299) admitted "the beauty of nature must always seem unreal and mocking, until the land-scape has human figures, that are as good as itself. If there were good men, there would never be this rapture in nature." Thus, inspirited with divine beauty, but also the universal pattern of all beauty, transcendental nature offered humanity an aesthetic foundation, uniquely geographical, for moral goodness.

The ability of nature to prompt moral transcendent action in humans established it as an agent of social reform. Emerson (ibid., 216, emphasis in original) insisted that "nature has a higher end, in the production of new individuals ... namely *ascension,* or the passage of souls into higher forms." Assuming the soul was "progressive," Emerson (ibid., 192) believed that, "in every act [it] attempts the production of a new and fairer whole." It was not simply the soul that was progressive, however; so too was the body: "A man is a method, a progressive arrangement" (ibid., 84). The human form, for Emerson, was inherently malleable and capable of transcending the mundane, and eminently susceptible to the influence of nature. Thus, nature was teleological, its purpose in the human world to instantiate higher life in

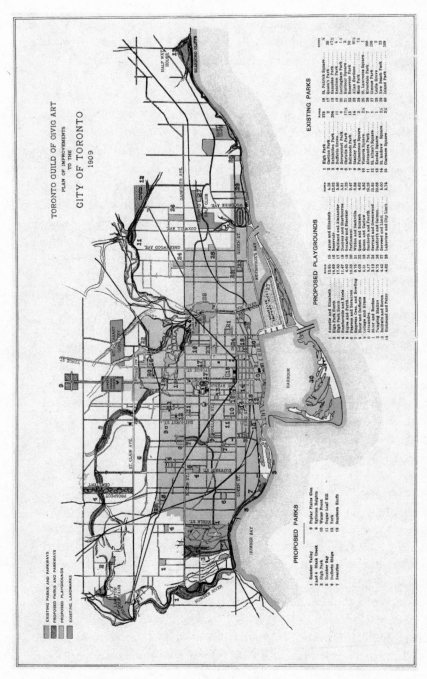

Figure 4.1   The Toronto Civic Guild's Plan of 1909, which also incorporated the natural elements of Toronto's urban landscape. The shaded areas represent proposed parks, playgrounds, and parkways (Toronto Guild of Civic Art 1909, n.p.).

morally and physically weak and/or inferior humans, whose own purpose in a hegemonic evangelical Protestant theology was to effect incremental personal improvement – especially bodily. Thus, God's spirit dwelt in perfectible corporeal "temples," to effect the human return to God's presence.

Emersonian theology may seem high-flown, but it nevertheless allowed city beautifier Charles Mulford Robinson (1901, 153) to assert there was "happily no need to present ... the arguments in favor of parks for cities, nor ... necessary to go deeply into the history of the movement in their behalf." By 1901 nature's ability to revivify the "soul" attained the status of common sense. Indeed, park planners enthusiastically recapitulated Emerson's (1963, 20-21) famous observation "To the body and mind which have been cramped by noxious work or company, nature is medicinal and restores their tone. The tradesman, the attorney comes out of the din and craft of the street and sees the sky and the woods, and is a man again. In their eternal calm he finds himself."[1]

The received wisdom of this transcendental theme and its variations pervades City Beautiful documents, appearing even in the following statement by the Toronto Civic Guild (1913, 5), the sponsors of Toronto's Plan of 1909: "When we think of city parks, and open spaces we must think of them as being, by necessity, utilitarian as well as by choice, beautiful, for we must have recreation and breathing spaces if we are to have healthy happy and contented citizens." Nature, implemented in the form of parks and filtered through transcendentalism, seemed destined to "contribute to the social renovation of Toronto's working and immigrant classes" (Mackintosh 2005, 693).

Parks and Propinquity

Park and playground building arrested the imaginations of professional and lay reformers who, by 1900, subscribed to the "redeeming power of nature" (Rosenzweig and Blackmar 1992, 2). The park occupied a significant portion of the city beautification impulse in the era shortly before the professionalization of city planning (Wilson 1981, 1989; Cranz 1982; Schuyler 1986; Sies and Silver 1996; P. Baldwin 1999; Peterson 2003). Professional planning guru Frederick Law Olmsted Jr. (1911, 16) contended in "The City Beautiful" that "well distributed public playgrounds and neighbourhood parks become one of the urgent needs if the health and vigor of the people are to be maintained." Olmsted did not equivocate. Why?

Van Wyck Brooks' acerbic depiction of transcendentalism as "a shining deluge of righteousness, purity, [and] practical mysticism" (Brooks, quoted

in Capper 1998, 510) could well describe beautifiers' belief in parks as manifest moral-aestheticism. Note Robinson's (1901, 288, emphasis added) conclusion to his planning treatise *The Improvement of Towns and Cities*:

> Looking out upon the world, let it note that if sunrise and sunset, if summer
> sky and winter night, if bending heaven and upreaching earth have beauty,
> nature giving constant example of its coupling with utility, we may accept
> beauty of environment as part of the divine plan and fear to shut it out from
> the crowded life of cities. For can we say there is no holiness of beauty, that
> it has no essentialness to creation's scheme, when we find it shaping the
> field flower, the fern in the densest forest, or the spray cap of a wave in
> trackless seas, lest in aeons of time these be seen? Consider how the grasses
> bend in broken beauty at our feet in virgin country, how the sky lavishes its
> wealth of glory before careless eyes, how the great trees sway and call, put
> forth tender leaves at spring or flaunt an autumn splendor; how the birds
> translate rapture into music; and the constant, changeless stars soothe
> weary hours with measureless majesty. When God does this for a lonely
> child, shall we relax our vigilance to bring beauty to the homes of huddled
> thousands? Dare we say that a city must be ugly?

Brooks' observation about transcendentalism's pietistic and mystical approach to nature and beauty pulses through Robinson's refulgent prose
(reminiscent of Emerson, even invoking his love of the sky).

Robinson's apparent socialized transcendentalism leaps from the page.
More forceful, however, is his environmentally determinate and planning-
oriented claim about the "holiness of beauty" and the implication that proximity to beauty – nature – would redeem the immigrant poor in cities.
Parks in propinquity to "the homes of the huddled thousands" – "huddled
thousands," "masses," "crowded," and "congested" being euphemisms for reformers' frustration with immigrants – was not an idea that Robinson alone
promoted.[2]

It seems that park planners were convinced that many parks placed near
the working and immigrant poor would effect social regeneration. For example, city beautifier and horticulturalist Horace McFarland believed, as
William Wilson (1981, 317, emphasis added) explains, that nearness to parks
could modify bad behaviour: "Chicago's 1910 crime statistics showed an
overall annual increase of 11 percent but [McFarland] claimed a plunge of
44 percent within a half mile radius of small recreational parks." In an
aside, Wilson suggests that, "if human beings were as malleable as

McFarland suggested, *dotting* the city with recreational parks a mile apart would have crippled crime in Chicago." This, of course, was precisely McFarland's point: increase park acreages – propinquity – and vice will decline proportionately. Montreal's Civic Improvement Committee made the same argument: "If Montreal were more generously provided with playgrounds, especially in the congested districts, juvenile crime and the mortality from tuberculosis and other ailments would be materially decreased" (W.S. Maxwell, quoted in Woodsworth 1972, 32-33). However, if in their zeal McFarland (and others) "misunderstood or misused statistics" (Wilson 1981, 317), they were not alone.

Many planners would *dot* the city with parks. Consider George Ford's (1909, 131, emphasis added) exhortation that parks and playgrounds "*should* be established in every section of the tenement district. They *should* be small and there *should* be many of them. They *should* have a southern exposure, open to prevailing summer winds. In all cases there *should* be lots of trees, grass, and flowers." Canadian reformer J.S. Woodsworth (1972, 35, 36-38), complaining that most Canadian "city streets f[e]ll far short of the standards of the City Beautiful," demanded that "scattered through the city, and surrounding it, there should be a series of smaller and larger parks that would enable every tired mother to wheel her baby out for an hour in the afternoon and the whole family to have a weekly half-holiday on the grass under the trees." Why? Woodsworth let Toronto child reformer J.J. Kelso (quoted in ibid., 360) reply: "Just consider for a moment the influence that [numerous and accessible parks and playgrounds] would have on the social life of the people of Toronto! You would have an object-lesson always before the people ... The happiness of the children playing there would reflect the lives of men and women passing by, who need something to cheer them up." A park on every street would allow nature to influence "the sad side of life" of those mired in hardscrabble neighbourhoods bereft of greenery, where children played on macadam, wood, or gravel streets, or in garbage- and rubble-strewn vacant lots behind inner-city buildings. "Proper" childhood eschewed such environments.

Reform beliefs in the park as "hygienic necessity" (Stubben 1885, n.p.) were even advanced in the press. A happy statistic on parks and mortality rates, reported in the *Toronto Daily Mail and Empire* (1898, 3), affirmed reformers' opinions of nature's hygiene. Though stressing the incompleteness of the study, the newspaper correlated quantity of park and general health: "It appears that Minneapolis with an acre of park land to each of 129 of its inhabitants, has a death rate per thousand of 9.93; while Cincinnati

TABLE 4.1

Persons per one acre of park in various cities, c. 1914

City	Population	Park acreage	Persons per acre
London	7,251,358	15,901	456
New York	5,333,539	7,738	689
Paris	2,847,229	5,014	554
Chicago	2,393,325	545	545
Berlin	2,082,111	1,034	2,014
Philadelphia	1,657,810	5,143	322
Hamburg	1,006,748	808	1,246
Birmingham	840,202	1,414	598
St. Louis	734,667	2,765	266
Boston	733,802	3,545	207
Baltimore	579,590	2,402	241
Washington	353,378	5,212	68
Kansas City	281,911	1,952	144
Rochester	241,518	1,836	133

Source: N. Lewis (1916, 134).

with a population 1,025 per acre of park land has a mortality rate of 18.74; and Chicago, which ranks next to Cincinnati in the number of inhabitants (745) [per acre] ... has a death rate of 16.93." The *Mail and Empire* did not offer a mortality statistic for Toronto, but then, Toronto's 1898 population of 186,517 co-existed with 1,573 acres of park space, a ratio of 118.5 Torontonians per acre of park.[3] Planner Benjamin Marsh (1908), who used planning to address social injustice, understood such statistics (Table 4.1) and employed them to advance the propinquity argument in New York City:

The Playgrounds Association of this city has estimated that there should be at least an acre of park for every 250 citizens. We may, however, in the built-up sections of the city assume a more conservative condition for health, and yet the condition in New York City makes it clear that we are in a very unhealthy state. In 1909 Manhattan had a population per acre of park area of 1589; Brooklyn, 1268; The Bronx, 83; Queens, 211; Richmond, 1127. The total park area of Greater New York, mapped in 1909, was 7221 acres. The normal park area, allowing one acre of park to every 250 people, would have been 15,944. New York City, therefore, lacks to-day 8,723 acres of ... normal park area. (Marsh 1910, 84-85, emphasis in original)[4]

Cleveland landscape architect and planner George Rettig (1912, 123, 126), in an address to the Canadian Club of Toronto in 1912, echoed Marsh. Cleveland had "added 1275 acres of park land ... to the 225 existing in 1894"; since then, "only 354 acres ha[d] been added, and not very much of a good nature has been done." Rettig admonished Toronto not to fail where Cleveland had, despite Cleveland's ratio of population-to-park acreage of 188:1.[5] Toronto must ensure that many parks and playgrounds be erected, "which should be within easy reach of every child in the city." Easy access would teach "the boy who has always been out for himself ... to understand the question of good citizenship when he is older," a politer way of saying "'the boy without a playground ... is the father to the man without a job'" (Rosenzweig and Blackmar 1992, 393). Thus, Rettig urged vigilant Torontonians to use parks and propinquity to effect the euthenic conversion of immigrant child to model citizen.

If parks and propinquity mattered in the effort to employ transcendentalism to transmogrify immigrants and their neighbourhoods, did examples of it exist in Toronto? The following discussion of both Toronto's Plan of 1909 and the Elizabeth Street playground illustrates the ease with which the propinquity idea fit with planners' motivations.

The Plan of 1909

Reformers' belief that their city lacked park and playground space was not new: "For some time past there has been a general belief among citizens that the number of public squares, parks and playgrounds in Toronto was not adequate to the needs of the city, especially when its future growth is considered" (*Toronto Globe* 1890b, 4). And though some aldermen believed that Toronto was not as "badly off in this respect as many people suppose[d]," council still moved to secure "additional park sites before the increased value of the land place[d them] beyond ... reach" (*Toronto Globe* 1890a, 6). The city council's Committee on Park and Gardens, which had become the Committee on Parks and Exhibitions (CP and E) by 1900, was charged with the task of supervising the construction of park space, if only in piecemeal fashion in an era that clamoured for comprehensive reform.

However, council's practice of ad hoc parking was insufficient and compelled the Toronto Civic Guild (TCG, formerly the Toronto Guild of Civic Art), a consulting body to Toronto City Council in matters of civic art and city beautification, to hire British architect and planner Sir Aston Webb in 1907. Webb, who worked on the Mall approach to Buckingham Palace (Carr 1996, 162), drafted a comprehensive park and parkway plan for Toronto.

The result, the *Report on a Comprehensive Plan for Systematic Civic Improvements in Toronto* (Toronto Guild of Civic Art 1909), detailed a method to increase the park, parkway, and playground space of the city. It would also help the rapidly populating city, which by 1909 topped 325,000, maintain the morals and health-promoting persons-per-acre-of-park standard – 250:1 – noted above.

The Plan of 1909, which sought to establish a continuous ring of green space around the city and to add hundreds of acres of new parks and playgrounds, was conceived partly "to create a more comely, a more spacious and a more inspiring Toronto" (Toronto Guild of Civic Art 1909, n.p.). More importantly, building parks, parkways, and playgrounds "would directly re-shape" what James O'Brian, president of the Toronto Civic Guild, euphemistically "'called the working class (for want of a better term)'" (Mackintosh 2005, 693). These were new citizens who, more than all other Torontonians, embodied the "evils of congestion of population in cities" (Toronto Guild of Civic Art 1909, n.p.).

The nature-as-reform idea was popular in Toronto. School Inspector James L. Hughes, as "chairman of a committee of the Playground Association of Toronto, appointed ... to arrange that as many children as possible in the city have the opportunity of planting flowers and vegetables," importuned *Toronto Daily Star* readers to allow him to use their vacant lots. The compulsion to teach children the value of nature through gardening and horticulture revealed Hughes' and the Playground Association's transcendental proclivities: "There can be no question that the growing of flowers and vegetables ... would afford the children of the city practice in one of the most essential departments of their moral training" (*Toronto Daily Star* 1912a, 9).[6] How could it do otherwise when gardening obtained the putative ability to increase a child's "respect for the rights of others" (Miller 1904, 5)?

Likewise, the *Toronto Star* Fresh Air Fund raised funds, before 1915, to give immigrant children a chance to experience nature's morally rejuvenating influence (Mackintosh and Anderson 2009). The Fresh Air Fund financed day excursions and weekly trips to Toronto's exurban parks as well as to wilderness getaways, such as the Muskoka Lakes and Haliburton Highlands. The point was to expose children to both the healthful and transcendental influence of nature. Whether or not exporting immigrant children into the countryside actually gave them "a taste of life that is pure and ennobling," a life that would change "their thoughts" from "the color of pavement dust, with dark shadows, stagnant crevices and [a] hardness love can scarcely soften," was never pursued critically (*Toronto Daily Star* 1915a, 2). Reformers asserted only that cavorting in the "fields of buttercups out at Bronte," a rural village roughly fifty kilometres west of Toronto and popular Fresh Air Fund destination, would beneficently alter immigrant children confined to "the poorly housed and badly ventilated districts of the city" (*Toronto Daily Star* 1915b, 4; *Toronto Daily Star* 1902, 1).

Organized according to such principles, the Plan of 1909 (Toronto Guild of Civic Art 1909, n.p.) demonstrated a commitment to propinquity (Figure 4.1), which I reproduce in a long quote below:

THE PARK SYSTEM

The Park System consists of a practically continuous chain of parks and parkways surrounding the city ... linked by boulevards ... Starting on the water front at the Old Fort, the Garrison Common, Exhibition Park ... a continuous park system [runs along] the water front to the Humber River ... Both sides of the Humber River are reserved for parks as far north as the Military Grounds on the east side ... passing the Lambton Golf Club ... east through the Black Creek Ravine ... to the higher level at Prospect Cemetery, which it crosses ... to the Ravine ... [then] south east [to] intersect [with] Poplar Plains Road ... [then] northward to ... Avenue Road ... [where it divides] so as to pass on each side of Upper Canada College, and then ... north to a large park above Eglinton Ave. From Avenue Road the main parkway continues east, south of St. Michael's Cemetery, and connects with Reservoir Park ... skirting the southerly boundary of Mount Pleasant Cemetery in an easterly direction, turns south east ... crossing the CPR tracks [and entering] the Don Valley through ... [to] Riverdale Park. Rising ... to the higher level it skirts the east and south banks of the eastern branch of the Don, widening into a large park reservation ... [and] following a ravine until due north of Norway Hill it drops south, join[ing] ... Kingston Road and continu[ing] on ... to the Scarboro Cliffs ... east of Yonge Street, where a park reservation is suggested.

From the Scarboro Park the parkway turns westerly ... overlooking the lake and descend[s] ... through Balmy and Kew Beaches to Woodbine Park ... [then] returns to the city by ... [a] minor connecting parkway, ... while [another] park reservation continues on the lake front south of Ashbridge's Bay to the Island ... which extends almost to the point of starting.

[From] Queen's Park as the heart of the inner park system ... parkways run south via Queen Street Avenue, west via Wilcox Street, and [other] continuations ... to High Park, north through Hoskin Avenue, to St. George Street ... to the outer park system at Poplar Plains Road and east via

Wellesley Street to Riverdale Park. The west side of the city is divided by another parkway ... connecting with the outer park system, east of Prospect Cemetery ... down Dufferin Street ... east along the brow of Wells' Hill and south through Christie Street, continues south through the Trinity College ravine and Stanley Park to the Exhibition Park ... [via] a bridge over the railway tracks. To the east this parkway is continued through Wellington place to Clarence Square.

From Riverdale Park the present Rosedale Ravine drives run to the northwest, the south one terminating in Ramsden Park and the north one in Reservoir Park. A parkway runs south through the Don speedway and on to the park reservation south of Ashbridge's Bay and east through Gerrard Street to connect with the outer parkway at the Norway Hill, and at Coxwell Avenue, a branch running south through the ravine at Small's Pond, which connects with Woodbine Park.

The Plan of 1909 attempted to entwine Toronto in parks, building propinquity into the structure of the city. The green space totalled 2,078 acres and resulted in a person-per-acre-of-park ratio of 156:1.[7] Given the TCG's population statistic of 325,302 for 1909, Toronto's proposed ratio compares favourably to Minneapolis' mortality-inducing 129:1, bests other cities (see Table 4.1), and meets the 250:1 standard (Toronto Civic Guild 1911, n.p.).[8]

The Elizabeth Street Playground

In the 1910s, as the TCG lobbied to have its meticulous parkway plan adopted by the city, the Toronto City Council Committee on Parks and Exhibitions (CP and E) mandated itself to the further consideration of piecemeal park and playground building; the city seemed to have an aversion to comprehensive planning (Mackintosh 2001). Instead, the CP and E minutes are peppered with individual proposals that suit the committee's dedication to "park and playground purposes" (Committee on Parks and Exhibitions 1910-12, 30 March 1910, 39). One of these proposed a playground on Elizabeth Street, a well-known thoroughfare in St. John's Ward, or Ward 3, Toronto's notorious "slum" neighbourhood. The Ward's chaotic confusion of public and private made it "'a strange and fearful place into which it [wa]s unwise to enter even in daylight'" (R. Dennis 1997, 396n32), or so "respectable" Torontonians opined.[9]

Toronto's immigrant neighbourhoods, with their dearth of green space, were obvious choices for parks and playgrounds. Populous and impoverished places such as the Ward in the centre of the city, Corktown at the east

Figure 4.2   A child and chickens in the "yard" of a condemned rear, 1917. This dwelling, labelled on the photograph "Condemned: Unfit for Habitation," was located behind 149 Elizabeth Street in the Ward. A main complaint about such housing was its unsuitability for children: no trees, no grass, no shade, no supervision or safe play space. | Series 372, Subseries 32, item 505, City of Toronto Archives.

end of King Street, and the King-Niagara district at the west end of King Street had no playgrounds and few parks – King-Niagara had nearby Stanley Park and Bellwoods Park about a kilometre away, and the Ward had Queen's Park, but of course "children we[re] not permitted, as in American cities, to play in the park" (Clark 1898, 77).[10]

The general lack of trees and grass had become a chief characteristic of the neighbourhoods containing "squalid foreigners, who violate every law of cleanliness and aggravate conditions in themselves radically bad"; the Ward was called "shoptown" for its "gabbling" cosmopolitanism (Zucchi 1988, 39). The newspapers especially fulminated against the Ward, "where a great part of the foreign population is concentrated," over half of it east European Jews and 10 percent Italian (ibid.; *Charities and the Commons* 1906, 967; *Toronto Daily Star* 1908, 3). Life for the immigrant poor in the Ward was "one monotonous round of pavements, courts, ash heaps, rubbish piles, close stuffy bedrooms, badly cooked food when there is any, to say nothing of the scanty cast off clothing they must wear all year round." To experience the Ward

Figure 4.3 Numerous children play on the southeast corner of Elizabeth Street and Foster Place, c. 1913, outside Sarah Smith's grocery, Moses Rosenbaum's and Samuel Goldrash's plumbing shops at 91 1/2, 91, and 89 Elizabeth Street respectively (*Toronto City Directory* 1913, 165). Elizabeth Street was a busy Toronto thoroughfare, but note that it was not paved, at a time when the city laid tens of miles of asphalt and other pavements in the central business district (Mackintosh 2005). Yet the council spent a good deal of money to build the Elizabeth Street playground. Why would it privilege one infrastructure (a park) over another (a paved street), in an era when pavements were promoted as the chief facilitator of commerce in the central business district? | Fonds 1244, item 341, City of Toronto Archives.

and its treeless, colourless landscape was to know what a real "slum" was, according to the *Toronto Daily Star* (1908, 3).

One of the worst streets in the Ward was Elizabeth Street, if newspaper reports were accurate; "Elizabeth Street" was code for "immigrant trouble." It exemplified the rear cottage evil in Toronto, or the "rows" problem. According to the *Toronto Daily Star* (1901, 1), there were two rows of humble existence in the slum neighbourhoods of the city: a row of dilapidated roughcast housing (stucco on lath) along the street – "roughcast" was another code word – and then behind it a row of housing so squalid it beggared reformers' attempts to describe it (Figures 4.2 and 4.3). These were the rears, as reformers called them, entered "through a passage under the front building or an alley between two houses ... Frequently there is but

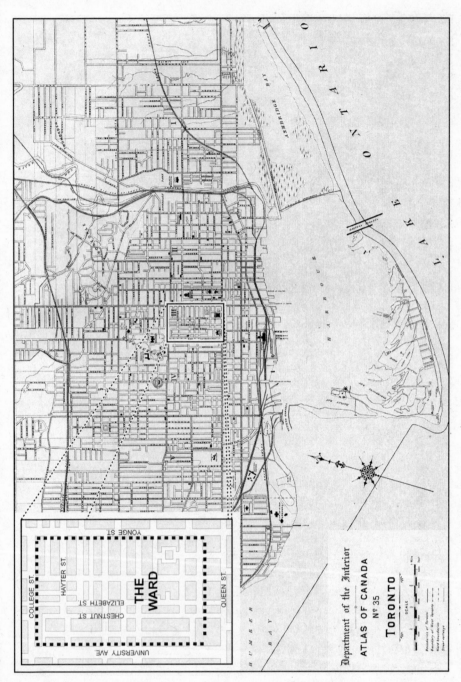

Figure 4.4   The location of the Elizabeth Street playground, between Elizabeth and Chestnut Streets at Hayter Street. | Taken from Toronto, No. 35, *The Atlas of Canada, Department of Interior* (Toronto: Toronto Lithographing Company, 1906). Altered by Loris Gasparotto.

one storey and one room, and in it lives a whole family, with its domestic animals" (ibid.).

Elizabeth Street (and surrounding neighbourhood) was home to a large percentage of renters and lodgers, who suffered the ills of absentee landlordism (R. Dennis 1997, 381-82). The resulting deplorable housing conditions created such animosity between renters and landlords that, when "three roughcast cottages" on "Foster Place, off Elizabeth Street" burned on a June night in 1912 – not surprisingly, the three families violently purged from their homes by fire, Malinsky, Olinsky, and Possava, were east European Jews – the arrival of the landlord, J. Ossilcar, caused an immediate riot. And peace was not restored until the landlord retreated "rather hurriedly up Elizabeth Street" (*Toronto Daily Star* 1912b, 2).

Such conditions fostered an apparent need for a park, so the CP and E forwarded a notice of motion in council by Alderman Maguire to establish "a playground between or in the district bounded by Hayter, Yonge, Queen St [sic] and ... [University] Avenue" (Committee on Parks and Exhibitions 1910-12, 17 February 1910, 24) (Figure 4.4). Indeed, there was an expediency to the motion; at the next monthly meeting of the CP and E, the parks commissioner had reported on an adequate site: "He recommended as the most suitable place the land lying between Elizabeth and Chestnut Streets and from the limits of the Public School Grounds to the new line of Christopher Street" (ibid., 9 March 1910, 29). Accordingly, the assessment commissioner was urged to "procure options on the property within the said district and submit an estimate to this Committee *at an early date*" (ibid., emphasis added).

Purchasing and then building the Elizabeth Street playground was not cheap. The park occupied a city block and required the expropriation of 200-202 Elizabeth Street, the site of the Union Soda Water Manufacturing Company, which would receive a bonus of $500 for vacating its premises. Payments of $4,072 were made to each of the owners of 196 and 198 Elizabeth, as well as $300 in "disturbance fee[s]" for disrupting their businesses (Toronto City Council 1911a, 24). The Board of Control also allocated $2,000 for the purchase of playground equipment (*Toronto Daily Star* 1911a, 2) (Figure 4.5). Upon receipt of the assessment commissioner's report in a "special meeting," the CP and E "recommended to Council that the report be adopted and that the Board of Control be requested (Committee on Parks and Exhibitions 1910-12, 3 May 1910, 53-54). This was a considerable sum of money in 1910-11, and yet it was to be spent on a playground in what was believed to be the most loathsome neighbourhood in the city, where

Figure 4.5 Newly planted greenery on the margins of the Elizabeth Street playground, 6 August 1913. | Series 372, Subseries 52, item 78, City of Toronto Archives.

"scores" of ragged children "rolled in the dust" and shot craps in the shade-less, stifling, dirt lanes, where entire families withered, "reduced to starva-tion and nakedness, in a strange land, unable to speak English" (*Toronto Daily Star* 1915b, 4). Why?

In part, the answer seems to be that the CP and E was ideologically com-mitted to the transcendentalist idea of parks and playgrounds as moral tu-tors, especially in immigrant and impoverished neighbourhoods. When it organized a search committee to identify a Toronto representative, and then expended funds to send that person – the park commissioner – to the Conference of the International Playgrounds Association held in Rochester, New York, from 7 to 11 June 1911, it did more than spend its budget. Rather, it demonstrated an affinity to the park and playground movement in North America, a principal expression of social reform from 1900 to 1930 (Boyer 1978; Cavallo 1981; Cranz 1982). A persistent idea in the playground move-ment was "the social value of playgrounds in crowded districts," which im-bibed the belief that children were the natural inheritors of flowers, trees, and blue skies (Veiller 1907, 509-10).

Further, the minutes of the CP and E show an enthusiasm for the demands of the Toronto Playground Association (TPA). When a Mr. A.J.
Russell Snow of the TPA asked it "to expropriate lands on the south side of
Argyle St. for the Playgrounds Association," the committee, without debate,
"recommended to Council that leave be given to introduce a By-law to expropriate the lots" (Committee on Parks and Exhibitions 1910-12, 17 March
1910, 33, 14 April 1910, 45). The TPA's request for the immediate improvement of the land purchased by the city for "playground purposes" on Brock
Avenue at Frankish Avenue received a typical response: "This is a very congested district ... [which] would make an excellent location for a Supervised
Playground and Social Centre as is proposed ... The Committee recommend
[sic] that the property on Brock Avenue ... be set apart for supervised playground purposes, under the direction of the Toronto Playgrounds Association" (Toronto City Council 1911b, 570-71).

Part of the CP and E's attraction to playgrounds came from its members,
for some were committed playground reformers. Alderman R.H. Graham,
CP and E chairman from 1910 to 1911, was a playground reformer in Toronto
and the city's representative at the Fifth Annual Convention of the Playgrounds Association of America in Washington, DC, 10 May 1911 (Committee on Parks and Exhibitions 1910-12, 24 April 1911, 143). Another CP
and E committee member, Alderman John Bengough, was the Toronto dele-
gate at the First Annual Convention of the American Playgrounds Association, in Chicago, 20-22 June 1907. Upon his return, Bengough moved
"that the Parks and Exhibition Committee ... take steps toward the opening
of supervised playgrounds for children" (*Toronto Daily Star* 1907, 8). And
George Geary (Toronto mayor from 1910 to 1912) demanded that "some
definite agreement be made to settle the respective rights of the [Toronto]
Playground Association and the city," and that "the controllers and the Park
Commissioner ... arrange a definite plan" to fund the aims of the Playground
Association (*Toronto Daily Star* 1911c, 7).

Curiously, the ironies of the TPA's and CP and E's uncritical transcendentalism were not lost on observers of the Elizabeth Street playground,
especially when proximity to nature did not produce moral outcomes, despite the small enactment of park relief in the Ward. The *Toronto Daily
Star*'s (1911b, 9) description of conditions in the new playground confirmed
what any critical observer would have known: "The Elizabeth Street playground [wa]s a nightly menace" to the children who used it. The park had
too quickly become "an open space with plenty of nooks and crannies,
hiding places for evil deeds." And with "no supervisors, no diversion to keep

young people busy, i[t] simply ... afford[ed] an opportunity for evil." And as
the mothers of children who frequented the playground would "pathetically
say, it fosters more harm in one night than the agencies for good can overcome in one year" (ibid.). This contradicted the truism of parks and playgrounds as an uncontestable good, in spite of "loafers and rowdies." Yet,
by March 1912, the city began "considering the advisability" of building a
"neighbourhood house" – a settlement house of sorts – opposite the
"Elizabeth Street civic playground" (*Toronto Daily Star* 1912c, 4).

Whether park statistics or their interpretations were correct, and there
are numerous (but unnecessary) ways to pursue the weakness of Edwardian
statistical assertions, is not the point. That reformers used statistics about
parks, however, confirms both their conviction that human nearness to nature had social efficacy in cities and that park building was an important
method of social reform, especially in its supposed ability to move immigrants into a higher and fairer form of citizen. This assumption not only
makes transcendentalist reformers simple moral environmentalists, but
also racists: they uncritically – euthenically – manipulated the urban environment to favour nature and parks, intending to produce a "better race of
[immigrants] in the future" (Richards 1910, viii).

Conclusion: Infrastructural Racism?

> *These Dagoes and Hunkies have got to learn that this is a*
> *white man's country, and they ain't wanted here. When we've*
> *assimilated the foreigners we got here now and learned 'em the*
> *principles of [North] Americanism and turned 'em into regular*
> *folks, why then maybe we'll let in a few more.*
>
> – Sinclair Lewis, *Babbitt*

The authors of Toronto's Plan of 1909 claimed that the desire for parks was
"characteristic of this generation" (Toronto Guild of Civic Art 1909, n.p.),
constituted, as J.S. Woodsworth implied, of concerned white bourgeois citizens labouring to reform decrepit modern cities "crowded with petty gro-
tesques, malformations, phantoms playing meaningless antics ... everywhere
an abnormal libidinousness, unhealthy forms, male, female, painted, pad-
ded, dyed, chignon'd, muddy complexions, bad blood, the capacity for good
motherhood deceasing and deceased, shallow notions of beauty, with a
range of manners or rather lack of manners (considering the advantage

enjoy'd) probably the meanest to be seen in the world" (Walt Whitman, quoted in Woodsworth 1972, 13). Yet it is just such a view of Toronto's immigrants and their neighbourhoods that allows us to think of transcendentalism as a type of white Anglo-Saxon and Anglo-Celtic Protestant reform: parks and playgrounds positioned as a method to erase immigrant identity. Indeed, the impulse to decrease the number of people per one acre of park suggests that planners held high hopes for the social efficacy of environmental determinism. Their embrace of transcendentalized parking embedded race in the very geography of parks and playgrounds, demonstrating the exigency of a racialized and rationalized environmentalism: the employment of quantifiable amounts of geography (acres of park) and numerical standards (250:1) to efface unseemly race in Toronto. Seen this way, Toronto's Plan of 1909 is nothing if not an attempt to place racially sanitizing nature near immigrant neighbourhoods. Little wonder that Toronto City Council went out of its way to build a playground on Elizabeth Street, within easy walking distance of every Jew and Catholic, Italian and eastern European "Hunkie" in the Ward.

Emerson's thinking about nature contextualizes the racial organization of infrastructure in modern North American cities. That proximity to quantifiable amounts of transcendental parking ostensibly produced a fairness of body and mind renders infrastructure development, in part, a spatial race therapy, remedying non-whiteness in "crowded" and "congested" cities. Non-bourgeois Europeans demonstrated a "whiteness of a different color" (Jacobson 1998), a condition wedded to the Victorian conceit holding that class could determine race (Clarke 1994, 34).[11] And if it is true that socially constructed markers of race garner no salience without substantiation through deliberate and sustained state public policy interventions (Sugrue 1996; Wilder 2000; Freund 2007), then, in Toronto, park policy making and park building had the dual and ironic role of not only alleviating infrastructural neglect, but also racializing and marginalizing immigrants.

This uncritical organization of public infrastructure abetting and affirming Victorian and Edwardian conceptions of race allows us to consider "infrastructural racism," where common physical structures and facilities of the street signify the logic of race. If parks spatialized race, it is hardly speculative to contend that City Beautiful's need to make the mundane physicality of the city osmotically beautiful (Mackintosh 2005, 713) has racial implications, especially given the beautifiers' infrastructural mania for parks, parkways, squares, gardens, playgrounds, boulevards, and greenswards, and their complementary pavements.

Charles Mulford Robinson (1970, 344) called the park "the cathedral of the modern city." Reformers in the English-speaking cultural capital of the Great White North in the early 1900s, with an imperious confidence in "white" Protestant values and appearances, viewed Toronto's urban modernity through the logic of race. Seeing only "the riff-raff of Europe and ... millions of ignorant foreigners" (*Toronto Daily Star* 1905a, 1), they intentionally and disingenuously tried to *dot* the city with metaphorical – and transcendental – cathedrals.

5

SARS and Service Work
Infectious Disease and Racialization in Toronto

CLAIRE MAJOR AND ROGER KEIL

In 2003 in Toronto, Ontario, two outbreaks of severe acute respiratory syndrome (SARS) hospitalized hundreds, put thousands in quarantine, and laid bare the fault lines of racialization in the multicultural city.[1] The crisis was a liminal experience that allowed the veneer of a working multiculturalism to be set aside, exposing the underside of normalized social relations and reconfirming the white settler core of Canadian society and its multicultural ethic. During the crisis, we defaulted as a community to the white male hegemony of Canadianness, leading to the villainization of the "other," predominantly people who were considered Asian, either phenotypically or by cultural markers. Although this event mostly hurt the Chinese Canadian communities of Toronto (immigrant or Canadian-born, including those in the latter group who may never have visited China), it also had an impact on other communities, such as Filipino immigrant workers in the city's diversified service industries.[2] This racialization raises important questions: who overcomes the barriers of latent (and perhaps institutional) racism, for whom does multiculturalism work, and in what ways? Anticipating a criticism that we put people under a microscope, we suggest this is perhaps a fitting metaphor; during SARS, Toronto was put under a microscope by the world. In the early days of SARS, the city was a carnival insofar as no one quite knew what role he or she played. As time went on, the messiness of non-exclusivity became apparent but not necessarily the roles: anybody who could be blamed for SARS typically was.

In order to address the complex and manifold issues involved in navigating the post-SARS landscape, we draw on a variety of sources that are rather eclectically consulted in this short review of the important literature on the bacteriological city (outlining the intellectual trajectory of this discussion). We reflect on how the experiences of those interviewed for this research may be explained, but we purposefully try to give room for workers – the frontline nurses, personal support workers (PSWs), hotel housekeepers, and those who represent them (trade unionists) – to speak for themselves, drawing on interviews conducted in Toronto between August 2005 and August 2006. Frances Abele and Daiva Stasiulis (1989) critique political economic analyses that add gender and race onto class, and we suggest that in the cases we discuss, gender and race co-determine class experiences of immigrants in Toronto. Rather than being located on the periphery of the SARS experience, the immigrant population was central to it, both in its mitigation and as victim, wearing the most fluid of masks (life-saving nurses one minute, Chinese immigrant nurses putting "us" at risk the next). We explore who are the racialized bodies saving lives and doing the city's dirty work during a moment of inversions, chaos, and unprecedented emergency.

Disorder and Bioterror in the Hygienic City

SARS transcended the usual mappings we use to negotiate our space and place in the city. It was a time of inversions, transgressions, and something of a macabre carnival. According to Stuart Hall's (1996, 291) discussion of the carnival metaphor of Mikhail Bakhtin, the carnival acts as "a metaphor for the temporary licensed suspension and reversal of order ... when the low shall be high and the high, low, the moment of upturning." With the usual rules in chaos, the racialization that lurks beneath the surface of our usual social relations was publicly exposed; but, as Hall notes, such liminal moments may not manifest as obvious inversions of binary oppositions. SARS was a disordered disembowelling when the inner came out, when racialized "back of the house" workers became the public face of the disease. Julia Kristeva, also drawing on Bakhtin, suggests that the carnival is not merely an inversion; rather, it is an act of ambivalence, when at least two meanings of gestures, signs, and symbols are inverted (Mol 1986). Thus, Bakhtin's carnival is expressed as the "logic of analogy and non-exclusive opposition" (ibid., 42). We wish to emphasize the latter in this discussion of a particular set of relationships that were subject to one of many possible reversibilities "of the 'logics' of ideological discourse" (Hall 1996, 296). Although we start, conceptually, with the carnival's inversions, during SARS nothing was predictable save for the oversimplifications about our neighbours and fluidity in the reading of immigrant bodies. Whereas, in Hong Kong, mask wearing was ubiquitous and a sign of social solidarity (Baehr 2008), donning such a medical device in public was rare in Toronto, often done only by health professionals and individuals with a background that customarily uses masks in case of illness as a sign of courtesy toward others. Needless to say, this exceptionalism increased the visibility and potential racialization of the mask wearers.

The post-structuralist metaphor of the carnivalesque moment has its perfect companion in Giorgio Agamben's (1998, 2004) work on the state of emergency. Agamben's biopolitical intervention aims to isolate a form of human life that exists outside the political realm that constitutes society. As Geraldine Pratt (2005, 1053-54) succinctly summarizes, "according to Agamben, what most characterizes modern biopolitics is the generalized suspension of the law – the state of exception – as a basis of liberal sovereignty." Agamben (2004) notes a particular liminality as he calls the state of exception a "threshold of indeterminacy," a "zone of indistinction" (9) or a "no-man's-land" (8) between democracy and absolutism. Those who have immigrated to Canada and are living in Toronto find themselves in precarious situations inside and outside of work, on the street and at home, where they face discrimination and eviction. In this "no-man's-land" are the built-in contradictions of, at best, celebrating our diversity while, at worst, simultaneously villainizing it. SARS – as a true state of emergency – lifted the normalcy of hardship into a liminal, carnivalesque, exceptional state. Vulnerabilities, previously considered "outside" in nature beyond society's borders (the virus, the other, the alien), reappeared. Therefore, "the state of exception is thus not so much a spatiotemporal suspension as a complex topological figure in which not only the exception and the rule, but also the state of nature and law, outside and inside, pass through one another" (Agamben 1998, 37). Agamben (2004, 9) himself makes the connection to the military order issued by the president of the United States on 13 November 2001, which suspended common civil rights in favour of the possibility of "indefinite detention" and other measures of exceptional law. In Toronto, such exceptional circumstances were not created by executive decree but rather by a biopolitical emergency stemming from the onslaught of a then unknown virus on what were presumed to be secure health care firewalls in hospitals and other institutions of the "bacteriological city" (Gandy 2005a).

More directly linked to the threat of disease is Philipp Sarasin's (2006, 221) analysis of anthrax. He reminds us of the long-standing pattern of linking infectious diseases with strangers such as illegal immigrants: "Terror is tantamount to the deadliest form of an infection that begins with streams of migrant workers swimming with individuals who 'penetrate' the national body, carrying deadly germs with them – infectious diseases of superbugs." There is a slippery slope – another liminal zone – between that twisted normalcy and an even worse state of emergency, bioterror. Sarasin (ibid., 222) writes, "Hence the signifier 'bioterror' turns out to be the quintessential expression of fear of 'infection' in the age of globalization. Whereas illegal migrant workers represent the average risk of infection, which the average tourist is also exposed to, 'bioterror' connotes the – apparently objective – maximal threat of pathogenic agents, against which there is no protection."

Once, a built and institutional environment of border stations was erected in an attempt to prevent foreign diseases such as the "Asian plagues" from reaching Europe and North America (Weindling 2000; Sarasin 2006). The post-modern media society, with its fine distinctions, allows more subtle if not less cruel forms of discrimination that work more pervasively through a complete governmentality of racialized social control. Part of this control has to do with the enlistment of very fundamental concepts of who belongs and who doesn't, used to establish lines of demarcation around virtual societal boundaries to create distinction between inside and out. Locally, this becomes wrapped into the arguments, discussed below, that Canada is constructed as a white settler colony that excludes the narratives of Indigenous peoples and juxtaposes an immigrant narrative to the hegemonic white one (Abele and Stasiulis 1989).

The city is central to this argument. Following Matthew Gandy (2004, 2005a, 2005b, 2006), we perceive Toronto as a city shaped – that is, mastered – by the specific modernity of the twentieth century in the West. Processes of purification isolated the modern bacteriological city from its natural environments via infrastructures and mechanized metabolic processes, an attempt at putting closure around threats, at constructing barriers to keep pestilence at bay. This city emerged from "the chaos of the nineteenth-century industrial city, driven by a combination of factors: advances in the science of epidemiology and later microbiology which gradually dispelled miasmic conceptions of disease; the emergence of new forms of technical and managerial expertise in urban governance" as well as other financial and administrative innovations (Gandy 2004, 375). The bacteriological city kept germs in check and allowed new types of socially cohesive urban governance institutions to take shape (ibid.). However, we must take our cue from Ash Amin (2004) when we think about urban regions, which are "unbound" entities in a globalized world. The social relations of globalizing cities are both place-specific and non-placed; they gel out of a set of relationalities that span the globe. Cities and urban regions are not entities unto themselves, but part of global processes and relations (Ali and Keil 2011), and the maintenance of clearly delineated insides and outsides is all but impossible. Thus, the urban, a place wrested from wildness, is unsettled by immigration, disrupting a misconception that where there is city there is no wildness. SARS reintroduced the threat of biophysical danger to urban lives.

Some words on Toronto as a global city are in order. Although some slippage appears to occur in our terminology – Toronto is synonymous with Canada and Torontonian with Canadian – we do not mean to imply that Toronto is the extent of Canadianness. Rather, we use it as shorthand to imply that Toronto is included and engaged in national-scale discourse, policy, and formulation of ideas of Canadian multiculturalism. Within that framing, Toronto (and the surrounding region) is one of the major gateway cities for newcomers to Canada. We do not mean to imply that it is more important than, say, Calgary. Rather, we are suggesting that SARS could unfold as it did precisely because Toronto is a major destination. Thus, though there may be some mythical place called Canada the Great White North, with its three-ocean perimeter and frozen endlessness, Toronto is a real place where lived notions of multiculturalism (Wood and Gilbert 2005) meet the hard realities of a culturalized racism, which covers up the growing socio-economic inequities that are defined through class but are more pronounced perhaps through ethnicity and gender. Racism and sexism provide the visible colour to the map of poverty and inequity that now characterizes Toronto. A recent and ongoing study finds "three cities" in Toronto, a "city of disparity," where 62 percent of the poorest 40 percent of the city are foreign-born and live in neighbourhoods where 43 percent of the population is black, Chinese, or South Asian (Hulchanski 2007). The latest census figures for Greater Toronto confirm this trend: more than 46.9 percent of Toronto's population identifies as "visible minority" (Statistics Canada 2008). That SARS hit such an ethnically and socio-economically diverse and divided city provided part of the overall explanation for why the disease was racialized in such stark terms: the virus found its victims in the most vulnerable areas of the city, not necessarily by inflicting bodily harm, but through the more pernicious pathways of collective hysteria that partly developed along lines of racialization (Keil and Ali 2006).

Multiculturalism in the Modern City

Canada is seen as a place free of disease, where modern infrastructure and medicine prevent the transmission of viruses. Historically, immigration policy functioned to keep undesirables out of the country through its written and explicitly racist directives (Walton-Roberts 2004; Sharma 2006) or through other means of exclusion such as head taxes (Abu-Laban 1998). Judgment is passed on who has the right to enter (Li 2003) and, during a time of crisis, extends to identifying who is a potential threat. Exclusion manifests at the urban scale because the story of multiculturalism, tied up with the narrative of Canadian urbanization and of the white settler cities in which we live (Razack 2002b; Blomley 2004), runs parallel to the history of the Canadian city as that of a white city.

Despite the messiness of global spatial and temporal relations, racialized immigrants are absorbed into Toronto's urban labour market in a particular way: through precarious positions that are designed to be part-time, flexible, and filled by racialized immigrant populations (Hardt 1999), or as a result of ethnic enclaving in particular industries (Galabuzi 2006). Through fulfilling such tasks, they become, and perform as, the "hard-working immigrant." Through SARS, we witnessed a rearticulation of past racisms. Bettina, who works at a legal aid clinic, said,

> The whole reason they brought in the head tax is because immigration from Asia is a threat to Canadian society, in terms of threatening jobs of white Canadians and also in that era, a lot of language of diseases is being used to justify this. The same exact belief system is still under the surface and it totally came out during the SARS outbreak, the danger, the disease. It's a deviant kind of thing. "Oh, Chinese people. They are so deviant so that the diseases are now coming down and they are going to threaten our society!" So it's exactly the same stereotype. People really feel symbolically that the tax should be redressed because nothing has changed, you know.[3]

As Farhana, another informant, stated, on one hand there was "a refusal to acknowledge the kind of racialization and isolation [that exists]" and on the other, "the celebratory stuff around the geography of China and Canada and the Chinese as the model minority, and then [the celebratory moments] just really split ... so quickly in a moment like this." Despite the formal exclusions, the experience of Chinese immigrants to Canada is riddled with inconsistency. To link SARS to the domain of immigration and visible minorities is perhaps not too far a step given the specific history of Canadian urbanization, when it is read in conjunction with immigration policy, a pantomime of equality premised on inequalities and inseparable from notions of white hegemony. Crucial to this discussion is recognizing how the perceived risks of contemporary Canadian urban life and expectations of how the modern city ought to perform become overlapped and intermingled with the poorly articulated policies of multiculturalism, creating a gap in which there is hegemonic demand for particular kinds of immigrant performativity. In short, immigrants and racialized people must become the "hard-working immigrant" to prove they "deserve" to be here.

In discussing the nightmarish disruption to life caused by SARS and the ensuing ethical challenges, Wang Min'an (2004, 596) states that "SARS is by no means a simple crisis of health and hygiene. Actually, it is a crisis of belief, it is yet another formation that challenges every possible optimism. We can see that Enlightenment humanism is facing an unprecedented challenge in this crisis: the human race is still not the domineering master of all it surveys." Crucial to the argument is the modernist, clean, predictable, hygienic urban and a post-modern, polite, multicultural Canada; however, the white male as the quintessential idea of a Canadian, as Nandita Sharma (2006) argues, is merely latent in Toronto, a multicultural city in which half of its inhabitants were not born in Canada. With the white male as the imperative, blame could be assigned and the location of fear of the crisis identified. As a city councillor who sat on the public health committee during SARS put it in an interview, "Toronto is a nice place, but in a rough patch racism rears its head. On the surface, officially we are all polite, but beyond that, under it, there is a lot of racializing."

National narratives of racialization are rearticulated to fit the scale at which lives are lived (the urban-regional). In 2001 nearly half of all immigrants settled in Toronto (Statistics Canada 2003), yet immigrants are selected federally and without urban input (Abu-Laban and Garber 2005). Still, the politics of ethnic difference and diversity are far from being a national domain. As Ash Amin (2002, 959-60) observes for the British case, it is "the everyday urban – the daily negotiation of ethnic difference – rather than the national frame of race and ethnicity" that may need to be the focus of our work in this period. He notes the "micropolitics of everyday social contact and encounter. The constitution of such micropublics, and the terms of engagement with them, are seen to be crucial for reconciling and overcoming ethnic cultural differences," further alerting us to "the very real cultural dynamism of minority ethnic (and White) communities." Thus, the context in which immigrants to Toronto find themselves is a multicultural city, the contours of which are also shaped by dominant white culture: "Multiculturalism policy has not dealt with systemic racism, nor has it adequately addressed the normalized qualities of uneven geographies that are integral to racist representations and practices. The latter include, for example, the fact that charter rights are rooted in particular places ... and are also dependent upon specialized representations (e.g., public versus private spheres) and spatial practices" (Peake and Ray 2001, 181). There is an institutionalization of managing and denying, of boundary construction of belonging (or not) that permeates "various non-white spaces" (ibid.). Patricia Wood and Liette Gilbert (2005) discuss how multiculturalism is contested, citing arguments that add to its ambiguity as a policy: from its inception, there has been no theoretical underpinning of what it is. In fact, one can also argue, as do Kanishka Goonewardena and Stefan Kipfer (2005), that perhaps multiculturalism, with its programmatic culturalization of socio-economic difference, constructs a particularly problematic form of racialization that glosses over any notion of class differentiation in the process. Therefore, during a crisis such as SARS, it is easy to revert to a racism that is not eradicated by the tenets of a poorly defined and ambiguously practised multiculturalism.

SARS on the Job

The jobs undertaken by Toronto's immigrant, racialized, gendered workforces are those that could put them at risk of SARS. Their racialized status compounded the risk of systemic discrimination, in part because of the neoliberalism to which personal support work, nursing, and the hospitality industry are subject (Major 2008). We do not wish to overstate the argument that the risky nature of the work is simply a function of neo-liberalism, given that Chinese immigrant workers were used in dangerous and dehumanized conditions during Canada's nation-building history; however, the pantomime of immigration parity and subject equality is a veneer. At the urban scale, racism lurks just under the surface of social relations, in a place where the very premise of the urban is a modernity that keeps plague and pestilence at bay, which happens, in part, through assigning blame to racialized peoples when threats to biosecurity arise.

The work of nurses, PSWs, and housekeepers has characteristics common enough such that these jobs can be considered together. First, neoliberalism enacted by both the state and multinational firms means these sectors are subject to organizational manipulation resulting in greater precariousness for workers and greater flexibility for employers. For instance, janitorial work in hospitals was likened to hotel housekeeping (Armstrong and Laxer 2006) and is now normalized as outsourced labour that is removed from the broader context of health care. Labelled "ancillary," it is not considered as part of the institution's operations. This shift makes containment of infectious disease and dissemination of information all the more difficult given that workforces within a particular location are employed by any number of firms that may or may not be briefed on outbreaks and that may or may not have the means to communicate this information to their staff. Lack of communication is particularly worrisome given that properly trained and protected cleaners are essential to helping manage and contain diseases in hospitals. Neo-liberalization also leads to shorter stays in the hospital, resulting in a greater reliance on PSWs and live-in caregivers, who are typically paid nine to twelve dollars per hour (unlike unionized nurses, who start at approximately twenty-five dollars per hour). Many PSWs are nurses who are trained abroad but who cannot afford (in time or money) to take the exams that offer them professional Canadian recognition.[4] Second, as part of the general trend from Fordism to post-Fordism in the Canadian urban labour landscape, the nature of work is such that the provision and creation of services supplants the production of things. All three sectors fall within this frame of service work that requires affective skills. Affective labour is the integration of one's emotion, humanness, skill, and attention into the post-industrial consumptive experience that is predicated on the interface of worker and consumer (Lazzarato n.d., n.p.). Its objective is customer accommodation through human support or the enabling and sustaining of life. Affective labouring requires reading cues through intuition and the management of unarticulated expectations. Some or all of it demands flexibility and polarized skill sets: quick thinking and constantly being "on" are foiled by enduring monotony. More interesting and autonomous affect work happens in the "high end service sector" and (recognized) skills lead to more enjoyable experiences of flexibility (Polanyi, Tompa, and Foley 2004, 68). Further, "flexibility for white, male workers tends to be about multiskilling, responsible autonomy, and task redefinition," whereas in deskilled jobs it is a "racialized and gendered concept," and for "many women and black workers it means lower pay, irregular employment, and harder work" (Peck 1996, 136).

How labour is absorbed into the local labour market is a function of the permutations and combinations of racialization transposed onto individuals and communities. Immigrants are often unable to perform work for which they are trained. Lisa, a hotel housekeeper, explained,

My impression was if you leave your country and you have an education and you meet the expectation, you can go in that field. When I left my country I was a nurse. When I came here, I thought, "Why do I have to do this? I cannot believe that I will start making beds for a living!" Is this it for all the minorities or anybody else that's coming [to Canada]? I went to the Ministry of Education and I went to a few places. They say, no, you have to go back to school. You have to have Canadian experience. I kept saying, "If nobody gives you a job, what's going to happen? You have to let me try." I was a nurse for about ten years before I came here and no way would I have done this in my country. I did school part-time, in the evenings, for four or five years. How will I survive? I didn't want to get into debt, I just came here. It's not only tiring physically, but mentally. After you finish up all the physical work, you're mentally tired. You cannot concentrate. I'm saying, "What's happening to me? I'm going crazy? What's happening to me?"

Despite the rhetoric of the need for skilled immigrants, federal entry criteria rarely meet provincial licensing requirements. Such credentialism keeps outsiders out even when they are accepted as citizens. The work in which they find themselves is deskilled, a process predicated on the gendering and racialization of who does the work, where skill comes to be "some kind of 'independent variable' which is [assumed to be] a fixed attribute of a particular job" rather than "a politically contested designation that reflects who is doing the work" (Herod and Aguiar 2006, 431). Local employers tend to deny jobs to people without "Canadian experience," a refrain that masks any number of reasons for not hiring someone (which may include mistrust of foreign credentials, concern that someone cannot do a job, racism, and everything in between). Many immigrants have no choice but to assume a place in the world of "survival jobs." Easily identified as "other," they fall into a liminal work zone of neo-liberalized lax protections on the job that are normal parts of the work they can get.

The SARS crisis put a spotlight onto the kinds of interrogations of private life that are experienced by racialized people during a crisis, with uneven impacts on public and private spheres. In their discussion of practised multiculturalism at the urban scale, Wood and Gilbert (2005, 685) argue that "the negotiation of multiple cultural identities (between and amongst 'different' and dominant groups) occurs in public spaces and institutions." Public space allows for both community building and stigmatization; the latter was not an uncommon experience of nurses in particular. During the crisis, there were ample reports of nurses who were told not to take their children to daycare, whose friends and family refused to see them, and of verbal abuse (while wearing masks over their noses and mouths) as they rode the subway or filled their cars with gas. Nurses were thrust into being the public face of SARS. Farhana explained: "We interviewed a nurse from Scarborough Grace [a hospital in the east end of Toronto] ... Buses wouldn't want to stop in front of their hospitals, so they would be dropped off farther down the road, and taxis wouldn't come to them. Those were the kind of difficulties that she experienced." Regardless of race, all nurses became the potentially life-threatening "other," all marked though their use of the carnivalesque N-95 mask of SARS. Nurses became "marked" members of society. Thus, the public realm – but only particular actors within it – became the venue in which public anxiety was directed.

Further, SARS led to peculiar disengagements and new engagements. For instance, due to the acute shortage of nurses given that many had to go into quarantine because of contact with SARS patients, hospitals did directly hire temporary nurses who normally get work through placement agencies. However, non-crucial staff (as determined by hospitals), including agency nurses, were not permitted at hospitals in part because agency nurses often work in hospitals across the city, and it was feared they could spread the disease from one site to another.[5] Similarly, because they are non-crucial staff, none of the nurses who were part of the Centre for Internationally Educated Nurses (CARE) program could attend their placements. Nevertheless, they were hired by hospitals to screen incoming patients, administer questionnaires, and make assessments about the likelihood of contact with the virus.[6] Given the lack of surge capacity in health care, the result of cost-cutting "efficiencies" implemented in the decade prior to SARS, their labour was essential. These foreign-educated nurses are not able to practise in Ontario, because they must complete courses and pass exams before being granted a licence, but they were given casual labour, literally on the frontline where SARS could reach the broader public. Although such work may have seemed attractive in that it offered a wage and was a marginal engagement in health care, the downside was that they assumed risk and filled gaps in ways that did not grant them protections (either to their bodies or as recognized workers with certain job-based rights).

As noted by workers in hotels, those who stayed on the job during SARS layoffs were managers (who are largely white).[7] This was costly, given the higher wages of management, but defended because management alone has knowledge about the entire operation of the hotel (which housekeeping staff lack because they are denied access to it) and ironic (management chose to be vulnerable to risk rather than to place others on the frontline). The hotel industry is engaged with the city's pandemic flu planning.[8] However, as for protecting the workers themselves, the industry representative with whom we spoke said the following about protocols and practices of training:

> Virtually every one of our association members belongs to a major chain, whether it is Starwood or Marriott or Hilton. Even if we develop something, brand standards operate worldwide. [They] are going to react and institute the programs they believe need to be in place to maintain their quality. If an outbreak occurs at one of those branded hotels, they have more to lose than anybody because it's their value that they have in their brands. For us to do anything here, quite frankly doesn't make any sense, because the hotels are going to do it the way they've been told to do it by the brands. The brand sets all the standards.

When asked if standards were changing (as in the way that guests were treated at reception or if hidden thermometers were put in place to test guests, unknowingly, for fever-like temperatures), the representative replied, "You would have to talk to the brand." This Tayloristic compartmentalization of brand standards developed by management and executed by workers, coupled with neo-liberal precarities, puts workers at risk because of the lack of comprehensive worker-informed (and possibly public-health-contrary) planning.

The comings and goings of racialized people were subject to scrutiny. Hotels were cautious about staff returning to work if they had been "south" (to Hong Kong or Vietnam) during the winter and spring of 2003. Those who had, as Sonya, a hotel housekeeper, mentioned, were asked to take a two-week period before coming to work.[9] Workers stated that they were asked to report anything "suspicious," although what this meant was highly subjective (Major 2008). More pressing is that hotels seem not to have mobilized to protect their workers, a failing made particularly serious because they house globally mobile travellers and because the transmission and contraction of SARS were so poorly understood.

Similarly, the comings and goings of women who worked as domestic caregivers and PSWs were scrutinized. Employers feared that they could come into contact with other "Asians." Gita, a representative of an agency that protects the rights of caregivers who come from overseas to work in Canada, said, "It was a very good time to use the excuse that you cannot take your day off because there's SARS. Employers said, 'If you're going to insist

on taking your day off, you don't have a job any more.' That was a very convenient excuse not to let them off. Maybe their fears were real for them that,
you know, 'If I let you go, you might go to some kind of grocery, some res-
taurant, some places we don't know of and you'll bring back SARS.'"

Some workers insisted on taking their day off and were fired as a result.
Technically, they could file a grievance with the Ontario Labour Board for
termination without notice, but Gita added "they never do" and cited the
difficulty in negotiating the employment acts of the provincial and federal
governments. She stated, "Whether there's SARS or not it's very hard for
them to file grievances on very legally admissible grounds" largely because
of time limits to make claims. Further, in the case of termination without
notice, the gap in employment is difficult to explain when one looks for a
new employer. The lives of these women, SARS or not, are precarious, with
limitations placed on mobility and freedom. Under the guise of something/
anything else, racialized workers can be subject to restraints that are foreign
to the white Canadian experience; they are treated as immature beings, as
teenage babysitters rather than autonomous adult women, a flexibility applied onto them – as a norm rather than an exception – through hybrid
combinations of citizenship, race, job, and gender.

One particular PSW, who went with her elderly employer to the hospital,
contracted SARS and was in a coma for eighty-one days. The family she
worked for compensated her while she was in the coma, but her job was
eventually terminated because her employer had died of SARS, a disease
that did not discriminate on the basis of one's country of origin or on racializations. However, what we wish to stress is that risk (incurred while being
the caregiver to the sick or the elderly) is a normal part of daily events for a
PSW, who *are* typically racialized bodies that lack workplace protections.
The violation of rights might be concealed or more explicit, including the
absolute absurdity to which racialized workers were subject. Heidi said of
her employer's household, "The worse thing I experienced in their house is
that the mother of my employer sprayed vinegar around my room. I think
it's not sanitizer." We can almost hear the puzzlement in her voice, the subject of a racism that is exercised in the otherwise mundane events of the
everyday. Finally, Estelle, who works with PSWs, stated that nannies and
PSWs from the Philippines were terminated during the crisis, some because
of their association with a church that was labelled as the site of SARS transmission. Employer control negated human rights and replaced them with
forced cloistering or termination of employment if the risk of the "other"
was too great.

Performance and Expectation

David J. Roberts and Minelle Mahtani (2010) raise the issue of the pre-determined racializing of immigrants; that is, "immigrant" is a word that practically implies a racialized body. Any person is a potential object of racialization, but in Canada that objectifying happens through a white lens of what must be negotiated (for instance, barriers to citizenship) and who is normalized (in what way, at what time, in what place) when performing as an immigrant body. Immigration discourse objectifies "others" as poster children of (white) Canadian multicultural policy. Whiteness defines multiculturalism through institutions, policies, and acts that are, if not literally drafted by white men, constructed in the spirit of colonialism, a process that continues to be reinforced through the shifting meaning and implications of words, including "immigrant" itself (ibid.).

This observation is particularly important because during the SARS crisis, this zone of indeterminate definition in which immigrants function became more inverted and non-exclusive than ever. Flexible social relations take on different meanings in different times and places, predicated, as David Lambert (2001) argues, on colonial rule itself existing as a hybrid; that is, there is no predictability in how "others" interface. The carnival-esque inversion is mutated through readings of individuals: SARS was very much a moment of rapid reassignments of identity and labelling onto bodies. Danica, a South Asian nurse who works at Scarborough Grace Hospital, spoke of the ways in which she was read during the crisis. In March 2003, early in the first SARS outbreak, she arrived at work with "all the symptoms of SARS, except for the fever. People were not comfortable with me but we were very short staffed. If they really needed me, they put aside my symptoms." Rather than being identified as a carrier or threat, Danica was valued for her ability to contribute as a nurse to the mediation and management of SARS. We suggest that this range of fluctuation is tempered both by an ill-defined multiculturalism and the need for workers given the lack of surge capacity in health care due to the neo-liberal measures enacted in Ontario during the 1990s. Similarly, a hotel housekeeper stated at a 2006 public meeting, "Without workers there are no hotels. We are all Canadians, why [do we have to] fight so hard for everything?" She suggests that work is always there, but the bodies who occupy the roles must first be devalued (through racism, gendering, citizenship status) and subjectified to an already always fluid set of definitions used in a white hegemonic multiculturalism to label them (as immigrants, racialized, othered). The mastered bacteriological city and a whitewashed multiculturalism intersect in the bodies of immigrants, who must perform in ways that make palatable their presence as others. Such a fixing is complex and necessary, as Charles L. Briggs (2004, 172) argues by way of Homi Bhabha, to maintain the myth of a conquered wild predicated on "colonial, national, racial, sexual, or other schemes of inequality" and that, in turn, covers up a mode of "splitting" subjects. These splits are created in the gap opened by a contradiction between a pedagogical process of projecting pre-given historical origins in the past and a performative one.

Yasmeen Abu-Laban (1998) posits that a universally applied criterion of skill, in which immigration policy is associated with the national economy, denotes an ulterior motive: ideal immigrants work hard to prove they deserve to be here (McLaren and Dyck 2004).[10] Yasmeen Abu-Laban (1998) posits that a universally applied criterion of skill, in which immigration policy is associated with the national economy, denotes an ulterior motive: ideal immigrants work hard to prove they deserve to be here (McLaren and Dyck 2004). Thus, if national immigration policy is the pedagogical process that suggests lives of immigrants will unfold in a particular way, performativity is enacted at the lived urban scale. There is no dismantling of their otherness or a state of full belonging; instead, racialized subjects create themselves in fetishized conditions, in wholly socially constructed spaces of inclusion and exclusion. Following Henri Lefebvre (1991, 33), we suggest that spaces provide order – of production, reproduction, continuity, and cohesion – that furnishes "a guaranteed level of competence and a specific level of performance" that is enacted through bodies, the same bodies that are read and ascribed meaning in convoluted, contradictory, villainized, or celebrated ways. Contradictions spring from the inconsistency of the bacteriological and contained city, on the one hand, posited in opposition to the lived urban reality, on the other, sometimes resulting in a denial of otherness and at other times a creation of "new concepts and meanings in which prior invocations are embedded, even if those antecedents are thereby rendered invisible" (C.L. Briggs 2004, 172). As a result, fetishized racialized subjects are in a permanent state of liminality.

Toronto did not experience large-scale biopolitical measures in terms of scapegoating groups in and through space, although quarantine was pervasive (but individualized), and Torontonians and visitors avoided areas such as Chinatown. Still, the spectre of medieval-type exclusions (think leper colonies, ghettos) became possible in principle (Sarasin 2008). A window was opened into a post-universal society where health care, for example, may not be a generally shared experience. The sudden onset of a massive biophysical threat pointed toward the particularization of social risk, which had previously been universally minimized through the processes of the modern bacteriological city, at least in the West. This spectre was more important in the aftermath of SARS as the city readied itself for a possibly much more pervasive onslaught of an avian flu pandemic and hearkens back to the ways in which past (re)introductions of plague and pestilence are associated with racialized peoples: Africans bring Ebola, the Chinese bring influenzas, Russians (and in the past, Irish and Jews) bring tuberculosis. Yet there is nothing about SARS that makes it a Chinese disease, or that makes it just a Chinese problem. For instance, Lara, a live-in caregiver who regularly visits Toronto General Hospital for dialysis, stated, "Some of the, some of the ... I should say Canadian, you know, doctors or nurses are a little bit more ... you know, um, aware ... I mean, like, distant with us. We are a few Filipinos there who are on dialysis and the fact that we're on dialysis they think that we're a little bit more susceptible." In no way do we mean to minimize the sacrifices made by health care professionals during SARS, but hospitals were perhaps the riskiest places in which to be working during the crisis. Like anyone else, Lara is a member of the general public; however, her pre-existing condition and regular use of hospital services were layered onto her as a racialized body, making her suspect. Yet SARS reinforced past fears about immigrants who can corrupt national well-being, exemplifying how a "cultural framework continues to influence the way Canada sees the security of its territorial boundary as well as the integrity of its social boundary. Thus to understand the warmth of the welcome also involves studying insiders' cultural representation of 'outsiders' and how the discursive frame enables insiders to maintain and safeguard the physical and symbolic boundary of the nation" (Li 2003, 3.). Peter Li defines how the recurrence of tuberculosis in British Columbia was linked to immigrants coming from places where it is described as "rampant" (India, China, the Philippines, and Vietnam), and the source of Chinese SARS follows this pattern. In *Yellow Peril Revisited,* Carrianne Leung (2004) cites Jian Guan's findings that the words applied to SARS – "deadly," "fearful," "mysterious," and "exotic peril" – are riddled with paranoia. As Charlotte stated, such talk led to "an excuse [for landlords and employers] to be more open about their racist behaviour." Immigrants are absorbed into the context of being Canadian in uneven ways, implying both that the identification of the other is fluid and that "a racialized cultural framework continues to influence Canada's representation of, and discourse about, outside threats to national security" (Li 2003, 6).

Conclusion: Systemic Racism and Pan-Asian Solidarity

SARS occurred at the intersection of modern infrastructure (and the associations of hygiene that accompany it) and the possibility of states of exceptions, in a national context that understands immigration and multiculturalism in an abstraction that does not match how they manifest on the ground. Toronto as a hygienic city is not only a materialization of modernity but also inscribed with a normalized institutional whiteness (Peake and Ray 2001).

We do not wish to minimize the impact that SARS had on people who lost loved ones to it, on those who risked their safety and lives at work, and on those who experienced great economic precariousness due to layoffs during the crisis. Yet the tone of the interviews around the issue of race and SARS indicates that the crisis – with its unpredictability, chaos, mask wearing, and name calling – was perhaps not especially remarkable. As Estelle pointed out, "It's only the majority, like, the mainstream Canadians who were so scared. It seems like this particular group of people were giving these kind of precautions or restrictions of moving, right, but they never take into consideration that they themselves have the responsibility." In times of emergency, rights of citizenship are negotiated and challenged. Advancing an argument similar to that of Wood and Gilbert (2005), that multiculturalism is practised in place, Nicholas Blomley and Geraldine Pratt (2001) suggest that broad claims about the recognition of "everyone" are continually contested. The logics of subjective fluidities of the upside-down world manifest in myriad ways. Although the crisis remapped relations, Estelle's comments inspire us to ask, for whom? SARS allowed the simultaneous construction and rearticulation of racializations – and where convenient, the ignoring of them – but always within the white hegemonic multicultural context. Before SARS, Toronto relied on racialized immigrants performing the undesirable work of the global city. SARS made clear the relations of local/global connectivities, but racialized immigrants continue to wear the mask of hard-working immigrant. They remain in the role of doing the city's dirty work. SARS gave them a new mask to wear until the crisis subsided, but they never stopped being others, never stopped being cleaners or nurses, never transcended their liminal vulnerability. And, in this world of inconsistent logics, just because one is an immigrant does not automatically mean that one is racialized in the same way all the time. Thus, racialization can run parallel with a poorly defined multiculturalism, filling in the gaps of an institutionalization in ways that are contradictory inversions. These inversions work through particular (il)logics on a case-by-case basis.

One of the logics that flowed from the crisis could be considered something of a "pan-Asian solidarity." When asked about how possible associations between racialized peoples manifested, Bettina responded, "Actually, now that you say that ... I think ... people kind of internalized [it] and somehow [thought] they should stay inside more, shouldn't move around the city. [Our association] tried to do a lot of stuff around the Chinese Asian Canadian network, and we try to use that network and share the information that we're doing, and get info from other communities. Especially the Filipino community was also one of the most affected, it was sort of pan-Asian Canadian solidarity ... Even Asians can't really tell all the time, [but] they'll still be affected by the stereotype."

This seems a manifestation of Lambert's (2001, 338) argument that, in order to maintain Bermuda's colonial order, there was a need to remove the liminal zone of white landless poor that could be associated with freedman blacks. Such liminality, "ambiguous and uncertain," distracted from the authority and hegemony of the colonial order. Similarly, the ambiguity caused by "Asians" needed to be solidified, by hegemonic default, so that they became one common group in order for SARS to be arrested, ironically villainizing "Asians" while leaving them exactly where they were: in their jobs doing global-city work.

Two further things are worth noting about Bettina's comment. First, there are shades of rearticulations exercised by the hegemonic white Canadian group that "belongs" in Canada. Although SARS was used in this way at the time, new demands of "other" were inscribed onto bodies using complex temporally differentiated bodies that come from many places. There was a recycling of the old ways of assigning plagues and pestilence to those from outside the modernity that Canada considers itself to be. Second, Bettina's recollection of the need to stay home experienced by people with whom her association worked dovetails with Estelle's observation that the rest of the city failed to take responsibility. Both of these comments hint at the shame associated with the SARS experience. Katherine McKittrick (quoted in Peake and Ray 2001, 181) suggests that "engagement with the white gaze results in an anxiety in black psyches and bodies that complicates their relation to place." This engagement complicates even further the ambiguous notion of multiculturalism and public places discussed above: the places and ideas of belonging extended to immigrants or racialized others are all too easily retracted.

We might further describe feelings of shame that are deeply rooted in Canadian history, bridging from the time of explicit racism to, and through, the SARS experience. History merges with the present. As Charlotte remarked,

> It seems the racism that existed during the time of the Chinese head tax still exists today. Nothing has changed. In BC they used to call the Chinese immigrants the yellow peril and this is still going on. I remember during SARS that no one sat beside a person of Chinese background on the subway. I noticed that a Chinese Canadian man was coughing and that a women seated some distance away got up at the next station, went out the door of the train, and entered the door of another train segment, just to avoid being close to the Chinese Canadian man.

The notion of the public is consolidated around the white middle-class space that behaves as the default (Peake and Ray 2001). Further, rights are problematized because the experience of SARS demanded that some members of the urban population subject themselves to self-censoring and limitations on their mobility from which the white population was exempt. Thus, SARS demonstrates that rights are grounded in ideas of "individual autonomy and freedom" that deny "historical-geographical relations of power and the deep structural conditions which perpetuate inequality" (ibid., 184).

Through this discussion, we have worked to establish three points. First, immigration contradictions work in tandem with a poorly articulated multiculturalism, creating a liminal zone in which immigrants live. Second, the labour of immigrant women is not only essential to Toronto as a global city, but also their efforts served to thwart the movement of SARS into the broader public. The modern city could not manage the new threat; the risks taken by these workers benefited everyone. Finally, in the performance of their labour, these workers move into a liminal zone where they retain their otherness, which is used against them when the broader hegemonic multicultural society requires someone to take responsibility for the failure of the modern city itself. There is unevenness in the terrain of the multicultural city. SARS emerged as a carnival in which there were indeed unequivocal starting points: depending upon one's relationship to the multiculturalism of Toronto and where one assumed one fell within its social relations, the ensuing mask wearing concealed some experiences while revealing others. Farhana said, "A man that I interviewed, he really went through his life very much identifying as status quo, as mainstream. This moment, it completely woke him up, the fact that he was now forbidden, the sense of shame that he felt. It sort of opened a lot of things for him to examine. There were a lot of complexities."

SARS was an upside-down moment, reordering the veneer of Toronto's multiculturalism when carnival masks were removed and reapplied. In that moment of liminality when the masks were removed, we might have seen things as they really are: predicated on particular kinds of inclusivity. Entire categories of legalities and of duties to citizens were abandoned, begging us to consider the nature of the multiculturalism in which we live, who gets what right to access what services, and how we want to live our urban lives.

Shimmering White Kelowna and the Examination of Painless White Privilege in the Hinterland of British Columbia

LUIS L.M. AGUIAR AND TINA I.L. MARTEN

The idea of the hinterland plays a central role in Canadian nation building.[1] The hinterland's distinctiveness has rested in the economic potential of the abundant forests, mines, terrains, lakes, and rivers whose goods are extracted or drawn by the hard hands, strong backs, and rugged personalities of the men and women who make up an apparently docile labour market for capital enticed to exploit natural resources. Canadians have dominated and domesticated nature by exploiting, abusing, polluting, and re-engineering its resources, as well as carving highways, laying rail, and channelling canals in order to tame, control, and make predictable spaces for investment, good wages, and whiteness. The regional identities of Canadian hinterlands rest on an unsaid but understood premise that solidarity in whiteness across class delivered responsible workers with a good work ethic for white capital investment in the economic development and colonization of Canada. Good wages and a relatively high standard of living sustained the "racial solidarity," even when class struggle undermined capital's profits. But workers' experiences of the labour processes in the hinterland came at the high cost of damaged bodies (Wolkowitz 2006) and have been accompanied by racialized campaigns of environmental devastation. It was largely the job of the state to coordinate, legitimate, and facilitate the terms of this arrangement. It was also the state that sought to weave the place of the hinterland into the "imagined community" of Canada (B. Anderson 2006).

Canada's "wilderness" too would be tamed, controlled, and made predictable and "safe" as Aboriginals were dispossessed, coerced, disposed, and pushed further into the bush (where they belonged, after all), corralled into the reserve system of the Indian Act (Hookimaw-Witt 1998), or positioned in "zones of contact" (M.L. Pratt 1992) where whites interacted primarily to socially surveil them while at the same time reinforcing their own "superior" values of civility, responsibility, and hard work. Historically, white colonizers saw First Nations peoples not as thoughtful men and women, but as a "natural feature" of the scenery in the landscapes where they lived (Korneski 2007, 172). And with the implementation of residential schools, First Nations families were torn apart and their children systematically deprived of their culture and language, often mistreated and at times even tortured to death (Annett, Lawless, and O'Rorke 2007). While countless families suffered nearly irreparable cultural deprivation, loss of identity, and trauma, white re-education and reculturation, or "civilization," were legitimated through the state and the church. This, of course, made the process of colonization and dispossession much easier to impose and implement largely without remorse. Only the resiliency, ingenuity, and imagination of First Nations people allowed some to resist long enough to make "Native spaces," even under colonizing forces (Harris 2002).

Ideologically, the exploited, sparsely populated hinterland was woven into a myth of separateness, distinctiveness, and distance from the metropolis (Dunk 1991), which represented all that the hinterland did not want to be: impersonal, crowded, noisy, and congested by cars, buildings, and diverse populations. This construction was solidified in the imaginations of Canadians via the state, as well as through cultural productions, literature, the arts, the media, and various important writings. The popularity of the Doug and Bob Mackenzie skits on SCTV is a case in point (Pevere and Dymont 1996). In addition, young left nationalist academics in the 1970s and 1980s found the (white) working class in the hinterland and debated the structuring, unionization, and consciousness of this class, along with analyzing the ownership of industry and the feasibility of developing an economy capable of sustaining an independent Canada free from foreign ownership, control, and above all American imperialism (see Luxton 1980; Clement 1981; Russell 1999; Lucas 2008). In these debates, the role of the hinterland and its relationship to the metropolis took prominence, especially in the work of Harold Innis (1954, 1970), who explained that "staples" (such as lumber, fur, and fish) drove economic and regional development as they were explored and exploited for exports to foreign markets as a result of a weak domestic manufacturing base and underdeveloped national markets (see also Watkins 1977; *Studies in Political Economy* 1981). These debates on national and regional development were set within the Fordist regime of accumulation of the second half of the twentieth century and the challenges of growing profit through increasing productivity and corresponding rising wages for the white male working class (Vosko 2000). It was possible at that time to sustain and reproduce the myth of the rugged hinterland where white men punished their bodies with physically exhausting and dangerous manual labour in the making and remaking of white masculinity so long as wages and standards of living continued to rise. Women too scarred their bodies with child-bearing and rearing responsibilities in the performance of waged and unwaged work in the reproduction of the hinterland as white (Luxton 1980) and the socialization in the reproduction of whiteness. Here in the hinterland, a "painless" white privilege remained unchallenged in the way that white was might and right.[2] However, the suffering endured by hard bodies in the labour-intensive work of extracting value from the various economic landscapes of the hinterland was anything but painless (Comish 1993; Colantonio 1997)! Perhaps for this reason privileged whites hide themselves in exclusive – often gated – communities in the Okanagan (J. Grant 2006).

Then Fordism changed, even collapsed in places, with restructuring severely affecting the country, including the hinterland. The economy jumped scale (Swyngedouw 2004) to the globe, transforming not only most economic sectors and regions, but also forcing its way into people's private lives (Sennett 1998, 2006). Now neo-liberal globalization is pushing hinterland localities to identify new economic roles by liberalizing local markets, leading to huge profits for some and polarizing class inequality for most (J. Harrison 2006; Allen and Cochrane 2007; Cohen 2008). Hinterland elites are coalescing in new power blocs to reinvent "their" communities through partnerships and competitive advantages schemes to compete in a global economy mad with structural adjustment programs and market fundamentalism (Harvey 2005; Whiteley, Aguiar, and Marten 2008; Marten 2009; Aguiar and Marten 2010). In this militant localism (Duncan and Duncan 2004), elites are supported by the provincial state as it reinscribes the hinterland as heartland and delivers neo-liberalism to the regions with a discourse of whiteness reasserted (British Columbia 2003). After all, who but whites in the hinterland have heart and the necessary work ethic, responsibility, and resourcefulness to feed the nation? Who but whites have fed the nation for generations from the interior geographies of the country? A hard-land reality, however, seems more apt at capturing the changes in British Columbia's hinterland as mills and manufacturing plants close, hospitals shut down, call centres relocate, and precarity is normalized (Bourdieu 2003; Sennett 1998). For instance, since the 2001 election of the Liberal Party in BC, forty-six mills have shut down, putting thousands of workers out of a job (*Kelowna Daily Courier* 2008, A2). Moreover, the time-space compression of globalization is leading to the increasing proximity – even presence – of the "other," often resulting in a backlash against new immigrants, especially those who are non-white (Harvey 1989). These new migrants are differently positioned in the nation-state as it seeks to regain a sense of coherent legitimacy in remaking the country as it changes rapidly. In the hinterland of Kelowna, our case study, a post-Fordist economy expands and its new service-based bourgeoisie reproduces the city as shimmering white (Carter 2007). How is this possible?[3] How is this racialization of place sustained? How is whiteness secured today? Labour recruitment policies have played a role in securing, reproducing, and maintaining whiteness in the Okanagan Valley. White high-skilled workers are brought in to fill jobs, settle, and reproduce, whereas non-white labour is on short-term contract with little or no possibility to stay, sponsor family members, or produce the next generation of Okanaganites. They are "wanted as unwanted" workers (Brodie 2008).

In this chapter, we argue that Kelowna's whiteness is no coincidence and that its securing has been sought and organized from the beginnings of "settlement" in the early twentieth century. Through generations, organized campaigns have been mounted to settle the place, but also to place people here who have the "proper" skin colour. In other words, Kelowna has been racialized as a space of whiteness offering sanctuary from a province and a country growing increasingly racially diverse. In securing whiteness, whites enlist the support of non-whites to maintain Kelowna as a white space. This is achieved through consensus about a claim that organized whiteness is proper and right, given the history of the place. In believing this, locals support the means by which their space is secured for whites and whiteness. Further, this racialization of place enables residents to practise in securing the hegemony of whiteness even when they deny such is happening. Though today's advertisements aren't as straightforward about who should move to Kelowna, the people pictured in the brochures are almost exclusively white. This, of course, communicates to the consumer of the advertisement about who is already in Kelowna and, by extension, who is not encouraged to move there (Aguiar, Tomic, and Trumper 2005b).

In what follows, we describe how whiteness was staked in the past and how it is being secured today. We do this by outlining the history of staking white space in the original settlement of the city, and then provide examples of how whiteness is being reproduced today. The issue is not that Kelowna is completely white – which, by all statistical accounts, it almost is – or exceptional of the hinterland of this country (which it is), but rather that new non-whites coming into the city are wanted only as migrant workers rather than permanent residents or citizens. Our aim is to provide contemporary examples showing how whiteness not only remains the organizing principle of the city but continues to be secured through reproductory policies of place such as targeted labour recruitment programs. The latter mimics the new racism perspective, which says that, at a time when overt racist acts and epithets are unacceptable, culture is invoked as the new discriminating characteristic to keep mobile black workers at bay. That is, cultural differences are so distinct that the "other" could not possibly integrate into "our" society, and besides, isn't it true that we all just naturally want to live among "our own kind" anyway (Brown and Miles 2003)? And who can argue with human nature?

Staking a White Hinterland

Canada never wanted visible minorities to settle or occupy this country (Calliste and Sefa Dei 2000; Wilmot 2005). The genocidal campaigns against First Nations peoples are one example of this (Barsh 1991, 1994; Annett, Lawless, and O'Rorke 2007). Another is the long periods of history whereby Canada practised a white-only policy of immigration, which even differentiated between white ethnicities: British and French were preferred to other northern Europeans, who were deemed more acceptable than southern and eastern Europeans (Jhappan 2007, 36).[4] The "brown invasion" of Indian immigrants at the turn of the twentieth century (Dua 2000; Handa 2003) resulted in Indian members of the British Empire being refused entry to Canada unless they managed to sail from India to Canada via a direct voyage, a difficult feat given the seafaring technology of the time. But the 1908 law of "continuous passage" was challenged by many Indians, as the 1914 *Komagata Maru* incident shows (Johnston 1989). There was too the hefty head tax levied on Chinese immigrants between 1885 and 1923, where newcomers were forced to pay a landing fee of $100 and later $500 (per person). Thereafter, the Chinese Immigration Act of 1923 (Morton 1974), also called the Chinese Exclusion Act of 1923, not only denied entry to Chinese migrants but sought to destroy the existing Chinese communities in Canada.

The Chinese men already living in Canada could neither bring Chinese women as wives nor, due to racism, could they turn to white women to reproduce their communities.[5] Those who still managed to come were met with hostility toward their customs and confined to Chinatowns (Choy 1995), only to be exploited for their labour power and racialized to embody vice and delinquencies threatening to white civility (Ward 1980). In Penticton during the 1920s, a public meeting to "keep Penticton white" sought to "consider ways and means of making our town unattractive for the Yellow man," and in Kelowna in the 1940s, billboards at the city's boundary warned "Japs" to stay out (ibid., 125).

For periods of Canada's history, white labour has been unavailable to do certain jobs, a fact that has prompted Ottawa to import non-white labour, even if doing so was contrary to its own principle and policies (Wong and Trumper 2007). But this imported labour has come into the country under strict regulations, often having to do with a government policy seeking only their labour power but not for their progeny to settle here. This biological eugenics has been more recently supplanted in the centres of the country by a social eugenics where class background is stressed over racialized identities (Aguiar 2006). But some jobs remain earmarked for black labour, and for them, especially constricting rules and regulations are adopted in the recruiting of visible minority workers. According to L. Wong and R. Trumper (2007), immigrant workers in the secondary labour market are recruited not on the basis of their ability but due to their ethnicity (see also Waldinger and Lichter 2003). We discuss this below as it applies to Kelowna and the Okanagan Valley more generally, after we fill in the background to whiteness in the Okanagan.

Securing a White Landscape

Europeans from Great Britain and France began arriving in the Okanagan Valley and Kelowna during the early nineteenth century. They came first as fur traders, then as missionaries, followed by gold miners, and finally as "settlers" (Wagner 2008, 4) who were "attracted by the prospect of unused land" (Harris 2004, 171). Land was abundant in the Okanagan Valley, and white settlers were able to secure claims to it with the help of the British government (Thomson 1994; Harris 2004). In fact, Governor James Douglas visited BC's southern interior in 1860, after proclaiming civil government on the BC mainland in 1858. There he struck imperial agreements with First Nations, implying that they might become equal subjects before the queen, enjoying the same protection under Her Majesty's government as all others (read non–First Nations) in BC (Thomson 1994). Coinciding with this was the conceptualization of First Nations lands as unused and empty *(terra nullius)* and of the First Nation way of life as uncivilized and backward, which paved the way for the "erasures of Aboriginal knowledge of time and space" (Harris 2004, 165) and of traditional ways of being. Over time, it became clear that those First Nations groups who accepted the new governance structure were not protected from systemic discrimination and exploitation but had in effect become deterritorialized from their land and cultural ways, and reterritorialized in reserves (ibid.). By the late nineteenth century, complicated bureaucratic accounting measures drastically reduced land available to First Nations as land allotment measures were revamped and the allowed acreage per adult male was reduced. Subsequently, the size of reserve land was drastically slashed (Thomson 1994), First Nations were forced to adjust their way of life, and the freed-up land was marketed to cattle ranchers. Cattle ranching soon became the main economic activity as settlers took advantage of the local topography, including its open grassland spaces, relatively low elevations, and easy access to lake and creek water to grow their feed and herds (Wagner 2008). Later on, however, some ranchers sold their property to British and European developers and to international land development companies who began to prepare it with irrigation systems for agricultural production (Thomson 1994). And whereas "fruit-lots" were selectively sold to other incoming Okanagan-bound British gentlemen, they were withheld from locals in Vernon, who were considered "mere colonials" (Barman 1981, 610).

In the early twentieth century, "fruit farming began to displace ranching as the primary agricultural activity" (Wagner 2008, 2), especially with the advent of an irrigation system throughout the farming areas of the valley (Murton 2007). And so, "irrigation agriculture ... quickly led to much denser populations, to the development of towns and villages, roads and railways and light industry" (Wagner 2008, 2).

From the initial colonial period, it was never in doubt which types of people were to settle in Kelowna and the valley itself. In one advertisement, fruit growing in the Okanagan was promoted here too: "Fruit growers as a class are among the most intelligent people in the world. They have leisure to read. By investing in ten acres of our land you are easily assured a splendid income for life. Can you earn $3,000 a year as easily in any other way? If you are a stranger you're one of us, for we all came here as strangers. Intelligent, educated and cultured English and Canadians form the bulk of the population" (Zoellner 2004, 112-13). This announcement targeted a certain class: the educated, white, rich, opportunistic, and obviously not local individuals with capital to invest. There was an attempt to bring rich, white, like-minded people to the Okanagan in order to persuade them to settle in the valley.

And so, campaigns to encourage, entice, and recruit white growers into the region were aggressively mounted and organized (Dunae 1981). One campaigner was Lord Aberdeen, the governor general of Canada (1893-98), who resided with his family in Kelowna during the 1890s and who is described as having brought "the height of luxury living to the valley" when he built his Kelowna ranch (City of Kelowna 2009). He placed advertisements in British magazines about the "beauty" of the Okanagan, continually drawing attention to the valley (Mitchell and Duffy 1979). The construction of the Okanagan was both about whiteness and class embedded in the "British aristocratic aura" of the place (Barman 1981, 611). In addition, several land companies ran advertisements in the *Times* and the *Illustrated London News* "filled with pastoral scenes of overladen fruit trees surrounded by beautiful children dressed in immaculate English style" (ibid.). One Kelowna land company went so far as to open an office in London in 1910 and to dispatch "a special photographer to tour England offering magic lantern exhibitions of genteel Okanagan scenes" (ibid.; Dunae 1981).

Whiteness was a foundational principle of the city's business class. Perhaps it was the point of re-creating England or building a "better Britain" (Korneski 2007) in the New World. Early settlers of Kelowna and the Okanagan Valley circulated brochures and pamphlets valuing the landscape of the region (J.B. Bennett n.d.). City boosters and promoters called it "paradise on earth," with its fruit gardens, sparkling lakes, and endless hours of sunshine. In their rhetoric, it was the "lost garden of Eden," and Kelowna was described as a "sun-drenched" city, or in today's local marketing parlance, the "Hawaii of the north" (Momer 1998; Keyes 2007; Wagner 2008).[6] These epithets drew the white viewer's attention to a "landscape aesthetics" that was captured in the images of Kelowna and the Okanagan, and that corresponded to a particular "way of seeing" whiteness as landscape construction. John Wylie (2007, 7) explains that the ways of seeing a landscape are tied to both what we see and how we look: "To landscape is to gaze in a particular fashion. And how we look at things is not only to do with the biological functioning of our eyes. How we look at things is a cultural matter; we see the world from particular cultural perspectives, the ones into which we have been socialized and educated." J. Duncan and N. Duncan (2004, 29) are more specific, writing that visual representations of the landscape do not occur outside political and economic interests: "Landscapes, especially those that are highly controlled, are integral to the performance of social identities. Collective memories, narratives of community, invented traditions, and shared environmental concerns are repeated, performed, occasionally contested, but more often stabilized or fixed in artifactual form." Thus, landscapes and their imagery are highly ideological and laden with political discourses (Hubbard et al. 2002). The internalization of the particular landscape helps individuals create mental maps. People situate themselves according to such maps, whereby their own positioning is influenced by their internalizations of the social vectors at work. Such cognitive mapping is extremely powerful in shaping people's perception of space and place (Hayden 1995).

During the late nineteenth century, a fruit culture emerged on the Pacific west coast to act as advertising material for, as an example, the California Dream (Don Mitchell 1996) with Okanagan extensions (Dunae 1981). This culture had a certain "biblical respectability" (Don Mitchell 1996, 19), best captured in the following passage: "Fruit culture nurtured the values of responsible land use, prudent capitalization, and cooperation among growers in the matter of packing, shipping and marketing. Above all else, fruit culture encouraged a rural civility in the care of homes, the founding of schools, churches and libraries, the nurturing of social and recreational amenities which stood in complete contrast to the Wild West attitude of wheat" (K. Starr, quoted in ibid.).

What is also important in the above is how respectability and the prudent capitalization tied to agriculture relate racially to who could and could not treat the land properly (see also Coleman 2006). In this racialization, some people were enticed to come and settle in Kelowna, whereas others were not. Thus, having claimed Kelowna for themselves, whites focused their next step of settlement on cementing whiteness as the organizing principle of industry and the culture of citizenship in the city. Race was constructed as a central element to be found and "not-found" there. The locals were very specific regarding which settlers they sought. Consider their recruitment criteria: "Fruit is the type of produce grown by a certain class of gentleman farmer, so one need not fear be 'surrounded with garlic eating, foreign speaking neighbours, with whom you could have nothing in common socially'" (Salting 1982, quoted in Keyes 2007, 1).

Whereas Canada was importing "garlic-eating" immigrants to the urban centres of the country, Kelowna would have none of them: it was a white space and sought very much to remain so. The metropolis could have its "exotic" immigrants who ate strange foods and smelled even worse, but Kelownians wanted no part of this influx of labourers. Their city was to be a sanctuary of whiteness, free from different-looking and strange-smelling immigrants. The passage above also implies that non-whites could not treat the land properly since they were not gentlemanly enough to so do. Only white English immigrants and residents were cultured enough to recognize the endowments of the land and make it yield properly and abundantly.

This rationale for whiteness was consistent in the writings of the early settlers and promoters of Kelowna. In fact, only the culture of whiteness had the experience and know-how to settle places as they should be. And though one can certainly point to the experience of the British in colonizing most of the world, the author quoted below isn't referring to this experience in quite the same sarcastic way we do here. F.M. Buckland (1966, 1), a local historian, wrote about the original settlers of Kelowna in this manner:

> The exploits as told of old pathfinders, traders and settlers, should be an inspiration when the tenacity and fortitude they displayed in their struggle to establish civilization in a wilderness are revealed. They were the foundation of our present happy position in this Okanagan Valley. "Canadian, you find them everywhere in this Western country," wrote one traveler and writer. And what class of men would be more likely to "be everywhere" than those who represented a fusion of Celt, the Saxon and the Norman races – a fusion that gave them courage, perseverance and strength to accomplish those undertakings which we are so proud to relate.

Not only is white the organizing principle of the city, but only white settlers of Anglo-Saxon background can perform the task of civilizing the "wilderness." This idea of Anglo-Saxon civilizing features has a long history in the Pacific Northwest, as Mathew Sparke (2000, 18) points out in his work: also called Cascadia, it was "one of the Earth's 'few favored regions' – a region 'which possesses all the basic requirements necessary and desirable for the development of the most virile types of humanity, and the highest attainments of civilization.'"[7] Such attainment could be achieved only by whites since Cascadia is a special "white site" with "a 'natural' base from which the White races can pursue their 'natural' talents for conquering the commercial world" (ibid.).[8] Much of this early-twentieth-century attitude, claims Sparke (ibid., 39), continues today under the promotion of a "postindustrial enviro-determinism" that invokes "a set of entrepreneurial possibilities rooted in the soil." Ultimately, Sparke (ibid., 40) says this is an exclusive vision for the region, a kind of gated community for the nouveau riche with a "postindustrial recreational landscape filled with the environmental amenities that will enable the new masters of the hi-tech universe to thrive." In Kelowna, the motto "Work Hard, Play Hard" is often invoked to marry the worlds of play and work for white residents with money. In our view, this motto too fits with geo-economics, as conceived of by Sparke, which seeks to naturalize neo-liberal ideology in the history of places, as in the argument that entrepreneurialism and the enterprising self are as natural to the region as is Okanagan Lake. Consider the following quote from a former BC prime minister, W.R. "Bill" Bennett (2006, n.p.), who hails from one of the wealthiest families in the Okanagan Valley. At the Kelowna Chamber of Commerce's 2006 centennial dinner, he remarked that "there has always been an entrepreneurial, community spirit that has beat just a little stronger here in Kelowna ... here in the heart of British Columbia ... a spirit that has always made Kelowna a good place to open a business and to raise a family."

Locating entrepreneurialism in human nature makes issues of class, patriarchy, and race irrelevant. And the role of the state is obfuscated in clearing land for whites and promoting white business through various support mechanisms, such as encouraging white landowners and depriving Aboriginals and other non-whites from owning land in the valley. Entrepreneurialism is nurtured, secured, and protected through the capitalist state rather than natural attributes of white men. But to make the latter claim is also to attribute naturalness to white ingenuity, in the process detaching privilege from social and political forces and conditions (Dyer 2005). In Kelowna and the Okanagan Valley, such enterprising and civilizing undertakings serve as inspiration for contemporary builders of the region. Not surprisingly, the old money of Kelowna claims this entrepreneurial spirit is what sets the place apart and that those who "succeed" there do so by their ability to take advantage of the entrepreneurial spirit characterizing the area.

Reproducing Whiteness in Kelowna

To this point, we have addressed whiteness in the history of Kelowna and the Okanagan. We now "attend to how whiteness is being (re)imagined and (re)configured" (Vanderbeck 2006, 642) in contemporary Kelowna.

Today, J. Couper (2004, 29) states, "close to 300,000 people make their homes in the Okanagan. Statistically it is difficult to find figures that show they are significantly different from other Canadians." But Kelownians and Okanaganites do indeed differ from "other Canadians," and ironically,

Couper himself provides the data! He writes that "English is the mother tongue of 84.9 percent of the Kelowna population according to Statistics Canada, virtually unchanged from 1996" (ibid.). This compares to 59.7 percent of Canadians elsewhere in the country, and the 2001 census shows that, though the numbers of people speaking a language other than English grew by 12.5 percent in Canada generally, they actually decreased in Kelowna (ibid.). How can this be in a country that is becoming increasingly more diverse? How is this possible in post-modern Canada?

With a population of close to 150,000 (Walton-Roberts 2005, 15, Table 1), Kelowna is the third-largest city/region in British Columbia. According to the 2001 census, the British constitute the largest group in the city, with 21.2 percent of all immigrants, followed by Germans at 13.4 percent and Americans at 9.7 percent (ibid., 17, Table 5). More revealing for our purposes is the fact that, according to the data cited by M. Walton-Roberts (2005, 15, Table 1), a minuscule 3.8 percent of Kelowna's population belongs to a visible minority. This figure compares to 36.8 percent for the province as a whole, 16.8 percent for Squamish, and 5.7 percent for the whole of the BC "hinterland." A recent study commissioned by the Intercultural Society of the Central Okanagan (2008) puts the 2006 visible minority percentage in Kelowna at 6.2. In the years between 2001 and 2006, this percentage almost doubled.[9] But even with such growth, the same study points out that Kelowna remains the least diverse city in Canada. Is it a coincidence that Kelowna is home to so few visible minorities? Is there some effort in place to reproduce Kelowna as so white? We have tried to show that history demonstrates a particular settlement pattern in Kelowna whereby whites were recruited as desired citizens. Next, we reveal how this pattern remains in place today.

The Okanagan economy is changing as its Fordist era shifts to that of post-Fordism, and sectors such as tourism, health care, and services are overtaking mills and manufacturing. Even the "old" industry of agriculture is changing, requiring new work methods, technologies, markets, and labourers (Tomic, Trumper, and Aguiar 2010). The regional business leaders recognize this change and have begun recruiting labour to take up jobs in the new industries. But old views of whiteness are evident in this process, and the purpose of solidifying it continues. The resulting economic expansion of capitalism, where temporary black workers are exploited, is fuelled by an ideology of racism (Brown and Miles 2003) that perceives nothing wrong with unequal relationships. White is the norm, placed securely at the top of the Okanagan social hierarchy, granting privileges to the dominant group (Rothenberg 2005). As Audrey Kobayashi and Genevieve Johnson (2007, 11) explain, "The challenge is to uncover the often unrecognized ways in which old prejudices and blatant racisms are received and repackaged in contemporary discourse – a discourse that includes the normalcy of whiteness." In Kelowna, whiteness is carefully nurtured as the norm, even while other places become multicultural: in Kelowna, whiteness is blinding. The city is portrayed as a place of a white everyday in pamphlets, advertisements, and other representations.

One stark example of this strong discourse is found in the envisaging of Kelowna and the Okanagan Valley of the future. The Okanagan Partnership (n.d.) has produced the video *Two Tomorrows,* in which a little white girl wonders what the future in Kelowna will be like for her.[10] The video shows skilled workers and knowledge workers, but what strikes the viewer is how the future of the Okanagan is imagined through the positioning and interests of this young white girl. It is she who is centred, who speaks, imagines, and marks out how the best path for her is also the best path for the valley. She imagines herself in ten years, when she is mature and of reproductive age. In this narrative, whiteness remains central, uncontested, unmarked, and normal in the future imaginings of the valley. In fact, the narrative, in which the girl and her personal goals are integrated into the whiteness of the region's future, could apply only to the Okanagan Valley. The video ends with the following words: "Time has brought changes but [the valley's] not so very different" (ibid.). Change here refers to economic shifts and adaptations; there is no mention of changes in the "racial" makeup of the region.

The imagining of the Okanagan's future is not normalized by a young white girl alone. For instance, in the November 2007 issue of *Okanagan Life Magazine,* a group of well-placed experts speak to the current and future challenges facing Kelowna and the valley. They say little, however, about the whiteness and cultural homogeneity of the region. The best we can get is the following statement: "We know that to offset the declining fertility rates that Gordon [another participant] was talking about, those two-thirds of this gap will be made up with international immigration. And so we've already seen Mexican labourers that have been brought into Kelowna, people from other countries that are living in hotel rooms to offset current labour shortages, and this will only increase and I think we all know that this is a community that's not used to diversity in many ways. And we have a lot of lengths to go before we really are a community that respects difference" (Mary Ann Murphy, quoted in *Okanagan Life Magazine* 2007, n.p.).[11]

Immigrants, then, are stereotypically categorized as a fertile group need-ed to replenish an aging population. But in the Okanagan, this is one stereo-type that does not stick, as only 7 percent of Kelowna's population comprises international migrants (Intercultural Society of the Central Okanagan 2008). And as we show next, this number conforms to the pattern of settle-ment outlined above rather than indicating a change in practice.

Whites Stay; Non-Whites Are Just-in-Time Workers

There are two employer-driven programs to bring skilled labour to the area: the BC Provincial Nominee Program (BCPNP) and the Temporary Worker Program. Under the auspices of the BCPNP, an employer brings skilled qualified foreign workers to work for him or her. The employees, who are issued a work permit, have a chance to become Canadians if they are nom-inated by their employer. The employer, together with the prospective em-ployee, submits a joint application to the program. Once approved, the nominee may apply to have his immigration process expedited (BC Statistics 2005). Furthermore, and perhaps most importantly, skilled workers may bring their families, and all family members have a chance to naturalize.

The Temporary Worker Program, on the other hand, is much more lim-ited, allowing workers entry to Canada with a work permit, albeit only after an employer's invitation. Moreover, the worker's family members must apply individually to join the applicant in Canada (Citizenship and Immi-gration Canada 2009), and they cannot fast-track their citizenship applica-tions. Currently, there are more temporary workers in Kelowna than PNP skilled workers, something that the Kelowna Economic Development Commission hopes to change, and there will be a push to increase the num-ber of PNP workers over the next five years.

Generally, PNP skilled workers come from western Europe, mainly the UK, Holland, France, and Germany. They are often recruited at overseas immigration shows, where they apply to an employer, resumé in hand. In 2006, Robert Fine, director of the Economic Development Commission (EDC), was accompanied by employers attending ten such immigration shows in Europe (MacNaull 2006, A3). As he explained, "The reason why we are so interested is that this will provide us with more young people and more families, people who move here to work as opposed to those who move here to live" (*Kelowna Capital News* 2006, A23). In addition, these coun-tries were apparently chosen because they are wealthy and because recruiting someone from, say, Poland was considered a waste of time since potential immigrants could not afford to live in Kelowna. This rationale does not hold, however, because the history of immigration shows many examples of migrants who cannot afford to emigrate but who, given the opportunity, nonetheless find the means to leave their country of birth to improve their lives and those of their children (Iacovetta 1992; Giles 2002). Most of those recruited to the Okanagan are master tradesmen who come to Canada with the hope of nomination by their employer. Often, they bring their families with them. It is argued that European workers are more compatible with the Okanagan lifestyle, particularly in connection with costs of housing and living. This sentiment is echoed by a government-commissioned report, which states that to qualify for the PNP, applicants must be "likely to contribute to BC's economic development and growth [while] successfully establish[ing] themselves in the province" (River Associates 2003, 1). Of course, many of those skilled workers are white and come from old-stock immigration countries. Enticed to the Okanagan by the quick process of becoming a landed immigrant with prospective formal citizenship, the overwhelmingly male skilled workers come with their wives to settle and produce the next generation of white Okanaganites. These racialized labour recruitment programs are justified with the assertion that European workers are culturally more compatible than other immigrants and that they hold the same values and work ethic as those already living in Kelowna. Here the shift to cultural racism seems obvious as community leaders argue that these immigrants will readily integrate into the population (Stolcke 1995; Fine 2008).

All temporary workers coming from Mexico to work on Okanagan farms have five- to seven-month contracts. To qualify for this program, they must be married and preferably have children. The main difference here is that their families live in Mexico and will continue to do so. This labour policy is about having a just-in-time workforce. But it is also about obtaining a disciplined workforce that must provide for families back home while never being able to settle, sponsor their families to come to the Okanagan, and produce the next generations of citizens of the valley. During the summer of 2007, there were approximately six hundred Mexican farm workers in the valley (Tomic, Trumper, and Aguiar 2010). Jamaicans too are moving into Kelowna under the temporary short-term work contract, and some come as international students.

Dionne Brand (2001, 35, 39) argues that the black body performs various metaphorical functions in/for the white gaze. The black body is "a place of captivity" that carries particular "cultural and political meanings." It is also a domesticated space, a common possession, a consumer item, a sign of physically and psychically open space, the most regulated body (after women's bodies), and a naturalized body. In her words,

> The Black body is a domesticated space as much as it is a wild space. It is domesticated in the sense that there are set characteristics ascribed to the body which have the effect of familiarizing people with it – making it a kind of irrefutable common sense or knowledge. It is a wild space in the sense that it is a sign of transgression, opposition, resistance, and desire. The Black body is culturally encoded as physical prowess, sexual fantasy, moral transgression, violence, magical musical artistry. These ascriptions are easily at hand for everyday use. Much as one would use a tool or instrument to execute some need or want. (ibid., 35-36)

Furthermore, the black body is a "space not simply owned by those who embody it but constructed and occupied by other embodiments. Inhabiting it is a domestic, hemispheric pastime, a transatlantic pastime, an international pastime" (ibid., 38).

Jamaicans in the Okanagan face even bigger hurdles. Since 2006, over a hundred international students and temporary short-term contract workers from Jamaica have arrived in the valley. However, to be eligible for a government-issued student visa, which is mandatory for enrolment at Kelowna's Okanagan College, a Jamaican student must have $20,000 in a Canadian bank account. Only after obtaining the visa may he or she enrol and attend the trades program at the local college. It is argued that employment in the Okanagan provides these students with global work experiences in new areas and fields, and that they have no desire to leave Jamaica permanently (Fine 2008). We disagree and reiterate our point that these are different labour programs intended to attract only white immigrants for settlement. Jamaicans have come to work on a new bridge and for a window-cleaning company (*Okanagan College News* 2007; Sun Valley Window Cleaners n.d.).

More importantly, Jamaicans must contend with racism while working under a temporary permit in the Okanagan Valley. For example, when it was announced that Jamaican students and contract workers were coming on a temporary basis to Kelowna and the Okanagan, a racial panic erupted as several locals wrote letters to the newspapers claiming that Jamaicans were unwelcome because their race, morals, and values differed from those of white Okanaganites. The director of the Kelowna Economic Development

Commission admitted that when the announcement was made, several racist messages were left on his office telephone voice mail (Fine 2008). In fact, the arrival of Jamaicans even prompted a study and public debate, which asked if Kelowna was ready for new faces in its midst. In this example of othering, whiteness was identified and marked, and Kelowna was defended as a white space free from the "polluting other" (Sibley 1995). bell hooks (1992) argues that, for blacks, whiteness is not invisible; instead, in the terror and fear with which it threatens them, it is starkly clear, even at the scale of the everyday (see also Brand and Bhaggiyadatta 1986). It was in anticipation of all these reactions and sentiments that the Jamaican liaison officer in Kelowna, Bertram Bailey, introduced a curfew for his countrymen: "[Jamaican workers] have been told they have an 11 p.m. curfew on work nights and should refrain from drinking when they have to work in the next morning. A sheet given to the workers reminds them the use of marijuana or any other non-prescription drug is illegal and tells them they are not allowed to have members of the opposite sex sleep over" (Nieoczym 2007, 4). And though there is good reason to believe that Jamaicans are hypervisible after dark (Walcott 2003) and thus in need of protection from racists and racism, the curfew could also be interpreted as unintentionally confirming the locals' myths about Jamaicans – as pot-smoking white-women chasers with poor work ethics who need to be surveilled and controlled.[12] On the other hand, it begins from the assumption that Kelowna is an unsafe space for blacks, especially after dark when they are most vulnerable to racism. This means that the inscription of Kelowna (and the Okanagan) as a place of whiteness and of Jamaicans as posing a threat to this whiteness has been recognized, stated, and now acted upon in a defensive manner by the Jamaicans themselves.

Conclusion

Whiteness has been most carefully constructed in Kelowna and the Okanagan since earliest settlement, and the history of the area gives witness to the deep entrenchment of white privilege there. While hinterland elites have striven to secure and strengthen their positions of privilege, non-whites have played central roles in the shaping of the valley, supporting and manifesting the hegemonic social order of Kelowna. Their sweat and labour have procured the white hinterland of BC, whereas they themselves have been continually discriminated against and exploited. Clearly, as Kelowna and the Okanagan Valley have been marketed and sold as white, as is depicted in brochures and literature, race has been one organizing principle.

Racialization was manifest as whites were enticed to settle in Kelowna and become its citizens. A white landscape was secured and occupied with white citizens.

This history rings true today, and though a post-Fordist Canada is becoming more diverse elsewhere, Kelowna is growing into a blinding, shimmering white city. We ask how racializing Kelowna in this way has been possible. One answer lies in the racist labour recruitment policies that allow white skilled labourers to immigrate as settlers, whereas non-whites are granted only limited temporary work visas to perform as just-in-time workers. Another answer lies in the fact that, in Kelowna, whiteness is the norm and that this discourse of the white everyday is not only strong but also staunchly hegemonic. In fact, whereas there is very little discussion about the racist recruitment policies and exploitative treatment of non-white labour in the Okanagan, there is absolutely no discussion of the white privilege that prevails and its resulting inequalities. We have no doubt that it is high time to scrutinize this blinding whiteness and, as Richard Dyer (2005) suggests, to make this whiteness strange!

ACKNOWLEDGMENTS
The authors thank Audrey Kobayashi, Andrew Baldwin, and the two anonymous reviewers for their advice and thoughtful comments on earlier versions of this chapter. We are solely responsible for the final text and any inconsistencies that may remain in this contribution.

PART 3

ARCTIC JOURNEYS

Inscription, Innocence, and Invisibility
Early Contributions to the Discursive Formation of the North in Samuel Hearne's *A Journey to the Northern Ocean*

RICHARD MILLIGAN AND TYLER MCCREARY

Whiteness is an elusive but pervasive construction. A fiction constituted through embodied encounters in specific times and places, it is also a marker of identity and belonging that, despite all of Canada's multicultural and pluralistic realities, often informs official, popular, and academic narrations of the nation. Anxieties about race arise most strongly in attempts to define national identity, as is exhibited in the First People's Hall on the bottom floor of the Canadian Museum of Civilization, where a visitor can read the following passage from Samuel Hearne's (1958, 78) *A Journey to the Northern Ocean* (the text in brackets was added by the museum):

> As I was the first [white man] they had ever seen, and in all probability might be the last, it was curious to see how they flocked about me, and expressed as much desire to examine me from top to toe, as an European Naturalist would a nondescript animal. They ... pronounced me to be a perfect human being, except in the colour of my hair and eyes: the former, they said, was like the stained hair of a buffaloe's tail, and the latter, being light, were like those of a gull. The whiteness of my skin also was, in their opinion, no ornament, as they said it resembled meat which had been sodden in water till all the blood was extracted.

With this placard, the museum attempts to establish a version of national origins based in a shared history between Indigenous peoples and colonizers. It offers a story free of gross inequities of power, violence, and dispossession. The foregrounding of Hearne's whiteness in the contact zone asks viewers to (re)imagine colonization as a joint venture marked by reciprocal othering but not a unilateral imperative of domination. The museum uses this passage from the exploration literature of colonization to encourage its visitors to remember a past of mutuality, to embody an ideal of reconciliation but not to acknowledge the vast dispossessions of a continent and the racial motivations that justified and ennobled this violence. Rather than paralleling the museum's recuperative impulse, which attempts to turn Hearne's racial visibility in this contact narration into an official version of national origins in which racialized power dynamics are equalized or invisible, we focus on critiquing Hearne's narrative constructions of race and geography. The inscription of whiteness across the Great White North has a direct genealogical connection to material processes and cultural productions of colonization. To begin to dismantle the centrality of whiteness in narrations of North in Canada, we seek to show some of its instabilities, movements, (dis)locations, gaps, and contingencies but also to expose more subtle facets of its persistent formulas. Following the discursive manoeuvres in Hearne's travel writing, we outline a core attribute common to articulations of white settler identity in Canada: a stabilizing posture of innocence that was a necessary precedent for white dominance to attain the status of powerful invisibility.

The question could be asked, why speak of whiteness and not simply power? To be sure, both are amorphous concepts. Who they belong to and what they mean vary, contingent upon geographical and historical circumstances. Nonetheless, to speak of whiteness, either in the period of "discovery" or our own colonial present, names the politics of racial domination that pervade the colonial project. Such naming is vital because, to borrow the words of Lyle Longclaws (quoted in Highway 1989, epigraph), "before the healing can take place, the poison must first be exposed." In our reimagination of the Great White North, the poison of colonization most fundamentally persists in the deployment of whiteness as the centre against which the strangeness and the inferiority of the other are marked. It is necessary to speak of whiteness and its gaze to denaturalize how it operates "as the normative, ordinary power to enjoy social privilege by controlling dominant values and institutions and, in particular, by *occupying space* within a segregated social landscape" (Kobayashi and Peake 2000, 393, emphasis in original). Studying the processes of racialization in the early colonial period helps to elucidate and denaturalize the colonial constructions that serve as normalized claims and identity positions today. Before whiteness could achieve its status of unmarked centre, vesting racial domination with a potent invisibility, it needed to establish its claim (through storying the land), its dominance (through the construction of an inferior other), and its innocence (through creating passive and even vulnerable subject positions in the colonial narrative). In mapping the headwaters of these colonial processes of identification and landscape production, we intend to contribute to the project of decolonization. As researchers, we need to develop "a more critical understanding of the underlying assumptions, motivations and values" that inform our society and our own research practices (L.T. Smith 1999, 20). It is important to realize that this more critical understanding toward which Linda Tuhiwai Smith urges us begins in part with realizing the difference between a flattened view of colonial power relations that simplifies the world into Europeans and Indigenous peoples and a view that allows for the complex play of bodies and discourses in space and in the production of space. Material and discursive relations of power in Canada, though certainly dependent on global relations between continents (Europe and North America), take on particular formations of whiteness and its others in the Canadian landscape. Thus, the poison to be exposed is not simply Europeans or something one might call European-ness but rather whiteness, the construct whose provenance and puissance is explored in this volume.

The late-eighteenth-century travelogue of Arctic explorer Samuel Hearne, *A Journey from Prince of Wales's Fort in Hudson's Bay to the Northern Ocean* (1958), engenders an early version of whiteness in the Canadian North simultaneously embedded within overt colonial articulations of power and the vestments of innocence. The text renders a prototypical account of the Great White North as a colonial landscape intelligible through resource speculation and the globally systemized knowledge of natural history that *de*territorialized Indigenous knowledge. It develops a harsh landscape aesthetic but also performs anxieties of identity and subjectivity as the explorer-narrator engages in intercultural exchange and negotiation. Indigenous people are both valued as knowledge-holding guides and systematically dehumanized through racist ethnography. In this complex play of spatial and cultural orientation, implicit claims to European authority through surveillance and intellectual management of "undiscovered" space are registered alongside, and softened by, explicit claims to innocence. Thus, landscape is not only a product of descriptive frames and screens but also a process whereby narrative identity is formed against a represented landscape (W.J.T. Mitchell 1994). This transformation of identity and simul-taneous construction of a represented space is a move that creates a geo-graphically specific whiteness, a political formation autochthonous to the contact zone.

The North, the Great White North, the "True North strong and free," and other variants on this particularly Canadian version of location-as-direction have long-standing resonances in popular, literary, and national cultures that have emerged following European colonization. Indeed, "North" in Can-ada is a richly limned and highly contested compilation of images, signs, tropes, themes, and technological representations with multiple valencies in deep-seated registers of identity, authenticity, and economy. The encod-ing and subsequent decoding of mythologized meanings of the North are activities that have long engrossed Canada's national icons and intellectuals. Here we aim to contribute to the elucidation of the North as it has been described as a "space-myth" that "has been appropriated as one symbol of specific Canadian nationalistic discourse which ... attempts to reconcile regional viewpoints" (Shields 1991, 163). The point is not to discuss what is (the real) North, but rather how in Canada, where multiplicity and dyna-mism are the central cultural and linguistic motifs, it is imagined that "the environment holds the transformative potential to condition and form a dis-tinct cultural identity, to facilitate acculturation, and to thus bring political unity" (Hulan 2002, 9-10). Particularly, we address Canadian nationalism based upon a racialized ideal of "the struggle to survive in a northern cli-mate" (Francis 1997, 154). The centuries-long development of national iden-tity along these lines has established a normalcy of racial domination and allowed (white) Canadians to know themselves as "not history-less but his-torical; not damned, but innocent; not a blind accident of evolution, but a progressive fulfillment of destiny," much as Toni Morrison (1992, 52) de-scribes the history of race in the United States.[1]

Thinking about Canadian nationalism entails thinking about race be-cause the desire for a deep spiritual connection between the settler nation's people and the land must first overwrite a far more deeply storied and en-coded connection – that of the region's Indigenous peoples and the land (Hulan 2002, 9). The identity formation associated with the modern nation of the latter nineteenth century, as Homi Bhabha (1990, 291) explains in *Nation and Narration,* "fills the void left in the uprooting of communities and kin, and turns that loss into the language of metaphor" by transferring "the meaning of home and belonging." The discursive formation of the

North as central to Canadian identity is a version of this turning. Also speaking to the concept of nation as narration, Edward Said (1993, xiii) explains that before processes of laying claim in colonial contexts could be legitimized, the "power to narrate" the land – to "block other narratives from forming and emerging" – had to be richly cultivated. And it is this phase of the development of the North as a psycho-mytho-social phenomenon in Canada that our analysis assays.

Samuel Hearne's *A Journey to the Northern Ocean* is an important text for such an analysis in that Hearne was one of the earliest anglophones to document his experience of living in the American North. Born in 1745, Hearne joined the Hudson's Bay Company (HBC) in 1766 and began working out of Prince of Wales's Fort at the mouth of the Churchill River on the western coast of Hudson Bay. He lived there for nearly three years before heading north in search of the Coppermine River and the Northwest Passage. This journey of discovery for the HBC, which was completed on the third attempt, took place between early November 1769 and the end of June 1772. After completing the expedition, Hearne remained in the area known to the British as Rupert's Land until his retirement. For most of his adult life, Hearne inhabited and travelled through the northern reaches of the Hudson Bay watershed, in the territories of Dene, Cree, and Inuit peoples.

Hearne provides one of the first representations of this contested and hermeneutically charged northern terrain attributable to a European (Shields 1991, 172-74). The processes of colonization and national narration that have since taken root and flourished in these spaces have at their headwaters Samuel Hearne's narrative. It is useful for analysis of the North in that it spans both the imaginary North critically construed as a blank space of symbolic function against which individuals can endlessly define themselves and the ideological North, which Renée Hulan (2002, 6) describes as a "repository of images defining the official national identity." Hearne's encounter with the North not only produces a text often referenced as an early entry in the repository of nation-defining images but, importantly, the construction of a subjectivity of a colonial agent practising surveillance and expansion in Indigenous territory provides a microcosmic example of the process of generating national identity discussed by the critics mentioned above. That is, Hearne as explorer and authorial voice defines himself, his motivations, and his spatio-temporal social and political context against a landscape that he creates and against an "other" developed as a part of this landscape. So we analyze his text dually: first as production of landscape, a

northern landscape that is now a part of the "repository of images" nourish-
ing claims to an official national identity, and second as process of subjectification whereby self and other are co-constructed against and within the
produced landscape in a synecdoche for the process of defining a national
identity in a colonial context. The elaboration of this process in spaces of
intercultural contact is foundational, not simply for European but for colonial claims to territory and identity, and from these claims emerges a distinct version of whiteness constituting the Great White North, a central
trope in the topographies of identity and power that situate and constitute
contemporary Canadian life according to critics such as Hulan and Rob
Shields.

Barren Landscape

In *A Journey*, Hearne surveys the North to ascertain the potential for profitability as well as the possibility of a northwest passage. Measuring the
potential for resource utilization and trade routes – and "discovering" an
absence that characterized his landscape aesthetics – he catalogued the
elements of this environment using systematic and scientific frames. The
objectives of the Hudson's Bay Company venture required that Hearne
contribute to the knowledge necessary to claim and administer the space,
and largely this process entailed transliterating Indigenous knowledge into
the frames of Enlightenment discourse. Although he had no training in
natural sciences before his excursions, Hearne participated in the extension of scientific taxonomies, comparing his own knowledge of species living around Hudson Bay and those he encountered on his journey with that
of Linnaean-styled natural histories, particularly Thomas Pennant's *Arctic
Zoology*. Hearne emulated popular scientific writing of the period as a
means of establishing his credibility with European audiences, recasting
his local botanical and zoological knowledge in the emergent discourse of
a global natural history. In this capacity, he not only contributed to resource speculation in colonial territories, but also to a version of the disciplinary regime Timothy Luke (1995, 58) has called "geo-power" through
"eco-knowledge." The popularity of Hearne's book and other books containing natural history in this period underscores the manner in which
"knowing" these faraway lands reinforced the colonial claim to them. Presenting itself as an intellectual authority over exotic landscapes by means of
scientific exploration, the empire reified the perception (from the centre)
that the colonies could be controlled and settled, while simultaneously
"naturalizing" that authority. The naturalization of authority via natural

knowledge, or knowledge of natural history, has the simultaneous effect of distinguishing peripheral colonial subjectivities from more centred ones, so that, we argue, European claims were legitimated in these discursive moves, but also white subject positions were initially established.

Although the most strongly constitutive frame for Hearne's landscape production was the significance of Linnaean methodologies in Enlightenment natural history, the most important innovation of *A Journey* is its development of an alternative aesthetic to prevalent European ones, a version of nordicity.[2] Reconnoitring little of value to his superiors during his journeys, Hearne's narrative initiated an evocative northern landscape aesthetic with implications well beyond those of his notably inaccurate surveys of the biophysical geography. His aesthetics of landscape give account of what the terrain looked like and what feelings it inspired. In a limited way, Hearne implements versions of the British picturesque and sublime in his landscape production, as I.S. MacLaren (1984) has argued. But it is important to notice that *A Journey* does not typically inflect natural description with awe-filled constructions of the sublime: "Hearne's narrative recounts little that resembles ... [a] sense of wonder, unless it is Hearne's occasional terror at the indifference of the Northern lands and peoples to him and his goals" (Greenfield 1986-87, 192). The narrator is almost never overcome emotionally by some terror in the landscape. The fierceness of cold, wind, and hunger are focused on as significant hardships, but these are treated in a sort of banal tone of practicability – as in a government or scientific report. Such treatment is fundamentally different from the Burkean descriptions of places such as Mont Blanc and Niagara Falls, which are more frequently characterized as instances of a sublime wilderness aesthetic.

Although the development of landscape in *A Journey* works to present the "predicament of an innocent, vulnerable character" – a fundamental aspect of the sublime outlined in Edmund Burke's *A Philosophical Enquiry into the Origin of Our Ideas of the Sublime and Beautiful* – Hearne's description of what he named the Barren Grounds functions mostly "to reverse Coleridge's definition of the Sublime" and instead offers "a boundless or endless nothingness" without the typical vertical structure of looming precipice or unfathomable abyss (MacLaren 1984, 29). MacLaren argues that a British readership would read the sublime in Hearne's landscape even if he presented it in ways contrary to typical deployments of the trope. It is possible, however, to argue instead that Hearne's narrative is innovative and, indeed, that it initially encodes aspects of a landscape topos distinct from the British picturesque and sublime – one of harshness and inhospitality, but also of purity, and one that has become distinctly Canadian over time. Along with European forms of natural history, these constructions did not simply establish a European claim to space but constituted the emergence of a specifically North American landscape that served as a vital fount for the imagination of the colony as possessing a unique rather than simply derivative character.

As Kathleen Venema (2000, 176-79) and others have pointed out, Hearne's anguished description of his Dene companions massacring vulnerable Inuit once they reach the Coppermine River provides a sublime and even gothic centrepiece and climax for his travelogue. At the rapids, to which Hearne (1958, 96) gives the appellation Bloody Fall, the climactic scene resounds with elements of the sublime and gothic terror.[3] Here the narrative motivation for exploration is superseded by an alternative "bloody design" of the Dene to "steal upon the poor Esquimaux the ensuing night, and kill them all while asleep." The description of the ambush that follows is wrought with gothic language, the sympathetic development of innocent and powerless victims, and the graphic inscription of cruel, grotesque violence. Calling it a "bloody massacre," Hearne (ibid., 99, 100) describes the "shrieks and groans of the poor expiring wretches" and self-dramatizes "the terror of [his] mind at beholding this butchery."

This narrative flourish – probably evidence of strong editorial influence (MacLaren 1993) – rendered the text legible for contemporary English readers by evoking, alongside "acts of barbarity," "a sublime landscape proper" (MacLaren 1984, 32). But, atypically, the episode at Bloody Falls uses the bleakness of the landscape produced throughout the rest of *A Journey* as a cold, nearly barren (empty) backdrop upon which to inscribe a frightening human drama more starkly. MacLaren demonstrates how some of the gothic and sublime language of the murder is transferred onto natural description that immediately follows the massacre. Hearne (1958, 107) writes, "the channel of the river has been caused by some terrible convulsion of nature." MacLaren (1984, 32-33) explains that, emulating the form of the English sublime, the "roaring cataract" at the massacre site is "wild" and "vertically-structured," a sharp contrast to the seemingly unending "desolate tracts" of "barren hills and wide-open marshes" that predominate throughout *A Journey.*

Although this climactic scene provides a hermeneutically navigable topos "for the English reader," as MacLaren (ibid., 32) notes, the bulk of Hearne's text traces the outline of an alternative landscape motif. This landscape aesthetic, neither picturesque nor concertedly sublime, is an important early manifestation of the Canadian North that has been elaborated and rehashed significantly over the intervening generations. Hearne's landscape can best be described as one of negation. By focusing on the "barrenness" and in-hospitable conditions of the Barren Grounds, Hearne develops an aesthetic motif that has become commonplace in descriptions of northern experi-ence: inhospitable, harsh, barren, forbidding, threatening, terrorizing, and cold. If, as Kerry Abel and Ken Coates (2001, 9) state in *Northern Visions,* "Canada is defined, in substantial measure, by its response to winter," Hearne's aesthetics of the Barren Grounds is an important first step in de-fining the nation. In "Winter and the Shaping of Northern History," their chapter in this same collection, Ken Coates and William Morrison (2001, 23, 30) declare that "'Winter' and 'northern' have become synonymous" and that "winter created a uniquely northern social world, one marked by isola-tion and loneliness, by a struggle to survive and hang on until spring." Just as Coates and Morrison highlight isolation, loneliness, and struggle, so does the following representative passage from Hearne's (1958, lxxi) text:

> I was invariably confined to stony hills and barren plains all the Summer, and before we approached the woods in the Fall of the year, the ground was always covered with snow to a considerable depth; so that I never had an opportunity of seeing any of the small plants and shrubs to the Westward. But from appearances, and the slow and dwarfy growth of the woods, etc. (except in the Athapuscow country), there is undoubtedly a greater scarcity of vegetable productions than at the Company's most Northern Settlement; and to the Eastward of the woods, on the barren grounds, whether hills or vallies, there is a total want of herbage except moss, on which the deer feed; a few dwarf willows creep among the moss; some wish-a-cuppa and a little grass may be seen here and there, but the latter is scarcely sufficient to serve the geese and other birds of passage during their short stay in those parts, though they are always in a state of migration.

Phrases in this passage work to exaggerate absence and to emphasize the difficulties Hearne experienced on his adventure. Typically limning the land by way of negation, he describes the "birds of passage," not as a significant aspect of biological diversity and production in the region, but rather to accentuate the motif of scarcity and as a means of naturalizing his own situ-ation. The bleak emptiness of the land portrayed in this summary seems to convey the sentiments of someone who had felt the pangs of its scarcity. And the invocation of a permanent "state of migration" in a land that is "scarcely sufficient" for subsistence echoes Hearne's own situation during his travels in what seems more an instance of projection than of naturalistic rigour.

Hearne's aesthetic development of a northern landscape fits right into a concept of "north as a negative, overwhelming presence," which figures such as Northrop Frye reiterated and popularized as the prevalent construction of the North and the nation (Grace 2002, 32). The power of the environment to define the Canadian national identity in Frye's version of North is famously less impressive than oppressive. So, at least as a contribution to the "discursive formation of the north," the aesthetic treatment of the Barren Grounds in *A Journey* is most significant in an archaeology of ideas of North that have become deeply imbricated in Canadian nationalism (ibid., 27).

Indian Ethnography

The cultural production of landscape is necessary for the stabilization of geographical identity, vital to laying claim to the land. Similarly, categories of race take on legitimating roles in the context of violent territorial dispossession (colonialism) through stereotyped constructions of difference that constitute ideas of superiority and inferiority. Hearne's *A Journey* functions as one of the linchpins of the early Canadian literary canon, famous, or infamous, for its depiction of life among the Dene ("Copper Indians" and "Northern Indians"). As such, it encodes a proto-Canadian colonial encounter that has been critically engaged to understand (or distort) settler-Indigenous relations then and now. Many readers focus upon Hearne's misogynist, racist, and Eurocentric representations, particularly in his description of the massacre at Bloody Falls (Goldie 1987, 1989; McGrath 1993; Venema 2000), but others have celebrated his inscription of cross-cultural bonding and occasional expression of anti-imperial sentiments (Greenfield 1986-87; K. Harrison 1995; Hutchings 1997).

A Journey does not simply catalogue a monological description of the Indigenous other as inferior and inhuman; but, of course, neither does it provide a polyphonic articulation of difference in which the subaltern speaks her own voice. Rather, it is marked by the recurrent doubling of male imperial discursive constructions of the other. Most ethnographic notes in the narrative harmonize with dominant colonial constructions of Indigenous inferiority, but it unexpectedly extols the virtues of Hearne's third guide, Matonabbee, in humanistic depiction that marks a departure from the unabated racism and ethnocentrism of most of the author-explorer's contemporaries. Although readers are right to note Hearne's exceptionalism in his treatment of Matonabbee, we must also acknowledge that these putatively contradictory exceptions serve to delineate further the rule of Indigenous inferiority. Rather than assuming that contradictions in performance and narration arising from colonial practices are exceptional and even recuperative, we should recognize these contradictions as inherent and perhaps even discursively practical features of colonial narrations. Recording the encounter necessarily entails negotiating between truth-claims of explorers' originating cultures and their own experiences of defamiliarization. At points, *A Journey* codifies uncertainty with regard to European values or embraces different cultural practices under the peculiar pressures of shifting geographic location; however, such apparently contingent incongruities are inherent elements of the colonial encounter, which Hearne mobilizes to negotiate the incompatibilities of his journeys with a colonial classification scheme that he ultimately upholds (Venema 1998).

Despite slippages, Hearne's text regularly represents Indigenous people as less-than-human savages. As he travels from Prince of Wales's Fort, his value and authority diminishes in the Indigenous cultural geography, a loss he palpably expresses as a bodily threat (ibid.). In his first two failed attempts, he uses two descriptions of individuals to establish a baseline characterization of Indigenous peoples: he represents Chawchinahaw, his first guide, as a back-stabbing villain, and Conne-e-quese, his second guide, as disinclined to extend basic hospitality and unable to protect him from robbery. Building with ethnographic generalizations, Hearne presents Indigenous people as callous and self-serving, and expresses fear regarding their hostility, his lack of cultural agency, and his inability to alter the threatening conditions of encounters so "distant from the fort" he depends upon for authority (ibid., 16).

Matonabbee, Hearne's final guide, who successfully leads him to his desired destination, is introduced into a tableau in which the white hero-explorer has experienced cultural devaluation and sustained bodily threat. Hearne regularly celebrates Matonabbee's civility in contrast to the stereotyped rule of indigeneity elsewhere established in *A Journey*, and Matonabbee is characterized as possessing the humane sympathies so lacking in the Indigenous people Hearne previously encountered: "The courteous behaviour of this stranger struck me very sensibly. As soon as he was acquainted with our distress, he ... furnished me with a good warm suit of otter and other skins" (Hearne 1958, 34). Thus, Matonabbee mitigated Hearne's vulnerability to the inclement landscape. Hearne (ibid., 35-36) reports that he found his "new acquaintance, on all occasions, the most sociable, kind, and sensible Indian I had ever met with. He was a man well known, and, as an Indian, of universal knowledge, and generally respected." Unlike his prior guides, Matonabbee possessed the knowledge, integrity, and social capital necessary to guide and protect Hearne's mission (Venema 2000).

Although Hearne occasionally records flaws in Matonabbee's character, these are regularly mitigated and justified, and he remains a celebrated figure throughout. However, Hearne's particular method of inscribing Matonabbee as exceptional does so by marking his difference against normalized colonial constructions of Indigenous depravity. Near the end of his book, Hearne includes an ethnographic chapter that is a robust display of Eurocentric and racist claims, in which it is difficult to discern many ethnographic details free from obvious biases. Hearne (1958, 197) notes of "the females" that "their skins are soft, smooth, and polished; and when they are dressed in clean clothing, they are as free from an offensive smell as any of the human race." In another moment of misogynist racism, he claims, "They differ so much from the rest of mankind, that harsh uncourteous usage seems to agree better with the generality of them ... for if the least respect be shown them, it makes them intolerably insolent" (ibid., 199). In this chapter, Hearne describes Matonabbee as distinct from Dene people, dedicating a separate biographic section extending well beyond the context of Hearne's journey section to inscribe his personhood. Hearne humanizes Matonabbee as distinct from the denigrated Indigenous population, accrediting him with "talents equal to the greatest task that could possibly be expected from an Indian" (ibid., 225).

The racist claims that permeate the general statements in this chapter, which is titled "Northern Indians," and the constant inscription of Matonabbee's exceptionalism function to reassure readers that Hearne had not, in fact, "gone Native." The strongest association of Matonabbee with that which is British occurs in the closure of his biography and life as he commits suicide after the French raze the fort. Hearne depended on Matonabbee for survival and in return attempted to distinguish him from his people and isolate him from their savagery for Euro-settler posterity.

Ennobling Matonabbee against cultural determinants elsewhere developed by *A Journey* is also very apparent in the climax scene where Hearne writes Matonabbee and his leadership out of the massacre of Copper Inuit at Bloody Falls. This episode renders the text legible to a European audience, deploying some central colonial motifs and stylings; however, it also resonates with the ambiguities of Hearne's colonial encounter. His description focuses on the death of a sensuous Inuit girl at the hands of violent, savage Dene men, and his own "neuter-ality" (Goldie 1987, 88) in the encounter:

> When they soon began the bloody massacre, while I stood neuter in the rear ... my horror was much increased at seeing a young girl, seemingly about eighteen years of age, killed so near me, that when the first spear was stuck into her side she fell down at my feet, and twisted round my legs, so that it was with difficulty that I could disengage myself from her dying grasps ... I solicited very hard for her life; but the murderers made no reply till they had stuck both their spears through her body, and transfixed her to the ground. They then looked me sternly in the face, and began to ridicule me, by asking if I wanted an Esquimaux wife; and paid not the smallest regard to the shrieks and agony of the poor wretch, who was twining round their spears like an eel. Indeed, after receiving much abusive language from them on the occasion, I was at length obliged to desire that they would be more expeditious in dispatching their victim out of her misery, otherwise I should be obliged, out of pity, to assist in the friendly office of putting an end to the existence of a fellow-creature who was so cruelly wounded. On this request being made, one of the Indians hastily drew his spear from the place where it was first lodged and pierced it through her breast near the heart. (Hearne 1958, 99-100)

Perhaps the best-known section of Hearne's published account, this passage relies upon and reproduces notions of Indigenous savagery and sexuality in relation to the colonial subject. As Venema (2000, 180) documents, the scene is rendered legible and lucrative to Europe's textual economy and colonial audiences through "recourse to the sign of the female body vulnerable to imminent and gothically menacing destructive forces." Although Hearne made passing references to Indian barbarity throughout, the massacre depiction constitutes an "emphatic irruption of the theme of savagery" (Hutchings 1997, 56). The striking serpentine simile for the Inuit girl, who struggles "like an eel," figuratively associates indigeneity and animality, reinforcing the image of indigeneity as nature (Goldie 1989, 45). This bare framing of Indigenous animality is in contrast, semantically and symbolically, to the complex construction of Hearne's own civil, humane supplications for an expeditious dispatch to end her suffering. Thus, in line with prevalent and enduring racist constructions, the episode presents the reader with the Indigenous woman as a suffering being but not a thinking subject.

The colonial encounter is marked by the ambivalence of "fear and temptation," as Terry Goldie (1989) discusses in his book of that title. Although Hearne figures himself as "neuter," distancing himself from both Indigenous peoples' sexuality and primal nature, the projected Indigenous state of nature both appealed to and threatened a repressed civility constituted through the domination of the rational intellect over the body. The girl's grasp upon his body, and the Indians' suggestion that he may desire "an Esquimaux wife," makes explicit the sexual undercurrents, the desire and threat of the embodiment that occurs upon entering the land of the other. As Goldie (1987, 88) notes, the "subtext of attraction shows the white approach/avoidance reaction to the sexual indigene, both as succubus of the land and potential liberation from repression." Thus, the girl exhibits a potent prone sexuality, unsettling the image of colonial restraint and registering the presence of hidden colonial sexuality.

Hearne (1958, 100) concludes his account of the girl's death in mournful contemplation, remarking "even at this hour I cannot reflect on the transactions of that horrid day without shedding tears," registering further ambivalences concerning his colonial encounters. *A Journey* resonates with powerful anxieties with regard to the realities of contact and progress. As Mary Louise Pratt (1992) indicates, though European enterprise is rarely noted within travelogues, the global colonial transformation is understood to be under way, and an explorer's narrative is itself an element of imperialist expansion. The supersession of new colonial modes was figured as inevitable, if tragic. Hearne's remorseful, reflective positioning in closing his description of the death of the Inuit girl underscores the position of Indigenous peoples as historical artifacts passing from a barbaric land (Goldie 1989, 46). This is an early encoding of what would become a dominant narrative of Indigenous peoples in Canada as historical, not contemporary (Francis 1992). Powerless before the superior advancing civilization, they are simply unable to adapt and sadly, romantically vanish.

The romanticized tragic passing of the Inuit girl, the fertile persona of the land, also figures as the (anti)climax of Hearne's explorations. As Bruce Greenfield (1986-87, 194) notes, Hearne's experience never fully accorded with the discovery plot, as he "discovered nothing." Although anticipation preceded his adventures, the mythologized landscape of discovery and plenty never appears. Instead, as he nears the ostensible goal of his pursuits, the Coppermine River, the journey becomes further contorted by the Dene's designs upon the Inuit. The emotional climax is underwritten by the barren nature of the virgin territory. As Anne McClintock (1995, 24) documents, the mythology of imperial discovery and conquest was "an erotics of engulfment" comprising both the fantasies of penetration and the fears of engulfment and impotence often figured in the encounter between the virile explorer and the supple Indigenous maiden as representative of the land. Whereas the massacre scene achieves legibility in the common colonial motif of the valiant explorer above the inviting female embrace, the girl's death represents the necrophilia of his entry into dead territory. Instead of the cavalier conquistador, Hearne stands as our impotent anti-hero.

The Anti-Hero

In *Imperial Eyes*, Mary Louise Pratt (1992, 4) traces the displacement of "older traditions of survival literature" by "scientific and sentimental travel writing" making use of the "anti-conquest" as narrative device. Pratt (ibid., 39) argues that systemizing nature according to the Linnaean gaze provided a means of shifting from "overt imperial articulations of conquest, conversion, territorial appropriation, and enslavement" to a "utopian, innocent vision of European global authority," while providing the framework of "territorial surveillance" necessary to render distant lands knowable. Within this form, the colonial agent transforms from an actor to an eye merely surveying the landscape. Although, in his final two chapters of ethnography and zoology, Hearne appends his attempt to emulate the objective scientific position, it is Pratt's sentimental anti-conquest that best describes the narrative structure of much of *A Journey*. Though Hearne "is composed of a whole body rather than a disembodied eye" of the purely scientific gaze, the narrator-explorer "is constructed as a non-interventionist European presence" in the contact zone: "He, too, is the non-hero of an anti-conquest ... Things happen to him and he endures and survives," but most importantly, he remains passive and innocent (ibid., 78). His production of landscape is significant in that there is almost "no landscape description at all" (ibid., 76, 77) except when natural detail "is textually relevant (has value) in so far as it bears upon the speaker-traveler and his quest." Even Hearne's zoology is marked by his attribution of human-use value to various animal resources. So, for the most part, his landscape was produced as "emblematic or composite" against which the narrative is arranged around his "personal experience and adventure" (ibid., 51, 75). Pratt's analysis locates this kind of "sentimental" travel writing as a complement to the scientific narratives of inland travel in colonial geographies of the eighteenth century. Crucially for

Pratt, despite the drastic differences in approach to the land, these two kinds of travel narration share a capacity to sanitize and mystify European expansion even as they contribute to it.

Whereas the anti-hero of scientific anti-conquest disappears from the narrative, the narrator of sentimental anti-conquest has a dogged determination to locate himself in the events reported. His feelings, hardships, responses, considerations, interactions, and most importantly, his actions dominate the field. Although this kind of writing was based on experiences in the contact zone that were explicitly a part of European expansionist enterprise, the narrator of the sentimental travel tale portrays these relations as fundamentally passive. In *A Journey*, "human agents abound" and the narrative process of sentimental writing "explicitly anchors what is being expressed in the sensory experience, judgment, agency, or desires of the human subjects" (M.L. Pratt 1992, 76). Whereas scientific travel writing dramatizes the "unfolding" self-presentation of landscape in a self-effacing way, Hearne is self-dramatizing because his authority primarily rests in the authenticity of his experience. Although this European presence in the contact zone is much more pronounced than the invisible all-seeing eye of scientific travel writing, the anti-hero of sentimental travel writing remains innocent and non-interventionist as he constructs himself with "submissiveness and vulnerability, or the *display* of self-effacement" (ibid., 78, emphasis in original).

Hearne's description of the natural world is deeply anthropocentric. The insistence on describing landscape occasionally with an emphasis on deprivation – hunger, cold, emptiness – and the manner in which he often focuses on issues of palatability are evidence of his deployment of a self-centred anti-conquest. By affixing his landscape production to his own situation, the traveller's body maintains its position on centre stage. But Hearne's body-centred account not only constantly demonstrates his vulnerabilities in the harsh ecosystems through which he travelled, it also highlights his submission to Matonabbee, his guide. He often reiterates how the success of his mission was entirely dependent on the leadership abilities and cultural know-how of Matonabbee, always diminishing the significance of his own performativity.

The inscription of innocence and passivity into *A Journey* is thus much more overt than in the scientific anti-conquest where it is the concentration on observation and not the display of powerlessness that elides colonial agency. Although, through his journeys, Hearne is composed of a double-body – the abstracted representational body of "institutionalized mercantilism and the corporeal body of visceral contact" – the authority of the former, and that of the colonial enterprise he represents, diminishes as the vulnerability of the latter is emphasized (Venema 1998, 21). Hearne is registered as a representative body through the inclusion of his official orders and the seven-gun salute that marks his initial departure from the fort. Only two pages later, he is already twenty days into his first attempt to reach the Arctic, engaged in recounting the severity of his hardships. In fact, the first two pages establish his dependence on and harsh treatment from his first guide, whom he calls "Captain Chawchinahaw," much more strongly than they establish the significance of his relationship with the fort.

Although Hearne relies on the colonial centre as the basis for his assumptions of Indigenous inferiority, the reference is implicit, and the centre (the fort) is marked by its "textual absence," which corresponds with the anti-conquest's absenting of colonial power (ibid., 16). Hearne regularly abstracts colonial trading practices as simply an object (noun) in the world – "trade" – erasing historicity as well as colonial participants and power relations in the processes of exchange. He presents the conflicts resulting from the development of trade as merely an internal issue of Indigenous communities. In some passages, his erasure of the violence of colonial activity comes through the overt dramatization of reciprocity, attributing to Indigenous peoples a willing acquiescence to colonization: "I smoked my calumet of peace with the principal of the Copper Indians, who seemed highly pleased on the occasion; and, from a conversation held on the subject of my journey, I found they were delighted with the hopes of having an European settlement in their neighbourhood" (Hearne 1958, 77). As Hearne's narrative translates his role from active agent on a colonial frontier to passive innocent under the care of Indigenous hosts, this passage encodes a passive naïveté into the Indigenous experience and engagement with colonial power. Hearne is a colonial agent, but he obscures the violence of colonialism and his relationship to it by distinguishing himself from the signs of that authority.

Nowhere is Hearne's self-effacement clearer than in his relationship of feminized dependence and subordinance to Matonabbee (Venema 2000, 168). Venema takes the title for her essay – "Under the Protection of a Principal Man" – from Hearne's (1958, 63) outright articulation of his relationship with Matonabbee as one that types the guide as a masculine, empowered agent, and the narrator as a feminine, vulnerable ward: "But as I was under the protection of a principal man, no one offered to molest me, nor can I say they were very clamorous for anything I had." Although Mary

Louise Pratt discusses the operation of anti-conquest in Mungo Park's feminized position in instances of "aggressive voyeurism" via the Indigenous "female gaze" recorded in his *Travels in the Interior of Africa,* the extent to which Hearne is transformed from masculine agent to feminine protector-ate is remarkable. As Bruce Greenfield (1986-87, 197) describes, Hearne is primarily a "passive dependent" instead of a heroic adventurer; "his actual role was that of an observer being led to his destination." Venema (2000, 171) argues that "after delegating heroism to Matonabbee, Hearne positions himself culturally as one of Matonabbee's many wives." Corroborating this claim, Venema (ibid., 168, 170) demonstrates that the narrative harbours an "unexpected ... focus on Matonabbee's wives," and, in fact, "much of what the text actually records specifically concerns Matonabbee's wives, his rela-tionship to his wives and his behaviour toward them, and the women's in-direct but powerful effect on the journey's advancement and success." All of this attention she calls "an inadvertent expression of [Hearne's] survival strategy in the cultural space" of contact (ibid., 171).

The contradictions in *A Journey* between Hearne's functionary role as agent of mercantile expansion and his visceral experience of contact, in which the "truth-claims of [his] originating culture" are called into question, inadvertently result in "records of the literal and symbolic slippages" such as his feminization (Venema 1998, 19). According to Mary Louise Pratt (1992, 74), the slippages arise in order to perform a discursive function during a crisis of legitimation. These two discussions are not contradictory. Venema seems to be concerned with how the space of contact necessitated these slippages. Pratt establishes the manner in which such slippages, whether or not they arise necessarily out of contact, retain and, in fact, build upon dis-courses that were required for the implementation and legitimation of col-onial practice. Two sides of a similar story. Most importantly, neither can coincide with a reading in which Hearne's slippages are "an early manifesta-tion of critical *self-reflexivity,* that anti-monological impulse which, if con-tinually 'improved' upon by intercultural discussion and debate, can help to provide the basis for sound cultural criticism, intercultural negotiation, and productive sociocultural transformation" (Hutchings 1997, 73, emphasis in original). In his analysis, Kevin Hutchings parallels much scholarship that seeks to celebrate the disjunctures that emerge from colonial encounters; however, a reader familiar with colonial discourses should not only expect these disruptions and contradictions, but as Venema and Pratt demonstrate, should also interrogate the manner in which such heterogeneities find contrapuntal resonance. Deployed as enactments of ideological and discursive transition, heterogeneous colonial narrations ultimately function with greater efficacy as a result of incorporating and narrating these very slippages and gaps.

It is important to continue to revisit our history not in the hopes of discovering a redemptive fount to reclaim an imagined mutuality between newcomers and Indigenous peoples that erases violence and elides power relations, but to orient us critically today in the enterprise of decolonization. It remains necessary to expose the power and appeal of a cloak of whiteness, shrouding colonial society in an air of innocence. The centrality of the mythos of survival in Canada, forwarding our common vulnerability while quieting the deterritorializations Indigenous peoples suffered to open the northern frontier both imaginatively and materially, must remain the subject of critical attention. Whether we be researchers, politicians, activists, or denizens, as we continue to narrate the North, we must maintain a constant vigilance. Retelling should aim not to recuperate the inscription of whiteness in the discursive appropriation of land and power, but to disempower it; not to erase the violent intrusion of whiteness in the semiotics of space, but to expose the toxicity of its grammar and rhetoric; not to wash away the sins that attend whiteness in all its articulations, but to disintegrate the power and privilege it continues to provide.

Conclusion

Indigenous claims to title and jurisdiction have long been contained or erased through colonial constructions of Aboriginal peoples as so primitive that they are merely part of the landscape, unable to transform the land or perform the higher functioning aspects of governance (Francis 1992). These constructions ideologically emptied the terrain for settlers, while colonial governments' land policies materially contained Indigenous space. But although powerful mythologies have naturalized the colonial grid and property relations, these are spatial relations that must constantly be performed and maintained. Two hundred years after Hearne, Indigenous land claims and blockades symbolically and materially mark the continued discordance between colonial and Indigenous topographies, generating spaces of negotiation over claims to the land (Morris and Fondahl 2002). And Canadian settler communities continue to rely upon and replay colonial mythologies present in Hearne's travelogue to claim the land and eschew Indigenous claims. These include the continued currency of the image of the untamed wilderness, demeaning stereotypes of Aboriginal peoples, and the wide-spread assumption of the historical inevitability of European domination (Furniss 1999).

Many researchers are currently working on the complex play of issues that constitute the colonial present. From debates about traditional ecological knowledge in resource management to the role of eco-tourism in political ecology, from post-colonial interventions in environmentalism to the role of literary theory and storytelling in land claim disputes, these projects often engage the manner in which recursive spatial relations, both material and discursive, reproduce raced bodies and relations in spaces mutually constituted by this play of whiteness against its others. Although whiteness was initially staged in the North American contact zone through the encounter between the European and his colonial other, the encoding of this moment has worked to authorize colonial subjectivities that maintain contemporary pertinence. The distinct tropes developed through the literature of early exploration not only authorized imperial claims, but fundamentally equipped future generations of colonists with the discursive resources to lay claim to a distinct national space and subjectivity. In this essay, we have focused on the ways in which Hearne's travelogue laid colonial claims to territory and identity, clothed in an innocence developed through motifs of vulnerability. This laid the foundations of what emerged as a distinct North American whiteness, eventually appropriated by autochthonic nationalist discourse as the roots of Canadianness. The precise career of these discursive tropes through the intervening years is more than we can or wish to develop here. Instead, we leave that to anti-racist researchers whose attempts to undermine whiteness today have inspired and informed our researches in the eighteenth century and to future work in the unwinding of whitenesses, both in Canada and wherever it has been central to politics of domination.

A Journey helps to recuperate colonial practice in its own discourses by offering examples of Europeans (or first-generation settlers) venturing out of the colonies and into the frontier, establishing a corporeal and intellectual authority, and most significantly, doing so in a way that insisted upon their own innocence – and that of the empire. As Mary Louise Pratt (1992, 57, emphasis in original) elucidates, "the *discourse* of travel that natural history produces, and is produced by, turns on a great longing: for a way of taking possession without subjugation." In this context it is important to realize that, despite earlier Eurocentric claims, humanist sentiments that acknowledged Indigenous culture and humanity came to be increasingly tolerated in colonial discourse from the eighteenth century onward as a means of resyncing colonial practice with prevailing sentiments. Therefore, we should not be surprised to find contradictory positions in texts such as *A Journey*. Constructions of race and landscape in Canada evolved in complex but deeply interconnected ways, staging the innocence of the white colonial agent protected by and yet vulnerable to the Indigenous other in a foreboding northern land. Given that Canadians may still embody this "great longing" for innocence and for an obviation of colonial national guilt – the guilt of imperial entitlement – the enthusiastic celebration of proto-Canadian exploration writing such as Hearne's as polyvocal needs to be curtailed by an acknowledgment of, and attendance to, the subjugative facility of a postured innocence.

Recently reissued by TouchWood Editions with a laudatory and even defensive foreword written by Ken McGoogan (2007), Hearne's travelogue remains vital because his narration laid foundational claims to both intellectual authority and innocence simultaneously, claims that persist in informing Canadian identity. Nonetheless, it continues to be framed within laudatory readings. Evoking the redemptive ideal that suggests that, somehow, the forefront of colonization is the place to find the groundwork for multiculturalism and decolonization, McGoogan (ibid., x) writes, "Hearne demonstrated that to thrive in the north, Europeans had to apprentice themselves to the Native peoples who had lived there for centuries – a lesson lost on many who followed." It is our argument that these are just the sorts of readings we need to debunk in retelling stories of contact. Rather than celebrating the transformative potential of the inclement environment to craft a shared national identity, we need to problematize how these normalized place frames have enabled us to misunderstand our relationships to the land and each other. The possibility of decolonization rests not within the restoration of an imagined guiltless past, but through a thorough engagement with socio-spatial processes, discursive and material, that have quieted other claims to the land. Rather than seeking absolution through the performance of (mis)remembered intercultural mutuality, we must pursue a justice that radically unsettles the dominant discursive and material ordering of Canadian society. This requires that we demythologize and destabilize governing Canadian myths and learn to read stories such as Hearne's contrapuntally. Robin McGrath's (1993) work on Inuit oral history begins the task of remembering against the veil of whiteness, but much work remains to decentre colonial histories and decolonize the Great White North. As Bonita Lawrence (2002, 46) suggests, "It is the voices of

Indigenous peoples, long silenced but now creating a new discourse, which will tell a fuller history." Recognizing the normalized ability for a text such as Hearne's to continue the long tradition of silencing these voices, we must trouble the unexamined repetition of "images that, because they are unique and irreplaceable, continue to turn up in new books on northern history" (McGoogan 2007, x).

Copper Stories
Imaginative Geographies and Material Orderings of the Central Canadian Arctic

EMILIE CAMERON

It has become almost a platitude to refer to the Canadian Arctic as a "changing" environment. There are dangers in this kind of rhetoric, but the past several decades have certainly seen enormous change in the region. The Nunavut Land Claims Agreement was settled in the early 1990s, just as diamonds were "discovered" in the central Arctic and a new wave of mineral exploration and extraction was initiated. Oil and gas exploration has similarly accelerated, renewing calls for the construction of a natural gas pipeline through the Mackenzie Valley, while multiple constituencies rally to address global environmental change and its impact at the poles. Indeed, the very lands and seas upon which Inuit claims to the territory of Nunavut were based are themselves changing. Ice is melting, the migratory patterns of birds and caribou are varying, and seasonal patterns are becoming radically unpredictable. The interests of multinational investors in northern resource extraction now mingle with federal interests in maintaining Canadian sovereignty in the region, in part through major expansions of military infrastructure and surveillance. Amid these pressures, the social and cultural legacies of colonial rule continue to affect northern communities and to intervene in efforts to govern the territory of Nunavut in the interests of its primarily Inuit citizenry. Far from the timeless place of nationalist imaginations, the Arctic is in fact a site of great political, cultural, environmental, and social change.

These changes do not occur in a historical or geographical vacuum. Contemporary Arctic geographies are shaped by histories of imperialism and colonialism, by the racializations elaborated in Canadian settler societies, by historical and contemporary flows of capital and resources, by state and missionary activities in the region, and by Inuit and other Indigenous political movements. Although some continue to imagine the Canadian North as an isolated, timeless, and far-flung region whose very isolation and starkness anchor the nation's symbolic economy, the Arctic is in fact deeply relational, a place constituted both imaginatively and materially by networks of people, ideas, and other things. Because of its immense symbolic and imaginative valence in Canada, moreover, the *narrative* articulation and organization of these networks of people, ideas, and things is particularly stark in the North (Grace 2002; Hulan 2002).

In other words, perhaps more than any other region in Canada, the North is constituted and ordered by stories – stories that make legible the connections between particular people, places, and ideas. By "stories" I refer not only to the classic tales of Farley Mowat and Pierre Berton (although these certainly make legible a particular form of relation between southern and northern Canada), and not only to the rich stories animating Inuit oral traditions, but also to the narrative construction of knowledge more generally and to the notion of story as "material ordering practice." Following John Law, I am interested in thinking about story as practice, performance, and network. Stories, Law (1994, 142) argues, are not something separate from, nor merely representative of, the world around us; they are themselves material and intimately bound up with "the materials in which they are carried." As such, the stories anchoring racialized and colonial imaginative geographies of the Arctic are significant not only because of their imaginative force, but also because of their influence over the material conditions of life in the region. Similarly, the shifting geographies of capital, resources, governance structures, and climate in the contemporary Arctic are made sensible, legible, and political through stories.

One of the most prominent stories shaping understandings of the central Arctic and particularly relations between Inuit, Dene, and Euro-Canadians is that of the Bloody Falls massacre, initially told as early as 1771 and reproduced countless times since then. It chronicles the alleged massacre of a group of Inuit camped along the Coppermine River in mid-July 1771, near present-day Kugluktuk, Nunavut. The Inuit were attacked by a group of Chipewyan Dene who had guided Hudson's Bay Company (HBC) explorer Samuel Hearne to the river from Prince of Wales's Fort, a distance of more than two thousand miles. Hearne had been dispatched by the HBC to look for copper rumoured to exist around the river's mouth, to establish good relations with the Indigenous peoples of the region, and to search for a northwest passage. His journey was essentially a failure on all three counts, but his description of the massacre, published in 1795, became an iconic Arctic story that was taken up with great enthusiasm in Britain and continued to be reinvoked and reimagined throughout the following two centuries. It is a brutal story. Hearne conjures images of ruthless, bloodthirsty Chipewyan Dene men and their unwavering compulsion to murder, torture, and pillage. He describes the massacre as an uncivilized ambush in which sleeping families of Inuit are jumped upon, helpless, in their tents, and naked young Inuit women are eviscerated with spears. Most importantly, Hearne presents himself as neutral, horrified, and helpless; he describes his pained efforts to prevent the massacre but laments that his efforts were in vain. Eventually, he opts to arm himself in self-defence, lest a fleeing Inuit victim come upon him and mistake him for an enemy, and casts his participation in the event as inert, observing, and deeply traumatic. Hearne named the massacre site Bloody Fall in memory of the event, a name that persists to this day and marks a series of rapids along the river and the adjoining land upon which the attack is alleged to have occurred.[1]

For contemporary critical scholars of racism, colonialism, and whiteness, this story offers rich opportunities for analysis and critique. It is not difficult to imagine how the story contributes to racialized understandings of Indigenous peoples and to imaginative geographies of the Arctic as a deeply inhospitable, unforgiving place in which death looms around every corner. One could draw lines between Hearne's story and more contemporary constructions of Euro-Canadian whiteness as neutral and observing, as a positionality in which one gazes upon the ills of colonialism but cannot quite think of oneself as involved, responsible, or actively constitutive of (and constituted by) those ills. One could argue that Hearne represented the first of a long line of outsiders who would claim the Arctic as their own and consistently marginalize the bodies and expressions of Indigenous peoples. Indeed, the story has been soundly critiqued on these and other grounds, critiques that are important and cogent (see, for example, Goldie 1989; McGrath 1993; Milligan and McCreary, Chapter 7, this volume).

My interest here, however, is to take the story in a slightly different direction. Inspired both by six years of qualitative research in Kugluktuk, Nunavut, and by feminist, anti-racist, post-colonial, and actor-network theories, my understanding of this event draws in particular on the notion of story as a material ordering practice. Rather than approaching this narrative in terms of colonialism, whiteness, and racism, which tends to demand in advance the casting of particular people and practices into binaries of colonizer/colonized, white/Inuit, power/resistance, and so on, I will attempt to narrate Bloody Falls (and the central Arctic more generally) by following a particular "thing" – copper.[2]

By following copper, different readings of the Bloody Falls massacre emerge, and a different understanding of relations among various people, places, and things shaping the central Arctic over the past two centuries becomes possible. These copper stories, I argue, are not counter-stories, subaltern stories, or even necessarily more true or just stories. They are *different* stories, and as such, they order the people and places of the region in different ways, calling into being not only a different understanding of the past but also animating different futures.

This approach, it should be noted, is "agnostic," in Latour's (1988) terms, with respect to the concept of discourse. Although the concept of discourse as the heterogeneous and yet patterned representations, practices, and performances through which meaning is produced and through which relations of knowledge and power are articulated is immensely valuable to studies of race, nature, and whiteness, discursive analysis tends to position individual stories in distinct and limiting ways. In an effort to emphasize the racialized and colonial work a single story can accomplish (which has perhaps been the biggest contribution of discursive studies of the colonial and post-colonial), scholars risk losing sight of the historical and geographical specificity of particular stories and the broader social practices and relations with which they are imbricated, casting them instead as iterations of broader discourses. They risk assuming to know in advance which discourses are relevant, how they work, and of what materials they are comprised. For all Michel Foucault's (1979) emphasis on the specificity and situatedness of discursive practice, discursive analyses tend to "scale up" the importance of a single practice, performance, or representation from the particular to the general and from the local to the global. A single story, in many discursive analyses, is meaningful and legible hierarchically: it is important because it is part of a broader and more powerful *meta*-story, a discourse.

Geographers have problematized such a hierarchical approach to scale in recent years, although not in relation to discursive analysis. Their cautions around scaling up from the specific to the more general are nevertheless highly relevant for scholars interested in rethinking something like the

Great White North, especially to the extent that this rethinking project involves the identification and invention of alternative, less racialized discourses. In a particularly polemical take on the question of scale, Sallie Marston, J.P. Jones III, and Keith Woodward (2005) argue for a flattened ontological approach to geographic research and a "human geography without scale." Alongside scholars such as J.K. Gibson-Graham (2002, 2008), Julie Cruikshank (2005), and Cindi Katz (2001), who have written extensively on the importance of taking seriously "the local" and the specific, Marston, Jones, and Woodward (2005, 427) argue that political possibilities are foreclosed by collapsing the specificities of particular places, movements, and experiences to the global, the general, and the structural: "We are convinced that the local-to-global conceptual architecture intrinsic to hierarchical scale carries with it presuppositions that can delimit entry points into politics – and the openness of the political – by pre-assigning to it a cordoned register for resistance." Their arguments suggest that by locating the meaning of the particular in the general, we shore up an understanding of power and the political as sweeping, pervasive, and hegemonic, thereby overlooking the very real political possibilities of the local and the specific.

Noel Castree has critiqued the ways in which critical scholars attend to the local and the specific in their efforts to make larger claims. In an essay about geographic research into consumption and commodities, Castree (2001, 1520) identifies a tendency among scholars who are critical of commodity fetishism to "ground commodities in a specific site and a particular constituency," usually the site of extraction or production. It is hoped that by specifying the "origins" of commodities some kind of justice will be served and a fuller understanding of our implication in networks of capital exploitation will be achieved. In doing so, however, Castree argues that scholars inevitably essentialize diverse and complex constituencies, particularly the peoples and places involved in extraction and primary production, in order to serve their political agenda. They forget, as Michael Taussig suggests, that the social relations exposed by the "unveiling" of commodity fetishism "are themselves signs and social constructs defined by categories of thought that are also the product of society and history" (Taussig 1980, 9, quoted in ibid.). "To critique the commodity fetish," Castree (2001, 1519, emphasis in original) argues, "thus *raises* – rather than answers – a key question: what imaginative geographies both of ourselves and of distant others are entailed in *any* attempt to make visible the geographical lives of commodities?"

Castree's point is highly relevant to any efforts to rethink the Great White North. If the commodity that critical scholars seek to unveil is a racialized and colonial notion of the North as a sweeping, natural, "white" Canadian space, it is crucial that we pay close attention both to our representation of the "distant others" inhabiting that space *and* to our own ambitions and desires as scholars. In whose name do we seek to reimagine the North? Who and what is legitimated in these reimaginative efforts, and on what terms? To what extent is this desire for a more just and nuanced imaginative landscape a *white* desire? And how might we account for the situated, specific contexts within which southern Canadian scholars operate as they aim to reimagine and re-present distant places such as the Canadian North?

My questions are partly informed by anti-racist literatures addressing efforts on the part of white scholars and activists to come to terms with racism through the study of whiteness. Scholars such as Sara Ahmed (2004) and Robyn Wiegman (1999) have critiqued the rise of whiteness as an object of study, pointing to the ways in which whiteness studies have generated a new white subject, one that is anxiously and emotionally invested in its own critical stance and "goodness" with respect to whiteness and racism. Wiegman (ibid., 119) argues, for example, that critical studies of whiteness are often invested in "actively forging ... a counterwhiteness whose primary characteristic is its disaffiliation from white supremacist practices." To take a critical stance with respect to whiteness is thus to perform an alternative white subjectivity, a subjectivity whose motivating importance, Wiegman suggests, has been downplayed by scholars of whiteness. Ahmed (2004, para. 11) argues that the performativity of this alternative white subjectivity is highly dependent on a "politics of declaration" in which, by declaring one's whiteness, privilege, racism, and crucially, one's anxieties with respect to this whiteness, one can claim to be anti-racist. She argues, on the contrary, that such declarations do not *do* what they claim to do. Instead, they reinforce an individualized, depoliticized, psychologized understanding of racism in which white subjects aim to transcend their implication in structural, systemic forms of racism and in so doing to "feel better."

But "what we might remember," Ahmed (ibid., para. 47) argues, "is that to be against something is, after all, to be in an intimate relation with that which one is against." It is to remain visible, implicated, and to "inhabit the [anti-racist] critique, *with its lengthy duration*" (ibid., para. 57, emphasis in original). It is, in other words, to refuse the notion that one might personally and individually move beyond one's whiteness or find a "right" and "good" form of relation with others – to become, in Ahmed's (ibid.) words, "the good white anti-racist subject." To the extent that critical white scholars remain fixated on their goodness (or lack thereof) and continue to equate racism with badness, non-white others can appear solely as signifiers of this goodness/badness and cannot be heard on any other terms. A turn away from being good and the personalized centre of anti-racist politics would thus imply a reconfigured relationship with the bodies and expressions of non-white others, including the fetishization of the expressions of non-white subjects as sources of guidance and absolution. As Ahmed (ibid., para. 59) states, "The task for white subjects would be to stay implicated in what they critique, but in turning towards their role and responsibility in these histories of racism, as histories of this present, to turn away from themselves, and towards others. This 'double turn' is not sufficient, but it clears some ground, upon which the work of exposing racism might provide the conditions for another kind of work. We don't know, as yet, what such conditions might be, or whether we are even up to the task of recognizing them."

The copper stories that follow are presented in this spirit of turning away from whiteness and toward others, not as sources of white recuperation or transcendence, but rather as part of a relational, ongoing effort to structure our material and imaginative landscapes on different terms. It is an effort to story the central Arctic in less racialized terms and in ways that do not limit the agency and expressions of Indigenous peoples to either pre-contact traditionalism or heroic subaltern resistance. It is, as Ann Laura Stoler (2008, 252) describes, an effort to tell a less "charmed" story of the central Arctic that "might dispense with heroes – subaltern or otherwise" and attend to the contradictions and ambivalent interests of the diverse people and things related to networks of northern copper.

Copper Stories

My attention was initially drawn to copper not so much because of its importance in Hearne's mission, but rather because during the course of many months of research in Kugluktuk, the importance of mining in the region was impossible to overlook. Every summer airplanes and helicopters filled with mineral survey teams zoom in and out of this tiny Arctic hamlet. Nearly every family has members employed in the mines south of Kugluktuk, and a significant portion of Crown land in Nunavut is under claim, exploration, or active extraction. As one woman in Kugluktuk made clear to me, moreover, this is by no means a recent phenomenon. When asked about the significance of the Bloody Falls massacre in local history, Millie Kuliktana (pers. comm., 16 August 2007) replied that Hearne represented the first of a long line of outsiders who have exploited and colonized her people and their land. "It's the monster of economy that made this happen," she said. "It was the first act of colonization."

This is not generally how Bloody Falls is storied outside of Kugluktuk. In the South, it is primarily known as the site of a savage and bloodthirsty act of violence on the part of a barbarous tribe of "Indians."[3] It is an event narrated through the eyes of a supposedly neutral, civilized, and horrified European witness, Samuel Hearne, who looks on as the poor innocent "Esquimaux" are ruthlessly murdered by their Chipewyan attackers, his own guides on the Hudson's Bay Company–sponsored expedition. Hearne goes to great lengths to establish not only his neutrality but also his efforts to prevent the killings and in so doing sidesteps the possibility that he might have been in some way responsible for the event. Kuliktana, on the other hand, along with a number of other Kugluktukmiut, considers Hearne to be both personally responsible for the event (because he led the Chipewyan into Inuit territory and failed to control their behaviour) and representative of a broader history of economic exploitation and colonialism in the North.[4]

Kuliktana's critique of Hearne is based on the fact that he was in her people's territory only because he was looking for copper. Although his journey is memorialized outside of Kugluktuk as an act of immense physical endurance (not so much as an economic venture), and his narrative is primarily known for its eyewitness account of the massacre, Kuliktana rightly pinpoints European interest in copper as its principal motive. An employee of the Hudson's Bay Company, Hearne was stationed at Prince of Wales's Fort through the late 1760s. During that time, the HBC was increasingly under fire in London for failing to explore and develop the large grant of land under its control. Mounting pressure was placed upon the company to make use of its sizeable monopoly or risk losing it to economic competition (G. Williams 1970). At the same time, the chief factor at Prince of Wales's Fort had been hearing reports from the Chipewyan Dene who came to trade there of a "Far Off Metal River" where lumps of native copper were so abundant as to ballast a ship. And so it was that Samuel Hearne was directed to set out and search for the river and to determine the richness of the copper deposited there.

Hearne took more than six months to walk to the river (prematurely named the Coppermine) and, once there, he and over thirty men spent hours searching for copper, only to discover a single sizeable lump. He and his guides promptly turned around and walked home. Hearne's journey would not have been worth publicizing had it not been for his alleged witness of the massacre at Bloody Falls the day before his futile search for copper began.[5] Indeed, Hearne's description of the massacre is the pinnacle of his published narrative; an early review of Hearne's *A Journey to the Northern Ocean* (1795) is almost entirely devoted to an excerpt of the massacre, noting that "throughout his work, Mr. Hearne speaks with a proper mixture of indignation at the brutalities, and of compassion for the miseries, of those wretched savages" (*Monthly Review* 1796, 250). The massacre scene itself has been reproduced countless times in novels, plays, documentaries, and poems (see, for example, Laut 1918; Mowat 1958; Gutteridge 1973; Carefoot 1980; McGrath 1998; Canadian Broadcasting Corporation 2001). It is almost impossible to find material on Hearne that does not mention and describe this event.

In his published narrative, Hearne emphasizes the senselessness and lack of motivation behind the violence. He conjures scenes of Chipewyan men gleefully torturing naked Inuit women and acting in a kind of primitive, bloodthirsty trance as they transact the massacre. If one reads the narrative closely, however, and particularly when one compares it to transcriptions of Hearne's unpublished travel notes, it becomes clear that the Chipewyan, too, were intensely interested in copper. Immediately after killing the group of Inuit, the Chipewyan raid their tents "of all the Copper Work and any other trifling things they thought worthwhile to take" (Hearne c. 1791, 29). Hearne makes extensive notes on the importance of copper in local trading economies, remarking on the annual journey undertaken by the Northern Indians to the region in search of copper to "shoe their arrows and make other necessary tools such as hatchets, Ice Chizzels, etc." (ibid., 31). He includes a list of trading ratios for copper tools and notes that among the Indians of the region, copper was almost as valuable as iron and was highly sought-after both for personal use and for trade. On more than one occasion throughout the journey, he records the plundering of neighbouring groups, explaining such events as economically motivated theft aimed at amassing goods sufficient to trade for copper and iron tools, not as acts carried out by an inherently uncivilized people. In fact, Hearne's unpublished notes are littered with references to his "surprise" at the civility of his companions and his admiration for their character traits (see, for example, ibid., 18). Clearly, the very metal Hearne had hoped to locate and claim for the British Crown was already circulating in a regional economy, embroiled in acts of war and trade throughout the central Arctic and sub-Arctic. It would seem plausible, then, that the Bloody Falls massacre was motivated as much by copper as by the "violent tendencies" of Chipewyan men.

Until very recently, however, explorers, missionaries, and scholars have persisted in the belief that copper use was not centrally important to the Indigenous peoples of the Arctic and sub-Arctic, believing instead that interest in metals emerged with the introduction of iron into the region by Europeans (Pringle 1997). More recent research challenges this long-standing belief and suggests that "throughout Arctic Canada, metal in one form or another appears to have been highly appreciated long before even indirect European contact" (D. Morrison 1987, 10-11). The Thule, who preceded today's Inuit populations, are now known to have relied upon metals traded over hundreds and even thousands of kilometres, and origin stories of the discovery of metals, particularly copper, have been recorded among multiple Indigenous groups occupying the central Arctic.

In the 1880s, missionary Émile Petitot recorded stories among the Dene about the discovery of copper, some of which involved the trading and stealing of women between Dene and Inuit. In one account, a Dene woman stolen by the "Esquimaux" escapes her captors and attempts to travel back to her homeland but becomes hopelessly lost. She is assisted by a white wolf who leads her to an iron tool with which she is able to kill some caribou to eat. Continuing on her route, she is distracted by a bright light glowing like a fire at the peak of a distant mountain. Curious, she makes her way to the source of the light and discovers a red metal that resembles beaver dung, which she collects and takes with her. Petitot understood this metal to be native copper. Eventually, she returns to her homeland and shows her people the valuable metal. Thereafter, the Dene make journeys to its source and use it to fashion knives, spears, and other tools; thanks to the metal the woman procured for them, they live with ease. But one day, some of the men want to take advantage of the woman, and she flees. They chase her all the way to the copper mountain, whereupon she disappears under the earth, taking the copper with her. And so it was that copper disappeared from their territory (Petitot 1886, 412-17).

It is important not to limit the storytelling work of this narrative to a question of origins, but rather to attend to the importance of copper in conveying a broader legal and moral framework within which the Dene operated. As Julie Cruikshank (1989, 1998, 2005) has made clear in her writing on oral traditions, storytelling is an important venue for teaching law and ethical conduct among the Indigenous peoples of the Yukon, a point Keith Basso (1996) has also made about Western Apache storytelling practices. Jean Briggs (1998) has made this point specifically in reference to Inuit (although not through work with the people who have traditionally lived around Coronation Gulf), profiling, for example, the ways in which fantastical stories are used to teach children the boundaries of ethical conduct. This story certainly alludes to a pre-contact copper economy in the region and is important on these grounds, but it also indicates that copper was "good to think with" (in Lévi-Strauss' terms; see Cruikshank 2005, 8) in Dene oral traditions.

Copper was an important part of the regional economies and imaginative geographies of the central Arctic and sub-Arctic long before Euro-Canadian involvement in the area, but it was also implicated in longer and larger networks of technology, labour, and trade. It was mined across the Americas (Abbott 1970; E.M. Barrett 1981) and in Britain (Burt 1995) from pre-industrial times through the early industrial era. The British copper-mining industry expanded rapidly in the mid-eighteenth century due to an influx of capital and technological expertise from Europe, and by the time Hearne left on his mission, Britain had become one of the world's leading producers (ibid., 29). Not unlike its uses in the Arctic, copper in Britain was used primarily in building and household utensils such as pots, pans, and pewter mugs, as well as in roofing, guttering, piping, and cisterns. Unlike the relatively circumscribed networks of extraction, manufacture, and trade characterizing copper networks in the Arctic, however, as the eighteenth century progressed, copper in Britain increasingly moved through more widely dispersed and longer networks of mines, smelters, manufacturers, distributors, and consumers, influenced by international capital and imperial acquisitions. In Law's and Latour's terms, we must see the difference between these networks as a matter of length and extension; what had hitherto been characterized as a very "local" industry in Britain was beginning to expand into other places and to involve more and more *things.* Hearne's journey, moreover, must be understood in relation to this burgeoning copper economy. His interest in connecting Arctic copper with networks extending outside the region is revealed in a brief anecdote he recounts shortly after his futile search for copper:

> The Indians imagine that every bit of copper they find resembles some object in nature; but by what I saw of the large piece, and some smaller ones which were found by my companions, it requires a great share of invention to make this out. I found that different people had different ideas on the subject, for the large piece of copper above mentioned had not been found long before it had twenty different names. One saying that it resembled this animal, and another that it represented a particular part of another; at last

it was generally allowed to resemble an Alpine hare couchant: for my part I must confess that I could not see it had the least resemblance to any thing to which they compared it. It would be endless to enumerate the different parts of a deer, and other animals, which the Indians say the best pieces of copper resemble: it may therefore be sufficient to say, that the largest pieces, with the fewest branches and the least dross, are the best for their use; as by the help of fire, and two stones, they can beat it out to any shape they wish. (Hearne 1795, 174)

Hearne includes this passage as a curiosity for the reader and uses it to underscore his own reliability and precision as an observer. But it can be read in quite another way; it also exemplifies the different narrative geographies within which eighteenth-century copper circulated. John Law (1994) argues that stories are material – they involve the assemblage and organization of people, objects, places, and ideas into networks of meaning that make the world coherent and sensible. The performance or inscription of stories over time and in different places contributes to the sedimentation of those same networks, lending them a bit more coherency and sensibility. Story, in that sense, is not only an imaginative practice through which we make sense of the world, but also a material ordering practice involving a diverse set of "things." By storying the copper as deer, the Chipewyan made connections between the piece of copper in their hands and a diverse network of things that enabled them to hunt, eat, and imagine their world. Their co-existence with copper enrolled a particular network of things. Hearne, on the other hand, was more interested in connecting copper to distant networks of trade and manufacture, to his own reputation as an explorer, and to the esteem and wealth that would surely follow. Indeed, Kugluktukmiut consistently critique Hearne for "wanting to make a name for himself" (C. Adjun, pers. comm., 20 August 2007; J.A. Evyagotailak, pers. comm., 7 August 2007; P. Taptuna, pers. comm., 3 August 2007), and in a sense that indictment gestures toward the very different narrative geography within which he operated, even as these geographies overlapped in 1771.

Exploration for copper deposits in the Coppermine River region continued after Hearne's time. Although the Hudson's Bay Company gave up on the project, subsequent British, American, and Canadian expeditions were explicitly interested in identifying and mapping copper resources in the Far North. The first Franklin expedition report included an appendix on "geognostical" findings (Richardson 1823) penned with "economic importance" in mind and emphasizing copper formations in the Coppermine region (Houston 1984, 292). Geologists were dispatched by various government and private organizations throughout the nineteenth century, including a venture by well-known geologist J.B. Tyrrell in 1893, which was sponsored by the Geological Survey Department of Canada. This widely publicized trip amplified expectations of "great mineral wealth" (Tyrrell, quoted in *Manitoba Free Press* 1894, n.p.) in the barrenlands, particularly in the form of copper. Tyrrell (who went on to edit a 1911 edition of Hearne's *A Journey to the Northern Ocean*) was cited in an imperial report on world copper reserves that anticipated the Canadian Arctic and sub-Arctic would yield "as much copper as is now mined in Northern Michigan" (Imperial Mineral Resources Bureau 1922, 50), thus reviving imperial dreams of copper riches in the region.

Inuit, Dene, and Euro-Canadian copper stories began to increasingly converge, however, in the first decades of the twentieth century. Copper tool use among Kugluktukmiut had virtually disappeared by the early decades of the twentieth century as iron and other metals became more readily available (D. Morrison 1987). Ironically, it was at this time that anthropologists first visited the region and assigned the name "Copper Inuit" to the people living around Coronation Gulf in reference to their historical use of copper tools. While Diamond Jenness, anthropologist with the Canadian Arctic Expedition, catalogued Copper Inuit language and culture throughout the summers of 1915 and 1916, J.J. O'Neill, geologist with the expedition, searched for copper deposits in the Coppermine River and Bathurst Inlet region. Jenness and O'Neill produced a detailed map of copper deposits in the area, and both recounted stories of copper trade, theft, and usage, including narratives of copper-related trade and conflict with the Dene (see Jenness 1922, 19, 52; O'Neill 1924, 60A). Indeed, the production of knowledge about Copper Inuit in the first decades of the twentieth century was deeply informed by a particularly colonial interweaving of anthropological, economic, legal, and scientific interests, one that would also characterize subsequent studies.

Several decades later, for example, as mineral surveying and mapping accelerated in the region, "traditional" copper stories were collected by missionary-anthropologist Maurice Métayer. Métayer recorded a series of stories in Coppermine (Kugluktuk) during the 1950s, including Texte 80, an account of a group of seal hunters that suddenly becomes stranded on an ice floe, told by James Qoerhuk. The full story was recounted and recorded in Inuinnaqtun but was summarized by Métayer for English readers, leading to a distinctive interpretation of its meaning and particularly its revelations about Inuit relations with copper. The English summary is worth quoting in its entirety:

> It probably happened before I was born. A group of seal hunters were out on the ice when it broke loose from the shore and a thick vapor filled the sky. Ulukhaq realized the danger they were in and cried: "The ice is broken." They started running towards the shore but it was too late: they were already drifting westward along with the ice. They built a snow house the following day, by the time the ice had stopped drifting, Nualiak urged them to try again to reach the land. However, they did not succeed and had to come back to their igloo where they remained for a good part of the winter. They were lucky enough to have among them real shamans who saved them from disaster by preventing the ice they were on to be crushed by an iceberg and by performing the rites that would bring them a good wind. One by one they let their knives sink in the water and offered them to the spirit of the sea. The last knife to be offered was a weapon made of solid raw copper; it floated a while before sinking. Qorvik also took a small block of ice and threw it towards the land. At the same time he asked the spirits to return them home, safe and sound. A short while afterwards the wind changed direction and brought them back home. The men leapt from an ice block to another finally making their way back to the shore. They reached it by the time darkness was falling. They yelled with joy, ate snow, cried, laughed, and walked home where they found their wives. Some of them, thinking that they were dead, had taken other husbands. Qinglorqana felt for a long time as though the roll of the ocean was still in his body, waking him up during the night. (Métayer 1973, 785-86)

The elements Métayer chose to emphasize in his abridged translation are notable. The copper "weapon," more probably a snow knife used to build igloos, the loss of which was particularly difficult for its owner Qinglorqana because it *audlartijjutiplu,* or "enabled him to travel" (Qoerhuk 1973, 565), is understood to be more valuable than the other knives, and its sacrifice is a central element of the abridged story. Although Qinglorqana laments its loss in the longer Inuinnaqtun version, and it is, indeed, considered the most valuable tool in their possession, he consents to its being offered because "ajornarhingman utilimaermik ... pingneramegoq audlartijun ... kivijaugame utqutilertainnarqaingoq kinranun kingunranun" (because there is no more hope, and they are not returning ... because it is beautiful and it was used for traveling ... [and then] because they let it sink, it brought them behind, to the land left behind) (ibid., 560-61). In the Inuinnaqtun version, the knife has agency; it is the knife that brings them home, not a sea god, as in Métayer's somewhat Christianized understanding of "sacrifice" to the "spirit of the sea." Furthermore, the fact that the knife leads them home is noted but not dwelled upon in Qoerhuk's account. The bulk of the story is devoted to extended descriptions of snow and ice conditions, to the subtleties of decisions made about how to travel and under what conditions, and to the painful separation and complications of reunion with their wives. As a story told in Inuinnaqtun to a white missionary in the late 1950s, recorded on tape, transcribed, and translated first into French and then into short English summaries, it has undergone multiple twists and translations. Texte 80 is thus as revealing of Euro-Canadian interests as it is of Copper Inuit oral traditions. Although Qoerhuk's account does seem to indicate that copper was storied by Kugluktukmiut, and in this story at least, some of its complex relations to travel and survival are considered, Métayer's summary produces its own distinctive assemblage of Inuit, copper, and other things. The capacity of the copper knife to lead and act is written out of his summary, rendering the knife a kind of de-animated fetishized object valuable because it can be offered to sea spirits. His version draws lines between the spiritual and the real; it places copper in an abstracted material hierarchy, one in which a copper knife is always more valuable than an iron or other tool, rather than conceptualizing copper's value relationally and contextually.[6]

Métayer's abridged version thus produces a particular kind of relationship between Inuit and copper, one in which copper is an inert natural resource whose value derives from its relative scarcity and its material properties, thereby rendering the metal object a particularly compelling sacrifice to external spirits that exert control over the fate of Inuit. The story conveys, in that sense, an essentially Euro-Canadian resource model of copper with a slightly Christianized Indigenous spiritual realm layered upon it. This reading, which works to naturalize Euro-Canadian resource extraction in the region as a more sophisticated iteration of traditional copper culture, should come as no surprise given the active mineral surveying taking place in Coppermine when Métayer recorded the story. This narrative strategy continues in corporate histories of diamond mining in the area. As a recent brochure produced by multinational mining conglomerate Rio Tinto begins, "For centuries, people of the North have used the resources wisely ... Diavik is continuing this tradition" (Diavik Diamond Mines 2002, i).

Donald Cadzow's catalogue of Copper Inuit material culture also frames Inuit copper tool use as a kind of primitive iteration of more "civilized" natural resource economies. In a leaflet describing the various copper artifacts he collected while travelling in the Northwest Territories, Cadzow (1920, 6) prefaces his tool descriptions with a short history of the region, beginning with the "discovery" of copper for Europeans by Samuel Hearne and mention of the massacre at Bloody Falls, an event alleged to have unfolded while Hearne was busy surveying and identifying copper reserves. After page upon page of photos and descriptions of copper artifacts, the report closes with the following comment: "The Copper Eskimo are at present rapidly becoming semi-civilized. The Hudson's Bay Company has opened a trading-post near the mouth of the Coppermine river, and the Northern Trading Company operates a trading schooner along the shores of Coronation gulf. Within a few years the utilization of native copper by these Eskimo for making weapons and utensils will have ceased, the white man's handy and practical materials having taken its place" (ibid., 22). In this publication, copper tools are made to make sense in terms of a historical progression from savagery to "semi" civility, an evolution that involves a shift from making copper weapons and utensils toward mapping and mining copper as capitalist resource.

Indeed, by the 1930s, as stories of a "traditional" copper culture proliferated in the South, airplanes had arrived in the North, revolutionizing mineral survey practices and enabling aerial identification of copper reserves (*Science News Letter* 1931). In the early 1960s, Echo Bay Mines began to mine copper near the headwaters of the Coppermine River, and mining has only intensified since then. The discovery of diamonds in the 1990s motivated the opening of three diamond mines within the Coppermine River watershed (Diavik, Ekati, and Tahera), and two copper-mining operations are proposed to open in the region within the next several years. Although some might wish to imagine that "Copper Inuit" resist this shift in their ancestral relationship to copper, such a view speaks more to southern imaginative geographies of the Arctic than to the views of Kugluktukmiut. As wary as some community members are about the impact of mining on the land, very few would advocate the stoppage of mining in the area. Mining offers the possibility of a viable economy in the North, if only for a short time and for a segment of the population, and the people of Kugluktuk are gravely concerned about the future of their young people. Kugluktukmiut will be hired to build the ice roads and port facility necessary to service the mine proposed at High Lake, 175 kilometres southeast of Kugluktuk, and they will drive the trucks carrying copper-rich ore to the sea. Ships destined for Europe will indeed be ballasted with copper from the district within the next decade, in a sense over two centuries late.

Kugluktukmiut insist, however, that they accrue benefits from mining activity in the region, and they have been politically active on this front for more than fifty years. In February 1953, alarmed at the increasing presence of prospectors in the area, the people of Coppermine (Kugluktuk) sent a petition to the federal government outlining their concerns and demands regarding mineral exploration and staking in their territory. Peter Kulchyski and Frank Tester (2007, 240) suggest that this may have been "the first time Inuit as a group in the Canadian Arctic formally petitioned the government." The petition, which is emphatic that Inuit have rights to the copper in the region, reads as follows (all sic):

Dear Sir,

Father Adam asked you what was our position regarding the copper deposits some of our boys have found around Coppermine.

You said that we had to follow the same laws as the whites regarding the staking and holding of the claims. We feel such a law is not right, because,

(1) The land is ours and we never gave it or sold it away and never will.
(2) We are one of the poorest people in the world; we have no money to buy a licence or to register a claim.
(3) We are too ignorant to steak a claim according to the regulations.
(4) We Eskimo feel we should be given a chance.

Therefore we send you a petition requesting that any Eskimo finding ore deposit will have the right to steak it, and hold it free of taxes, and hold it free of taxes, and that he may well sell it to any Company free of taxes whenever he wants to do so.

Although we have no leader amongst us our signatures will tell you that we agree on those points.

Hoping that we find the Government most co-operative we sign:
The Eskimos of Coppermine (Coppermine petition, quoted in ibid., 240-41)

This would be the beginning of a larger movement among Inuit to assert their rights to the land and resources of Nunavut, a process that gathered speed in the early 1970s following a meeting of Inuit leaders in Coppermine

(Indian-Eskimo Association 1970) that led to the creation of Inuit Tapirisat of Canada (ITC) the next year.[7] ITC (later ITK or Inuit Tapiriit Kanatami) was instrumental in articulating Inuit demands for land claims and resource rights, rights that became particularly urgent as "a new breed of explorer [came] to search for oil, natural gas, and minerals" in the North (Inuit Tapirisat of Canada 1977, 4). The Nunavut Land Claims Agreement (NLCA) was finalized in 1993, and the territory of Nunavut was created in 1999. The NLCA outlines Inuit mineral rights (notably, Inuit retain subsurface rights over only 2 percent of the territory's 1.9 million square kilometres, although royalties are collected from mining on non-Inuit land) and establishes protocols for environmental monitoring, land and resource management, and rights of entry and access to non-Inuit lands. Regardless of whether they hope to mine on Inuit or Crown land, mining companies must go through a process of community consultation, one that is poorly defined (McCrank 2008, 34) and in some ways moot. In practice, both the territorial government and Nunavut Tunngavik Incorporated (the corporation established to administer the NLCA on behalf of its Inuit beneficiaries) are tremendously supportive of mineral exploration and extraction, seeing mining as a potentially lucrative source of "employment opportunities (both direct and in service industries), business and investment opportunities, education and training, and infrastructure improvements in the communities" (Nunavut Tunngavik Incorporated 1997, 1). Some community members express concerns that land use planning documents and legal acts have yet to be implemented in the Kitikmeot region (of which Kugluktuk is a part), limiting the ability of Inuit to assess mineral development activities on a comprehensive regional basis (S. Buchan, pers. comm., 17 July 2007). Currently, environmental and community impact studies are done on a case-by-case basis, and no studies of the cumulative effect of multiple mines have been undertaken. In spite of these concerns, however, mineral exploration and mine development continue to be a priority in the territory.

In effect, Kugluktukmiut are as tied to copper today as they were two or three hundred years ago, although copper is now connected to networks of commodity pricing, multinational capital investment, federal and territorial bureaucracies, and the expansion of shipping into an increasingly "warm" Arctic. Whereas in 1771, the Dene saw caribou shapes in the native copper chunks they would fashion into hunting tools, mine development today threatens the calving and feeding grounds of these same herds of caribou, even while the revenues from mines allow more Kugluktukmiut to access the capital and equipment necessary for hunting. Kugluktuk teenagers who occasionally steal skidoos for a night of joyriding are intimately familiar with the copper wiring systems that allow them to cut an ignition wire and jump-start the machine. The copper mined in the region will soon find its way into the GPS units that help them navigate unfamiliar lands and into the televisions that light up their living rooms. And ironically, the same copper that contributed to generations of conflict between Inuit and Dene has recently brought them together in a peace and reconciliation process. The rapid increase in mining in the territories of these groups has motivated them to resolve their conflicts in regular peacemaking visits so that they might better coordinate their responses to proposed mineral development plans (M. Kuliktana, pers. comm., 16 August 2007). In fact, these reconciliation processes began with an apology from the Sahtu Dene for past wrongdoings and a clarification that it was not their ancestors, but rather the ancestors of the Chipewyan Dene, who transacted the massacre at Bloody Falls. Stories of cooperation, trade, and collaboration between Inuit and Dene were shared by elders in a recent visit, calling into being not only a different understanding of the past but also forging new terms for future relations.

Conclusion

What, then, do these copper stories offer as we set out to reimagine the Great White North? Part of their value lies in their ability to help turn away from the often self-referential "post"-colonial impulse to document the ravages of whiteness and to open a space to think differently about the central Arctic. These copper stories are not counter-stories, even if they do provide openings into alternative understandings of the Bloody Falls massacre. They do not address dominant narratives directly, but instead aim to order and make legible a different set of relations than those demanded by hegemonic Arctic stories, and in so doing to foster different kinds of life. As Donna Haraway (1994, 62) notes, "The point is to get at how worlds are made and unmade, in order to participate in the processes, in order to foster some forms of life and not others ... The point is not just to read the webs of knowledge production; the point is to reconfigure what counts as knowledge ... I am calling this practice *materialized refiguration;* both words matter. The point is, in short, to make a difference – however modestly, however partially, however much without either narrative or scientific guarantees."

To the extent that dominant Arctic stories mobilize binary understandings of race, place, culture, and history, tracing the region through copper has allowed me order the region differently, to refigure stories rather than simply critique them. A focus on copper has enabled me to account for some of the complexities and contradictions inherent in relations between various people, places, and things, and to challenge some of the binary notions that tend to structure understandings of the contemporary North, such as traditional versus modern, Inuit versus white, and so on. Rather than presenting contemporary copper mining in the region as a wholly "modern" undertaking that alienates Inuit from a "traditional" way of life, for example, these stories suggest a longer, more complicated history of relations. They blur racialized lines between different constituencies and refuse to fetishize an authentic Inuit voice that might "speak back" to colonial or capitalist oppressors. Stories like these more closely attend to the complex relations shaping the contemporary Arctic and open up important lines of inquiry and intervention.

Although a focus on copper helps in stepping outside of dominant representational frameworks, there is a risk of avoiding issues of power and scale in this kind of approach and of tending to treat all copper stories as equal insofar as they assemble diverse people and things in relation to copper. If, as Law (1994) and Latour (2005) argue, we are intimately interconnected with things and, indeed, constituted by the assemblage of diverse bits and pieces, we must take seriously the ways in which copper has both constituted and undermined life in the central Arctic, and not lose sight of the very real and material effects of these networks. Networks are not neutral; they are ordered, powerful, and strategic, and one's position in a network matters. How, then, to balance the need to loosen dominant representational frameworks and allow alternative perspectives with the need to maintain an acute focus on relations of power and to keep in mind the consequences of being positioned in particular ways within networks of capital, technology, resources, and governance?

There are no easy answers to this question. Arguably, the ethical and political tensions generated by bringing actor-network theory into conversation with whiteness studies are productive and not necessarily amenable to "balance"; actor-network theory works best by destabilizing, not by claiming to offer a coherent and stable alternative. Indeed, as Noel Castree argues, actor-network theory must be kept in check if it is to assist us in intervening in the prevailing inequalities structuring networks of people, places, and things. Castree (2002, 135) suggests that a "weaker" version of actor-network theory may thus be of greater use to critical scholars. He describes such a version as one that remains "critical of binarist thinking, of asymmetry, of limited conceptions of agency and of centred conceptions of power" and yet that acknowledges that, notwithstanding their differences, "many actor-networks are driven by similar processes, ... that these process-es might be 'global' and systematic even as they are composed of nothing more than the ties between different 'localities'; that these processes are so-cial and natural but not in equal measure, since it is the 'social' relations that are often disproportionately directive; ... and that power, while dispersed, can be directed by some (namely, specific 'social' actors) more than others." Castree (ibid. 116) advances this weaker version of actor-network theory as part of an effort to challenge what he perceives as a "false antithesis" be-tween eco-Marxian and actor-network approaches to nature-society rela-tions. It is a suggestive and important attempt to bring conflicting theoretical traditions into conversation.

My effort in this chapter has been to consider what kinds of productive tensions might be introduced to critical studies of race, nature, and white-ness in the Canadian North by actor-network-inspired storytelling, and I would argue alongside Castree that the openings offered by actor-network accounts must be tied to a wider political project if they are to realize their radical potential. To the extent that actor-network accounts trace and de-scribe relations that tend not to appear in critical whiteness studies, they signal ethical possibilities and responsibilities that are crucially important. As Haraway (2008, 37) has observed, when we "touch and are touched" by a story, we "inherit" different relations and begin to "live" different "histories." That is, our relations demand responses of us, and to the extent that critical whiteness studies trace the relations between white and "other" subjects in self-referential terms, they demand self-referential responses. The copper stories I have traced in this chapter have a certain political *potential,* then, but their potential is not realized merely in the tracing and describing; there are no guarantees that the telling of different stories will lead to the kind of touching Haraway describes.

Geraldine Pratt's (2009, 17) recent contemplations of the capacity for stories to circulate and affect "a wider witnessing public" are thus central to the kind of renarrating project I have considered in this chapter. As Pratt (ibid., 6) makes clear with respect to her study of the affective capacities of Filipina mothers' life narratives, efforts to ensure that "the testimony [is] heard" are formidable in and of themselves and carry with them additional concerns about "what dangers attend" the successful circulation of such stories. There is always the risk that the story of an "other" "preserves rather than disrupts the status quo." Pratt's efforts to think carefully and strategic-ally about how, where, and on what terms stories are told (and heard) is thus an important check on the sense of radical possibility and contingency in actor-network accounts. The capacity to connect, affect, and relate, Pratt reminds us, is shaped by an already structured political and ethical field that is not as malleable and open to possibility as we might hope.

"In any narrative tradition," writes Barnor Hesse (2002, 146), "it is always possible to remember otherwise, although this can be studiously avoided." The telling of alternative stories about the central Arctic is an important part of remembering otherwise, not because they are the right stories, the more just stories, or the more comprehensive stories, and neither under the pretense that remembering otherwise will necessarily dismantle the studious avoidance (what Stoler 2008, 18, calls the "educated ignorance") enabled by hegemonic narratives. As Alootook Ipellie (1997, 96) has observed:

> No living generation of Arctic narrator will ever get enough satisfaction out of spinning yarns about the Arctic and its cast of thousands, from the by-gone days to this very moment. I am standing here in front of you to announce, unfortunately, that none of us will ever live long enough to finally complete the elusive final book on the Arctic and its people ... The Great White Arctic will remain an unfinished story to the very end of human habitation on planet Earth. How sad.

Faced with the impossibility of writing the "right" story about the Great White North, it seems to me that this unfinished and unfinishable project demands our active attention and participation.

ACKNOWLEDGMENTS
Thank you to Andrew Baldwin, Laura Cameron, and Audrey Kobayashi for organizing the workshop that led to this collection and for their editorial comments. Thanks also to Caroline Desbiens and Julie Cruikshank for their thoughtful reflections on an earlier version of this chapter, and to Darryl Leroux for his suggestions. Research leading to this essay was supported by the Social Sciences and Humanities Research Council of Canada, the Canadian Polar Commission, the Northern Scientific Training Program, the Network in Canadian History and Environment, the *Antipode* Graduate Student Scholarship, and Queen's University.

PART 4

NATIVE LAND

Temagami's Tangled Wild
The Making of Race, Nature, and Nation in Early-Twentieth-Century Ontario

JOCELYN THORPE

From its popularity beginning in the early twentieth century as a wilderness tourism destination to its fame in the late 1980s as an imperilled wilderness region, Temagami, Ontario, has long enjoyed privileged status as one of Canada's most important sites of wild nature. This chapter interrogates the Temagami wilderness by reading early travel narratives about the region through the dual lens of anti-racist and social nature scholarship, arguing that there is nothing natural about the Temagami wilderness. Cultural processes and relationships of power, including those associated with Temagami tourism at the turn of the twentieth century, created Temagami as a wilderness space for white men to visit as tourists.

Anti-racist scholars offer important insight into how race and racism have shaped the building and maintenance of the Canadian nation, thus challenging the prevalent understanding of Canada as a naturally white settler nation that later incorporated a diverse population to become the multicultural Canada of today. These scholars demonstrate that Canada has long existed as a "racially plural" society (Perry 2001, 3). From the seventeenth century onward, the diverse Aboriginal peoples who inhabited the North American continent for thousands of years before the encroachment of outsiders (Dickason 2002) were joined by Asian, black, and white people who came from many places, including China, Japan, India, the United States, and Europe, to settle in Canada (Satzewich and Liodakis 2007). Although colonial officials and early nationalists aimed to create Canada as a white settler nation (Berger 1966; Dua 1999), this desire often conflicted with the need for labourers who would do the work of building it (Abele and Stasiulis 1989, 241). Thus, members of "non-preferred races" were allowed to enter Canada in limited numbers, but whereas Europeans were welcomed as the "exalted subjects" of the Canadian nation, Aboriginal people and non-European immigrants were constituted as the nation's external others (Thobani 2007, 93). Racism permeated all facets of Canadian life, including the law (Culhane 1998; Backhouse 1999), Aboriginal and immigration policy (Bolaria and Li 1985; Harris 2002; Lawrence 2004), the making of "ethnic" communities (K. Anderson 1991; Dua 1999), and labour wages and working conditions (Adachi 1976; Kobayashi and Jackson 1994). Discourses of race worked not only to justify the preferential treatment of Euro-Canadians, but also to naturalize the link between whiteness and Canadian identity. Scholars argue that this link continues to inform the present (Razack 1998, 2002a; Dua and Robertson 1999; Thobani 2007). Himani Bannerji (2000) and Eva Mackey (2002) show, for example, how the policy of multiculturalism that emerged in the 1970s worked both to manage the crisis brought about by marginalized groups' challenges to the nation and its racism, and to recentre whiteness as the normal mode of being in Canada.

Whereas anti-racist scholars often analyze the gendered and classed dynamics of race and racism in Canada, they have not in general engaged with the literature that understands nature, as well as gender and race, to be a social category (for exceptions, see Sandilands 2004; Mawani 2005). Though seemingly counterintuitive – what is nature if not natural? – the concept of social nature has in recent decades gained popularity among scholars interested in examining the "traffic between what we have come to know historically as nature and culture" (Haraway 1989, 15; see also Haraway 1992; K. Anderson 1995a; Cronon 1996a and 1996b; Castree and Braun 2001; Braun 2002; Moore, Kosek, and Pandian 2003). Just as anti-racist scholars trace various processes through which whiteness and Canadian identity have become linked in order to reveal the connection as a product of history and power rather than nature (see Erickson, Chapter 1, this volume), social nature scholars describe the mechanisms through which nature appears separate from culture in order to make it clear that the nature-culture binary is a cultural product that has benefited some groups at the expense of others. Both clusters of scholars are interested in denaturalizing what often appears as the self-evident truth and in showing that particular truths are not universal, but rather the result of complex power relations. This chapter suggests that anti-racist scholars in Canada might productively engage with social nature literature. By analyzing the social construction of the Temagami wilderness, I show that a thorough denaturalization of the link between whiteness and Canadian identity requires attention to the ways in which this link has been created, and made to appear natural, in part through discourses about land. Social nature literature, then, might provide anti-racist scholarship with deeper understandings of how whiteness and Canadianness have become integrally related.

A focus on land might also allow critical scholars of the nation to attend more carefully to the struggles of Aboriginal peoples. Bonita Lawrence and Enakshi Dua (2005) have recently argued that anti-racist scholarship in Canada does not always take seriously the colonization of Aboriginal peoples upon which the Canadian nation was, and continues to be, premised. In part, they contend, this is the result of scholars' failure to take up the contested character of "Canadian" land and to recognize that the reclamation of lands is central to First Nations' struggles for self-determination. Analyzing the ways in which the land itself is made to appear "naturally" wild, white, and Canadian through the disappearance of Aboriginal people and their claims represents one way that anti-racist scholars might begin to draw connections between the colonization of Indigenous people and lands and a racist nation-building project in the Canadian context. By showing that the Temagami wilderness is a contested term and place, I hope to demonstrate how critical scholarship on the nation might more effectively support the anti-colonial efforts of Aboriginal peoples.

Wild Temagami Present

Before turning to my analysis, I offer a brief background about Temagami. Today, the region makes mainstream sense as part of the Canadian wilderness. Located in northeastern Ontario, Temagami is forested with pine and other tree species, and contains many lakes and the rocky shores and soils typical of the Canadian Shield. In the late 1980s, Temagami received widespread attention when environmentalists staged a media campaign as part of their effort to stop the logging of the region. This campaign, which emphasized the wilderness character of Temagami, produced posters of big pine trees with the heading "Temagami: The Last Great Pine Wilderness" and held a benefit concert called "Temagami: The Last Wild Stand" (see Bray and Thomson 1990). It garnered a good deal of public support, including that of prominent Canadians such as Margaret Atwood, David Suzuki, and Bob Rae (Rae was arrested with environmentalists for blockading a logging road), and succeeded not only in drawing attention to the region but also in securing the protection of "a particularly sensitive area" of the Temagami forest (Allen 1989, A2). Alongside environmentalists, others have also contributed in recent years to the idea of Temagami as a site of wild Canadian nature. Summer camp brochures, for instance, advertise that Temagami promises "Canadian wilderness canoe trips" (Camp Wabun 2007) and "the peace and quiet of Canada's wide open pine forests and pristine waterways" (Camp Keewaydin 2007).

In spite of the prevalence of the present-day association between Temagami and the Canadian wilderness, however, Temagami has not always or for everyone existed as a site of national nature. Long before the first tourist arrived there, the Teme-Augama Anishnabai knew the region as n'Daki Menan (our land). They regulated the use of their lands according to their laws, customs, and beliefs, central among them being a system of family hunting territories in which each family had a responsibility to steward its two- to three-hundred-square-mile territory (Trails in Time 2001). For the Teme-Augama Anishnabai, n'Daki Menan provided the cultural and spiritual basis of their identity as a people as well as their means of support. They made extensive use of its hundreds of species, relying on everything from bear fat for lamp oil to moss for baby diapers, and from stewed birch-bark for healing wounds to spruce tree roots for making fish nets (ibid., 80-89). Although this brief description does not begin to do justice to the Teme-Augama Anishnabai's vast knowledge and use of, respect for, or belief system regarding n'Daki Menan, it does show that, for them, the region was never a wilderness area but rather a homeland to live in and use. Indeed, they continue to constitute the region in this manner, although their ways of living on and with the land have also changed over time. During the 1980s, while environmentalists struggled to save the pristine Temagami wilderness, the Teme-Augama Anishnabai were enmeshed in a legal battle with Ontario in order to have a Canadian court recognize the region not as wilderness, but as their territory. Due to the findings of the Supreme Court of Canada in that case, the Teme-Augama Anishnabai are currently in negotiations with Ontario to secure greater access to the resources of n'Daki Menan that have been denied to them for many generations.[1]

In spite of the Teme-Augama Anishnabai's continued understanding of n'Daki Menan as their territory and persistence in endeavouring to get non-Native governments to recognize their claim to land, according to Canadian law and popular imagination, the region is, with the exception of the Teme-Augama Anishnabai's one-square-mile reserve, part of Ontario. In this chapter, I focus on cultural rather than legal explanations for how n'Daki

Menan came to make sense as part of the Canadian wilderness, and I concentrate specifically on Temagami travel literature written around the turn of the twentieth century. This travel writing, I argue, did not merely reflect a self-evident Temagami wilderness, but rather created the region as part of the Canadian wilderness and, in so doing, made it appear as a tourist destination for white men, thus obscuring Teme-Augama Anishnabai claims to, and some of their relationships with, n'Daki Menan. The making of a Temagami wilderness in travel writing constituted part of the larger process through which Aboriginal lands were remade, albeit never completely, as white and Canadian.

Scholars have established that whiteness is a thoroughly relational category that gains its power and legitimacy from its appearance as the power-neutral norm (see, for example, Dwyer and Jones 2000). In Canada, whiteness is "literally founded upon Indigeneity," since the "liberal, bourgeois, propertied self" came into being only through the appropriation of Aboriginal lands (Lozanski 2007, 224). As this chapter shows, however, it is not only whiteness, but also wilderness, that is constructed in relation to aboriginality. The inherent instability of both whiteness and wilderness is revealed by paying attention to the multiple ways in which Temagami tourism depended upon the active participation of the Teme-Augama Anishnabai, who variously assisted, resisted, and ignored tourists' imaginations of themselves and n'Daki Menan itself. In spite of this instability, the idea of Temagami as a wilderness region remains prevalent, and for this reason, it is important to demonstrate how this story about Temagami, to paraphrase Julie Cruikshank (2005, 242), has come to adorn, cover, and ultimately obscure prior stories. By revealing some of the processes through which Temagami came to be understood as a wild space, I aim to participate in the effort to break this story's hold on the truth, thus creating room for alternative stories to be heard and different futures – which include Teme-Augama Anishnabai self-determination on n'Daki Menan – to be imagined.

Temagami Tourism in Context

From Almost Unknown to Far Famed

I chose to study travel literature written between 1894 and 1915 because it was during this time that the Temagami region transitioned, in less than ten years, from a place known mainly to the Teme-Augama Anishnabai to a famous wilderness tourism destination. The travel writing offers the opportunity to examine how the region was represented by, and for, tourists when it first became widely known to non-Native people. In 1899 Temagami was still considered a "little known district amid the wilds of Canada" (Jones 1899, 3), but by the summer of 1905, the opening of the government-run Temiskaming and Northern Ontario Railway had brought the region within easy access of major urban centres in eastern Canada and the United States. As a result of the new railway and promotional efforts by the Canadian Pacific and Grand Trunk Railways, both of which ran connections to the government line, hundreds of tourists began pouring into Temagami each summer. Although opinions differed regarding the greater numbers of visitors in Temagami – some complained that it was being "tamed fast" (*Rod and Gun* 1905, 425), but many appreciated the new ease with which they could access the area – none denied that as early as 1905 and definitely by 1910, Temagami had become a "far famed sportsman's paradise of the north" (T.J.T. 1910, 18).

Tourism, Romanticism, and Colonialism
Patricia Jasen's *Wild Things: Nature, Culture, and Tourism in Ontario, 1790-1914* (1995) provides an important historical context for my reading of Temagami travel writing, for Temagami tourism did not occur in a vacuum. Jasen shows that tourism in Ontario started as early as the 1790s, when tourists began to seek out places where they might experience the sights and feelings associated with romanticism. In turn, promoters of tourism packaged and sold romantic images in an attempt to get tourists to spend their money on experiencing the wild in nature (ibid., 13). Jasen convincingly demonstrates that the culture, economics, and politics of nineteenth- and early-twentieth-century Ontario tourism relied upon the romantic sensibility. One feature of romanticism that Jasen (ibid.) contends requires closer analytical attention is the fascination with places and people considered primitive. In the context of pre–First World War Ontario tourism, this fascination played out in the commodification not only of specific localities, but also of their Aboriginal inhabitants, as tourists sought to understand themselves and the nature of civilization through contact with "wild" others (ibid., 16, 13). European tourists regularly figured Native people as a race in decline and often saw themselves as civilized by comparison in a process that had the effect of making the advance of European civilization onto Native lands seem inevitable (ibid., 17). Because this kind of thinking was so embedded within the sensibility that profoundly shaped Ontario tourism, Jasen insists that tourism provided a link between culture and imperialism in the Canadian context.

Temagami tourism must, then, be considered as playing a role in European colonialism. As Mary Louise Pratt (1992, 5) demonstrates, European travel writing produced "the rest of the world" for a European readership. She uses the term "anti-conquest" to describe the representational practices through which travel writers asserted European hegemony because, unlike more obviously imperialist ventures, travel writing appeared innocent: the writers who created it did not actively seize foreign lands or appropriate foreign resources. Pratt shows, however, that the "imperial eyes" of travel writing were no less implicated in shaping economic and political realities than were other techniques of imperialism. Pratt's work is instructive for this chapter both in its exploration of the material effects of travel writing and in its insistence that colonial travel writing is a product of "transculturation," not of one-way (Europe-to-colony) knowledge production (ibid., 6). Encounters between tourists and Teme-Augama Anishnabai in the contact zone of n'Daki Menan/Temagami were highly ambivalent affairs. Certainly, tourists' experiences of the region were shaped by the formidable amount of "cultural baggage" that they brought with them (Jasen 1995, 26) but also by encounters with real places and real people. Similarly, although the Teme-Augama Anishnabai did not write Temagami travel narratives, they influenced what tourists could write, as well as where they could go in n'Daki Menan. (For an exploration of a similar point in the context of British Columbia, see Loo 2001.) They also had, and continue to have, their own stories about the area, stories into which tourists sometimes fit (see, for example, Theriault 1992).

Who Went, Who Wrote, and Who Worked

Although wilderness vacations became more popular near the close of the twentieth century, not everyone enjoyed the privilege of a yearly holiday in the wilds of Canada. Tourism in Temagami, as in the rest of Ontario before the First World War, was largely an activity of middle- and upper-class women and men (Jasen 1995, 20-21). Until the railway stretched north as far as Temagami, getting to the area via train, steamer, and portage before even putting a canoe in the water was something that only those who had leisure time and spare money could afford to do. Even after railway service began, the more than day-long train ride from Toronto or Buffalo to Temagami made the destination largely inaccessible to urban working-class people, who usually did not have paid holidays and commonly worked six days a week until well into the First World War (ibid., 21). Some rural people who lived close to Temagami did visit the area for day trips, such as with the annual excursion organized from nearby New Liskeard (*New Liskeard Speaker* 1906). However, these people did not tend to write about their experiences, and members of the more privileged classes were both the authors of and target audience for Temagami travel literature.

Both white women and white men went on Temagami wilderness vacations, but of the several dozen travel narratives written about the area between 1894 and 1915, all but a few were by white men. Jasen (1995, 24) suggests that the predominance of men's writing is probably due to the fact that the wilderness travel genre was largely gendered male, and women were at least sometimes actively discouraged from writing in this form (see also Mills 1991). In part because women wrote so few of the published Temagami narratives, it is difficult to assess how many women travelled to the region. This difficulty is compounded by the fact that, as both Mary Louise Pratt (1992, 155) and Jasen (1995, 22) point out, men's narratives are not always reliable sources of information about women's participation in travel. It is probable that male writers sometimes failed to mention the presence of white women who may have been in their parties or encountered during their journeys. One example will clarify the reason for this: As a woman writer recalled about her hunting trip in Temagami, "I went out to call my husband to breakfast, when one of them [a party of hunters from Toronto] exclaimed, 'Is that a woman's voice? Why, we're not out of civilization yet!'" (A.G. Adams 1909, 400). When a white woman was acknowledged as entering wilderness space, the space ceased to be wild. In this example, she stood as a "boundary marker" in Anne McClintock's (1995, 24) sense of the term, a threshold figure through which "men oriented themselves in space, as agents of power and agents of knowledge." If white women marked the boundary between civilization and wilderness – where they were, wilderness was not – it makes sense that white men writing about their wilderness experiences might avoid mentioning the presence of white women. The absence of women in men's travel narratives had the effect of making wilderness appear not only wild, but also a domain for white men, even as white women also travelled through the region.

Like white women and men, the Teme-Augama Anishnabai participated in Temagami tourism, but for them, tourism was work rather than leisure. Indeed, they did much of the work that made the leisure of white tourists possible and enjoyable, not necessarily because it was their first choice of activities, but because their options had become limited in recent years. During the late 1870s, they began to petition the Department of Indian

Affairs (DIA) to set aside a reserve for them because their lands were being impinged upon by non-Native timber interests, and they wanted to ensure that at least some portion of n'Daki Menan remained under their control. Although the DIA agreed that they required a reserve, the Ontario government refused to participate in creating one because it wanted to control the valuable timber in the region. In 1901, having ignored the Teme-Augama Anishnabai's requests for a reserve for over twenty years, Ontario created the Temagami Forest Reserve, banning settlement in the area in order to secure future timber supplies. Suddenly considered "squatters" in the forest reserve, the Teme-Augama Anishnabai found their activities policed and criminalized by government officials (Hodgins and Benidickson 1989; Thorpe 2008). Within this context, tourism became an important means of economic survival for them. Teme-Augama Anishnabai men worked as guides (women did not, probably due in large part to tourists' gendered expectations), securing decent wages because the demand for guides far outstripped their supply (Carrell 1907b). Teme-Augama Anishnabai women worked as cooks at camps and as helpers and waitresses at hotels on Lake Temagami. They also did laundry for tourists, cleaned cottages at private camps, and sold butter, bread, and handicrafts to tourists (A.W.C. 1903, 344; Carrell 1907a, 937; Theriault 1992).

The Making of Wild Temagami Past

Temagami consistently featured in travel literature as a feminized wild place. Authors described it as "utterly wild" – an "as yet wholly unsurveyed" (Wadsworth 1899, 151) region where nature "is to be found in practically her virgin state" (*Toronto Daily Star* 1905b, 28). Even after it had become a well-known tourist destination, writers continued to represent it as "thousands of square miles of primitive forest intersected by innumerable lakes and rivers, many of them practically unexplored" (Camp Temagami 1915, 7). Temagami figured not only as virgin, but also as part of the past. One author described a voyage down the Temagami River as a tour through "regions of grand antiquity," where it became possible to "lose yourself among the shades of former ages when the forest patriarchs and the red-man dwelt in unmolested security" (Barry 1905, 168).

According to Jasen (1995, 82-83), the association between wilderness and the past was a consistent feature in nineteenth-century romantic tourism. The idea that wild places would inevitably pass away made them all the more attractive as tourist destinations. Banking on the idea that these "silent places" were disappearing with the "march of Empire" and the "white man['s] ceaseless search for the earth's endowments" (Grand Trunk Railway 1908), promoters advertised Temagami as a place where tourists could escape the forward movement of progress and access both traces of a past era and the nostalgia associated with the passing of a previous time. The narrative of progress is embedded in the understanding that the virgin forest exists in the past, for its destruction appears as the necessary result of European history's inevitable unfolding. Travel writers took it for granted that the emergence of "civilized conditions" in Canada necessitated the disappearance of the wild forest. As an advertisement for the Grand Trunk Railway put it, "A little while and the 'forest primeval' shall be no more ... Therefore, it behooves you, O mighty hunter, to go forth and capture your caribou or moose while you may" (ibid.).

Constructing the Temagami forest as virgin and existing in the past also had a political significance. As Anne McClintock (1995, 30) argues, the "myth of the virgin land is also the myth of the empty land, involving both a gender and a racial dispossession." To be virgin within patriarchal narratives "is to be empty of desire and void of sexual agency, passively awaiting the thrusting, male insemination of history, language and reason" (ibid.). And within colonial narratives, the myth of virgin land "also effects a territorial appropriation, for if the land is virgin, colonized peoples cannot claim aboriginal territorial rights" (ibid.). The creation of a virgin Temagami in travel narratives relied on the female gendering of wilderness space in order to empty the region of agency and an Aboriginal claim to it. As its moose, waterfalls, and old trees became incorporated into a tourist gaze that valued them because they could conform aesthetically and imaginatively to romantic ideals, they could no longer have their own reasons for being or uses for one another. Similarly, as will be discussed below, as the Teme-Augama Anishnabai came to exist within travel writing as part of the romantic nature that tourists travelled to encounter, their territorial claims disappeared. With no other reasons for its existence and no prior claims impinging upon it, n'Daki Menan could be reinvented within travel literature as a tourist destination.

Temagami tourists faced a dilemma, however. They learned from travel writing and promotional materials that Temagami was an empty, wild place, and yet their own travels through it depended fundamentally upon the labour of the Teme-Augama Anishnabai, who clearly both inhabited the region and knew it intimately. Although these facts probably caused confusion for individual tourists, no dilemma appeared in travel writing. Authors simply accepted, and indeed lauded, the Teme-Augama Anishnabai's presence in space while adamantly denying an Aboriginal presence in the contemporary moment. The Teme-Augama Anishnabai became racialized as, to borrow McClintock's (1995, 30) phrase, "the living embodiment of the archaic 'primitive.'" Writers constructed Native people as fixed in the past in part through romantic nostalgia about the supposedly inevitable decline and disappearance of Native people and ways of life. One author, for instance, devoted an entire article to reflecting upon all the work the "woods Indian" did to help the white race get its footing in the North and noted with a sense of regret that Aboriginal people "led the way and did the work for the civilization which eventually will swallow them up" (Sangster 1912, 124). Other writers similarly found it sad that the "race [was] dying out" (Farr 1902, 2), and some went so far as to pre-empt its disappearance, stating that "here it was that the Ojibways had their home ... The wigwams, with the circling smoke, have disappeared, and in their place are the tents of holiday-makers or prospectors" (*Toronto Globe* 1907, 4).

Native people became the living embodiment of the archaic primitive in Temagami travel writing not only through their displacement in time, but also via their representation as fixed at an early stage of development, with no hope of becoming full adults or even fully human. They consistently appeared as "children of the wild" (Yeigh 1906, 326) and "children of nature, ... notwithstanding that some of them are grey" (*Rod and Gun* 1903, 409). As one writer bluntly stated, "the average Indian differs from the average white in character as the child differs from the man – he is less developed" (The Chief 1894, 412). Other contributors offered more nuanced analyses. An author who called himself St. Croix, for example, asserted that context was everything. "Capture one of these wild men of the woods," he said, "bring him to our civilization, and his intelligence seems far below that of a child; but in his own wilderness he is a different creature, and, pitted against him, we are forced to acknowledge his infinite superiority" (St. Croix 1902, 103).

The common message given by travel writers – that Aboriginal people belonged in the bush and could not survive in civilization – also worked to contain Native people in the past. Such representations disallowed the possibility that they had the potential to become "civilized" and thus to survive in the modern era. In fact, when tourists found evidence that some Teme-Augama Anishnabai negotiated modernity quite well – for example, one writer commented that many of them spoke fluent English and French (Carrell 1907a, 936) – they seemed unsure of how to interpret this, and generally tossed it off as out of keeping with true Aboriginal character. On the other hand, writers seemed to relish moments when Aboriginal people appeared "properly" Aboriginal. One author, for example, felt disappointed that he had dropped his camera into the lake because he had planned to photograph "a few favorite poses of my guide David, which I knew would interest my friends" (Carrell 1907c, 146). By insisting that Native people belonged in the wilderness, travel writers attempted to keep them in wilderness time, a time, as they presented it, that was nearing its end.

Wild with Some, Wild for Others

Even when travel writers extolled the virtues of Aboriginal people, and particularly of Native men for their abilities in the bush, they simultaneously asserted their own cultural superiority. One writer admired the "wonderful power the adult Indian possesses" but contended that it was the "Anglo-Saxon spirit of adventure ... more than any other force under Providence, [that] has been the civilizing factor in the world's progress" (St. Croix 1901, 8). This author was willing to grant brute strength to Aboriginal people but restricted the ability to move forward to British colonizers. Thus, European culture appeared civilized and progressive through the construction of Aboriginal people as savage and fixed in time and space.

In fact, authors did not generally believe that Aboriginal people had the capacity to develop or learn skills, referring instead to guides' abilities in the bush as innate instincts. One writer, for example, commented that his trip offered many opportunities for "our Indians to display their ability of keen scent" (Carrell 1907c, 138), and another made note of the "instinctive sureness" with which two guides carried canoes over a portage (M. Cameron 1911, 1020). In this way, Aboriginal people appeared in travel narratives as having more in common with wild animals than with white tourists. Indeed, one writer, stating that he craved land "untrammeled by the foot of man, unsullied by his hand," was thrilled to find Temagami, which, he observed, was inhabited by "the bears, the moose and even Indians" (Me 1914, 569). The representation of Temagami as *wild with* Aboriginal people made it easy for the region to become imagined as *wild for* white tourists. It also allowed tourists to forget that guides went on Temagami trips for work rather than pleasure, a lapse that allowed them to ignore as well the fact that guides were people trying to make a living from their land *in the present.*

Yet writers also valued the savagery and wildness that they imagined they could find in their encounters with the Temagami wilderness and its Aboriginal inhabitants. Many tourists went to Temagami for the explicit purpose of having such encounters. Their appreciation of savagery and the wild must be understood within the then popular intellectual climate of anti-modernism, in which modern life seemed not only artificial and meaningless, but also threatening to the racial health of the nation (see Valverde 1991; Jasen 1995, 106-7, 140; Loo 2001; 2006, 29-35; Boag 2003). L.O. Armstrong (1904a, 60-61) articulated the concern about racial degeneracy when he rhetorically asked, "Are we Anglo-Saxons degenerating? Is the Englishman, the American and the Canadian less hardy than his forefathers?" The answer, according to Armstrong and other social commentators, was a clear yes. North American men were "becoming effeminate, as [had] done so many of the advanced civilizations of the past" (Armstrong 1904b, 15). The cure, many thought, for the "over-civilization" caused by modern urban life lay in "the outdoor life," where activities such as camping, canoeing, and portaging allowed men to become physically and mentally fit like their forefathers, who had been "hewers of wood and drawers of water" instead of office workers (ibid.). Indeed, Armstrong (1904a, 61) called for outdoor activities to become "national pastimes." Contact with wild nature thus became increasingly associated with a healthy, white, male-led nation. In an article titled "Why We Take to the Woods," one writer predicted that it would be "a shame and a blow to the health of the nation when hunting is a thing of the past" (*Rod and Gun* 1911, 560). After all, he continued, no activity except hunting removed men from civilization entirely (ibid.). Travel writers insisted that it was imperative, particularly for men, to take regular breaks from civilization in order to recuperate from the pressures of modern urban life and to become "energized and built up, stronger in body and mind" (Another Wet Bob 1899, 53).

Given the potentially dangerous effects of modern life and the promise that a wilderness vacation could prevent degeneracy, it makes sense that tourists and travel writers came to appreciate what they considered the savage in nature. Particularly attractive was the idea that a wilderness encounter could bring out the savage assumed to be embedded in every civilized man. As two contented tourists wrote of their Temagami vacation, "With each mile breath came freer; with each hour we grew delightfully more savage" (E. and S.W. 1908, 10). Tourists appreciated wild Temagami nature for what they perceived it did to them: made them (temporarily) uncivilized. This positive evaluation of wilderness was also connected to their appreciation of supposedly savage Aboriginal people. Tourists not only enjoyed regarding Native people's abilities in the bush, but also valued wilderness trips because they themselves could become similar to Aboriginal people.

For instance, one article enthusiastically stated that on a Temagami canoe trip, a young man was "as free as the wind to act like the original red-man himself" (Raney 1910, 191).

Although many Temagami travel writers placed value on wilderness, they simultaneously drew a boundary between civilization and savagery, placing themselves on the side of civilization and Aboriginal people on the side of savagery. They did so primarily by asserting that encounters with wilderness had value to the success of their own civilization. White men, they stated, became savage for a reason: to become more effective contributors to civilization. As one author put it, a wilderness vacation allowed "the brain-fagged, nerve-racked, denizens of our great cities" to recover from "the hurry and the worry of the ten months' grind in the treadmill of business life," so that they might return to work refreshed (Parkinson 1914, 167). Tourists' status as visitors to the Temagami wild further separated them from its Aboriginal inhabitants. White tourists encountered wilderness, became temporarily savage, and emerged from their encounter better fitted for the challenges of civilization. Aboriginal people, on the other hand, were at home only in the wilderness and thus were unfit for civilization.

As Jasen (1995, 16) observes, no matter how writers characterized Aboriginal people, the very act of defining them and their culture in the context of European colonial expansion was an assertion of control. But the specific ways that travel writers represented Aboriginal people and the Temagami area mattered too, since these portrayals influenced how readers understood the region and its inhabitants. As described above, Temagami travel literature constructed Aboriginal people as part of the wilderness, fixed in wilderness space and prehistoric time, dying, savage, and undeveloped. This kind of depiction made it easy for tourists to imagine Temagami as a wild space existing only for them to discover. Forms of representation that could challenge the idea of Aboriginal people as anachronistic or savage – for example, the Teme-Augama Anishnabai's self-representation in letters to the DIA, which revealed them to be a creative and intelligent group coping in the present and planning for the future – did not usually appear in the tourist literature. As a result, those who read it were not forced to confront the possibility that another group might have a prior claim to the Temagami wilderness or, worse, that the region might not be a wilderness at all.

Of course, tourists' sense of entitlement to Temagami did not come solely from travel writers' convenient representations of Aboriginal people; it stemmed as well from the larger project of imperial expansion and white settler nationalism in which Temagami tourism was situated. Elite white subjects travelled in droves to Temagami because they felt they had an absolute right to do so, a right they asserted simply by getting off the train at Temagami Station. For them, the question was one of logistics rather than ethics: not of whether they *should* go to Temagami, but rather of how to get there. Once the railway reached the area, the question of how to get there was answered for many, and so, therefore, was the question of whether to go. According to one article, now that "the pathfinder has passed that way, has opened a steel trail ... you, who are tired of the old, worn trails, may have your first peep into this new sportsman's Paradise" (*Toronto Daily Star* 1905c, 29).

The Anti-Conquest of Temagami Tourism

Late-nineteenth- and early-twentieth-century Temagami tourism was what Mary Louise Pratt might call an anti-conquest: it simultaneously asserted European hegemony and rendered its own power invisible. It appeared innocent in part through the previously discussed depiction in travel writing of the region as wild with Aboriginal people, a representation that made it possible and logical to consider the area as wild for tourists. More directly, however, Temagami appeared as wild for tourists because travel literature stated just that: God or nature had created the region for the pleasure of tourists. As one writer asserted, God had provided Temagami's "most beautiful scenery ... for the refreshment of his children" (Norris 1909, 703). Others characterized Temagami as "truly a sportsman's Garden of Eden" (Beswick 1905, 316) and a "practically virgin territory for the sportsman" (*Toronto Daily Star* 1904, 5). The construction of Temagami as a natural space made for (male) tourists implicitly produced them as innocent subjects who merely received the place, and it created tourism as an act of passive consumption rather than active appropriation. Thus, though travel writing helped make Temagami into a wilderness space that could be consumed by tourists, the disappearance of this creative act from the writing itself made the process unintelligible, thereby allowing Temagami to appear as wild – thanks to nature (or God) – for tourists. As Mary Louise Pratt (1992, 31) states in another context, travel writers were able to "subsume culture and history into nature."

The innocence of tourists and tourism was also maintained through the presentation of sportsmen as having no choice but to travel: they simply had to respond to the call of the wild. A member of a canoeing club explained the call of the wild as "a strange feeling of unrest" that came upon men in the spring (K.K.K. 1906, 1380). Unable at first to understand its significance, they soon realized that "the wild has begun to call" them "back to the free life of the natural man" (ibid.). Contemplating the call of the wild, one Temagami canoe tripper concluded that since the current industrial age discouraged individuals from conducting activities that did not produce material wealth, the call must be instinctive in men, touching "the most responsive chords of a man's nature" (The Guide 1915, 1207). Even as he ignored the increase of wilderness vacationing in industrial society, he demonstrated the gendered character of the call of the wild and the way that it reinforced tourists' sense of innocence. Travel writers understood that the call was primarily heard by men, since they were not meant to sit at "a desk year in and year out, to stand behind the counter, or at the bench – nor in fact to do incessantly any of the hundred and one occupations of our civilized life" (Barton 1909, 71). Although some women insisted that men and women had the same instincts and therefore that women also required wilderness holidays (Walton 1899), travel writers generally constructed Temagami as a region for sports*men.* One writer stated that "*the* story of Temagami" was "a story of men, rods and fish" (Angus 1908, 864, emphasis added). Whether tourists understood the call of the wild as their own primitive instincts insisting that they travel, as Temagami nature calling to them, or, most likely, as a combination of the two, the idea that they did not travel of their own volition worked well for them. The call of the wild represented "nature's invitation to conquest" (McClintock 1995, 26); as such, it justified tourists' infiltration of Teme-Augama Anishnabai territory, simultaneously obscuring the connections between this onslaught and the larger colonial processes of which it constituted an important part.

Conclusion

Anti-racist scholars have firmly established that, as a result of cultural rather than natural processes, "whiteness" and "Canadianness" are linked social categories. This chapter has endeavoured to show that such cultural processes include not only methods of racialization but also the social construction of nature. In the case of Temagami travel writing at the turn of the twentieth century, racialization and the social construction of nature worked together to make Temagami appear "naturally" as a wilderness space for white men to visit. Even as Temagami tourism depended on the labour of the Teme-Augama Anishnabai, Aboriginal people became racialized within travel literature as part of the wilderness and the past, through the simultaneous construction of the region as untouched and wild. White tourists, and particularly men, were at the same time encouraged to come to know themselves, in opposition to Aboriginal people, as the natural inheritors of the wilderness that called them to visit it and that promised to make them properly national, and properly male, subjects. Since discourses about land can also facilitate the idea that Canada is a naturally white nation, anti-racist scholars might benefit from an examination of the co-constitution of race and nature in other Canadian contexts as well.

In creating the Temagami region and its Aboriginal inhabitants as part of the fading Canadian wilderness for white men to visit, travel writing simultaneously rendered unintelligible both the Teme-Augama Anishnabai's existence and claim to land. Yet this process did not take place easily, largely because of the actions of the Teme-Augama Anishnabai themselves. Trained to expect a picturesque wilderness on their Temagami vacations (including noble, and doomed, Indians), tourists found instead a confusing new place, full of lakes and rocks and dense forests, one they did not know how to negotiate, but that the Teme-Augama Anishnabai knew well. And, as some writers uncomfortably acknowledged, tourists were "helpless to get about" without the assistance of Aboriginal guides, who occasionally deserted one tourist party for another offering better pay (Ontario 1906, 248). But even when tourists were not abandoned by their guides, they remained helpless, for their guides carried their luggage, set up their tents, cooked their food, taught them how to fish and hunt, did their laundry, and waited their tables. Travel writers seem to have dealt with this awkward situation by controlling the actions of the Indians on the page, voicing satisfaction when they looked and acted like the Indians they had in mind (see King 2003) and expressing anxiety and displeasure when they did not. Frank Carrell (1907a, 939-40; 1907c, 146), for instance, wanted to photograph favourite poses struck by his guide but was offended when a guide sat with his party on the hotel veranda. The anxiety expressed by some writers in their Temagami travel narratives was caused by going to a place imagined as a Canadian wilderness tourism destination and finding that it was no such thing. Temagami became part of the Canadian wilderness not so much due to tourists' encounters with the region – which were full of ambivalences, of un-imaginary Indians, of getting lost in an unfamiliar landscape – but with their writing of those encounters and with readers' consumption of that writing. Over time, and with the repetition of stories, Temagami came to be imagined as a site of national nature. But possession and dispossession, like the stories themselves, were never complete. Other stories always existed.

Resolving "the Indian Land Question"?
Racial Rule and Reconciliation in British Columbia

BRIAN EGAN

No challenge is more central or integral to British Columbia's geopolitical identity than "the Indian land question." This issue, as Paul Tennant (1990, ix) puts it, "is as old as British Columbia itself." The phrase, which has largely fallen out of circulation in recent years, is colonial in origin. For the officials charged with establishing a British colony in this place during the mid-nineteenth century, the question had to do with taking possession of Indian land: that is, how to properly arrange for the displacement of Indigenous peoples so that their lands could be taken up by British settlers. For the provincial and federal officials who assumed this task after BC joined the Dominion of Canada in 1871, the question was always understood as being about where Indigenous peoples should be put and how much – or, more aptly, how little – land they should be allotted. Their answer, formulated during the final decades of the nineteenth century and the first few decades of the twentieth, was to restrict First Nations to a dispersed network of Indian reserves, which represented a tiny fraction of the territory they had traditionally used and occupied, and to define the rest of the land base – more than 99 percent of the province – as "Crown land" (Harris 2002). This vast expanse of Crown territory, and the rich resources it encompassed, provided the economic base for the establishment and expansion of British Columbia's settler society.

Throughout the late nineteenth and early twentieth centuries, Indigenous peoples were largely excluded from debates about the Indian land question in BC. This is not to say that they did not seek to address it or, more typically, to expand and redefine its terms. Indeed, during this period, they continually pressed for a more expansive allocation of lands to their communities and, more fundamentally, asserted jurisdiction or sovereignty over their extensive territories. Through such actions, they sought to challenge both the validity of the spatially constricted Indian reserve system and the Crown's assumption that it could rule unilaterally and unchallenged over the province (Tennant 1990). These Indigenous assertions, which yielded little result in earlier periods, began to gain legal traction in the 1960s. Since then, Aboriginal groups in British Columbia have had considerable success in using Canadian courts to advance their claims to land and territory, the primary gain being a measure of legal and political recognition of the continuing existence of Aboriginal title and rights in this province.

In the legal formulation of the courts, "Crown sovereignty" in BC – defined as having been established in 1846 – was "burdened" by pre-existing Aboriginal rights to land and resources.[1] Indeed, in the landmark *Delgamuukw* (1997) case, Aboriginal title is posited to have come into existence or "crystallized" at the moment when Crown sovereignty was asserted. The unburdening of the Crown was to come, it was argued in *R. v. Van der Peet* (1996, para. 31), through "the reconciliation of the pre-existence of aboriginal societies with the sovereignty of the Crown." In time, the Crown has come to see reconciliation as a vehicle to move beyond the challenges posed by Aboriginal title and rights. From its perspective, what has been important is the shaping of this vehicle to its own ends – in other words, controlling the definition of what reconciliation is and isn't, as well as what and who is to be included and excluded in reconciliation processes.

In this chapter, I focus on what I refer to as British Columbia's official contemporary reconciliation project, defined here as the attempt to achieve a reconciliation of Aboriginal title and Crown sovereignty within the province's territory. My reference to an *official* reconciliation project indicates my intention to examine the project primarily as it has been shaped by Crown-led policies and processes. My main focus is on the BC treaty process, which has been the key instrument created to achieve this reconciliation. I am concerned here with a reconciliation project that operates predominantly in the juridical-political domain and is fundamentally about resolving competing jurisdictions over land, natural resources, and peoples. I argue that British Columbia's reconciliation project can be understood as a response on the part of the Crown to the challenge posed by the assertion of Indigenous rights to land and territory. Given the absence of formal processes (historical treaties) providing for the extinguishment of Aboriginal territorial rights or claims across much of the province, the contemporary assertion of Indigenous land rights – an assertion given considerable legal weight by court rulings that recognize Aboriginal title and rights – undermines the Crown's ability to freely allocate and manage the province's lands and natural resources. Strongly controlled and shaped by Crown interests, the BC treaty process (along with other elements of the reconciliation project) has functioned – not always successfully – to contain the challenge posed by the assertion of Indigenous territorial rights and to stabilize Crown control over the province's land and resource base.

If British Columbia's reconciliation project is about stabilizing Crown sovereignty, it is also about stabilizing a certain understanding of BC's racial constitution. The province, to use David Theo Goldberg's (2002a) term, was founded on the idea of "racial rule" – that Europeans, or "whites," would naturally rule over Indigenous peoples – and the reconciliation project is about stabilizing this regime and maintaining BC as a "white province." Among other things, racial rule involves the displacement of First Nations from their larger territories or homelands and their confinement to Indian reserves, a spatial project that constituted a fundamental part of the effort to produce British Columbia as a white place. From this perspective, the assertion of Crown sovereignty in 1846 was also an assertion of white sovereignty, which itself relied on an active denial of Indigenous land and territorial rights: colonial officials not only argued that Aboriginal peoples had no rights to extensive lands and resources but were also incapable of governing either themselves or their larger territories. As I hope to demonstrate in this chapter, these racial conceptions remain with us today, albeit in modified and more nuanced form, and are evident in the BC reconciliation project. The project, in other words, attends to the need to stabilize the notion and practise of white sovereignty.

Racial Rule

As Audrey Kobayashi (2003, 544) notes, race is a social and historical construct whose origins can be traced to the Enlightenment period; between the eighteenth and twentieth centuries, she argues, race "became a fundamental part of western understanding of what is human, normalized in every aspect of common discourse, from the intellectual to the political, the economic and the social." From the start, race was defined as a marker of human worth or value, with lighter skin tones indicating human beings with superior moral, social, and intellectual qualities and darker skin tones indicating the opposite. Also from the start, there was a spatial dimension to the idea of race, with lighter skin tones – and hence superior human subjects – located in temperate zones (broadly, Europe), whereas inferior and darker-skinned peoples were located in tropical regions. This conflation of race with space allowed for the production of a spectrum of human worth based on geographical location, which, in turn, helped establish the basis for Europe's imperial and colonial adventures – it helped legitimate the rule of one group of people, those defined as European, or white, over all others. Space itself, Kobayashi (ibid., 552) reminds us, is also a social and historical construct, and one "that has been mobilized in the major projects of modernity." It is the working together of representations of race and space, and how these are entangled with relations of power, that is of central concern to my arguments in this chapter.

Focusing on the imbrications of race and space has yielded important insights into the operations of colonial power. Edward Said's (1979) work on the discursive production of "the Orient" (a particular space) and "the Oriental" (a racialized subject), and how these representations formed the basis for European domination of the Middle East and the peoples that inhabit it, laid the foundation for a large body of work on this theme. Geography was central to Said's work, particularly to his assertion that racialized spaces are produced through discourse and, further, that this discourse establishes "configurations of power" between different peoples and places. In this way, race and racism are closely linked to certain geographical imaginaries, integral to the way that places and spaces are constructed or imagined to be. Important to my arguments, Said saw the symbolic and cultural dimensions of colonialism as inseparable from the material project of taking possession of territory, which itself was something that he perceived as lying near the core of the colonial project. Said (1993, 7) understood the discursive production of certain peoples and places to be inseparable from the colonial effort to settle on and control land that was "lived on and owned by others."

In Said's wake, much of the critical work on the links between colonialism and Western representations of race has focused on the discursive production of the colonial other, on colonized or non-white peoples. Until fairly recently, scholars have paid less attention to the production of colonialism's companion subject, the colonizing or white subject. Over the past decade or so, this gap has begun to be addressed by studies dealing with the white subject and the operation of what has been termed "whiteness" (see, for example, Goldberg 1997; Hill 1997). A fundamental starting point for any study of whiteness is a recognition of "white" as a socially constructed racial category (Dyer 1997). Kobayashi (2003, 550) defines whiteness, on the other hand, as a historical form of racism that "involves not only depicting those who are non-white in prejudicial terms, but also reinforcing the centrality and superiority of white cultural, social and aesthetic forms." The "project of whiteness," she notes, can take on myriad forms – indeed, its adaptability, flexibility, and variability are key aspects of its power. Also key to the function of whiteness is its ability to remain hidden from scrutiny or to be only vaguely perceived, to act as the invisible and non-racial backdrop, and as the norm against which all other subjects are measured (Vanderbeck 2006). Other scholars have highlighted the geographic nature of whiteness, showing how white identities and privilege are "inseparable from the production of space and places, from geographies of inequality, and from the territorialization of definitions of normalcy and deviance" (McCarthy and Hague 2004, 388). These authors write from the perspective that to focus on whiteness is not to further privilege the white subject, but rather to better understand the different ways that white identities – and the project of whiteness – develop, adapt, and are defended and challenged in different places (Bonnett 1997; Pulido 2000).

I draw here on Goldberg's (2002a) idea of racial rule in an effort to better understand how whiteness operates to subjugate peoples who are deemed non-white and to rule over both them and their territories. Goldberg (ibid., 82) argues that "increasingly sophisticated forms and techniques of racial formation, power, and exclusion" have been central to the development and governance of modern states. Racial rule is based on the assumption that not only are non-Europeans inferior to Europeans but that they are incapable of governing themselves. Goldberg draws out two different, yet overlapping, traditions of racial conception that are evident in racial rule. "Naturalist" conceptions of race are founded in ideas about nature and biology. From this perspective, European superiority is a product of genes and an unalterable natural fact. "Historicist" racial conceptions, on the other hand, draw on ideas about social and historical development; the notion here is that European superiority is due to the fact that whites have progressed further along the historical or evolutionary process toward civilization. Although Goldberg distinguishes between these two forms of racial conception and how they shape the governance of non-white peoples and places – naturalists favour racial segregation and more coercive forms of social control, whereas historicists lean toward paternalism, ambivalence, and the requirement that non-white subjects assimilate into European society – he notes that they co-exist historically and tend to blend together and reinforce each other. As highlighted in the following section, both variants of racial rule are evident in the conception of British Columbia as a white province.

Producing a White Province

As was the case in other British colonies, early narratives of the white settlement of British Columbia drew on the idea of populating a wild and barren space. Where the presence of Indigenous peoples was acknowledged, they tended to be depicted as "primitive" or "savage" and yearning for the gifts that white civilization would bring. European colonization of, and rule over, Indigenous peoples and territories was portrayed as a natural effect of progress, part of the inevitable spread of Western civilization across the globe. Reflecting such ideas, early chroniclers of BC history represent the province's founding as "a quiet and effectual redemption from savagery" and assert that the white settlement of it was "a matter of easy and frictionless accomplishment" (Kerr 1890, 1-2). Here we find fertile soil for the construction of what Sherene Razack (2002b, 2) calls, in the broader Canadian context, "white founding mythologies," stories of creation and identity that serve to define "who belongs and who does not belong." A quintessential feature of such stories, she argues, is a disavowal of certain difficult and unpleasant aspects of the history of the place – namely, the forceful and often violent dispossession of Indigenous peoples. The central white fantasy in such founding stories is the denial of conquest and colonization, and the assertion that these areas were peacefully settled.

In the British Columbia context, Daniel Clayton (2000, 56) describes efforts to construct a "white history" of the province, a project undertaken in the late nineteenth and early twentieth centuries by a small group of prominent white intellectual and political figures. In this project, Captain James Cook's contact with Nuu-chah-nulth people at Nootka Sound in the late eighteenth century marked a critical starting point for BC's white history, and Captain George Vancouver's detailed mapping of the coastline a few decades later signalled an important further step in giving shape to this place. According to this perspective, these European explorers began to lift a veil of mist, bringing light and meaning – and history – to what was hitherto a vaguely defined space. This intellectual project involved an effort to build a local master narrative, Clayton argues, based on a myth of the white founding of British Columbia. This was to be a history that was comforting to the inheritors of this colonial space and a narrative that would serve to consolidate and stabilize a place built on shaky foundations. Building a white history of British Columbia required, for one thing, that a neat and untroubled image of a pioneer settler society be constructed, of an idealized white settler society that, in other words, was untainted by meaningful contact and conflict with other races. It also required that Indigenous peoples be obscured, or at least confined to particular representational categories (such as "savage"), and that the early relations between European visitors and First Nation hosts be rendered in simple and unidirectional terms. In relation to this, it demanded that a spatial trick be performed – that Indigenous attachments and claims to a larger territorial base be erased and replaced by a more restricted understanding of Indigenous land and resource use and governance.

Recent scholarship has begun to dismantle the myth of the white founding of British Columbia and to add greater complexity and nuance to our understanding of the early encounters between Europeans and First Nations in this place. The work of ethno-ecologists, for example, has documented the extent and depth of Aboriginal land and resource management in precolonial times, undercutting colonial claims that much of the land was unused or ungoverned (Deur and Turner 2005). Robin Fisher (1977) has shown how early relations between Indigenous peoples and Europeans were complex and multidirectional, mediated largely through the maritime fur trade, a system of exchange that was of benefit to both parties. Fisher suggests that it was in the transition to land-based colonization that conflicts between Indigenous groups and Europeans became more prevalent, and relations of domination began to be established. In examining this early phase of colonization, Adele Perry (2001) notes the extent to which the project of establishing a model British colony, encompassing an orderly white settler society, was troubled by a more complicated and "messy" reality on the ground, including the prevalence of "mixed race" relationships, primarily between Aboriginal women and white men. The ideas or fantasies of a pure white colony and of an unchallenged whiteness were projected, in these early colonial days, against the reality of a much larger Indigenous population and against a landscape where white rule or control was marginal and restricted to very limited areas. Later, particularly in the late nineteenth and first half of the twentieth century, these same aspirations of whiteness would be articulated against a growing Asian immigrant population (K. Anderson 1995b). As Perry points out, British Columbia has never actually been a white province, despite efforts to construct it as such.

White Property, Crown Land, and Indian Reserves

As Said reminds us, colonialism is at some fundamental level about taking possession of land. Thus, the planting of European settlements in what was to become British Columbia, beginning at Fort Victoria in the 1840s, required the taking possession of Indigenous lands and the imposition of boundaries around Aboriginal subjects and spaces. During the early colonial period, this process was effected through land purchase agreements "negotiated" with Indigenous groups. Between 1850 and 1854, James Douglas, the chief colonial authority in the colony, signed fourteen such agreements – known today as the Douglas treaties – with Indigenous groups on Vancouver Island, providing for the appropriation of some ninety-three thousand hectares of land for an expanding settler population. These agreements stipulated that, apart from the village sites and enclosed fields used by the Indigenous communities in question (which would be reserved for their exclusive use), the land would become "the Entire property of the White people for ever" (Duff 1969, 11). Although important questions have been raised about the validity and meaning of the Douglas treaties – Chris Arnett (1999, 36-37), for example, has argued that some of the Indigenous signatories understood them as peace and friendship agreements rather than land cession treaties – these agreements do provide evidence that colonial authorities, and Douglas in particular, recognized Aboriginal title to extensive territories (Tennant 1990, 20).

After 1854, however, no further land purchase agreements or treaties were negotiated with Indigenous groups either on Vancouver Island or the mainland colony of British Columbia.[2] Rather than pursuing treaties, Douglas sought to resolve the Indian land question through the creation of a system of Indian reserves, which would provide Aboriginal communities with certain lands for their exclusive use while freeing up the rest for white settlers. Before retiring in 1864, Douglas directed his staff to establish "anticipatory reserves" – to map out Indian reserves prior to the arrival of white settlers in a region – and he sought to create reserves of a size that might satisfy Indigenous communities' needs for land; indeed, as Cole Harris (2002) documents, he ordered colonial surveyors to allow local First Nation leaders to choose the boundaries of their own reserves. Importantly,

Douglas also provided Indigenous peoples with the right to pre-empt lands outside their reserves, the same privilege afforded to white settlers in the colony. Under Douglas' instructions, a number of Indian reserves were mapped out in the Okanagan and Kamloops region, and also in the lower Fraser Valley, which Harris (ibid., 42) notes were "the most generous ever identified in British Columbia." Although Douglas' actions indicated an understanding of the importance of providing Indigenous communities with an adequate land base, it is clear that he believed in the rightness of racial rule; influenced by a historicist conception of race, he questioned neither the distinction made between the civilized European and the savage Native nor the legitimacy of the former ruling over the latter. And, as Harris shows, he firmly believed that the future of Aboriginal peoples lay in their assimilation into a more advanced white settler society.

After Douglas' retirement in 1864, control over Indian land policy fell into the hands of officials who had much less understanding of, and sympathy for, Indigenous peoples and cultures. Much of Douglas' approach to the Indian land question was cast aside: most immediately, the larger reserves he had allocated were reduced in size, and the right of Aboriginal peoples to pre-empt land was withdrawn (while the pre-emption rights of white colonists were simultaneously expanded). The new approach to dealing with the Indian land question was shaped by a small group of white settlers who, perhaps reflecting more of the naturalist conception of race, viewed Indigenous people as little better than primitive wanderers with little real connection to the land – apart from their village sites, cultivated fields, and burial grounds – let alone any claim to jurisdiction over more extensive territories. Rather than serving, as Douglas saw them, as a temporary space of refuge for Indigenous peoples while they made the difficult journey into becoming part of settler society, Indian reserves under this new regime were to become spaces of confinement, places to house a dying culture. Under the leadership of Joseph Trutch, the commissioner of lands and works, colonial officials sought to minimize the space allocated to Indian reserves and maximize the land made available to settler society.

There is neither space nor need to describe here in any detail the highly unequal division of land produced in British Columbia through the Indian reserve system. Harris (2002) describes this project, spanning some seventy years and involving decades of wrangling between federal and provincial authorities, in great detail. By the time it was complete, in the mid-1920s, a tiny part of British Columbia had been set aside for Aboriginal communities

– about 340,000 hectares of land, or approximately one-third of 1 percent of the province's land area, scattered across some fifteen hundred reserves – with the rest of the province established as Crown land and open for white settlement and development. The line separating Indian reserves from the rest of the province, argues Harris (ibid., xviii), became the "primal line on the land in British Columbia, the one that facilitated or constrained all others." This was a profound and durable boundary, across which inclined steep gradients with respect to socio-economic status, civil and political rights, and the law.

Harris notes that the production of this colonial geography was a decidedly asymmetrical process, not only in the unequal division of land but also in terms of how Indian reserves were laid out, with Indigenous peoples having little real say in the demarcation of these spaces. This is not to say that they did not resist the taking of their lands; they certainly did, employing tactics ranging from peaceful petition to violent rebellion, but were effectively marginalized and pushed aside at nearly every turn (Harris 2004). In the early decades of the twentieth century, for example, First Nations in British Columbia began to seek justice on the land question through Canadian courts, often relying on the services of white lawyers. In 1927, however, in an effort to forestall any further Indigenous resistance in the legal sphere, the federal government amended the Indian Act to make it illegal for Aboriginal people to raise or accept funds for work on land claims, a measure that effectively barred them from engaging legal counsel or even organizing in support of their claims. As Tennant (1990, 113) writes about this point in BC history when the Indian reserve system had been fully mapped out and Indigenous legal challenges closed off, "From the white perspective, the Indian land question in British Columbia had been resolved."

Aboriginal Rights and Modern Treaty Making

In retrospect, of course, the Indian land question had clearly not been resolved – and certainly not in the minds of British Columbia's Indigenous people. After the Indian Act was amended in 1951, removing the section that had prohibited them from raising or accepting money for land claims activity, the Indian land question quickly came to the fore again. Particularly important during this period, and what would become a key strategy in the decades to come, was the focus on using the courts to assert Aboriginal claims to jurisdiction over lands and resources. Throughout more than four decades, starting with *R. v. White and Bob* (1964), which provided the first tentative judicial recognition of Aboriginal title, and continuing through to the present day, First Nations have used the courts to pursue recognition of their rights to lands and resources, and more broadly, to self-determination. Over this period, court rulings have established a legal recognition that Aboriginal title and rights continue to exist in British Columbia. These judgments functioned, initially, to undermine, and then later to dismiss altogether, long-standing arguments advanced by provincial officials that denied the validity of any Aboriginal claims to territory. Through these court actions, in concert with other resistance strategies, First Nation activists have slowly but surely dismantled a central pillar of the province's white settler mythology – namely, the idea that Indigenous peoples have no serious legal claim to lands outside of the limited Indian reserves that were allocated to them during the late nineteenth and early twentieth centuries.

The undercutting of this settler narrative, and of the Crown's denial of any form of Indigenous jurisdiction over territory, eventually convinced both the federal and provincial governments of the need to sit down with First Nations and seek a resolution of the Indian land question. Ottawa was the first to relent. After the Supreme Court decision in the *Calder* (1973) case provided clear recognition of Aboriginal title under Canadian law, Canada moved to establish the federal comprehensive claims commission, which would allow for the negotiation of Aboriginal land claims in areas of Canada, including much of British Columbia, that were not covered by treaties. The BC government, on the other hand, continued its policy of denying the existence of Aboriginal title well into the mid-1980s until a series of Indigenous blockades and associated court victories – the opposition to logging at Meares Island by the Nuu-chah-nulth in 1984 and by the Haida at Lyell Island in 1985 being the most important and high-profile actions – posed a major threat to its ability to plan and approve resource extraction activities across much of the province (Blomley 1996).[3] By the end of the 1980s, the provincial government had joined Ottawa in concluding that the Indian land question had not in fact been resolved and could no longer be ignored.

In 1990 the BC Claims Task Force was created – a body with representation from Victoria, Ottawa, and leading Aboriginal groups in British Columbia – and given the assignment of discovering a solution to the land question. The task force released its findings in 1991, acknowledging that the land issue was central to the historic conflict between "aboriginal and non-aboriginal societies" in the province and that Indigenous land claims needed to be resolved. What was needed, the task force argued, was a "political and legal reconciliation between aboriginal and non-aboriginal societies" in BC (British Columbia Claims Task Force 1991, 4). This reconciliation was to come through the development of a "new relationship" between Indigenous peoples and the federal and provincial governments, one that would be based on recognition and respect for "First Nations as self-determining and distinct nations" whose "traditional territories are their homelands" (ibid., 7).[4] The development of this new relationship would require that the conflicting territorial interests of First Nations, through the claim to Aboriginal title, and of the Crown, through its claim to sovereignty, be reconciled. What was needed, in other words, was not simply a new relationship and a reconciliation in legal and political terms but also a reconciliation in a spatial or territorial sense.

The task force argued that the path to reconciliation lay through the negotiation of modern comprehensive treaties, negotiations that would deal not only with the central issue of jurisdiction over land and natural resources but also with questions of Aboriginal self-government, the provision of government services, and financial support for First Nation governments and communities.[5] The task force recommended the creation of a tripartite treaty negotiation process, involving Canada, British Columbia, and First Nations, with Indigenous participation in the negotiation process to be entirely voluntary and self-directed. In addition to reconciliation, a central goal in the BC treaty process was to be the achievement of "certainty" in the natural resource sector – that is, to create legal clarity about who owns and has jurisdiction over land and resources in the province. Although the task force noted that this was of interest to all parties, the achievement of what might be called territorial certainty was of particular immediate interest to the BC government. In a province highly dependent on natural resource extraction – especially of timber, minerals, petroleum resources, and fish – the BC government needed the assurance that its land and resource development plans could be implemented and would not be blocked by Aboriginal protest or court action (Woolford 2005).

As the BC treaty process was being developed, federal and provincial officials advocated for an approach to achieving certainty based on the "cede, surrender, and release" model: here, Indigenous peoples would agree to the extinguishment of their Aboriginal title claim in most of their traditional territory, which would give the Crown the certainty it desired. In exchange for surrendering their claim to a larger territory, First Nations would gain ownership and some level of jurisdiction over a smaller portion of it, in what are typically called "treaty settlement lands." This approach in some ways resembles a complex real estate transaction whereby an Aboriginal group's traditional territory is subdivided into two distinct subterritories, one in which the First Nation holds primary jurisdiction and one in which Crown sovereignty prevails and where, with the burden of Aboriginal title removed, non-Aboriginal governments can operate freely.

Although the cede, surrender, and release model was attractive to the Crown, it was anathema to many Indigenous people. Chief Edward John of the First Nations Summit, a group that represents the interests of First Nations engaged in the BC treaty process, described the difficulty that Indigenous people had with this approach: "When government asks us to agree to surrender our title and agree to its extinguishment, they ask us to do away with our most basic sense of ourselves, and our relationship to the Creator, our territory and the other peoples of the worlds. We could no longer do that without agreeing that we no longer wish to exist as a distinct people. That is completely at odds with our intentions in negotiating treaties" (quoted in McKee 2000, 72).

Here, it is clear that First Nation and Crown parties to the treaty negotiation process have much different perceptions of Aboriginal title. Whereas the former understand it as something inseparable from a larger Indigenous identity, the latter see it as little more than "a collection of quasi-property entitlements ... that can be traded once and for all to the Crown in return for treaty-based rights with respect to land governed by the treaty" (McKee 2000, 72). For Aboriginal peoples, Chief John and other First Nation leaders argue, treaties should provide for a clear recognition of Aboriginal title rather than its extinguishment. Precisely because of such reasoning, the BC Claims Task Force had counselled against the adoption of an approach to treaty making that required the extinguishment of Aboriginal title.

To achieve certainty without resort to extinguishment, a second approach was proposed, what Mark Stevenson (2001, 126-27) refers to as the "exhaustive definition" model of treaty making. This necessitates the description, in exhaustive detail, of all the rights that the Indigenous group would come to possess with the signing of the treaty, including the geographic extent of those rights and their various limitations. Through this model, Aboriginal title and rights would be "modified" – once the treaty was signed and ratified by all parties – into treaty rights, which would then come to be protected under section 35 of the Canadian Constitution. Although this approach makes no reference to the extinguishment of Aboriginal title, it nonetheless requires that First Nations agree to "release" (that is, to not pursue) any claim to Aboriginal rights not specifically defined in the treaty agreement. Under this model, Indigenous peoples also agree to release the Crown from any "claims, demands, actions, or proceedings, of whatever kind" related to the past infringement of their Aboriginal rights (Canada, British Columbia, and Nisga'a Nation 1999, 21). These modification and release clauses are contained in the 1999 Nisga'a Final Agreement, the first modern-day treaty signed in British Columbia, and this general "modify and release" approach has been adopted by the Crown in the BC treaty process.

Although the modify and release model makes no reference to the extinguishment of Aboriginal title, one can argue that the effect is much the same. The end result of a treaty under this model, in other words, is the division of an Indigenous group's larger traditional territory into two distinct subterritories, one composed of treaty settlement lands predominantly under First Nation control and one in which Crown sovereignty is unimpeded by any claims to Aboriginal rights and title. It must be noted at this point that the division of these territories into distinct Crown and First Nation subterritories is highly asymmetrical: the Crown seeks to make this division based on a formula in which it would be allocated approximately 95 percent of the territory, and the First Nation would receive the rest (McKee 2000, 70).[6] This formula, which federal and provincial negotiators have shown little inclination to stray from, has certainly been one of the main stumbling blocks to the finalization of treaties under the BC process.

By early 2011, after almost eighteen years of negotiation at some four dozen treaty tables across the province, and after the investment of well over $1 billion in the process, only two (relatively small) treaty agreements had been finalized. At one level, this lack of progress can be traced to the Crown's formulaic and inflexible approach to treaty making, as well as the meagre land and cash offers that have been extended by federal and provincial negotiators to Indigenous communities. For most First Nations engaged in the process, what is being offered – about 5 percent of their traditional territory, approximately $40,000 in cash per member of the nation, certain limited self-government powers, and assorted other benefits – is simply not enough to entice them to cede their claim and attachments to their larger territories and to surrender, as Ed John put it, this integral part of their Indigenous identities.[7]

Conflicting Understandings of Reconciliation
The difficulties of the BC treaty process may also be traced to fundamentally different understandings of what the treaty-making process is about and

how reconciliation, a central objective of treaty making, is to be achieved. For the Crown, it seems, the process is primarily a way of redrawing the province's "primal line," the line drawn, via the historical process of mapping out the Indian reserve system, to clearly delineate and separate Indigenous space from the space that would be occupied by members of settler society. Given the contemporary need, as directed by the courts, for the Crown to address the recognition of Aboriginal title, this redrawing of the old line would allow somewhat more space for Indigenous peoples than has been the case so far; full implementation of the treaty model, based on the current formula, would see the allocation of about 5.0 percent of the province's land base to First Nations, a significant increase from the 0.3 percent currently allotted to Indian reserves. Nonetheless, the spatial division of the province would remain highly lopsided. Moreover, this unequal division aside, the Crown's intent through the treaty process remains largely unchanged from that of the colonial Indian reserve system; to demarcate and maintain clearly separate spaces for Aboriginal peoples while at the same time keeping them firmly under Crown rule. In the post-treaty world, despite these separate spaces, Indigenous peoples would remain fully within the juridical-political bounds of the Canadian state.

As Jim Tully (2001) points out, there is another way of understanding the treaty-making process, one that is more attractive to many Indigenous peoples. From this alternative perspective, he argues, treaty making is seen as being not so much about defining Aboriginal title and rights in exhaustive detail and negotiating a complex real estate transaction, but rather as a way of determining how to share land, resources, and jurisdictions in their traditional territories. For many First Nations, he notes, the purpose of treaties is "to work out relations of *mutual sharing* among equal and co-existing partners" (ibid., 10, emphasis in original). A shift to this way of understanding the treaty process has spatial implications: rather than dividing a First Nation's territory into distinct and separate subterritories, Indigenous on one side of the line and Crown on the other, treaties could serve to explore ways that Aboriginal title and Crown sovereignty could co-exist and overlap within the same territory. This approach would allow Indigenous communities to maintain some degree of control over, and connection to, a much larger portion (if not all) of their traditional lands; this control or connection need not mean full control or ownership of land and resources, but rather some form of shared jurisdiction with the Crown. This approach, which holds considerable appeal for many First Nations, is something that, to this point, the Crown has seemed loath to consider.

Tully argues that the Crown and First Nations also seem to have very different ideas about reconciliation and how this might be achieved in the treaty process. For the Crown, he states, reconciliation is typically seen as coming through a "full and final settlement" of Aboriginal title and rights, which is achieved with the signing of a final agreement between the treaty negotiating parties (Tully 2001, 13). Seen in this way, reconciliation is something that is achieved at the signing of the treaty agreement, and once this is done, the treaty process – and any reconciliation efforts associated with it – is brought to a speedy conclusion. As one Indigenous observer suggested, the notion of reconciliation embodied in the Crown's model is more like a divorce than a marriage (Blackburn 2007, 627). An alternative approach, one that Tully sees as more attractive to many Indigenous groups, is to view reconciliation as an ongoing process of engagement and discussion, and a way to build new relationships. From this perspective, rather than being completed and then set in stone, treaties become living documents subject to review and renewal as conditions change and relationships develop. The emphasis in this understanding of reconciliation is on co-existence, on learning about each other and how to live together in the same place. In this way, the reconciliation of Aboriginal title and Crown sovereignty, a central goal of treaty negotiations, becomes just one aspect of a broader project of reconciliation.

It should be noted that though the BC treaty process is the main, and most long-standing, instrument for seeking reconciliation between Indigenous peoples and British Columbia's settler society, it is no longer the only one. In 2005, with the treaty process bogged down and First Nations increasingly frustrated by the lack of progress in resolving their land and territorial concerns, the provincial government – led by Premier Gordon Campbell – committed itself to developing a "new relationship" with Indigenous peoples in British Columbia. Provincial and Indigenous leaders developed a vision document that spelled out, in broad strokes, what this relationship would look like. According to this document, the new relationship was to be based on "respect, recognition and accommodation of aboriginal title and rights" (British Columbia 2005, 1). Furthermore, the right to Aboriginal title was to be recognized "in its full form," which was to include "the inherent right of the community to make decisions as to the use of the land" (ibid.). The new relationship was also to be on a "government-to-government" basis, with the parties committing themselves to the "reconciliation of Aboriginal and Crown titles and jurisdictions." Finally, the parties to this vision agreed to "establish processes and institutions for shared decision-making about the land and resources and for revenue and benefit sharing" (ibid.).[8]

With its clear recognition of Aboriginal title "in its full form" and its commitment to a government-to-government relationship and to shared decision making and revenue sharing on land and resource use, this vision addressed many of the key points that Indigenous leaders had long been pushing for. Given this, it is hardly surprising that the new relationship statement was warmly welcomed by most Indigenous leaders in the province; indeed, many viewed it as a critical breakthrough and as the most important policy statement on Aboriginal issues ever to come from the provincial government. Many prominent Indigenous leaders, including several who had been highly critical of Campbell and his government, heaped praise on the premier.[9] Although the words in the new relationship statement were welcomed, the more material effects of this initiative have been slow in coming. The government has demonstrated a greater respect for First Nations in symbolic form – for example, it appointed Steven Point, an important member of the Sto:lo Nation, as lieutenant governor – and has brought forward a number of projects designed to improve the lives of Indigenous people, including a few that provide First Nation communities with greater access to lands and resources, as well as a share in the revenues generated from their development. The gains accruing from the new relationship vision, however, have been modest at best, and importantly, the initiative seems to have had little if any impact on the treaty process. By early 2011, the extent to which the ambitious goals set out in the new relationship vision could be accomplished was unclear, and many of the Indigenous leaders who had greeted the new relationship initiative with such warmth found themselves questioning whether anything had really changed.

Conclusion

British Columbia was founded and constructed on the principles of racial rule. It was built on an unquestioned belief in the superiority of Europeans and the inferiority of non-Europeans – from which naturally flowed the imperative that the former should rule over the latter. Indeed, as Goldberg (2002a) points out, racial rule is predicated on the belief that non-Europeans are incapable of governing themselves and their territories, and therefore must be ruled over. In British Columbia, these ideas about race underpinned the colonial project and legitimized the appropriation of Indigenous lands and the construction of separate spaces – Indian reserves –

for Indigenous peoples and cultures. Both the naturalist and historicist conceptions of race are evident in the discourses and actions of settler officials in early colonial and post-colonial British Columbia. For James Douglas and like-minded officials, Aboriginal subjects possessed the potential for civilized life, but this was to be achieved only through assimilation into settler society. By the mid-1860s, however, Douglas and those who shared his views were marginalized by colonial officials who saw little of redeeming human value in Indigenous peoples and who worked (with considerable success) to confine them permanently to small patches of land and to deprive them of the rights enjoyed by settlers. The next century would be characterized by continuous denial that Aboriginal peoples had any rights to land or to self-determination, beyond what settler society had allotted them through the Indian reserve system and the Indian Act.

British Columbia's settler society invested considerable energy in the production of the province as a white space. Thus, in the Douglas treaties, it was specified that the land was to become "the Entire property of the *White* people for ever" (Duff 1969, 11, emphasis added). At the same time that Douglas was purchasing Aboriginal land to be possessed by "White people for ever," he was also asserting the Crown's possession of Indigenous territory that had not been ceded by treaty. For example, in a speech given to a group of Cowichan people in 1853 – while leading a military expedition into unceded Cowichan territory in pursuit of an Indigenous man suspected of killing a white shepherd – Douglas informed his audience that "the whole of their country was a possession of the British crown" (quoted in Arnett 1999, 43).[10] In this way, at this early stage of the colonization process, the Crown was directly linked to a particular racial category – white – and its assertion of sovereignty over this place can be interpreted as the simultaneous assertion of white sovereignty. British Columbia was thus confidently defined as a white possession, and the confinement of Aboriginal groups to tiny "postage-stamp" reserves served to put the idea of white sovereignty into effect. However, rather than seeking to codify the white possession of Indigenous territories through resort to formal legal declaration, as James Douglas had done with land purchase agreements or treaties, white political authorities in the late nineteenth and through most of the twentieth century simply denied the existence of any valid Aboriginal claims to land.

Writing in the Australian context, Aileen Moreton-Robinson (2007) notes that what she calls "patriarchal white sovereignty" in that country is based on illegally taking possession of Indigenous territory and is dependent on the continuing denial of Aboriginal sovereignty. Moreton-Robinson (ibid., 88) argues further that patriarchal white sovereignty is a regime of power, which "operates ideologically, materially and discursively to reproduce and maintain its investment in the nation as a white possession." Elsewhere, Moreton-Robinson (2006, 384) has suggested that white sovereignty or white possession functions as a mode of rationality "within disciplinary knowledges and regulatory mechanisms, defining and circumscribing Indigenous sovereignty in particular ways." In post-colonial settler societies such as Australia and Canada, in other words, Indigenous sovereignty has been defined and limited within a narrow juridical-political framework of Western notions of law, rights, and sovereignty. Despite the seeming progress made in the court decisions – in both Canada and Australia – that recognize certain Aboriginal title and rights, these legal judgments continue to define these rights as subject to the Crown or the state, as subject, in fact, to white sovereignty. Such legal recognition falls far short of any fuller or more fundamental understanding of Indigenous sovereignty. Moreton-Robinson (2007, 4) argues that what Indigenous people have been given "by way of white benevolence" is a "white-constructed form of 'indigenous' proprietary rights that are not epistemologically and ontologically grounded in indigenous conceptions of sovereignty. Indigenous land ownership, under these legislative regimes, amounts to little more than a mode of land tenure that enables a circumscribed form of autonomy and governance with minimum control and ownership of resources, on or below the ground, thus entrenching economic dependence on the nation state." In this way, Western legal discourse tends to reproduce Indigenous peoples as colonial subjects.

Writing on the self-determination struggles of Indigenous peoples in Canada, Glen Coulthard (2007) echoes Moreton-Robinson's arguments. In Canada, Coulthard states, the past three decades of Indigenous self-determination aspirations have been largely shaped and contained within a liberal rights discourse, focused on the recognition of a limited set of specific rights related to self-government and treaties, as well as the right to occupy and use certain lands and resources. He suggests that this contemporary "politics of recognition" serves to reproduce "the very configurations of colonial power that Indigenous demands for recognition have historically sought to transcend" (ibid., 437). Recognition of Indigenous peoples and their rights has been limited and constrained by the state – especially by courts and by policy makers – so as to preserve the status quo. Even though courts and policy makers in Canada have recognized Aboriginal title and rights in certain ways, Coulthard (ibid., 451) emphasizes that this recognition fails to challenge "the racist origin of Canada's assumed sovereign authority over indigenous peoples and their territories." That is, this politics of recognition fails to confront the fundamental tenets of racial rule.

Tightly bound up in the politics of recognition and embedded in the legal discourse of Aboriginal rights and title, British Columbia's reconciliation project functions to contain or manage the problem posed by the open-ended Indian land question. Indigenous assertions of jurisdiction and sovereignty over ancestral territories, beginning anew in the 1960s and gathering strength in the decades since, have posed a serious threat to the Crown's ability to unilaterally govern the province's lands and resources, and to maintain resource revenue flows. This challenge to Crown sovereignty and to the province's prevailing development model, one predicated on the unrestricted extraction and export of natural resources, had to be addressed. With the reconciliation of Aboriginal title and Crown sovereignty as a central goal, the treaty process has served as an effective instrument for the Crown to manage and contain this threat in several ways. First, it has enabled the Crown to continue the exploitation of natural resources, albeit in a somewhat more restricted context, while treaty negotiations drag on. Second, it has allowed for the Crown to draw Indigenous peoples into the resource economy, as junior partners with the Crown and with corporations that seek to profit from resource exploitation.

Although the Crown's efforts to shape the treaty process so as to contain and constrain Indigenous claims to territory have been evident from the start, they were perhaps most visible during the Campbell government's first term in office as it pushed for a province-wide referendum on the treaty process. This referendum, held in the spring of 2002, was described as an attempt to establish a set of principles supported by a majority of the public that would guide treaty negotiations. Voters were asked to respond with a simple "yes" or "no" to eight statements that addressed a number of key issues or concerns related to treaty making, including whether private land and private interests on Crown land (forest tenures, water licences) should be subject to treaty negotiations and whether existing Crown land and resource uses (fishing, hunting, enjoyment of parks) should be maintained "for all British Columbians" (British Columbia 2002). The referendum also asked whether "Aboriginal self-government should have the characteristics of a local government, with powers delegated from Canada and British Columbia" (ibid.). Not surprisingly, the vast majority of those who completed and returned their ballots – about 36 percent of those eligible to vote in the referendum actually did so – indicated support for the eight statements. As David Rossiter and Patricia Wood (2005) point out, at root the referendum was about confining the treaty process and Indigenous claims to territory within a neo-liberal frame that gave precedence to private economic interests and capital accumulation.[11]

The treaty-making process, and British Columbia's official reconciliation project more broadly, has also functioned to draw Indigenous peoples into the legal and political mainstream. In her analysis of the reconciliation discourse in the negotiation of the Nisga'a treaty, for example, Carole Blackburn (2007) argues that Nisga'a Aboriginal title and rights, and Nisga'a identity (which is tied to these territorial rights), were transformed or modified in such a way as to be made compatible with the legal and political structures of the Canadian state.[12] Through the existing treaty model, more expansive and flexible understandings of Aboriginal title and rights – and Indigenous sovereignty – are fixed in place, and are in fact formalized within section 35 of the Canadian Constitution. In this way, Indigenous claims to land and resources are neatly "folded back into the parameters of the state" (Bhandar 2004). Interestingly, while the treaty process exhibits this tendency toward the incorporation or assimilation of Indigenous subjects into the Canadian and British Columbian legal and political body, it simultaneously seeks to re-establish a line between Indigenous peoples and contemporary settler society. This line is spatial, reflected in the mapping out – or, more accurately, the remapping – of separate Indigenous spaces, which remain nonetheless politically and legally subordinate to the more extensive and overriding Crown jurisdiction. The line is also re-established or reaffirmed around a particular Indigenous identity, still subjected to the Crown but now also a marker of a new and somewhat expanded set of territorial and monetary benefits and costs, to be dispensed and demanded by the state. This tendency toward both assimilation and segregation marks an ambivalence at the heart of racial rule, a desire to both fold Indigenous peoples into settler society and to hold them apart.

British Columbia's official reconciliation project, then, is a deeply racialized process that seeks to reconfirm and reassert the basic structures of racial rule set in place during the nineteenth century: the superiority of European peoples, the inferiority of Indigenous peoples, the "natural" ruling of the former over the latter, and the imperative of assimilating Indigenous peoples and subjectivities into a white settler state. To say that this project is racialized is not to suggest that it actually neatly divides peoples and spaces along clear racial lines; it doesn't, and racialization should be understood as a messy and contradictory process. In contemporary British Columbia, the lines between Indigenous and settler spaces and subjectivities are clearly as blurred today as they have ever been, not least by the presence of a large urban Indigenous population, and the idea of BC as a white province is troubled by an increasingly multicultural citizenry. To a great extent, however, the structures of white sovereignty remain largely in place, perhaps most visible in the continuing dominance of white faces in key centres of political and economic power. If British Columbia's contemporary settler society is more open and accepting of Indigenous claims and subjectivities – it is now common, for example, to see white political leaders happily don traditional Indigenous clothing during ceremonies celebrating the latest Aboriginal political or economic agreement – this shift has taken place on terms that ultimately do not threaten the stability of white sovereignty.

Indigenous sovereignty, in the larger sense of the word – encompassing, among other things, a First Nation's ability and right to fully govern itself and its territory – continues to be denied under the Crown's notion of reconciliation. British Columbia's reconciliation project does allow for the recognition of a set of more limited Indigenous rights, reflected in the political and legal acknowledgment that Aboriginal title and rights do exist, and it encourages the reconciliation of these rights *to* Crown sovereignty, which itself remains unchallenged and is reaffirmed. As Fiona Nicoll (2004, 17-18) states, the "semantic ambivalence" of the term "reconciliation" proves useful to the project of limiting recognition of Indigenous sovereignty – "reconciling with" and "reconciling to" mean two very different things. The former indicates the harmonious bringing together of two equal bodies, whereas the latter indicates a resignation or submission of one group or person to another. "As a consequence," Nicoll notes, "reconciliation is conducive to parallel conversations conducted at cross-purposes that usually deliver power and resources to the colonial party."

In concluding, I stress that I am not arguing that some sort of reconciliation is impossible or, indeed, is not already under way. Rather, my central point is that the official reconciliation project shaped by the Crown falls far short of what is needed to dismantle the regime of racial rule upon which British Columbia is founded and the relations of domination inherent to this construction. Nor does it create possibilities for Indigenous peoples to be fully engaged in governing themselves and their territories. Ultimately, resolution of the Indian land question will come only through a more expansive and mutual project of reconciliation, one that allows for the recognition and consideration of a much wider range of perspectives and approaches.

Changing Land Tenure, Defining Subjects
Neo-Liberalism and Property Regimes on Native Reserves

JESSICA DEMPSEY, KEVIN GOULD,
AND JUANITA SUNDBERG

The "colonial present" is alive and well in Canada. The United Nations Development Index consistently ranks Canada among the top ten states, yet First Nations communities in Canada compare with many countries from the global South (Assembly of First Nations n.d.). One out of four First Nations children lives in poverty, whereas for non–First Nations Canadian children this ratio is one in six. These discrepancies are compounded by the fact that non-Aboriginal Canadians earn almost twice the annual income of Aboriginal people. This situation led the UN Office of the High Commission on Human Rights' Committee on Economic, Social and Cultural Rights to criticize the Canadian government for its deplorable record on First Nations' poverty. In 1998 the committee called for an urgent national strategy on the issue, and in 2006, it expressed serious concern about Canada's lack of progress on First Nations poverty (CESCR 2006). At the same time, a number of recent Supreme Court verdicts have challenged the legacy of colonial history in Canada. Through a stream of rulings on Aboriginal rights and title, such as Supreme Court decisions in *Delgamuukw* (1997) and *Haida* (2004), and the December 2007 BC Supreme Court decision known as *Xeni Gwet'in,* or the *William* decision, the courts have clarified the Canadian government's legal responsibilities to First Nations. However, as Glen Coulthard (2007, 451) states, "even though the Court has secured an unprecedented degree of protection for certain 'cultural' practices within the state, it has nonetheless repeatedly refused to challenge the racist origin of Canada's assumed sovereign authority over Indigenous peoples and their territories" (see also Alfred 2005).

The Canadian government has been inconsistent in its efforts to address these ongoing inequalities. Stephen Harper's Conservative government rejected the Kelowna Accords, which would have invested $5 billion in First Nations communities over ten years. Yet the former premier of British Columbia, Gordon Campbell, recently reversed his government's position on First Nations relations by moving toward a policy of reconciliation. In March 2009, the Campbell government announced it would introduce recognition and reconciliation legislation that would finally acknowledge Aboriginal title within the province. The main Aboriginal institution in the province, the Union of BC Indian Chiefs, welcomed this move (UBCIC 2009), although only a couple of days afterward, the government and First Nations leadership decided to postpone the initiative. At the same time, Aboriginal scholars such as Glen Coulthard (2007) draw attention to the colonial logics in such "politics of recognition."

It is within these contradictions of the colonial present that Tom Flanagan, who is a professor of political science at the University of Alberta, a senior fellow with the conservative think-tank the Fraser Institute, and a close advisor to Canada's prime minister, Stephen Harper, has put forth a proposal to address "Aboriginal self-determination" and poverty reduction. In conjunction with his colleague, University of Toronto political science professor Christopher Alcantara, Flanagan has penned a series of academic and policy papers (Flanagan and Alcantara 2002, 2004, 2005) advocating the expansion of *private* property rights in land on Indian reserves. They frame these rights as "a necessary ... precondition to attaining widespread prosperity" there (Flanagan and Alcantara 2002, 4). Although these authors build their arguments around case law and oral testimony from particular First Nations territories, their work maintains an unwavering and overarching faith that "collective property is the path to poverty, and private property is the path to prosperity" (ibid., 16). Most recently, in 2010 Flanagan, Alcantara, and André Le Dressay published *Beyond the Indian Act: Restoring Aboriginal Property Rights,* in which they propose a First Nations Property Ownership Act. Some Aboriginal people are allied with Flanagan and Alcantara. Manny Jules, head of the First Nations Tax Commission and former Secwepemc band chief, has emerged as the leading Aboriginal proponent of reserve land privatization. However, Aboriginal leaders such as former chief Art Manuel have strongly opposed these new proposals (Manuel 2010; see also Coulthard 2007).

We do not attempt to determine whether Flanagan and Alcantara's proposal will or will not help to end systems marginalizing First Nations; those decisions lie with others. Nor do we wish to idealize life on contemporary reserves. Rather, our intention is to complicate the smoothness of Flanagan and Alcantara's policy narrative and in so doing, develop a counter-narrative that refuses the self-evidence of private property rights discourse and foregrounds the historical geographies of First Nations peoples.

Flanagan and Alcantara's proposal to promote private property on reserves is framed as a transparent and self-evident reform intended to give First Nations people living there the freedom to participate in the marketplace, a freedom that, they argue, is available to all *other* Canadians. This chapter examines how Flanagan and Alcantara's suggestion is rendered intelligible, desirable, and potentially implementable in Canada. Specifically, we explore how their proposal articulates with national imaginaries of land and citizen, and we examine how neo-liberal debates about property rights on Aboriginal reserves articulate with the construction of whiteness in Canada. To do so, we analyze the discursive practices through which Flanagan and Alcantara draw boundaries around appropriate land management regimes and subjects, and how these, in turn, script other forms as inappropriate. Such boundary-making practices are built on hegemonic and normative models of land management and subjectivities, which, we argue, are entwined with ongoing colonial processes of whitening. For instance, as we detail below, appropriate land management regimes for Flanagan and Alcantara are those that facilitate the acquisition of credit, and the ideal Canadian subject is one who is self-sufficient and enterprising, and who never demands special rights based on history/geography/culture. Far from universal, these racialized conceptions of human-land relations and subjectivity now articulate through neo-liberal technologies of inclusion that invite First Nations individuals to become *equal* with other Canadians by becoming property-owning entrepreneurial citizens. Such a shallow sense of equality, we suggest, is made possible only by a complete bracketing of historical geographies of dispossession. We conclude that this policy seeks to manage heightened claims for Aboriginal self-determination, especially those demanding increased redistribution of wealth toward First Nations people (transfer payments and land) and full recognition of Aboriginal rights and title, which would increase both decision-making powers and autonomy on traditional territories and First Nations' ability to collect resource rent/royalties (see, for example, Royal Commission on Aboriginal Peoples 1996; *New Socialist* 2006; websites of the Union of BC Indian Chiefs and Assembly of First Nations).

Some might argue that Flanagan and Alcantara's proposal should be dismissed as right-wing ideological positioning; however, we take it seriously as it reflects and advances an increasingly popular neo-liberal program. Indeed, two developments in the past few years demonstrate that the logic underlying this scheme is becoming naturalized in Canadian law and policy. First, in April 2007, the Conservative government established a $300 million fund that encourages individual home ownership on reserves. Second, as well as influencing policy, ideas similar to those of Flanagan and Alcantara circulate widely in the media. For instance, from 19 January to 20 February 2008, the *National Post* (Toronto) ran a series of articles titled "Rethinking the Reserve," which focused on "aboriginals who are finding creative, often market-driven ways out of the dependency trap." The subtitle of Part 1 read "Real Warriors Hold a Job" (Libin 2008a, A1); the headline of Part 2 was "Shackled by Red Tape" (Libin 2008b, A1). These headlines and the accompanying articles fit neatly alongside the policies articulated by Flanagan and Alcantara, as both have a similar neo-liberal vision for reserves, one focused on creating the conditions for proper markets in both land and labour as a way out of poverty and dependency, and into "self-sufficiency." The current federal government also appears to share this vision, as indicated in a 2008 interview with Chuck Strahl, who was then minister of Indian and Northern Affairs Canada (Strahl 2008).

In this context, we find it imperative to formulate a critical counter-discourse that points to the ways in which neo-liberal technologies of inclusion – in this case, private property rights – articulate with and further colonial practices of whitening, potentially constraining the possibilities for Indigenous sovereignty and autonomy.[1]

Colonial Imaginaries and Neo-liberal Environmental Formations

In this section, we present Flanagan and Alcantara's argument in more detail and outline our approach in analyzing it. To this end, we first describe how the two authors have positioned and supported their proposal to expand private property rights on reserves. We then describe the analytical framework through which we interpret their project. The objective of our analysis is to understand how Flanagan and Alcantara's proposal is made commonsensical and even seductive in Canada.

Private Property for All

In advocating for expanded private property rights on reserves, Flanagan and Alcantara (2002, 2004, 2005) argue that such a measure will help alleviate poverty and allow First Nations people to become more productive members of Canadian society. The authors (2002) contextualize their enthusiastic embrace of private property rights on reserves in relation to the "end of history" interpretations of Cold War geopolitics, which they also see as a triumph of private property. They write, "Communist polities either collapsed (the USSR) or reformed themselves by introducing major elements of private property (China)" (ibid., 4). Going on, they cite private-property-rights advocate Richard Pipes, himself referencing the fall of communism: "The benefits of private ownership for both liberty and prosperity are acknowledged as they had not been in nearly two hundred years" (Pipes 1999, 63, quoted in ibid.). In this context, they equate First Nations land tenure arrangements with these outdated communist models to substantiate the argument that First Nations property regimes are in need of transformation. They also present their proposal in relation to the ostensible success of a specific property rights approach to development in the global South. Noting the "success" of development programs that distribute state-sanctioned property rights to poor people throughout the South, they suggest that the same approach will be successful in Canada. Hence, First Nations reserves are equated with the global South and therefore are considered appropriate targets for development policies that (supposedly) have been successful there.

Having positioned their proposal in this way, Flanagan and Alcantara (2002, 2004, 2005) present empirical analyses of current property arrangements on reserves, which they base on case law and interview testimony. Such arrangements, they note, are complex, not simply "communal." The point of their research is to study "the embryonic systems of private property now existing on reserves to see how they can be expanded and perfected" (Flanagan and Alcantara 2004, 494). These social scientific descriptions of tenure arrangements on reserves function as a kind baseline data for a policy that would seek to transform these arrangements. To counter potential critiques that private property would be an imposition on reserves, the two authors draw from what they describe as "not widely known" studies suggesting that private property existed as a part of pre-conquest First Nations culture (for citations, see ibid.) and that where it exists in the present, economic productivity is enhanced (T.L. Anderson 1995). They note the benefits of "other" types of property, but their research and writing are permeated with a wholehearted belief that private property is the path to prosperity.

Environmental Formations

In order to analyze and critique Flanagan and Alcantara's seemingly simple and technical solutions to poverty on reserves, we frame private property regimes as an *environmental formation,* by which we mean a hegemonic and normative discourse that establishes appropriate and inappropriate conceptions of human-land relations and, by extension, standards for how land and subjects should be managed and/or governed.[2] Understanding private property as an environmental formation allows us to treat it as a set of historically contingent discursive practices that are productive of the territories and subjects of which they speak. To make sense of what is at stake politically in Flanagan and Alcantara's support for this particular environmental formation, we draw on key insights in the fields of political economy, governmentality, and post-colonial theory. For heuristic purposes, we address each field in turn, although they become intermingled in our analysis.

Flanagan and Alcantara's plan to establish private property on reserves makes perfect sense in the context of the neo-liberal policies pervasive in many parts of the world. Geographers have described neo-liberalism as a suite of political economic reforms associated with a turn to laissez-faire policies including rolling back state supports in social services and welfare, reducing taxation, privatizing government services such as education and health care, extending private property rights, liberalizing trade, and re-scaling governance (Peck and Tickell 2002; Harvey 2005; Heynen et al. 2007). In many instances, neo-liberal policies are strategies by corporations and the state to deal with crises of profitability and growth. Strands of these neo-liberal rationalities are manifest in Flanagan and Alcantara's work, and in Canadian governance more broadly (as in the downsizing of welfare and other government safety nets). Flanagan and Alcantara suggest that under the right conditions, reserve lands are sites for increased market efficiencies and private investment, and that if such efficiencies and private investment can be gained, First Nations can achieve increased self-sufficiency and reduce government dependency. Their proposal, then, is not simply about increasing efficiencies or creating increased value in First Nations land, but also a project that seeks to privatize reserve lands, make them more available to investment, and ultimately decrease government supports to First Nations people in Canada. Such a venture may be described as accumulation by dispossession (Harvey 2003; Glassman 2006). Indeed, the predominance of this type of economic thinking/practice in Canada, and elsewhere, is critical to making Flanagan and Alcantara's proposal so seductive and commonsensical. Of course First Nations need competitive and private land markets; of course they need to depend less on the government: how could it be otherwise?

At the same time, neo-liberalism is much more than a set of policies for obtaining economic efficiency or cutting people off government support. As Wendy Brown (2005, 38) argues, it is best understood as a political rationality that "both organizes these policies and reaches beyond the market." Brown (ibid., 39) suggests that the implications of neo-liberalism reach "from the soul of the citizen-subject to education policy to practices of empire." Following from this, she asserts that neo-liberalism is a normative and constructive project in that it involves developing institutional discourses and practices that produce the market as the central plank organizing all dimensions of human life (see also Dean 1999). Brown's approach to neo-liberalism is grounded in Michel Foucault's (1991) concept of governmentality, a neologism combining two terms: government and rationality. Foucault described government as "the conduct of conduct," or the art of regulating the conduct of individuals or collectives. He applied the term broadly to the management of states, to disciplinary institutions such as schools and factories, and to the individual (Gordon 1991, 2). Governmentality, then, refers to the formulation and organization of rationalities of government in this broad sense. Crucial to our project is the insight that "governing always involves particular representations, knowledges and expertises [rationalities] regarding that which is to be governed" (Larner and Walters 2004, 496). Paying attention to these representations is imperative because they do not merely describe the spaces and subjects to be governed. Rather, they are productive of spaces and subjects both epistemologically and ontologically in that governing rationalities help to constitute the targets of government. For instance, Nikolas Rose (1996, 1999) suggests that neo-liberal forms of governmentality are designed to produce normative subjects by shaping and inciting aspirations for self-management and self-actualization. Rose (1996, 158-60) calls this subject "the enterprising self," one who comports him- or herself rationally and prudently. Seen from this perspective, Flanagan and Alcantara's proposal seeks to produce particular kinds of First Nations subjects: property-owning entrepreneurial subject-citizens.

Building on Rose's work, Jonathan Inda (2006, 18) argues that constructions of ideal neo-liberal subjects simultaneously work to constitute a "realm of abjection." In other words, neo-liberal political rationalities and technologies "produce a division between active citizens and anti-prudential, unethical subjects, between a majority who can and do secure their own well-being through judicious self-promotion and those who are judged incapable of managing their own risks" (ibid.). In the case of the US, welfare recipients, the homeless, the poor, and undocumented immigrants are scripted as the abject. This is very much a racialized division, states Inda, for the figure of the prudential subject is a projection of the dominant white elites, whereas abject subjects are racialized minorities.

Inda's insights into the ways in which neo-liberal subjects are racialized leads us to a body of post-colonial and critical race scholarship emphasizing how space is racialized through specific legal practices (Kobayashi and Peake 2000; Pulido 2000; Razack 2002a; Mawani 2007). Although contemporary conceptions of private property are often represented as universal, they are outcomes of very particular philosophical and geographical histories (Blomley 2004). Private property was codified in the context of European colonialism, including in the Americas (Goldberg 1993; R. Williams 2000). Indeed, those serving imperial administrations (such as John Locke) defined property rights in specific ways to legitimate violent colonial processes of dispossession of Native peoples (Hulme 1990; K. Anderson 2007). Claims to universality mask the constitutive processes that make property – namely, its partiality and racialized origins. Private property, in other words, comes from somewhere and therefore embodies racialized assumptions regarding appropriate resource management, social relations, and the human subject.

As a hegemonic environmental formation, private property is one modality through which Canada was produced as a white settler society. Settlers travelled to Canada with notions of civilized land use and governance; as Cole Harris (2002, 267) explains, "most immigrants took a regime of private property rights, backed by the state, for granted ... These rights were assumed to be at the heart of a civilized society in which owners should be entitled to do what they wished with their lands: fence them, sell them, or evict trespassers." Private property became a key site through which First Nations peoples were racialized as uncivilized and inferior due to their apparent lack of this particular land management regime. As Harris (ibid., 268) notes, debates about land use, and private property in particular, were not only about the distribution of wealth, "nor even an argument between different economies, but rather a far more elemental, polarized, and characteristically racialized juxtaposition of civilization and savagery." The institutionalization of private property rights in Canada, therefore, was a crucial mechanism in colonial projects of whitening both space and subjects. In short, conceptions of private property in Canada are deeply entwined with colonial and capitalist systems of governance that sought to create a white settler society in which Euro-American models of land and subject reigned supreme. For this reason, we argue that Flanagan and Alcantara's scheme to develop private property regimes on reserves articulates with and furthers colonial practices of whitening.

In sum, we frame private property – as operationalized in Flanagan and Alcantara's research and policies – as an environmental formation, a hegemonic and normative vision of human-land relations that is productive of specific conceptions of land and subjects. To analyze what is at stake in their proposal for reserves, we draw on crucial insights offered by political economic and governmentality approaches. However, such approaches seldom recognize how neo-liberal discursive practices are entwined with colonial practices of whitening. In contrast, our analysis emphasizes the importance of whiteness in rendering Flanagan and Alcantara's suggestion so "sensical" in Canada. This approach allows us to treat their idea not as representing a historical break with past colonialism in Canada but as an extension of national projects of colonial racialization, one that seeks to place rigid boundaries around both Aboriginal land management and subjectivity.

Bounding Environmental Formations, Bounding Racialized Subjects

In what follows, we examine how Flanagan and Alcantara's proposal seeks to bound appropriate environmental formations and therefore subjectivities. In the first section, we analyze the boundary-making practices that work to constitute appropriate and inappropriate human-land relations. In the next section, we consider how their proposal attempts to narrowly circumscribe appropriate Aboriginal subjectivity in accordance with neoliberalism. In both cases, we show how the self-evidence of the project depends upon bracketing the historical geographies of colonial violence, dispossession, and regulation, which were instrumental in producing the reserve system and guaranteeing First Nations' poverty. In this context, and without idealizing life on contemporary reserves, our aim is to examine how Flanagan and Alcantara build their arguments and how those arguments articulate with colonial processes of racialized exclusion.

Bounding Appropriate Land Management and Tenure Systems

Flanagan and Alcantara analyze customary property rights on reserves through implicit and explicit reference to fee simple ownership, a form of private property characterized, as per the liberal tradition, as the ideal tenure regime from the perspective of efficiency and economic productivity. Customary property rights, as described by Flanagan and Alcantara, are those originating in the historical property practices of individual First Nations. Although we recognize that customary rights also reflect legal and normative frameworks of the colonial and later national administrations, we are interested in the discursive work accomplished by the notion of "customary property rights" in Flanagan and Alcantara's work.

According to these authors, customary property rights do have some advantages, particularly the ability for a First Nation to determine how it wants to govern land use to achieve collective rather than individual goals. But the disadvantages, they argue, are many. Here we examine three of Flanagan and Alcantara's conclusions: customary property rights are often subject to "political management," which can result in unfair land allocations; customary property rights "sap" incentives to develop and improve reserve lands; and customary property leads to mortgage defaults and rent arrears (what they call non-payment).

Perverted Land Management

According to Flanagan and Alcantara, many of these disadvantages stem from the fact that customary property rights are neither recognized nor enforced by the Canadian court system. As many customary allotments on reserves go unregistered (either with the First Nation or Indian and Northern Affairs Canada), they are subject to band council decisions, or what Flanagan and Alcantara (2004, 501) term "political management," which they say can be a problem "since the small size of bands usually means that politicians are well connected to many of the members of the community." Although they are careful in their word choice, Flanagan and Alcantara (ibid., 502, 529) repeatedly suggest that decisions may be subject to nepotism, thereby implying that customary property regimes on reserves are informed by "perverse political incentives."

Here we begin to see the boundary being drawn: legally enforceable property rights found elsewhere in Canada are neutral, and through the legal system, they tend to yield "fair" outcomes that are not influenced by political perversions and nepotism. This hegemonic environmental formation is made through juxtaposition with abject customary systems that are not legible to the state and the legal system, and cannot be enforced in the courts. As such, they are labelled "perverse" and said to form "an inadequate basis for participating in a modern economy" (ibid., 530). This claim reproduces colonial dichotomies between private property and customary or collective property, in which the former is associated with the modern civilized world and the latter with backward traditionalism. In doing so, it suggests that property systems must be identical in order for Canada, and within it First Nations, to function and thrive as a modern economy: there is simply no space for different forms of tenure. Indeed, where difference exists, poverty and perversions will follow.

The irony of this kind of thinking is demonstrated well by Carol Rose (1994), who argues that private property is a form of persuasion that requires massive collaboration among property owners and others in society. For Rose, property is always a social and political relation involving all kinds of actors, regardless of whether it is privately owned or customary. Thus, the suggestion that private property rights are somehow able to do their work outside of, or independently of, politics is blind to the innumerable relations that make private property stick.

Insecure Tenure Saps Development and Improvement

This boundary between appropriate and inappropriate environmental formations is deepened when Flanagan and Alcantara reflect on the insecurity of customary tenure, which they say stems from politicized management and a lack of legal recognition by the courts. The problem with this system, they argue, is that without security in tenure, individuals have little incentive to pursue economic development projects on reserves (Flanagan and Alcantara 2004, 502). Without citing research or giving references, they (ibid., 502-3) state that First Nations people invest off-reserve rather than on-reserve because of the greater tenure security available there and that this partially explains poverty on reserves. They add that customary rights inhibit the ability of the holder to mortgage and sell his or her property. Again, their argument seems to stem less from empirical research conducted on reserves (at least, they cite no data in their article) and more from their faith in the benefits of private property. In this case, their analysis relies on Hernando de Soto's famous *The Mystery of Capital* (2000), which asserts that poor people all over the world are poor because they are unable to use their assets as capital. Providing state-sanctioned property rights to poor people, de Soto states, will turn their "dead capital" into "living capital," permit them to make prosperity-enhancing investments, and allow them to pull themselves up by their bootstraps – without any redistribution. Customary property rights, in Flanagan and Alcantara's eyes, are inappropriate because there is less incentive to develop or improve them, and it is difficult to secure loans against such insecure property.

Given the importance of *The Mystery of Capital* as the apparent inspiration of Flanagan and Alcantara's proposal, it is logical to take a closer look at de Soto's claims and accomplishments. If de Soto had led successful development projects, one might expect at least some of these to have occurred in his native Peru. In fact, the Institute for Liberty and Democracy (ILD), which he directs, participated in a massive project to provide state-sanctioned private property rights (land titles) to urban areas of Peru between the early 1990s and 2004. By the end of the project, 920,000 land titles had been distributed (including 200,000 by ILD) to 1.2 million families. Studies indicate that "property titles had no significant effect on access among the poor to business credit" and that mortgage lending merely increased after the "Peruvian government abandoned de Soto's neoliberal prescriptions and began to subsidize low-income mortgages" (Field and Torero 2002, quoted in T. Mitchell 2005, 300). Timothy Mitchell (2007, 268) provides a more generalized critique of the "fallacies of de Soto's arguments" in the context of an ILD property rights project carried out in Egypt. Mitchell (ibid., 250-52) concludes that de Soto's success stems from his capacity as a self-promoter and the support that he has received since the early 1980s from elites within the North American and European neo-liberal movement (see also Peck 2008 for a history of the wider neo-liberal movement).

It would be insufficient to rely only on Mitchell's critique of de Soto to unsettle the connection that Flanagan and Alcantara are trying to make between development projects in the global South and their proposal for First Nations reserves. After all, de Soto is not the only promoter of private property rights as development panacea. For the last two decades, various international organizations – notably the World Bank – have sought to reduce poverty and increase economic productivity in the global South through projects designed to strengthen private property rights and increase access to formal credit. Such work has rarely been successful in the way that Flanagan and Alcantara claim (Bruce, Migot-Adholla, and Atherton 1994; Hendrix 1996; Ballantyne et al. 2000; T. Mitchell 2007). Brian Ballantyne, a professor at the University of Calgary, is the lead author on an essay that reviewed forty-four studies of cadastral reforms in Latin America, eastern Europe, and Africa, and concluded that land titling projects were unsuccessful at "increasing security of tenure; promoting improvements to land; facilitating access to credit, and creating a viable land market" (Ballantyne et al. 2000, 693). Experts from the World Bank and the Wisconsin Land Tenure Center, conducting research in western Africa, assert that there is good reason to doubt "the wisdom and cost-effectiveness of large-scale, systematic programs of compulsory titling for smallholders in rain fed agriculture" (Bruce, Migot-Adholla, and Atherton 1994, 261). Furthermore, according to the World Bank's top land experts, the success of the bank's biggest land titling project ever – carried out in Thailand – is largely the result of the credit market advantages of titles, not to title-induced changes in ownership security (Binswanger, Deininger, Feder 1995, 2723; see also Feder 1993). Although many World Bank land experts continue to support these projects (such as Feder and Nishio 1998; Deininger 2003), virtually all social justice organizations agree that they are a threat to marginalized groups such as women, Indigenous people, and the poor (see Mollett 2006; Rosset, Patel, and Courville 2006).

Our point is not that de Soto's work is unsuccessful or that his brand of land policy in the global South has failed. Rather, we highlight the checkered record of land policy projects in the South to draw attention to the uncritical way that they – and de Soto's work in particular – have been incorporated into Flanagan and Alcantara's arguments.

Mortgage Defaults and Rent Arrears

From Flanagan and Alcantara's perspective, a related problem with customary rights is the issue of high mortgage default or rent arrears on reserves. Their research found non-payment rates ranging from 12.5 percent to 97.0 percent among customary title holders; and yet, they note (with some incredulousness), these customary title holders are not evicted even though band councils have the legal right to do so. The lack of payments is portrayed as a market distortion that hinders efficient land use, a problem that stems from "the community-held idea that housing is either a band responsibility or a treaty right," nepotism at election time that "paralyzes housing departments," and a lack of resources to enforce and account for housing payments (Flanagan and Alcantara 2004, 504). Although housing may be considered a right by some First Nations people (see, for example, Manuel 2005), Flanagan and Alcantara focus most of their attention on the financial impact of these non-payments, pointing out that the Cowichan tribe is losing $600,000 per year in unpaid rent and noting that non-payments are leading to "rapidly deteriorating housing conditions and very few new housing constructions per year" for the Piikani Nation.

What is not considered, however, is whether the people living in those houses actually can pay their mortgages and rent. Average real incomes for

Aboriginal people in Canada hover around $13,500 annually, compared with $22,400 for non-Aboriginals (Libin 2008a); thus, there is little doubt that many First Nations people have difficulty paying for basic necessities, including their mortgage or rent. Yet Flanagan and Alcantara bracket out the low incomes of many First Nations people, the stunningly high unemployment rates, and the problem of homelessness that could result if band councils did begin to enforce mortgage and rent payments. Their claim that non-payment is "fuelling the poor housing conditions that exist on many reserves in Canada" (Flanagan and Alcantara 2004, 504) makes sense only according to a narrow market logic, but it completely fails in the context of the larger issues of social, political, and economic marginalization that First Nations face in Canada.

Combining their concern with nepotism, insecurity of title, and rent arrears/mortgage payments, Flanagan and Alcantara (ibid., 530) make the broad claim that customary property is subject to "political management" and therefore will not bring maximum benefit. Customary property rights, they conclude, "are an inadequate basis for participating in a modern economy where boundaries need to be clearly defined, land may need to be transferred from one user to another in order to realize its value, and investors require security" (ibid.). In other words, they argue that the best, and most efficient (valuable), use of land cannot be realized, because reserve lands are burdened by customary forms of property where land management is too political, too insecure, and where rent and/or mortgages are not adequately enforced. In doing so, the authors are attempting to circumscribe what appropriate land management and tenure systems are, to bind the perhaps infinite variety of ways that land might be managed and governed into fee simple private property.

In our interpretation, their reasoning is based on weak foundations. First, it asks us to believe that the Canadian legal and economic system is somehow uncontaminated by politics and that politics and political interference are somehow completely (and miraculously) disconnected from the creation and dissipation of "value" in off-reserve private lands. As the numerous analysts of neo-liberalism have shown, the state is central to propping up corporate entities and in maintaining flows of capital to particular groups and institutions such as auto manufacturers and banks. Second, Flanagan and Alcantara ask us to believe their arguments about the power of secure land tenure by drawing upon land titling/privatization projects in the global South, projects that have yielded far less than ideal results. And finally, they ask us to believe that poor housing on reserves is a product of non-enforced mortgage or rent payments, somehow not related to the larger issues of social, political, and economic marginalization of First Nations people in Canada.

But unsubstantiated or bad arguments about what private property does, or can do, are not all that is at stake in this proposal. We have suggested that this wholehearted private property boosterism is connected to the long history of valuing particular types of property as civilized, progressive, and natural, and some as not. In drawing narrow boundaries around appropriate property rights, Flanagan and Alcantara's neo-liberal policy recommendations script what people *need to be,* in effect attempting to regularize what *they can be.* In the following section, we elaborate on these arguments by examining the formative visions of the subject latent in Flanagan and Alcantara's research and arguments. What are the characteristics of this subject, and how are they made intelligible and desirable in the context of Canada as a white settler society?

Bounding the Economic Citizen, or Whitening by Another Name

Flanagan and Alcantara's (2005, 1020) analysis of the specific forms of property rights on reserves begins as follows: "Secure, well-documented and enforceable property rights give people options for improving their economic situation. With secure title, individuals can extract resources from their land, use it as collateral for a loan to build a house or start a business, sell it for a price or lease it for a fee." Entwined with these normative visions of property, we argue, are normative conceptions of the subject who enjoys secure property rights. As the quote suggests, this is a subject with investment options, one driven to make improvements – in short, an enterprising subject.

Flanagan and Alcantara provide many examples of such enterprising individuals on reserves. However, they argue that these individuals often face limitations in their attempts to realize their projects. In what follows, we analyze how these limitations are explained in order to highlight the boundary-making practices at work. Specifically, Flanagan and Alcantara's subject – autonomous, disembodied, and free to do as she or he pleases – is cast against a First Nations subject bound by culture or customary law. Their idealized subject, we suggest, is not only a neo-liberal subject who embodies the politico-economic rationalities of the market place, it is also a white subject who embodies the national capitalist values upheld by white Canadian settler society.

Colonial Scripts, Neo-Liberal Narratives

In contrast to those who suggest that Aboriginal "cultures ha[ve] no room for institutions of private property," Flanagan and Alcantara (2004, 491, 494) frame their research as studying the "embryonic systems of private property now existing on reserves to see how they can be expanded and perfected." In using the word "embryonic," the authors deploy a developmentalist narrative that scripts one specific form of private property rights as an end point or ultimate achievement, while framing another as incomplete, at an early stage of development. This teleological narrative also works to present colonial and national white settler societies as having achieved maturity – as demonstrated by the development of this particular environmental formation – while casting First Nations societies as child-like, still burdened by tradition and therefore in need of guidance to achieve mature and transparent forms of environmental governance.

The notion of "not yet ready" is a well-analyzed colonial trope used to legitimize inequality in citizenship rights and responsibilities, and to rationalize intervention to guide Native peoples out of the darkness and into enlightenment and civilization (Chakrabarty 2000). Within this trope, racialized peoples are cast as inferior, but not inherently so; rather, the right guidance and training will enable them, over time, to resemble the racially superior group. For instance, Eric Olund's (2002) analysis of property reforms in Native territories in the late-nineteenth-century United States illustrates how white land reformers linked together the so-called deficiencies in Indian people with their deficiencies in land governance and management practices. "Indians could only become Americans if 'lawless' Indian Country were *actively reconstituted* as a governable space comprising individual, private properties," notes Olund (ibid., 133, emphasis in original).

Flanagan and Alcantara support this developmentalist narrative by treating fee simple title as universal, transparent, and unquestionably superior, and customary rights as locally specific and therefore not transparent, but also as lacking or burdened. Building on colonial tropes, their analysis locates the origin of such lacks and burdens in First Nations *culture*. Customary rights on reserves are not enforceable in Canadian courts; instead, they are subject to the authority of the band. This is a problem, Flanagan and Alcantara (2004, 501) suggest, because "politicians are well connected to many members of the community." An "example of politics intruding in dispute resolution" is taken from conflicts that arose between the Blood tribe and the Piikani Nation in Alberta when the Indian Act called for fencing of property boundaries. Flanagan and Alcantara (ibid., 502) suggest that, instead of resolving the resulting disputes, the bands resisted making decisions "so as to avoid antagonizing voters at election time"; when they did try their hand at resolution, they "sometimes made decisions based on nepotism." Here, the Canadian court system is set against band authorities, and only the latter is said to be marked by political interference. Underpinning this discourse lies the neo-liberal contention that the hand of the market is invisible as compared to the distorting influences of politics.

To demonstrate how and why this rationale is caught up in ongoing processes of racialization, we situate it in relation to Flanagan's comments made in a review of Tsimshian lawyer and business person Calvin Helin's recent book *Dances with Dependency* (2006). In his review, published in the *Fraser Forum,* Flanagan (2007, 30) highlights the "intractable factors" in "traditional tribal culture" that create unemployment on reserves and therefore dependency upon the government. The "cultural issue" of relevance to our argument is said to be "the tendency to rely heavily on the support of kin, which is sometimes associated with outright discouragement of self-improvement through formal education and work experience" (ibid.). When placed in relation to this statement, the above arguments about political interferences and nepotism imply that Native cultures lack formal institutions of governance and therefore are at the whim of traditions as interpreted by powerful individuals or families.

Given such "perversions," Flanagan and Alcantara (2004, 502) want to expand and perfect the "embryonic systems of private property" on reserves, to bring them in line with the fully developed and rational property rights system within the Canadian nation at large. Their reasons for doing so are placed in relation to characteristics lacking in First Nations subjects as well. Without security of tenure, "the individual has little incentive to pursue economic development projects on-reserve" (ibid.). Indeed, fear of the band's (arbitrary?) authority is said to "sap the individual's desire to build a house or start a business on-reserve" (ibid., 503). Here, Flanagan and Alcantara put forward an idealized universal subject who aims to buy property and become an entrepreneur. Indeed, they naturalize these characteristics as "individual desire," thereby establishing the notion that the entrepreneurial subject is repressed within all First Nations people and that these characteristics will be enabled once private property is made available. For this reason, we argue, discourses about perfecting private property regimes are also about inciting citizens to assimilate into a normative white capitalist culture.

Many of Flanagan's claims about why First Nations people are not entering the workforce, investing, and becoming entrepreneurs are applied by neo-liberal proponents to social programs more generally, especially welfare. And, as Inda (2006, 18) points out, such narratives invariably draw lines between the prudential subject and the "oft-racialized anti-citizen unable or reluctant to exercise responsible self-government." For instance, Flanagan (2007, 30) suggests that "many intractable factors discourage reserve residents from entering the work force. The reserve offers tax-exempt status, welfare payments," and more. But government policies are not alone in sapping the work ethic on reserves; Flanagan (ibid.) claims that another major problem lies with "traditional tribal cultures," which "do not generally include the concept of regular work hours in a hierarchically structured workforce." As noted above, he also suggests that tribal cultures rely upon their kin instead of seeking "self-improvement" and states that "changes in government policy can address the perverse incentives of the reserve system" (ibid., 30). He adds, however, that "native people themselves will have to tackle their cultural issues, following the lead of pioneers like Calvin Helin" (ibid.). Here we see that, if Flanagan's project for private property is to work, First Nations people must be transformed into *individual labourers*. Indeed, as Flanagan and Alcantara (2004, 532) state, "private property rights are not a panacea for all the economic and social ills of native communities."

Ultimately, Flanagan and Alcantara are suggesting that First Nations must subscribe to an ethic of individual responsibility, which means becoming good Canadian subjects who pay their bills no matter what their circumstances may be. Homelessness – a consequence for those who cannot do so (as it is for many in Canada) – should incite them to become self-reliant.

It is critical to analyze the line drawn between responsible and irresponsible subjects, writes Inda (2006, 19), as such "dividing practices" have "radical implications for the way [subjects] are governed." Inda identifies two principal governance strategies for those deemed abject: technologies of inclusion and containment. Of relevance to our argument are the former, policies to govern the abject by preparing them "to take upon themselves the responsibility for managing their own well-being and that of their kin" (ibid.). We treat Flanagan and Alcantara's proposal to perfect existing private property regimes on reserves as a technology of inclusion. From this perspective, the government's role is to create the conditions for inclusion by removing the legal obstacles that prevent First Nations from joining all other Canadians in becoming entrepreneurial subjects. It is the task of First

Nations individuals to take on this subject position. When land titling projects fail to produce the desired outcome – prosperity – for marginalized groups, project proponents tend to place the blame upon the beneficiaries, whose cultural traditions limited their vision or their behaviour.[3] For example, in eastern Europe, after years of bad results from land titling and privatization, World Bank land policy experts are still urging landowners to be patient and work harder (Deininger 2003, 134). For First Nations, the danger of this discourse of inclusion is that if and when they lose their land – either because of foreclosure or not being able to earn enough from land-attached investments – their dispossession is rationalized by land market discourse: they didn't work hard enough, or their culture held them back. According to this discourse, there is no dispossession, only the market-driven – and prosperity-enhancing – *reallocation* of land to those who will manage it most productively.

Multicultural Neo-Liberalism and the Colonial Present

Flanagan and Alcantara's proposals for inclusion are made in a society that has enshrined multiculturalism in law, ostensibly having given up previous national imaginaries that explicitly fostered whiteness. *Equality in diversity*, the slogan reads. But in our view, Flanagan and Alcantara's project demonstrates a kind of multicultural neo-liberalism, an emergent national imaginary and form of governance that furthers colonial whitening projects but under a different guise. Multicultural neo-liberalism is framed as a project of economic rather than cultural assimilation, as though these are ontologically separate and separable realms. Unlike colonialist practices of explicit economic exclusion and cultural assimilation (Royal Commission on Aboriginal Peoples 1996; Harris 2002), Flanagan and Alcantara's proposal is presented as an inclusionary project to give everyone the opportunity to freely engage in entrepreneurial activities, to buy, sell, profit, save, and – most critically – to become indebted (A. Roy 2010).

We see multicultural neo-liberalism as a reconfiguration of liberal democracy, however, in the sense that whiteness figures as its core. "Differences" from the white norm are allowed, as long as they are contained and limited to language, art, food, and folk festivals. Thus, First Nations may participate or even "self-determine" their futures, but only under the conditions specified by a white capitalist elite.[4] Notions of self-determination are hijacked by concepts such as responsibility and self-reliance. Indeed, the concept of equality begins to take on a very specific meaning within multicultural neo-liberalism, one that relates to the development of a level playing field to compete in capitalist systems. *Equality in land equity,* the slogan might read. Ultimately, inclusion in this colour-blind multicultural society seems also to entail giving up the right to make special claims about historical entitlement and redistribution.

A remark made in 2008 by the minister of Indian Affairs, Chuck Strahl, helps us elaborate this point. During an interview with Kevin Libin, author of the *National Post* series "Rethinking the Reserve," Strahl (2008) commented,

> People pay lip service to this idea of equality or levelling the playing field ... and as soon as you say, "How about we'll take these steps – a market housing fund?" people say, "That's outrageous. They need to have a separate deal where they don't actually own their houses but the government of Canada somehow funds them." And you roll your eyes and say, well, all of these things are part and parcel of getting ahead economically ... And yet, there is resistance at every level ... I think there is some paternalism within the whole Indian industry, if you will, that says, "Of course they should be treated equally – but not quite yet."

This very rich passage helps demonstrate what we mean by neo-liberal multiculturalism, where equality means constructing a level playing field so that First Nations can compete in the economic system.

Conclusion: The Anti-Politics Machine at Work

Clearly, Flanagan and Alcantara are concerned with what they, and many neo-classical economists, see as inefficient uses of land on reserves and the untapped potential of these so-called underutilized lands. What makes their view and the subsequent proposal for change intelligible in Canada today is their ability to bracket out historical and geographical factors shaping reserves. In particular, what is missing from their analysis is any explanation of how reserve inhabitants came to be poor other than the fact that private property rights have not been extended to them. In other words, they avoid any discussion of colonialism and the colonialist legacy, while simultaneously calling forth dichotomies rooted in the colonial era such as backward/modern to describe property systems on reserves.

This is perhaps best demonstrated in their vision of the reserve. For them, it is a site of possibility and hope that can be realized if only the right conditions for investment are created, conditions that will allow a modern economy to flourish. Prosperity is within reach of those living on-reserve, if only it were managed properly. But their imaginaries of the reserve have little in common with those of other analysts of the reserve system and with the "place" of the reserve within the colonial project and in contemporary settler–First Nations relations.

In describing the logics and tactics behind the creation of the reserve system in British Columbia, Harris (2002, xxi) argues that a profound shrinking of Aboriginal space lay at the heart of colonialism: "The confinement began almost as soon as a colony was created," with "a tiny fraction of the land set aside for Natives, the rest available, in various tenures, for development." The logics behind such confinement were grounded in economics and self-interest on the part of settlers, but confinement was also laden with the belief that the First Nations were using their lands inappropriately and inefficiently, and thus should be replaced, a rationale that sounds startlingly like that elaborated by Flanagan and Alcantara. Government officials believed that if Natives were moved to small reserves and surrounded with settlers and their private property, they would be introduced to and eventually assimilated into "civilization" (ibid., xxii). As noted above, Harris (ibid., 268) argues that the question of property in colonial BC (ca. nineteenth to early twentieth century) was an "elemental, polarized, and characteristically racialized juxtaposition of civilization and savagery." In this settler context, "use rights of a different, and in most settlers' eyes, a lesser people, were essentially invisible" (ibid.). The reserve, through Harris' analysis and research, is a carceral space, one that was explicitly created to assimilate First Nations people into colonial white society. Given this, customary rights on reserves are not traditional as Flanagan and Alcantara would have it, but forms of tenure practices that have been densely articulated with the legal and normative frameworks of the colonial and later national administrations.

Further, Harris (ibid.) demonstrates that many First Nations people/communities were simply unable to make a living on the small space of the reserve and were excluded from pursuing their economic activities elsewhere. On reserves, colonial officials encouraged particular kinds of economic activities as a part of the civilizing mission, of which agriculture was prominent. Harris explains that First Nations who did pursue agrarian economies on reserves often found that their land holdings were too small and the soil too infertile and dry to secure livelihoods for most people living on the reserve. The size of the reserve, he notes, was critical in ensuring that many First Nations would seek work elsewhere. The problem of land distribution was recognized by many First Nations: "From the late 1860s, Native leaders had protested their small reserves in every way they could, claiming, fundamentally, that their people would not have enough food and that their progeny had no prospects. In retrospect, they were right. The spaces assigned to Native people did not support them" (ibid., 291). Also emphasizing the carceral nature of the reserve, Mary-Ellen Kelm (1998) states that the reserve, high mortality rates, increased concentration of Native populations, and restricted mobility are all interconnected. As Harris (2002, 290) concludes, "the confinements imposed on Native lives took their toll on Native bodies."

We have pointed out that Flanagan and Alcantara's boundaries between appropriate and inappropriate property and subjects call forth similar dichotomies made in colonial periods between civilized and primitive environmental formations and subjects. Although seductive, their arguments about the potential lurking in more secure forms of private property rest upon a full-scale bracketing of history and geography. They fail to consider the lack of resources and land allocated to many First Nations along with the colonial violence of dispossession that built the reserve system. Only through these exclusions can their research and policy conclusions become intelligible, desirable, and potentially implementable within Canada as a white settler society.

This bracketing reminds us of James Ferguson's (1990) anti-politics machine, although with a distinctly neo-liberal flavour. In Lesotho, he argues, development policies were based upon a particular discourse of how poverty and "underdevelopment" were created and maintained. In this discourse, explains Ferguson (ibid., 63, 64), colonialism/land grabbing are "completely eradicated," and "history as well as politics is swept aside." Such is the situation in Flanagan and Alcantara's discourse regarding poverty on reserves. In Ferguson's (ibid., 256) words, this anti-politics machine (of development discourse) "suspends politics from even the most sensitive political operations" and makes issues such as poverty amenable to technical interventions. But whereas the effects of the anti-politics machine in Lesotho are a reinforcing and expansion of bureaucratic state power, an amplified military presence, and increased governmental services (services that "serve to govern"), the effect in Flanagan and Alcantara's case is to perpetuate the colonial Canadian myth that "we" (settlers) have had no hand in creating the dire situations on reserves.[5] David Rossiter and Patricia Wood (2005, 354) reach a similar conclusion in their analysis of the 2002 British Columbian referendum on treaty making, which they assert worked to "cleanse debates over Native land rights of the very historical geographies that led to the present day negotiations and thus denies the possibility of a full Aboriginal citizenship in BC and Canada."

Although Flanagan and Alcantara's proposal purports to advocate self-determination, freedom, and autonomy for First Nations, it does so through a very specific environmental formation, one that continues to narrowly constitute who belongs in the national body as well as the characteristics they ought to have. Their policies for reconfiguring land on reserves are about defining and circumscribing Indigenous sovereignty, governance, and economies in particularly Western, white, and capitalist forms. Thus, they seek to bind the *political* claims of many First Nations leaders and communities, who advocate for redistributions of land and resource rents on regions beyond the reserve, for increased transfer payments to deal with the immediate crisis of poverty on reserves, and for governance and autonomy over traditional territories.[6]

ACKNOWLEDGMENTS
We thank the organizers of the workshop (Andrew, Laura, Audrey, and Cheryl). We thank Christopher Reid and Joanna Reid, and the editors of the volume for commenting on drafts of this essay. Jessica Dempsey acknowledges the help of the Social Science and Humanities Research Council and the Trudeau Foundation for doctoral support. Kevin Gould acknowledges the generous support of the John Sloan Dickey Center for International Understanding at Dartmouth College, NH. Juanita Sundberg appreciates the support provided by the University of British Columbia Hampton Fund.

INTERLOCATIONS

Extremity
Theorizing from the Margins

KAY ANDERSON

Much like Great White North, Australia's Wide Brown Land is a rich and resilient myth of nation. Said to sit tenuously on both sides of the North-South divide, Australia is often characterized as a Western country under southern skies in a Third World environment. It is the flat, scorched land of far horizons and endless skies whose narrative force finds its inverse congruence in the rugged and icy terrain of Arctic Canada. If landscape is a key mode of human signification, Great White North and Wide Brown Land are its defining instances, all the more dramatized in the characteristic staging of their antipodality. From furthest north to deepest south, ice storm to heat wave, cold feet to sunburnt noses, these iconic categories share in the spatialized trope of *extremity*. How might this be so? And what matters of concern does it call up?

These myths depict a land that most Australians and Canadians traverse by avoiding altogether. Flyover country. Australia, in particular, is one of the most urbanized continents on earth, its arid centre a site of fear and yearning for city-dwellers who know it more in fable than on foot. The desolate expanse of Arctic Canada has also become the defining landscape aesthetic of a largely metropolitan constituency for whom "wilderness" is variously performed. Like Australia's Red Centre, Canada's White North has long been a currency for tourist production and consumption, both national and international.

It is not by accident that these parallels across frontiers and hemispheres can be drawn out for special interest here. Great White North and Wide Brown Land are modes of subjectivity that adhere not only to the apparently benign scripts of tourist brochures and mantras of human connection to a pristine nature. They also shape the imaginaries of governmental unities or "nations" that were themselves born in the turbulent experiences of settler colonialism and Indigenous dispossession. As the essays gathered in this volume amply demonstrate, a mythologized equation of North/nature/Native has been a thick thread in the discursive formation that became the modern Canadian nation. Because Inuit and First Nations people (in all their diversity) were thought to live closer to nature than those who assumed the right to define and produce Canada in their image, a "whitewashing" of Indigenous modes of living and being took hold. Stereotyped as remote savages, they stood outside the march of time, mute and motionless as a mountain itself. From this more critical perspective, Great White North appears in stark relief as a *white* metaphor that has been variously mobilized in the nationalist organization of racialized difference.

In foregrounding the historical co-constitution of race, nature, and nation in Canada, this volume brings a fresh perspective to now familiar critiques of the exclusionary politics of nation building. Using the optic of "whiteness," it charts the diverse characterizations and deployments of Native/nation/nature/North that acquired their (neither consistent nor coherent) force in the Canadian nation-building project. The lens of whiteness also affords a productive conversation *across* the typically split knowledge and policy spheres: of race and ethnic studies, on the one hand, and Indigenous and post-colonial/colonial studies, on the other. For this is an opposition whose strictly binary operation has itself inscribed "white settler" as an unmarked norm and status. It follows that a dialogue – however awkward – across the multiple diversities of migrant, indigene, *and* settler is needed to advance citizenry rights in ex-colonial immigrant-receiving nations such as Canada and Australia.

Welcome too are the efforts to augment the analytical frame of "identity politics" that has pitted race *against* (all things made to stand as) nature. The important refrain of critical race theory – that race and racism are modes of discursive practice – is now standard orthodoxy. For over two decades, it pursued the claim that there is nothing foundational – no fact of nature or biology – underpinning racialized difference, hierarchy, and prejudice. So, in the area of colonial discourse analysis, for example, the dispossession of

Indigenous people was traced not to any inherent ethnocentrism, but (after Michel Foucault and Edward Said) to a discursive operation of symbolic othering that justified colonial power and privilege.

But as noted in the Introduction to this volume, recent efforts in geography and elsewhere to historicize nature issue a fresh challenge to this still useful (though by now conventional) move – one that depended for its logic on a theorization of nature as a timeless essence set apart from culture and politics. For if nature can no longer be accepted as an external entity of environment "out there," or an unproblematic animal-like corporeality "within" people (human nature), then an analytic that closes its ontological gates around the intersubjective sphere of identity politics needs to be thought again. The implications of this move are multiple and far-reaching. And they are still to be comprehensively worked through in the field of race, which has so far been considered as an issue to be addressed only on the human side of the modern divide of culture/nature.

To that end, more can be said here by way of theorizing the immense power of the iconography of frontier called up by "Wide Brown Land" – a detour that tracks us back to the notion of extremity, with which this essay opened. This frontier references an environmental presence that under conditions of colonial contact became figured not only as a space of difference, a space of abstract otherness, a vacant space *(terra nullius)* of generic savagery. More specifically, and in the critical register of recent post-humanist problematizations of the human, the parched surface of the Wide Brown Land became intelligible in modern Christian thought as a barrenness to be *overcome.* If to be human was to realize a universal potential to separate from everything assembled under the sign of nature, this was a space to be *transcended.* Shifting ontologies not only of race, then, but also of "the human," stake their claim for analysis here.

Elsewhere, I have charted the affective dynamics of colonial shock, awe, and perplexity through which the continent that became Australia was apprehended from the late eighteen hundreds (K. Anderson 2007). This work was an insistently "situated" effort to rethink the rise of racial discourse from a specific space of empire. It demonstrated the sense in which Australian encounters – far from folding neatly into the European legitimation projects at which so much colonial discourse critique has been levelled – *deranged* European knowledges. Nature/Native encounters did not confirm prevailing discourses of savagery as a difference that would inevitably be surmounted. They *upset* them. In a land of "singular creatures" and "vegetable vagaries" – where it was said "a different Creator must have been at work" – the non-farming inhabitants of this apparently uncultivated surface posed an intractable challenge to the presumption that people universally realize their character *as human* in a progressive movement *out* of nature. Aborigines were construed not as yet another savage race, but as the *most* miserable of people. They stood as figures of remoteness and antiquity – succinctly, of *extremity*. They had the "feeblest" canoes, the "flimsiest" of huts, and later on, for observers starting to think in more physical terms, the "leanest" limbs and the "smallest" skulls. They shook up craniocentric ideas of civilization and culture, not least in defying colonial efforts to bring them into cultivation and settlement. Sitting at the limit of what it meant to be human in the nineteenth century, the Australian cast doubt on the cherished assumption that an interval of "agency" separated human from non-human.

In rattling the humanist paradigm that was fraught with anxiety about the human place in nature, Australian encounters disrupted the very logic and conceit of human distinction. It was a southern crisis of confidence that prompted the speculation that if Aboriginal people *don't* move out of nature, then perhaps they inherently *can't*. And perhaps they won't ever. Perhaps the human is not a unified family after all. Racial determinism thus presents itself for analysis here as a *hypothesis* – as an (uncertain) ordering of anomalous people, theorized within broader ecologies of culture and violence.

The place of people in relation to the non-human world elicits a confusion that persists, unresolved, in Western cultures today (Anderson and Perrin, forthcoming). The very precariousness of that place is registered for twenty-first-century audiences in the mounting evidence of environmental stress and depletion. The matters at stake bear not only on a field of human-environment relations from which the subject of race can be quarantined. On the contrary, it is from the racialized spaces and bodies of empire that suspicion about the modern assertion of human distinction might be actively stimulated. For, in their thoroughly white colonialist figuration as *extremity*, margins such as Great White North and Wide Brown Land hold up a mirror. They stir the pot of that which has been held in all its anxious instability as referential. They unsettle white normativity. Theorizing from the edge, as this book broadly attempts, is not only therefore the gesture of counter-discourse. It is not only the defensive voice that "speaks back" from margin to metropole. The interjection here, from Australia, of a secular ethics of race and the human has a transformative potential of much wider reach. It anticipates a fresh sensibility to the diversity and vulnerability of all modes of being on earth, human and non-human, from furthest north to deepest south.

Colonization
The Good, the Bad, and the Ugly

SHERENE H. RAZACK

Notwithstanding the centrality of race to notions of nature and the environment, the politics of environmentalism have until recently been so entangled
with white identities (the academy's politics on this point are no exception)
that when a white colleague invited me to participate in a discussion on
sustainability, my initial response was no. "That's such a white thing," I
thought, the idea of sustainability and the environment calling up for me
images of white environmental activists talking about eco-tourism and the
greening of daily life with little thought to the capitalist and white supremacist economies in which such practices are embroiled. My colleague patiently persisted, asking me to reflect on where my own scholarship and teaching
on race already takes up environmental issues. Anxious to dissociate myself
from a politics and scholarship that have often failed to challenge white supremacy, I had offered up a knee-jerk reaction that failed to see that concepts of nature and the environment are centrally about race and subjectivity,
an area I would describe as my predominant scholarly interest. This volume
makes abundantly clear why those of us who explore questions of race and
subjectivity in education can only profit from an engagement with those
scholars who unmap the geographies of whiteness: the constructions of
nature, the wilderness, and the Great White North. Colonial masculinities
and femininities are produced in and through such spaces, and a decon-
struction or unmapping of them reveals a great deal about the production of
racial hierarchies.

Whiteness helps to understand wilderness: This is one of the key claims made by several of the contributors to this volume. To desire whiteness is to desire overcoming difference, Kalpana Seshadri-Crooks (2000) has argued. Overcoming difference first requires that difference be produced and maintained. Indian and white must be fundamentally different. Wilderness is one way in which these two things, constituting and then overcoming difference, can be accomplished (see Erickson, Chapter 1, this volume; Sandilands, Chapter 3, this volume). Many critical geographers have tracked these processes. Jake Kosek (2004, 126), for example, offers the compelling argument that ideas of wilderness are "infused with racialized notions of purity and pollution." A land grant activist whom Kosek quotes goes further: "Wilderness is something that is entirely a white man's invention" (De Vargas, in ibid.). For one thing, wilderness is achieved though the eviction of Indigenous people. Although Kosek's and others' insights on race and nature are now regularly taken up in critical geography, they are likely to shock the average person for whom wilderness and national parks are unqualified good things and thus not something they would associate with white supremacy. This collection provides a salutary lesson: it takes many bad things to make a good thing. Want a nice view? A lovely hiking trail? A sustainable resource? Call a colonizer. The matter goes far beyond the theft of land and the dispossession of people, however. The routing of race through notions of nature shows how racial, class, and, I would add, gender identities are "formed, naturalized, and contested" through concepts such as wilderness (Kosek 2004, 126). If "unspoilt nature" is where white men and women must go to know themselves as white, then it is indeed imperative to understand the relationship between subjectivity and the beautiful things that come with colonization.

The Emplacement of White Settlers

For Kosek, the fear of race contamination, provoked by the emancipation of slaves, the accelerated flow of non–Anglo-Saxon immigrants at the turn of the twentieth century, and a general crisis of white masculinity brought on by the closing of the frontier, left the white settler anxious to protect the purity of the white race. In the need for pure places – places, that is, unsullied by racial others and offering civilized man a chance to test his mettle and develop his character – wilderness and later parks were born. If wilderness is about "unsoiled bloodlines" and the shoring up of white subjectivity, the contributors to this volume track in minute ways the historical, contemporary, and geographical basis of the settler's preoccupation with miscegenation (ibid.). In Chapter 9, Jocelyn Thorpe shows how, in early-twentieth-century Ontario, the forests of northern Ontario provided a setting for the staging of white masculine identity. White male travellers, and a few white women, tramped through the wilderness that Temagami came to represent, assisted, ironically, by Aboriginal guides. The Teme-Augama Anishnabai would spend the rest of the century in court trying, and largely failing, to win the right to the territories so exalted by white travellers as spaces of unsullied nature. If, as Thorpe shows, wilderness is anything but natural, one can only wonder at the tenacity of these early white travellers, anxiously repeating the founding colonial fiction of terra nullius, determined to write themselves into colonial fantasy, all the while steadfastly ignoring the Aboriginal men and women on whom they necessarily relied. The compulsion to perform the colonial fantasy suggests that the settler's crisis of identity is an ongoing one, born of a psychic and material need to emplace himself. Where the land is stolen, when entitlement to it must be performed over and over again in anxious repression of those indigenous to it, emplacement is the most urgent of tasks. This volume offers insights into *how* settlers gain a sense of who they are and how they come to *feel* that they are owners.

The colonial project involves dispossession and displacement. As Nicholas Blomley (2004, 109) suggests in *Unsettling the City*, "while dispossession is complete, displacement is not." Dispossession "refers to the processes through which settlers come to acquire title to land historically held by aboriginal people." Displacement, "while related, refers to the conceptual removal of aboriginal people from the city, and the concomitant 'emplacement' of white settlers" (ibid.). Place making and enactments of claims to land, Blomley (ibid., 114) points out, are "partial and incomplete." The city, for instance, has to be "made into a white place through physical settlement and occupation." As I argue elsewhere (Razack 2011), the regular and violent eviction of Aboriginal bodies from urban spaces is one important practice of emplacement, a violence that is visible in the numbers of Aboriginal people who die in police custody after being rounded up from city streets. The conceptual and material removal of Aboriginal people from the land, when the land is transformed into something called wilderness, complements these urban strategies of emplacement. The land must bear visible evidence of the colonizer, signs, that is, of modernity's presence. It is mapped, place names are changed, and a steady Europeanization of the landscape begins and continues apace. Wilderness and parks are parts of this Europeanization as spaces are created for modern man to know his modernity.

The relentless imprinting of colonial power on landscapes and racialized bodies is accomplished though law; law transforms this violence into a story of peaceful settlement. Iterations of processes of emplacement mimic the original fiction of reciprocity, terra nullius, and the story of modern peoples assisting pre-modern peoples into modernity. In later instalments, colonization continues by other names. Reconciliation and conservation replace notions of civilizing and modernizing. Brian Egan (Chapter 10, this volume) shows how British Columbia's reconciliation project simply coats the original theft of land in law, beginning with the fiction that the land was originally purchased, not stolen, and title to it negotiated rather than imposed. From Douglas' treaties in the 1850s, to a more ruthless colonial administration for the next hundred years, to today's "negotiations" in BC's current treaty process, the fiction is installed of a historical and mutual relationship between white settlers and First Nations. Like reconciliation, conservation is another name for this process of turning dispossession into relations of contract. Colonialism through conservation (Bocking, Chapter 2, this volume) transforms white authorities into protectors of wildlife who must keep in check the excesses of Aboriginal hunters.

Tartans and Highland Cattle: The Neurosis

In a documentary on race and police brutality, filmmaker Richard Fung (1991) introduces the black man whose encounter with the police is explored by the film. In the first frame, we see the man paddling a canoe on a lake in cottage country. Fung means to disturb the viewer's expectations. We immediately ask ourselves, What is a black man doing on a lake in a northern landscape? Fung's opening gambit messes with citations. As Bruce Braun (2003) comments, drawing on Judith Butler (1993, 1997), images are viewed with other images in mind; the black canoeist makes no sense to us because there are no prior images to which we can connect it; on the contrary, the images upon which we most easily draw, black men handcuffed and splayed across police cars, do not prepare us for black bodies in a canoe on a pristine lake. What does it mean when a black man is out of place in a canoe and when a Canadian, as Pierre Berton is widely remembered as saying, is defined as someone who knows how to make love in one?

Whiteness has to be spatially consolidated, and it is the white subject for whom wilderness and nature provide an opportunity for the making of self (ibid.). Yet these evident strategies of emplacement have a febrile character to them that tells us something about the colonial project's instability. How else to read the suggestion that the staff of Cape Breton Highlands National

Park wear the tartans of Scotland, and that the park be stocked with high-land cattle? However absurdly, the landscape must express a European story of origins; anything remotely Indigenous or "ethnic" must be removed and declared out of place. Acadians, whose claim to whiteness is an in-secure one, are evicted from the lands that would become a national park (Sandilands, Chapter 3, this volume). Violently cleansed of anything that would threaten the integrity of the settler's story, the national park, like the wilderness, becomes a place where whiteness can be experienced in full. The hiker-consumer is invited into this continuous but nonetheless precarious staging of identity. Adventure and extreme sport industries offer newer and bolder options for the purification of bloodlines. Non-white subjects know that they cannot participate in this return to nature and savagery since they are imagined as never having left it in the first place (Braun 2003). The script simply doesn't work when the bodies are not white.

Triumphal encounters with savagery have their academic equivalents. In Chapter 11, Jessica Dempsey, Kevin Gould, and Juanita Sundberg strongly argue that neo-liberal debates articulate with whiteness, and I want to sug-gest that the journeys into aboriginality that such intellectual forays demand resemble the wilderness journeys from which white men emerge confirmed in their own superiority. As Dempsey, Gould, and Sundberg show, Tom Flanagan and Christopher Alcantara, for example, two white political sci-ence professors, journey to reserves (if only on paper) and find tribes unable to fling off the chains of collective life. They propose developing private property rights for reserves, urging that First Nations be apprenticed into the cadre of entrepreneurial citizens. We might also understand their cor-porate version of the white man's burden as a domestication of the wild. Necessarily, dispossession falls out of the picture. If Aboriginal people lag behind their white counterparts, it can only be because they lack skills and knowledge; it cannot be because the land was stolen and their impoverish-ment deliberate state policy. An unmarked neo-liberal subject, wise enough to jettison community and kin, and to remain suspicious of collective solu-tions, can light his or her way into the modern, although the risk of failure is high.

Law offers white subjects the same opportunity for material and sym-bolic entries into whiteness as does the academy. In today's Kelowna, a western town imagined as the preserve of enterprising white people, mi-grant workers remain temporary brown stains on an otherwise pristine landscape. Law makes this possible. Luis Aguiar and Tina Marten (Chapter 6, this volume) detail the material basis for preserving Kelowna as a land of gentlemen farmers. In their argument that the hinterland as heartland is simply reinstalled with neo-liberal labour policies, we ought to recall the settler's psychic and material need for emplacement and the disavowal of racial others that this reinstallment requires. The migrant workers of Kelowna are under surveillance, like their immigrant forebears of the early twentieth century whose bodies and spaces were the "unhygienic geographies" written upon in this collection. They are also improved (as was the case with park planning in Toronto's poor districts, as explored by Mackintosh, Chapter 4, this volume). And they are contained (as they are when the threat of contagion is thought to be acute, such as during the Toronto SARS crisis, which is detailed by Major and Keil, Chapter 5, this volume). Bodies that threaten the wholeness of whiteness, as many of the contributors argue, are nevertheless indispensable. They cannot be banished forever, for how else is the settler to know and materially accomplish his own superiority?

Perhaps in these performances of whiteness and spatialized enactments of superiority there lies the possibility of rupture. I often wonder if I cling to the idea of the instability of the colonial project out of desperation. However, I am reassured by the chapters of this volume that track colonial performances of the nineteenth and early twentieth centuries, for they reveal that such performances have never proceeded seamlessly. They have always included a mix of good and bad things, of desire and repulsion. How do we thread our way through the good, the bad, and the ugly? Is it good to want immigrant and poor communities to have parks? To conserve forests? To improve the landscape? Was Grey Owl, the Englishman who passed as Indian and who urged the preservation of the wilderness, someone we should vilify, or can he be recuperated, as Margaret Atwood (1995) intends that he should be (Erickson, Chapter 1, this volume)? What are we to make of those white scientists and anthropologists who recognize the value of Indigenous knowledge but who nevertheless cannot imagine Aboriginal peoples as constituting nations in their own right, nor see the role of whites in their dispossession? Accountability is nowhere more necessary than when we feel that some good has come out of practices of dominance. Colonizers always claim a commitment to the improvement of racialized peoples. Land claims often flounder in Canadian courts due to the notion that Aboriginal peoples did not properly manage the land or know how to develop it.

The uneven, contradictory character of the colonial relationship should not therefore disguise its violence. Colonization is always announced as "for their own good." On this we should be clear. The contributors to this volume offer ways to map the geography of violence, first, by tracking the omissions on which the stories of goodness and progress rely, and second, by examining their productive function. When Samuel Hearne tells the story of the Bloody Falls massacre as an instance of the savagery of the Dene toward the Inuit, he neglects to mention both his own implication in the story as an agent of the Hudson's Bay Company and the ways in which copper already circulated in the local economy, giving rise to tensions and conflicts among Aboriginal peoples (Cameron, Chapter 8, this volume). Hearne produces himself as the disinterested observer, outside of the savagery and perfectly positioned to champion the massacred Inuit, all the while expressing through the pornographic tale of the violence his own ambivalence of attraction and repulsion (Milligan and McCreary, Chapter 7, this volume). Grey Owl, playing Indian, appoints himself as the saviour of the Indians and of the wilderness, mourning the passing of what whites have themselves destroyed. Grey Owl's playing primitive, Bruce Erickson suggests, is an integral part of modern identity; settlers must take the place of the Indian, however fantastic a story or violent a dispossession this requires.

Race, Desire, and Knowledge Production

Hearne, Grey Owl, Flanagan, and Alcantara are anti-conquest men par excellence, undertaking the colonial mission not as conquistadors but as men of science, believing deeply in the innocence of the scientific and travel narratives they construct. To know the land is to claim it, and if knowing cannot come from having occupied the land for generations, it must come from science. As Richard Milligan and Tyler McCreary (Chapter 7, this volume) argue, the stories settlers tell of the North contribute to resource speculation and to a disciplinary regime where to know the land and its peoples is to lay claim to it. In this way, such stories render the settler indigenous to the land by virtue of his knowledge and control over it. Aboriginal people can play only bit parts in this drama, limited by the storylines to the role of Friday, Native servant of Robinson Crusoe. Hearne's Friday, the good Native Matonabbee, guides him through the North, but Matonabbee's virtue lies not in his knowledge of the land but in his love for and devotion to Hearne. Eternal *bricoleurs,* or handymen, who possess only intuition and experience (Indigenous knowledge) rather than the science possessed by engineers (Lévi-Strauss' 1966 division of human intellectual activity into two unequal ways of knowing), Indigenous peoples reside permanently in the premodern, destined to be dominated by those who make maps, classify plants, and offer neo-liberal economic solutions. The indigene, Radhica Mohanram

(1999, 14) argues, remains "immobile against the repeated onslaught of the settler."

Is the white desire to re-examine the North itself a story that reinstalls white dominance (Cameron, Chapter 8, this volume)? The contributors to this book worry that in deconstructing the work done by settler narratives, they might be joining the ranks of those whom Robyn Wiegman (1999, 143) describes as anxious to be "former white people," those who imagine that they can leave their race privilege behind through participating in critical projects. Whiteness cannot be so easily transcended, the authors warn, because it is a strategy of visibility; skin still means a great deal, even when, and perhaps especially when, it is the asset deployed in anti-racist and anti-colonial struggles.

There is reason to worry. I expect that some readers will notice that most contributors to this volume are white. All are non-Indigenous, including myself. How, then, are we held to account in a space where we are not directly challenged by Indigenous scholars? The relationship between academic knowledge production and white supremacy is an intimate and long-standing one, and an intense vigilance is warranted. In this practice, we can be guided by the insight that whiteness has a geography, but we must also remember that scholarship too has a geography and work to challenge the conditions that have made us once again the knowers. How are we not Samuel Hearne and Grey Owl?

Notes

INTRODUCTION: WHERE IS THE GREAT WHITE NORTH?

1 This was a documentary for the weekly radio program *Ideas.*

2 Whether Berton made such a reference is open to debate. James Raffan (1999, 255n5) attempted to settle its attribution by appealing to Berton himself. According to Raffan, Berton is on record as saying, "Although I have been for the last twenty years, credited with the quote you use, 'A Canadian is someone who knows how to make love in a canoe', it is not actually my own – at least I don't think so, it's been so long. It seems to me I saw it somewhere else and used it with attribution, but the attribution has long since been lost and I'm tired of telling people I didn't actually think of it. So I'm afraid I can't help you much. I notice I'm even in the *Canadian Book of Quotations* as having said that; so at this late stage it's difficult for me to say I didn't. Maybe I did, but I don't think so."

CHAPTER 1: "A PHANTASY IN WHITE IN A WORLD THAT IS DEAD"

1 See, for example, Harris (1993), McIntosh (1995), Roediger (1991), and Sullivan (2006), who envision whiteness as a problem that focuses upon the investments and privileges it bestows on people.

2 By asking this question, McWhorter (2005) is not dismissing the fact of the economic or social privileges of whiteness. Rather, she wants to emphasize that our mode of action should not merely address providing equal social and economic relationships, but should also question the forms of subject construction that are necessary for the benefits of whiteness.

3 An excellent illustration of this process is Chris Bracken's *The Potlatch Papers* (1998), which investigates the postal networks and letters that attempted to legislate the

potlatch out of existence. Bracken reveals that an anxious need to differentiate European and primitive identities lay at the heart of the potlatch legislation.

4 See, for example, Bracken (1998) on incorporation and death, Francis (1992) on death and assimilation, and Slotkin (1973) on the death of the Indian.

5 Several biographies are devoted to Belaney, with Donald Smith's *From the Land of the Shadows* (1990) being widely recognized as the most authoritative. Much less reliable are the three biographies written by his publisher, Lovat Dickson (1960, 1976, 1984). His third wife, Gertrude Bernard, wrote about her life with Grey Owl in *Devil in Deerskins* (Anahareo 1972), but much of Grey Owl's life is related only as he told it to her.

6 It is, of course, no surprise that he ended up in Temagami, which was already heavily produced as a premier space of wilderness (see Thorpe, Chapter 9, this volume).

7 The most complicated investigation of Belaney's life, failings and all, is Armand Garnet Ruffo's *Grey Owl: The Mystery of Archie Belaney* (1996), a series of narrative poems. Ruffo's investigative and imaginative take on Grey Owl suggests an ambivalence; at times, he gives Belaney the benefit of the doubt, portraying him as a soul emotionally tortured by thoughts of the women he had abandoned and the lies he had told. Although the book does mention how Belaney's actions affected these women, it nonetheless celebrates his intentions over his deception. Thus, the environmental message triumphs over its very flawed racial coding, an ethical decision made by Ruffo and others in their memorializing of Grey Owl, which is illustrative of the whiteness of Canadian nature.

8 Although he had taken on the story of his mixed Apache and Scottish parentage in 1918, for his public appearances he did not object to the claim that he was a "full-blooded Indian" (Anahareo 1972, 138) in hopes that it would help his cause.

9 This points to the significant boundary-crossing abilities of the Indian masquerade, an issue that is discussed at length by David Chapin in "Gender and Indian Masquerade in the Life of Grey Owl" (2000). Chapin suggests that the masquerade allowed Belaney to adopt less rigid performances of masculinity. Although I agree that it was a significant factor in letting Belaney take up a different image of masculinity, the path of his life, the colonial image of a dying Aboriginal past, and his treatment of the women upon whom he depended are all warnings to any claim that this was a benign form of masculinity.

10 As Tina Loo (2006) notes, this surrogacy, with its roots in anti-modernism, was in large part the reason why Grey Owl was a more successful figure than other contemporary conservationists, such as the sportsman Jack Miner.

11 It is important to see that both Grey Owl's and Fernow's projects arose in the Depression era, during a time when citizens felt the vulnerability of their economic circumstances.

12 On wilderness as a concept made legible by the discourse of civilization, see Cronon (1996a) and Jasen (1995). On the Indian, see Deloria (1998).

13 The combination of Lacan and Lefebvre that I promote here attempts to highlight the possibility that our spatial understandings are linked to unconscious processes. For other analyses of the relation between Lacan and Lefebvre, see Blum and Nast (1996) and Gregory (1997).

14 For more on the role of misrecognition in the construction of race, see Seshadri-Crooks (2000) and Winnubst (2006).

15 Seshadri-Crooks (2000) makes clear that this desire to overcome difference is a fact for all racial subjects, including those who conceive of themselves as white (and perhaps more so, since they have more to lose). Whiteness exists as an impossible ideal, and when white subjects confront this impossibility, anxiety ensues.

16 For more on the role of the master signifier, see Žižek (1989), especially Chapter 3.

CHAPTER 3: CAP ROUGE REMEMBERED?

1 These plaques follow the tradition of including the name or nickname of the father in the son's name: for example, Joseph à Cacoune Deveau is the son of Cacoune Deveau. All five families had at least nine children.

2 For an interesting (if highly partisan) account of the building and development of the Cabot Trail, and especially the segment between Cap Rouge and Pleasant Bay, see MacMillan (1993).

3 A travelogue published in 1936 indicates that the Cap Rouge community was clearly visible from the Cabot Trail at the time of the expropriations: "As we move along between the green sides of the road we suddenly get a magnificent vista of red scarred headlands. Near at hand we see good crops and well painted houses" (Brinley 1936, 94). This account tends to suggest that, in large measure, Cautley saw what he wanted to see.

4 MacEachern offers a much fuller discussion of the establishment of CBH than I do here, including the responses of several landowners who lost their homes in the process. Working from Creighton's views of the negotiations, MacEachern considers that landowners were fairly compensated for their woodlots (especially the Oxford Paper Company, whose single settlement was nearly twice as large as all the rest combined), but that the expropriation of homes was much more problematic. Anselme Boudreau, a prominent political figure in Chéticamp during the period, notes in his memoirs (n.d.) that the people of Cap Rouge were not happy with the settlements; his own opinion was that they were fair. Disagreement on this issue lingers among the descendants of the Cap Rouge dispossessed (see A. Boudreau n.d.).

5 In about 1922, New Yorker Lillian Burke began to market locally hooked rugs from Chéticamp internationally. After some skirmishing about profit, the business became independently successful in the form of a co-operative artisanale. Rug hooking remains an active industry in Chéticamp.

6 MacEachern (2001) notes that James Smart, who was in charge of the early development of the park, favoured the name "Cape Breton Highlands National Park" because it included both the Highlands and the *Cap Breton,* thus acknowledging both the Scottish and the Acadian presences in the region (nobody mentioned including a Mi'kmaq name). Indeed, Smart was quite active in his attempts "to ensure that the French culture of the park region was represented in the park theme" (ibid., 70). Still, as MacEachern (ibid.) states, "the Parks Branch could tolerate the associations with people but not the people themselves."

7 Peggy Archibald's (2000) description of the lodge's history includes everything from early publicity brochures bearing "Ciad Mile Failte" (originally misspelled), to the

1949 construction of "Ceilidh Hall," to the adoption of the thistle on the Keltic Lodge crest, to a picture of the gift shop with rows of tartan ties.

8   McKay argues that Macdonald was not himself overtly racist (and did not subscribe to ideas of degeneracy), but that he certainly promoted ideas of racial essence that supported such racist agendas.

9   McKay notes that, in the Victorian imagination, Cape Breton had even been portrayed as "cosmopolitan" because of its rich mix of cultures and traditions. This view is apparent in Vernon (1903), which makes an interesting comparison to Clara Dennis (1942) and Walworth (1948).

10 McKay also points out that the establishment of the Lone Shieling in the park, a simulacrum of a Scottish crofter's cottage, was among the first of Angus Macdonald's acts of tartanization. Clara Dennis (1942, 299) specifically mentions it and quotes the Canadian boat song that was part of its inspiration: "From the lone shieling of the misty island/ Mountains divide us, and waste of seas;/ But still the blood is strong, the heart is Hieland,/ And we in dreams behold the Hebrides."

11 Her Lacanian argument is that the system of racialized difference is an attempt to overcome the failure of sex to appear in language, and that whiteness "tries to fill the constitutive lack of the sexed subject" (Seshadri-Crooks 2000, 6). The argument is compelling, but the important point for this chapter is that whiteness (which is not the same thing as being Caucasian) is an overcoming of the system of racial difference itself.

12 Shannon Winnubst's (2004, 41) psychoanalytic argument about whiteness differs from that of Seshadri-Crooks, but on the important question of universality and disavowal, she agrees: "Whiteness operates as the universal, unmarked signifier through its disavowal of embodiment itself."

13 Seshadri-Crooks (2000, 36) focuses on the regimes of visibility that produce the racialized *body:* "To be subjected to Whiteness ... means that certain marks of the body then become privileged and anxious sites of meaning." My argument here is that spaces are also part of the regime of whiteness.

14 I have made the argument elsewhere (Mortimer-Sandilands 2009) that parks are institutional sites for the naturalization of the nation: they create spaces for a singular natural/national experience out of previous complex landscape relations by erasing those relations in favour of a narrative of ecological/geographic origin.

15 It is not unusual to see Aboriginal inhabitations of landscapes thus rendered as *firmly* past by referring to them using "archaeological evidence"; the *Management Plan* at least dates their inhabitation as "from about A.D. 1000 to *the present*" (Environment Canada 1987, 2, emphasis added).

16 Of course, this is not to say that no one in Parks Canada recognizes that parks embody many conflicting desires for the landscape: such disagreements are the texture of their everyday lives, including everything from the conflict embedded in their mandate between preservation and recreation to the policing of so-called poachers, some of whom are Aboriginal people asserting traditional subsistence rights to lands that have not been ceded, and some of whom are Euro-Canadian urbanites who insist on picking the orchids as souvenirs because one flower is just one flower.

17 The whiteness of park nature-desires is also present in the fact that, for heterosexual white men in particular, such activities as camping are a way of "getting away from it all," whereas, for people of colour and sexual/gender minorities, they are sources of some justifiable anxiety about the possibility of violence. The particularity of the white heterosexual male position is not challenged; it is the "others" who are understood as failing in relation to the reputedly "human" desire for wilderness.

18 Given the archaeological evidence of Mi'kmaq presence in northern Cape Breton, it is doubtful that the Acadians were "the first." In CBH there is almost no public interpretation of Aboriginal presence, although several internal park documents do acknowledge it.

19 Another interesting quality of the guidebook description – one that underscores the fact of the tourist audience – is their unremarked seasonal particularity. There is no snow on the trails, flowers are in bloom, and birds' nests contain young.

20 Les Amis is a park cooperating association, a non-profit group formed (in response to dramatic cuts in Parks Canada during the 1980s) to supplement Parks Canada activities, including revenue generation and park interpretation. Based in Chéticamp, Les Amis also runs the bookstore in the Visitor Centre at the southwestern entrance to CBH.

21 The panels at Le Buttereau are also vague. One states that "you will see traces of the homes of the last five families who were living here when Cape Breton Highlands National Park was created." No mention of expropriation, but at least the park is named as the thing that was created on top of the traces.

22 One interesting image also included in the La Bloque display, and echoed in a different form on both a Le Buttereau panel and the back cover of Aucoin (n.d.), is a map of the individual properties that were expropriated, including a list of the property owners' names. There is also a map of the original land grant from 1864 that highlights the size of the expropriation and the solid long-standing legality of the families' claims to ownership – they had been there for generations.

23 An unpublished report by Pat Rousseau (1972) indicates an even more extensive presence, including a mill, farms in several locations, a mine shaft from the late nineteenth century, a school, widely cleared pasture-land, and the lobster cannery and processing plant.

24 The pamphlet is available in French only, emphasizing its orientation to Acadian rather than Anglo memory. In this respect, it is very unusual: all official Parks Canada interpretive materials are published in both French and English, marking the Les Amis interpretive authority as unique.

25 Again, I would argue that First Nations, whose lands are often directly implicated in park creation, frequently and effectively challenge this universality: at Pacific Rim National Park Reserve, for example, some Nuu-chah-nulth communities have consistently refused to accept the park's infringement on their territory and activity. Although, in some corners, Parks Canada has attempted to include First Nations perspectives in its rewriting of park policies and practices, these perspectives are often reduced to questions of "traditional ecological knowledge" and subsumed into the hegemonic articulation of preservation with progress. See Mortimer-Sandilands (2009).

CHAPTER 4: THE "OCCULT RELATION BETWEEN MAN AND THE VEGETABLE"

1 Mary Kupiec Cayton (1989) has addressed the overt masculinism of Emersonian transcendentalism.

2 Emma Lazarus famously used the phrase "huddled masses" in "The New Colossus," her 1883 sonnet to immigration, which was dedicated to America's immigrants and is engraved on a plaque on the pedestal of the Statue of Liberty.

3 The acreage is based on a figure in *Report on a Comprehensive Plan for Systematic Civic Improvements in Toronto, 1909* (*RCPSCIT* 1909, n.p.). The population figure is from Toronto Civic Guild (1911, n.p.).

4 Hugo Grosser et al. (1905, 152) complained that Chicago's "total park area of only 2,463 acres [was] a smaller area per capita of population" than any of America's larger cities.

5 This is an estimate based on the total number of acres. Rettig noted that not all the Cleveland park acreage statistics he used represented "improved" land; though the lands were purchased, not all the parks were built.

6 This undoubtedly fit well with other efforts in North America to use gardens to reform children. For example, Miller (1909) discussed school gardens for "defective" children in Cleveland.

7 Acreage figures for proposed parks are available only for York Park – 200 acres – in *RCPSCIT* (1909). I conservatively estimate the other twelve proposed parks and reservations, Humber Valley, two at Black Creek, High Park, Dufferin Ridge, Beatrice, Poplar Plains Glen, Eglinton Heights, Water Front, Sugar Loaf Hill, York, and Scarboro Bluffs, at sixty acres. Later, the Harbourfront Plan of 1912 would "add nearly 900 acres of [park land] across the City's lakefront" (Toronto Civic Guild 1913, 5).

8 There is in fact no direct evidence that the guild was aware of this standard or that it actually thought in terms of ratios.

9 How strange, then, that a quick glance at the *Toronto City Directory* (1913, 165-66) reveals that Elizabeth Street was lined with largely Jewish and Chinese small businesses. We find a fishmonger, baker, butcher, watchmaker, poulterer, tinsmith, milliner, bookseller, and shoemaker, as well as grocers, plumbers, confectioners, woodworkers, barbers, Chinese laundries and dry goods stores, a liquor store, a Home of Industry, and the Hester How School, listed among the street's residents identified in the city directory. This hardly seems a congregation of shiftless and dangerous immigrants, yet the directory churlishly notes the occupants of 168 Elizabeth as simply "Foreigners."

10 This ironic barring of children from parks (which did not persist past the 1900s), as well as the seemingly incongruous erection of "keep off the grass" signs in parks, came from certain restriction-happy park boosters who regarded the park as "municipal art." As Julius Harder (1898, 25-45), a New York architect and park and playground reformer, suggested of children, who in modern cities were often treated as "insufferable nuisance[s]," they were not permitted to "'walk upon the grass' because this would destroy the only 'municipal art' which the municipality prides itself in possessing."

11 Why transcendentalism's hope of white transmogrification was not extended to North American Aboriginals, who were aggressively denied their traditional propinquity with nature, needs explaining.

CHAPTER 5: SARS AND SERVICE WORK

1 This chapter is based on research done under the umbrella of "SARS and the Global City: Severe Acute Respiratory Syndrome (SARS) in Toronto," a project funded by the Social Sciences and Humanities Research Council of Canada and led by S. Harris Ali and Roger Keil of York University, which develops a comprehensive analysis of the spread and response to the SARS virus by investigating how processes of globalization affected the transmission and response to it within the context of Toronto as a global city. One issue the project specifically explored is the racialization of the disease (Ali and Keil 2006; Keil and Ali 2006, 2007). The two authors of this particular chapter are white, the research project is headed by a South Asian male, and the group that conducted these particular interviews consisted mostly of visible minority researchers.

2 As we argue elsewhere, the racialization of SARS in Toronto was a complex multilayered process that worked through several scales and topologies of meaning making during and after the crisis. This non-linear process was fraught with contradictions, as some of the medical and community heroes who were lionized during the crisis – first and foremost municipal officer of health Sheela Basrur – were also visible minorities (Keil and Ali 2006).

3 All interviewee names are pseudonyms.

4 Due to a policy change by the Ontario College of Nurses, after January 2007, all foreign-trained nurses must complete a Canadian bachelor of nursing science, regardless of their formal education and how long they may have practised nursing elsewhere.

5 Nursing agencies typically attract newcomers through word of mouth or advertisements in the ethnic media. Agency workers may or may not get predictable hours and locations of work; generally, the more predictable work is for PSW jobs, which pay less. Although many agency workers are foreign-educated nurses, they lack the requisite provincial approval to practise.

6 The Centre for Internationally Educated Nurses (CARE) program counsels internationally educated nurses, offers funding opportunities for assessment testing, and arranges internships at hospitals and health care providers.

7 Hotels are a crucial site for SARS analysis given that the SARS super-spreader stayed at the Metropole Hotel in Hong Kong in February 2003.

8 This includes plans for hotels as sites for the temporary housing of emergency workers, families, and casualties of the illness should a pandemic flu arise.

9 Sonya did not indicate whether employees were remunerated during this time of employer-imposed quarantine.

10 Complicating this discussion is the fact that those workers who perform in Toronto as a global city are not necessarily immigrants per se (that is, with citizenship) but may be temporary workers who undertake specific jobs. It is beyond the scope of this chapter to explore their experiences during SARS.

CHAPTER 6: SHIMMERING WHITE KELOWNA AND THE EXAMINATION OF PAINLESS WHITE PRIVILEGE

1 There is a large literature on the connection between the hinterland and regionalism. Often, these concepts are used interchangeably. We are careful to keep them separate.

2 Steve Pile (1994) uses the concept of "painless privilege" to describe the practices of the privileged and their spatial and visual insulation from uncomfortable questions of race, poverty, and indeed privilege itself. (See Duncan and Duncan 2003 for a discussion of this concept and how it relates to whiteness.) We have inserted "white" into painless privilege to racialize Pile's concept and make it more specific to our case study.

3 Labelling Kelowna a hinterland, as we do in this chapter, is resisted by many. City boosters and interest groups are quick to point out that major political gatherings have taken place in Kelowna and to suggest that this is evidence of its prominence in the political landscape of the country. Also, two provincial premiers (W.A.C. Bennett and his son W.R. "Bill" Bennett) were from Kelowna. Some will go so far as to call Kelowna a "world city." And indeed, if we judge according to its housing prices, it does rival Vancouver and Toronto in this unenviable category (it is the thirteenth most expensive city in the world). On the other hand, we feel this argument constitutes an effort by its elites and business people to inflate the status of Kelowna for financial gain, rather than to truly evaluate its position in the era of globalization. There is, of course, some merit in the view that globalization has reshaped the metropolis-hinterland relationship of the Fordist regime. But this is now about the reinvigoration of places rather than a complete restructuring of their position in the global economy. Practically speaking, Kelowna doesn't have a children's hospital, is often virtually inaccessible by land during the winter months when snow and ice cover the Coquihalla Highway, and remains a four-hour drive from Vancouver.

4 This white-only immigration policy was never fully realized as several writers have demonstrated (P.E. Roy 1989; Ward 1980).

5 This was the case in Kelowna, where a vibrant Chinese community was eventually effaced, its Chinatown buried beneath new urban development projects in the downtown core (Waters 2001; Steeves 2002, 2005; MacNaull 2002).

6 As recently as 2008, Allan Casey (2008) referred to the Okanagan in these idyllic terms.

7 Cascadia is usually defined as the geography of the Pacific Northwest, which includes British Columbia, Washington, and Oregon. A "more grandiose vision" of Cascadia adds Alaska, Alberta, Montana, and Idaho (Sparke 2000, 5, 7).

8 James Ridgeway (1995) shows that the "future homeland" for the extreme right in the USA is the Pacific Northwest.

9 We are not entirely confident of this number, because the study failed to provide a source for it and did not indicate how it defined "visible minority." The latter point is especially important as there has been some movement of Jamaican international students and short-term contract workers into Kelowna and the Okanagan Valley during the years 2006-08. The numbers of Mexican migrant agricultural labourers working on Okanagan farms are also growing. They too are on short-term contracts, usually of five to seven months. None of these groups have permanent residency

status in the Okanagan, and so the 6.2 percentage figure for visible minorities may be a skewed number, making the Okanagan appear more diverse than it really is.

10 Leaders from the regional power bloc have banded together under the helm of the Okanagan Partnership to bring prosperity to the Okanagan region. In other words, they support and foster the neo-liberalization of the region under the guise of sustainable and prosperous development (see also Whiteley, Aguiar, and Marten 2008).

11 The fact of the matter is that Mexicans in Kelowna (and the Okanagan generally) are temporary migrant agricultural workers on short-term contracts. Their status is that of non-citizen, and they are only temporary residents in the confines of farms deep in the woods of the Okanagan Valley. In other words, diversity will not come from this source.

12 For examples of neo-Nazis in the valley and their disturbing activities, see Lethbridge (1994) and Aguiar, Tomic, and Trumper (2005a).

CHAPTER 7: INSCRIPTION, INNOCENCE, AND INVISIBILITY

1 As the United States and Canada have different histories of racialization, we must condition our understanding of the processes of national subjectification with an attendance to geographic and historical specificity (see Bonnett 2000), as well as congruences. Whereas Toni Morrison argues that the presence of the enslaved African American other in the United States is the necessary basis for the development of a national American consciousness as autonomous, free individuals, it is our argument that Canadian identity relies on the abjection of Aboriginal others to construct settler entitlement to the land (see Schick and St. Denis 2005 for an extended discussion of the relevance of and problems with Morrison's work in the Canadian context). This is not to say that the dispossession of Indigenous people was not central to the process of American nation building, for indeed it was. Rather, the distinction between Morrison's emphasis and our own should be read as a reflection of the differing prevailing intellectual predilections between scholars in the two nations. Morrison's emphasis on the formative role of black-white race relations, and her taken-for-granted assumptions that the American land mass was a blank slate for these developments to play out, unfortunately reflects a significant and all-too-common gap in critical race theorizing south of the border. Canadian race scholars, by contrast, have accorded more significant weight to the ways that whites secure dominance in settler societies vis-à-vis both the Indigenous and the racialized immigrant other.

2 Our argument here is not that Hearne's innovation was simply to narrate the North, but that his text is concomitant with the naissance of a new aesthetics in the narration of North. Other versions of nordicity were in circulation. Carolus Linnaeus, for example, went north to Sami territory in Sweden (although he did not travel far) and produced a version of nordicity in concordance with European aesthetics. Unlike Hearne, who described a disorientingly horizontal and horizonless Barren Grounds, Linnaeus ascribed a stark verticality to the North, inventing an Arctic of towering alpine cliffs. Although he also exaggerated his own hardships in the North, Linnaeus ultimately limned an Edenic North (like all natural regions in his combination of natural and economic philosophy) that could produce a viable and self-sustaining

local economy (Koerner 1999, 56-81). Though Hearne's text is typically Linnaean in that it contributed to the extension of a mechanized and systemized view of the natural world throughout the entire globe in an age when exploration and discovery were primary national interests in Europe, his aesthetic rendering of nordicity is distinct, indeed innovative. For an interesting discussion of Hearne's aesthetics of nordicity, see I.S. MacLaren (1984, 1993). For more on Linnaeus' version of nordicity, see Lisbet Koerner (1999), particularly "The Lapp Is Our Teacher."

3 For details on the history of the name, see Cameron, Chapter 8, 169.

CHAPTER 8: COPPER STORIES

1 Hearne's original name, Bloody Fall, which the first Franklin expedition later varied to Massacre Rapids (see Franklin 1823), gradually evolved to Bloody Falls. The rapids are known as Kugluk among Inuinnaqtun speakers (a general noun for "rapids"), and specific parts of the rapids and adjoining land are also named in Inuinnaqtun. Onoagahiovik, for example, refers to a gravelly stretch of land along the western edge of the river known as the "place to stay all night and fish" (J.A. Evyagotailak, pers. comm., 7 August 2007; R. Meyok, pers. comm., 18 August 2007).

2 This approach has obvious resonances with recent geographic, ethnographic, and actor-network interests in "following things," but it is also rooted in earlier northern scholarship, particularly Harold Innis' (1962, 3-6) study of the fur trade in Canada, which traces Canadian economic history in part through the habits of the beaver. Hailed as a "fundamental reinterpretation of North American history" (Winks 1962, viii), Innis' attention to "things" and the specificities of geography allowed for a greater emphasis of the importance of Indigenous peoples in the fur trade. His project was carried forward by a number of scholars, particularly Arthur Ray, whose *Indians in the Fur Trade* (1974) focused on the storying of Indigenous peoples in fur trade historiography. Both Innis' and Ray's sensitivity to the weight of dominant intellectual ideas and the importance of dismantling received approaches to the study of the Canadian North has significantly shaped northern and Indigenous scholarship.

3 My use of the terms "Indian" and "Esquimaux" is reflective of the eighteenth- and nineteenth-century sources from which I draw. When not referencing these sources, I use the name of the specific Indigenous group in question whenever possible or the collective term "Indigenous."

4 The term "Kugluktukmiut" means "people of Kugluktuk" in Inuinnaqtun, a dialect of Inuktitut spoken in the Kitikmeot region of Nunavut and in parts of the Northwest Territories. Kugluktuk was not established as a permanent settlement until the mid-twentieth century, and its Inuit population (roughly 85 to 90 percent) includes people from multiple regional subgroups.

5 Both Hearne's witnessing of the massacre and the occurrence of the massacre itself have been called into question over the past two hundred years. For a discussion, see Emilie Cameron (2009). Because the story continues to circulate as "truth," however, its importance in imaginative geographies of the central Arctic remains relevant.

6 In Qoerhuk's version, the copper knife's value is relational. He suggests that Qinglorqana drops it into the sea because its value as a survival tool has shifted: the men

no longer require it as an igloo-building tool; they need to get off the ice floe, and the knife can lead them home from under the sea. By contrast, Métayer implies that the absolute value of copper knives makes Qinglorqana's "offering" the ultimate sacrifice and appeasement of the spirits of the sea.

7   "Nunavut," which means "the people's land" in Inuktitut, refers to both a territory within the Canadian federation and an Inuit land claim. Although Inuit comprise 80 to 90 percent of Nunavut's population, and some of its governance structures are modelled upon Inuit cultural values, the territory is not inherently Inuit. It is a jurisdiction within the Canadian federation that is predominantly populated by Inuit, but its relationship with Ottawa is similar to that of the Yukon or the Northwest Territories. The Nunavut Land Claims Agreement, on the other hand, outlines the rights and benefits of Inuit with respect to the settling of their claim to the lands contained in the territory of Nunavut. In exchange for converting the majority of the territory into Crown land, a cash settlement was made, Inuit surface and subsurface rights were determined for particular parcels of land, and rights to hunt and fish throughout the territory were articulated. (For a fuller description of the Nunavut Land Claims Agreement and the creation of Nunavut, see Hicks and White 2000.)

CHAPTER 9: TEMAGAMI'S TANGLED WILD

1   The Teme-Augama Anishnabai were unsuccessful in having n'Daki Menan recognized as their territory. The Supreme Court, however, determined that the Crown breached its fiduciary obligation to members of the First Nation by failing to comply with some of its duties under a treaty between itself and the Teme-Augama Anishnabai. For the relevant court decisions, see *Ontario (Attorney General) v. Bear Island Foundation* (1984, 1989, 1991). For information about the current negotiations, see Ontario Ministry of Aboriginal Affairs (2009).

CHAPTER 10: RESOLVING "THE INDIAN LAND QUESTION"?

1   In *Delgamuukw* (1997), the court traced the assertion of Crown sovereignty to 1846, the year in which Britain and the United States signed the Treaty of Washington, establishing the boundary between American and British territories on the west coast of North America at the forty-ninth parallel (Barman 2004, 48-49).

2   It should be noted that the northeastern corner of the province – the area lying to the east of the continental divide – was included in Treaty 8, which is a land cession treaty signed in 1899 between Canada and Indigenous groups. The BC government was not involved in this agreement.

3   The Nuu-chah-nulth appealed to the courts for an injunction to halt logging on Meares Island until their Aboriginal claim had been resolved. In the *Martin* (1985) case, the court ruled in their favour, a decision that undermined the provincial government's ability to unilaterally allocate natural resources in this area to non-Aboriginal groups for economic development purposes.

4   The term "First Nation" came into use during the 1980s, reflecting a desire to move away from more colonially inflected terms such as "Indians" and "Indian bands" and, often, to assert the idea that Indigenous people belong to nations that predate European contact and colonialism.

5   Although the Crown has always been reluctant to use the term "compensation" in the treaty process, the task force report makes it clear that the "financial component" of a treaty agreement – that is, the Crown's provision of financial support to Indigenous governments – stems, at least in part, from the recognition of "past use of land and resources and First Nations' ongoing interests" (British Columbia Claims Task Force 1991, 11).

6   This formula stems, it seems, from a commitment made in the early 1990s by the provincial government of the day, under New Democratic Party premier Michael Harcourt, that resolution of all outstanding land claims in British Columbia would involve no more than about 5 percent of the province's total land area (McKee 2000, 70).

7   In addition, treaty agreements under the BC process may also provide Aboriginal signatories with some access to certain natural resources (such as specific allocations of fish, wildlife, and water) and allow for a measure of Aboriginal involvement in the management (through co-management) of certain lands and resources.

8   The new relationship document also described a number of other goals to be pursued through this initiative, including strengthening First Nations communities and families, eliminating the socio-economic gap between First Nations and other British Columbians, achieving self-determination for First Nations, ensuring that lands are managed in a sustainable manner in accordance with First Nation laws, knowledge, and values, and revitalizing First Nations cultures and languages (British Columbia 2005).

9   In a speech to the BC Liberal Party's 2006 annual convention, for example, Grand Chief Stewart Phillip – head of the Union of BC Indian Chiefs and traditionally a harsh critic of the provincial government's position on Aboriginal matters – described Campbell as "an exceptional, extraordinary, visionary leader" (quoted in Hunter 2007, n.p.).

10 Arnett's source is the 7 January 1853 entry in Douglas' diary, which is located in "Private Papers of James Douglas, First Series," 34-35, BC Archives.

11 It is important to note, as Rossiter and Wood (2005) document, that the referendum, which was highly controversial, generated considerable resistance from Indigenous peoples and organizations as well as from a broad range of individuals and groups in the province.

12 Although the Nisga'a treaty, which settled the Nisga'a claim to territory in northwestern British Columbia, was negotiated outside the BC treaty process, it was nonetheless closely watched by all of those involved in treaty negotiations in the province and came to serve as a model for negotiations taking place within the BC treaty process.

CHAPTER 11: CHANGING LAND TENURE, DEFINING SUBJECTS

1   We recognize that some First Nations people and leaders put forth arguments similar to those of Tom Flanagan, such as Tsimshian lawyer Calvin Helin (whose 2006 book *Dances with Dependency: Indigenous Success through Self-Reliance* is one of Flanagan's favourites), Chief Clarence Louie of the Osoyoos First Nation, and Patrick Brazeau, national chief of the Congress of Aboriginal Peoples. Indeed, many First

Nations subscribe to a great diversity of political approaches and views, although, in writing about Helin, Louie, and Brazeau, *National Post* journalist Kevin Libin (2008a, A20) notes that they are "frequently at odds with the establishment, epitomized by the Assembly of First Nations." He suggests that they are on the margins of contemporary First Nations politics. Here we focus on the research and arguments made by Flanagan and Alcantara, particularly because Tom Flanagan is a mainstream politically influential person in Canadian politics. We feel it is not appropriate for us to interrogate the claims of the others, particularly as the goal of this chapter is to understand how neo-liberal debates about property rights on Aboriginal reserves articulate with the construction of race and whiteness in Canada.

2 Our framing of environmental formations draws from Michel Foucault's notions of discourse and "discursive formation." For Foucault (1972), discourses are productive of objects, and discursive formations are identifiable by regularities in discursive relations.

3 Take, for instance, the title of the recent piece in the *National Post:* "Real Warriors Hold Jobs" (Libin 2008a). In focusing on the so-called universal subject's essential capacity for self-reliance, the headline precludes questions about what kind of job, or why jobs may not be obtainable. The issue becomes simply one of individual success or failure, or how hard an individual tries.

4 Flanagan's most recent edited collection of works on this subject (Anderson, Benson, and Flanagan 2006) is titled *Self-Determination: The Other Path for Native Americans.*

5 We recognize that the expansion of private property rights is also an expansion of state bureaucracy within the reserve, just as Ferguson (1990) suggests. Private property rights are defended at the last instance by state violence, and they are maintained through state bureaucracies.

6 See, for example, *New Socialist* (2006), which focuses on Indigenous radicalism. But see also the websites of the Assembly of First Nations (http://www.afn.ca) and the Union of BC Indian Chiefs (http://www.ubcic.bc.ca/), which are relatively "mainstream" organizations. These points are also emphasized by current or recent Indigenous demonstrations and blockades at Six Nations, Grassy Narrows, and Sun Peaks.

References

A.W.C. 1903. A cruise in the Ojibway paradise. Part 2. *Forest and Stream,* 2 May, 343-44.

Abbott, C.M. 1970. Colonial copper mines. *William and Mary Quarterly* 27(2): 295-309.

Abel, K., and K.S. Coates, eds. 2001. *Northern visions: New perspectives on the North in Canadian history.* Toronto: Broadview Press.

Abele, F., and D. Stasiulis. 1989. Canada as a "white settler colony": What about Natives and immigrants? In *The new Canadian political economy,* ed. W. Clement and G. Williams, 240-77. Montreal/Kingston: McGill-Queen's University Press.

Abu-Laban, Y. 1998. Keeping 'em out: Gender, race, and class biases in Canadian immigration policy. In *Painting the maple: Essays on race, gender, and the construction of Canada,* ed. V. Strong-Boag, S. Grace, A. Eisenberg, and J. Anderson, 69-82. Vancouver: UBC Press.

Abu-Laban, Y., and J. Garber. 2005. The construction of geography of immigration as a policy problem: The United States and Canada compared. *Urban Affairs Review* 40(4): 520-61.

Adachi, K. 1976. *The enemy that never was: A history of Japanese Canadians.* Toronto: McClelland and Stewart.

Adams, A.G. 1909. A lady's hunting trip. *Rod and Gun* 11(5): 400-3.

Adams, J.C. 1896. What a great city might be: A lesson from the White City. *New England Magazine* 14(20): 3-13.

Adams, W. 2003. Nature and the colonial mind. In *Decolonizing nature: Strategies for conservation in a post-colonial era,* ed. W. Adams and M. Mulligan, 16-50. London/Sterling, VA: Earthscan.

Agamben, G. 1998. *Homo sacer: Sovereign power and bare life.* Stanford: Stanford University Press.

–. 2004. *Ausnahmezustand* [State of exception]. Frankfurt: Suhrkamp.

Agrawal, A. 1995. Dismantling the divide between Indigenous and scientific knowledge. *Development and Change* 26: 413-39.

Aguiar, L.L.M. 2006. The new 'in-between' peoples: Southern-European transnationalism. In *Transnational identities and practices in Canada,* ed. V. Satzewich and L. Wong, 202-15. Vancouver: UBC Press.

Aguiar, L.L.M., and T. Marten. 2010. Wine tourism and post-Fordist restructuring in the Okanagan Valley, British Columbia. In *Labour and work in the new economy,* ed. N. Pupo and M. Thomas, 173-93. Peterborough: Broadview Press.

Aguiar, L.L.M., P. Tomic, and R. Trumper. 2005a. The letter: Racism, hate and monoculturalism in a Canadian hinterland. In *Possibilities and limitations: Multicultural policies and programmes in Canada,* ed. C. James, 163-74. Halifax: Fernwood.

–. 2005b. Work hard, play hard: Selling Kelowna, BC, as year-round playground. *Canadian Geographer* 49(2): 123-39.

Ahmed, S. 2004. Declarations of whiteness: The non-performativity of anti-racism. *Borderlands* 3(2). http://www.borderlands.net.au/vol3no2_2004/ahmed _declarations.htm.

Alfred, Taiaiake. 2005. *Peace, Power, Righteousness: An Indigenous Manifesto.* Ontario: Oxford University Press.

Ali, S.H., and R. Keil. 2006. Global cities and the spread of infectious disease: The case of severe acute respiratory syndrome (SARS) in Toronto, Canada. *Urban Studies* 43(3): 491-509.

–. 2011. Global cities and infectious disease. In *International handbook of globalization and world cities,* ed. B. Derudder, M. Hoyler, P.J. Taylor, and F. Witlox. London: Edward Elgar.

Allen, G. 1989. Ministry wants freeze on Temagami logging. *Globe and Mail,* 21 November, A1, A2.

Allen, J., and A. Cochrane. 2007. Beyond the territorial fix: Regional assemblages, politics and power. *Regional Studies* 41(9): 1161-75.

Amin, A. 2002. Ethnicity and the multicultural city: Living with diversity. *Environment and Planning A* 34: 959-80.

–. 2004. Regions unbound towards a new politics of place. *Geografiska Annaler Series B Human Geography* 86: 33-44.

Anahareo. 1972. *Devil in deerskins: My life with Grey Owl.* Toronto: New Press.

Anderson, B. 2006. *Imagined communities.* London: Verso.

Anderson, D. 2004. Reindeer, caribou and "fairy stories" of state power. In *Cultivating Arctic landscapes,* ed. D. Anderson and M. Nuttall, 1-16. New York/Oxford: Berghahn Books.

Anderson, K. 1991. *Vancouver's Chinatown: Racial discourse in Canada, 1875-1980.* Montreal/Kingston: McGill-Queen's University Press.

–. 1995a. Culture and nature at the Adelaide Zoo: At the frontiers of "human" geography. *Transactions of the Institute of British Geographers* 20(3): 275-94.

–. 1995b. *Vancouver's Chinatown: Racial discourse in Canada, 1875-1980.* Montreal/Kingston: McGill-Queen's University Press.

–. 2007. *Race and the crisis of humanism.* London: Routledge.

Anderson, K., and C. Perrin. Forthcoming. Mind over matter: Race, aesthetics and the human. *Body and Society.*

Anderson, T.L. 1995. *Sovereign nations or reservations? An economic history of American Indians.* San Francisco: Pacific Research Institute.

Anderson, T.L., B. Benson, and T. Flanagan, eds. 2006. *Self-determination: The other path for Native Americans.* Stanford: Stanford University Press.

Anderson, W. 2002. Introduction: Postcolonial Technoscience. *Social Studies of Science* 32: 643-58.

–. 2003. The natures of culture: Environment and race in the colonial tropics. In *Nature in the global South: Environmental projects in South and Southeast Asia,* ed. P. Greenough and A. Lowenhaupt Tsing, 29-46. Durham/London: Duke University Press.

Anderson, W., and V. Adams. 2008. Pramoedya's chickens: Postcolonial studies of technoscience. In *The handbook of science and technology studies,* ed. E. Hackett, 181-204. Cambridge, MA: MIT Press.

Angus, E. 1908. Temagami. *Rod and Gun* 9(9): 864-69.

Annett, K.D., L. Lawless, and L. O'Rorke. 2007. *Unrepentant Kevin Annett and Canada's genocide.* Hidden from History: The Canadian Holocaust. http://www.hiddenfromhistory.org and http://video.google.com/videoplay?docid=-6637396204037343133#.

Another Wet Bob. 1899. Temagaming. *Rod and Gun* 1(3): 53.

Apffel-Marglin, F., and S. Marglin, eds. 1996. *Decolonizing knowledge.* Oxford: Clarendon Press.

Archibald, P. 2000. *Sixty years of tradition: Keltic Lodge, 1940-2000, Diamond Jubilee album.* Ingonish, NS: Keltic Lodge.

Arendt, H. 1973. *On the origins of totalitarianism.* New York: Harcourt, Brace, Jovanovich.

Armstrong, L.O. 1904a. Down the Mississaga. *Rod and Gun* 6(2): 55-61.

–. 1904b. Out of doors. *Rod and Gun* 6(1): 15-18.

Armstrong, P., and K. Laxer. 2006. Precarious work, privatization, and the health-care industry: The case of ancillary workers. In *Precarious employment: Understanding labour market insecurity in Canada,* ed. L. Vosko, 114-38. Montreal/Kingston: McGill-Queen's University Press.

Arnett, C. 1999. *The terror of the coast: Land alienation and colonial war on Vancouver Island and the Gulf Islands, 1849-1863.* Vancouver: Talon Books.

Asch, M. 2001. Indigenous self-determination and applied anthropology in Canada: Finding a place to stand. *Anthropologica* 43: 201-20.

Assembly of First Nations. N.d. Unequal treatment of First Nations questioned. http://64.26.129.156/cmslib/general/UTFNQ.pdf.

Attenborough, R. 1999. *Grey Owl.* Culver City: Columbia Tristar.

Atwood, M. 1995. *Strange things: The malevolent North in Canadian literature.* New York: Oxford University.

Aucoin, R. N.d. *Cap-Rouge: Sur les traces des habitants.* Chéticamp: Les Amis du Plein Air.

Bacchi, C. 1982. "First wave" feminism in Canada: The ideas of the English-Canadian suffragists. *Women's Studies International Forum* 5(6): 575-83.

Backhouse, C. 1999. *Colour-coded: A legal history of racism in Canada, 1900-1950.* Toronto: Osgoode Society for Canadian Legal History and University of Toronto Press.

Baehr, P. 2008. City under siege: Authoritarian toleration, mask culture, and the SARS crisis in Hong Kong. In *Networked disease: Emerging infections in the global city,* ed. S.H. Ali and R. Keil, 138-51. Oxford: Wiley-Blackwell.

Baldwin, A. 2003. The nature of the boreal forest: Governmentality and forest-nature. *Space and Culture* 6(4): 415-28.

–. 2004. Ethics of connection: Social-nature in Canada's boreal forest. *Ethics, Place and Environment* 7(3): 185-94.

Baldwin, P. 1999. *Domesticating the street: The reform of public space in Hartford, 1850-1930.* Columbus: Ohio University Press.

Balikci, A. 1989. Ethnography and theory in the Canadian Arctic. *Études/Inuit/Studies* 13(2): 103-11.

Ballantyne, B., M. Bristow, B. Davison, S. Harrington, and K. Khan. 2000. How can land tenure and cadastral reform succeed? An inter-regional comparison of rural reforms. *Canadian Journal of Development Studies* 21(3): 693-723.

Baltzell, E.D. 1966. *The Protestant establishment: Aristocracy and caste in America.* New York: Vintage.

Bannerji, H. 2000. *The dark side of the nation: Essays on multiculturalism, nationalism and gender.* Toronto: Canadian Scholars' Press.

Barman, J. 1981. The world that British settlers made: Class, ethnicity and private education in the Okanagan Valley. In *British Columbia: Historical readings,* ed. P. Ward and R. McDonald, 600-26. Vancouver: Douglas and McIntyre.

–. 2004. *The West beyond the West: A history of British Columbia.* Toronto: University of Toronto Press.

Barrett, C. 2002. *Cape Breton Highlands National Park: A park lover's companion.* Wreck Cove: Breton Books.

Barrett, E.M. 1981. The king's copper mine: Inguarán in New Spain. *Americas* 38(1): 1-29.

Barry, J.W. 1905. Timagami, a region organized by nature for real sport. *Rod and Gun* 7(2): 165-68.

Barsh, R. 1991. Ecocide, nutrition, and the "vanishing Indian." In *State violence and ethnicity,* ed. P. van den Berghe, 221-51. Boulder: University Press of Colorado.

–. 1994. Canada's Aboriginal peoples: Social integration or disintegration? *Canadian Journal of Native Studies* 14(1): 1-46.

Barton, J.W. 1909. The health value of a summer vacation. *Busy Man's Magazine* 18(2): 70-73.

Basso, K. 1996. *Wisdom sits in places: Landscape and language among the Western Apache.* Albuquerque: University of New Mexico Press.

BC Statistics. 2005. Immigrants to British Columbia under the Provincial Nominee Program – Strategic occupations. *Infoline* 05-34 (26 August): 1-2.

Bennett, J.B. N.d. Apple of the empire: Landscape and imperial identity in turn-of-the-century British Columbia. Department of History, University of Victoria.

Bennett, W.R. 2006. Reflecting 100 years (1906-2006) – A legacy of leadership. Speech delivered at the Kelowna Chamber of Commerce Centennial Dinner, Kelowna, 1 June.

Berger, C. 1966. The true North strong and free. In *Nationalism in Canada,* ed. P. Russell, 3-26. Toronto: McGraw Hill.

Berkes, F. 1999. *Sacred ecology: Traditional ecological knowledge and resource management.* Philadelphia: Taylor and Francis.

Beswick, G.P. 1905. After fish in Temagami. *Rod and Gun* 7(3): 316-19.

Bhabha, H. 1990. DissemiNation: Time, narrative, and the margins of the modern nation. In *Nation and narration,* ed. H. Bhabha, 291-322. London: Routledge.

Bhandar, B. 2004. Anxious reconciliation(s): Unsettling foundations and spatializing history. *Society and Space* 22: 831-45.

Binswanger, H., K. Deininger, and G. Feder. 1995. Power, distortions, revolt and reform in agricultural land relations. In *Handbook of development economics,* ed. J. Behrman and T.N. Srinivasan, vol. 3, 2659-72. Amsterdam: North Holland.

Birney, E. 1990. Can. Lit. In *An anthology of Canadian literature in English,* ed. R. Brown, D. Bennett, and N. Cooke, 405. Toronto: Oxford University Press.

Black, J.E. 2002. The "mascotting" of Native America: Construction, commodity and assimilation. *American Indian Quarterly* 26(4): 605-22.

Blackburn, C. 2007. Producing legitimacy: Reconciliation and the negotiation of Aboriginal rights in Canada. *Journal of the Royal Anthropological Institute,* n.s., 3: 621-38.

Blomley, N. 1996. "Shut the province down": First Nations blockades in British Columbia, 1984-1995. *BC Studies* 111: 5-35.

–. 2004. *Unsettling the city: Urban land and the politics of property.* New York/London: Routledge.

Blomley, N., and G. Pratt. 2001. Canada and the political geographies of rights. *Canadian Geographer* 45(1): 151-66.

Blum, V., and H. Nast. 1996. Where's the difference? The heterosexualization of alterity in Henri Lefebvre and Jacques Lacan. *Environment and Planning D: Society and Space* 14: 559-80.

Boag, P. 2003. Thinking like Mount Rushmore: Sexuality and gender in the Republican landscape. In *Seeing nature through gender,* ed. V.J. Scharff, 40-59. Lawrence: University Press of Kansas.

Bocking, S. 2004. *Nature's experts: Science, politics, and the environment.* New Brunswick, NJ: Rutgers University Press.

–. 2007. Science and spaces in the northern environment. *Environmental History* 12(4): 867-94.

–. 2009. A disciplined geography: Aviation, science, and the Cold War in northern Canada, 1945-1960. *Technology and Culture* 50: 320-45.

Bolaria, B.S., and P.S. Li. 1985. *Racial oppression in Canada.* Toronto: Garamond Press.

Bonnett, A. 1997. Geography, "race," and whiteness: Invisible traditions and current challenges. *Area* 29(3): 193-99.

–. 2000. *White identities: Historical and international perspectives.* Harlow: Prentice Hall.

Boudreau, A. N.d. *Chéticamp: Memoirs.* Trans. Jean Doris LeBlanc. Chéticamp: Boudreau.

Boudreau, L. N.d. History of Chéticamp. Cape Breton Highlands National Park.

Bourdieu, P. 2003. *Firing back.* New York: New Press.

Boyer, P. 1978. *Urban masses and moral order in America, 1820-1920.* Cambridge, MA: Harvard University Press.

Bracken, C. 1998. *The potlatch papers: A colonial case history.* Chicago: University of Chicago Press.

Brand, D. 2001. *Of the map to the door of no return.* Toronto: Penguin.

Brand, D., and K.S. Bhaggiyadatta. 1986. *Rivers have sources, trees have roots: Speaking of racism.* Toronto: Cross Cultural Communication Centre.

Braun, B. 2002. *The intemperate rainforest: Nature, culture and power on Canada's west coast.* Minneapolis: University of Minnesota Press.

–. 2003. "On the raggedy edge of risk": Articulations of race and nature after biology. In *Race, nature and the politics of difference,* ed. D.S. Moore, J. Kosek, and A. Pandian, 175-203. Durham: Duke University Press.

Braun, B., and N. Castree, eds. 1998. *Remaking reality: Nature at the millennium.* New York: Routledge.

–. 2001. *Social nature: Theory, practice, politics.* Oxford: Blackwell.

Bravo, M. 1996. *The accuracy of ethnoscience: A study of Inuit cartography and cross-cultural commensurability.* Manchester Papers in Social Anthropology 2. Manchester: Department of Anthropology, University of Manchester.

Bray, M., and A. Thomson, eds. 1990. *Temagami: A debate on wilderness.* Toronto/ Oxford: Dundurn Press.

Briggs, C.L. 2004. Theorizing modernity conspiratorially: Science, scale, and the political economy of public discourse in explanations of a cholera epidemic. *American Ethnologist* 31(2): 164-87.

Briggs, J.L. 1998. *Inuit morality play: The emotional education of a three-year-old.* New Haven: Yale University Press.

Brinley, G. 1936. *Away to Cape Breton.* New York: Dodd, Mead.

British Columbia. 2002. *Backgrounder: Treaty referendum.* Victoria: Ministry of Attorney General, Treaty Negotiations Office.

–. 2003. *The B.C. heartlands economic strategy: A plan to revitalize our entire province.* Victoria: Province of British Columbia.

–. 2005. The new relationship. Ministry of Aboriginal Relations and Reconciliation. http://www.gov.bc.ca/arr/newrelationship/default.html.

British Columbia Claims Task Force. 1991. *The report of the British Columbia Claims Task Force.* Vancouver: BCCTF.

Brodie, J. 2008. Review of Nandita Sharma, *Home Economics: Nationalism and the Making of "Migrant" Workers in Canada. Journal of International Migration and Integration* 9(2): 229-30.

Brody, H. 1981. *Maps and dreams.* Vancouver: Douglas and McIntyre.

Brokensha, D., D. Warren, and O. Werner, eds. 1980. *Indigenous knowledge systems and development.* Washington, DC: University Press of America.

Brown, M., and R. Miles. 2003. *Racism. Key ideas.* London/New York: Routledge.

Brown, W. 2005. *Edgework: Critical essays on knowledge and politics.* Princeton/ Oxford: Princeton University Press.

–. 2006. *Regulating aversion: Tolerance in the age of identity and empire.* Princeton: Princeton University Press.

Bruce, J.W., S.E. Migot-Adholla, and J. Atherton. 1994. *Searching for land tenure security in Africa.* Dubuque: Kendall/Hunt.

Buckland, F.M. 1966. *Ogopogo's vigil: A history of Kelowna and the Okanagan.* Okanagan Mission, BC: Kelowna Branch, Okanagan Historical Society.

Burt, R. 1995. The transformation of the non-ferrous metals industries in the seventeenth and eighteenth centuries. *Economic History Review* 48(1): 23-45.

Bussidor, I., and Ü. Bilgen-Reinart. 1997. *Night spirits: The story of the relocation of the Sayisi Dene.* Winnipeg: University of Manitoba Press.

Butler, J. 1993. *Bodies that matter.* London: Routledge.

–. 1997. *Excitable speech: A politics of the performative.* London: Routledge.

Cadzow, D. 1920. *Native copper objects of the Copper Eskimo.* New York: Museum of the American Indian.

Calder et al. v. Attorney-General of British Columbia, [1973] S.C.R. 313.

Calliste, A., and G.J. Sefa Dei, eds. 2000. *Anti-racist feminism: Critical race and gender studies.* Halifax: Fernwood.

Cameron, E. 2009. "To mourn": Emotional geographies and natural histories of the Canadian Arctic. In *Emotion, place, and culture,* ed. L. Bondi, L. Cameron, J. Davidson, and M. Smith, 163-86. London: Ashgate.

Cameron, M. 1911. A day's journey in the wilds. *Rod and Gun* 12(8): 1018-22.

Camp Keewaydin. 2007. Ojibway family lodge. http://temagami.keewaydin.org/ article/view/2582/1/298/.

Camp Temagami. 1915. *Camp Temagami: A summer camp for men and boys, established 1900, conducted by A.L. Cochrane.* Camp brochure. N.p.

Camp Wabun. 2007. Canadian wilderness canoe trips for boys and girls. http:// www.wabun.com/.

Canada, British Columbia, and Nisga'a Nation. 1999. Nisga'a Final Agreement. http://www.ainc-inac.gc.ca/al/ldc/ccl/fagr/nsga/nis/nis-eng.asp.

Canadian Broadcasting Corporation. 2001. *Canada, a people's history.* Episode 6, *The pathfinders.* Toronto: Canadian Broadcasting Corporation.

Capper, C. 1998. "A little beyond": The problem of the transcendentalist movement in American History. *Journal of American History* 85(2): 502-39.

Capra, Fritjof. 1983. *The turning point: Science, society, and the rising culture.* Toronto: Bantam Books.

Carefoot, E.H. 1980. Matonabbee: A play in twenty scenes. University of Saskatchewan Archives, Saskatoon, 25th Street Theater fonds.

Carr, A. 1996. *Toronto architect Edmund Burke: Redefining Canadian architecture.* Montreal/Kingston: McGill-Queen's University Press.

Carrell, F. 1907a. Our fishing and hunting trip in northern Ontario. Part 1. *Rod and Gun* 8(11): 931-43.

–. 1907b. Our fishing and hunting trip in northern Ontario. Part 2. *Rod and Gun* 8(12): 1080-91.

–. 1907c. Our fishing and hunting trip in northern Ontario. Part 4. *Rod and Gun* 9(2): 137-50.

Carter, S. 2007. *New England white.* New York: Knopf.

Casey, A. 2008. The lost Eden of the Okanagan. *Canadian Geographic,* July-August, 40-56.

Castree, N. 2001. Commodity fetishism, geographical imaginations and imaginative geographies. *Environment and Planning A* 33: 1519-25.

–. 2002. False antitheses? Marxism, nature, and actor-networks. *Antipode* 34: 111-46.

Castree, N., and B. Braun, eds. 2001. *Social nature: Theory, practice, and politics.* Oxford: Blackwell.

Cautley, R.W. 1934. Report on examination of sites for a national park in the province of Nova Scotia (selections), in searching for the Highlands National Park. *Cape Breton Magazine* 43: 17-29.

Cavallo, D. 1981. *Muscles and morals: Organized playgrounds and urban reform, 1880-1920.* Philadelphia: University of Pennsylvania Press.

Cayton, M.K. 1989. *Emerson's emergence: Self and society in the transformation of New England, 1800-1845.* Chapel Hill: University of North Carolina Press.

CESCR (UN Committee on Economic, Social and Cultural Rights). 2006. Concluding observations of the Committee on Economic, Social and Cultural Rights: Canada. UN Doc. E/C.12/CAN/CO/4, E/C.12/CAN/CO/5. Office of the High Commissioner for Human Rights. http://www.unhchr.ch/tbs/doc.nsf.

Chakrabarty, D. 2000. *Provincializing Europe: Postcolonial thought and historical difference.* Princeton: Princeton University Press.

Chapin, D. 2000. Gender and Indian masquerade in the life of Grey Owl. *American Indian Quarterly* 24(1): 91-109.

Charities and the Commons. 1907. Immigration restriction in Canada. (2 March): 967.

Chief, The. 1894. Away "up North." Part 3. *Forest and Stream,* 12 May, 412.

Choy, W. 1995. *The jade peony: A novel.* Vancouver: Douglas and McIntyre.

Citizenship and Immigration Canada. 2009. Working temporarily in Canada: Who can apply. http://www.cic.gc.ca/english/work/apply-who.asp.

Clark, C.S. 1898. *Of Toronto the good. A social study. The queen city of Canada as it is.* Montreal: Toronto Publishing.

Clarke, G.E. 1994. White niggers, black slaves: Slavery, race and class in T.C. Haliburton's *The Clockmaker. Nova Scotia Historical Review* 14: 13-40.

Clayton, D.W. 2000. *Islands of truth: The imperial fashioning of Vancouver Island.* Vancouver: UBC Press.

Clement, W. 1981. *Hardrock mining.* Toronto: McClelland and Stewart.

Coates, K.S., and W.R. Morrison. 2001. Winter and the shaping of northern history: Reflections from the Canadian North. In Abel and Coates 2001, 23-36.

Cohen, M.G. 2008. Labour policies worsen wage gap. *Okanagan Saturday,* 31 May, A10.

Colantonio, F. 1997. *From the ground up: An Italian immigrant's story.* Toronto: Between the Lines.

Coleman, D. 2006. *White civility: The literary project of English Canada.* Toronto: University of Toronto Press.

Comish, S. 1993. The Westray tragedy: A miner's story. Halifax: Fernwood.

Committee on Parks and Exhibitions. 1910-12. Minute Book, 1910-1912. Fonds 200, Series 638, RG17A, file 14, box 12, City of Toronto Archives.

Coulthard, G.S. 2007. Subjects of empire: Indigenous peoples and the "politics of recognition" in Canada. *Contemporary Political Theory* 6: 437-60.

Couper, J. 2004. *Discovering the Okanagan: The ultimate guide.* Vancouver: Whitecap.

Cranz, G. 1982. *The politics of park design: A history of urban parks in America.* Cambridge, MA: MIT Press.

Creighton, W. 1994. Interview with Kenneth Donovan. Wilfred Creighton and the expropriations: Clearing land for the national park, 1936. *Cape Breton Magazine* 69: 1-20.

Cronon, W. 1996a. The trouble with wilderness: Or, getting back to the wrong nature. *Environmental History* 1(1): 7-28.

–, ed. 1996b. *Uncommon ground: Rethinking the human place in nature.* New York: Norton.

Cruikshank, J. 1989. Oral traditions and written accounts: An incident from the Klondike gold rush. *Culture* 9(2): 25-31.

–. 1998. *The social life of stories.* Lincoln: University of Nebraska Press.

–. 2005. *Do glaciers listen? Local knowledge, colonial encounters, and social imagination.* Vancouver: UBC Press.

Culhane, D. 1998. *The pleasure of the Crown: Anthropology, law and First Nations.* Vancouver: Talon Books.

Damas, D. 2002. *Arctic migrants, Arctic villagers.* Montreal/Kingston: McGill-Queen's University Press.

Dawson, C. 1998. Never cry fraud: Remembering Grey Owl, rethinking imposture. *Essays on Canadian Writing* 65: 120-40.

De Soto, H. 2000. *The mystery of capital.* New York: Basic Books.

Dean, M. 1999. *Governmentality: Power and rule in modern society.* London: Sage.

Deininger, K. 2003. *Land policies for growth and poverty reduction.* Washington, DC: World Bank and Oxford University Press.

Delgamuukw v. British Columbia, [1997] 3 S.C.R. 1010.

Deloria, P. 1998. *Playing Indian.* New Haven: Yale University Press.

Dennis, C. 1942. *Cape Breton over.* Toronto: Ryerson Press.

Dennis, R. 1997. Property and propriety: Jewish landlords in early twentieth-century Toronto. *Transactions of the Institute of British Geographers* 22(3): 377-97.

Deur, D., and N. Turner. 2005. *Keeping it living: Traditions of plant use and cultivation on the Northwest Coast of North America.* Vancouver: UBC Press.

Diavik Diamond Mines. 2002. *Diavik – Our foundation, our future. The story of the Diavik Diamonds Project.* Edmonton: Quality Colour Group.

Dick, L. 2001. *Muskox land: Ellesmere Island in the age of contact.* Calgary: University of Calgary Press.

–. 2009. People and animals in the Arctic: Mediating between Indigenous and Western knowledge. In *Method and meaning in Canadian environmental history,* ed. A. MacEachern and W. Turkel, 76-101. Toronto: Nelson.

Dickason, O.P. 2002. *Canada's First Nations: A history of founding peoples from earliest times.* New York: Oxford University Press.

Dickerson, M. 1992. *Whose North? Political change, political development, and self-government in the Northwest Territories.* Vancouver: UBC Press.

Dickson, L. 1960. *Half-breed: The story of Grey Owl (Wa-sha-quon-asin).* London: Davies.

–. 1976. *Grey Owl, man of the wilderness.* Toronto: Macmillan of Canada.

–. 1984. *Wilderness man: The strange story of Grey Owl.* Toronto: Macmillan of Canada.

DiPiero, T. 2002. *White men aren't.* Durham: Duke University Press.

Diubaldo, R. 1978. *Stefansson and the Canadian Arctic.* Montreal/Kingston: McGill-Queen's University Press.

Du Bois, W.E.B. 1966. *Black reconstruction in America: An essay toward a history of the part which black folk played in the attempt to reconstruct democracy in America, 1860-1880.* New York: Russell and Russell. (Orig. pub. 1935.)

Dua, E. 1999. Racializing imperial Canada: Indian women and the making of ethnic communities. In *Gender, sexuality and colonial modernities,* ed. A. Burton, 119-33. London/New York: Routledge.

–. 2000. "The Hindu woman's question": Canadian nation building and the social construction of gender for South Asian-Canadian women. In Calliste and Sefa Dei 2000, 55-72.

Dua, E., and A. Robertson, eds. 1999. *Scratching the surface: Canadian anti-racist feminist thought.* Toronto: Women's Press.

Duerden, F., and R. Kuhn. 1998. Scale, context, and application of traditional knowledge of the Canadian North. *Polar Record* 34: 31-38.

Duff, W. 1969. The Fort Victoria treaties. *BC Studies* 3(Fall): 3-57.

Dunae, P.A. 1981. *Gentlemen emigrants: From the British public schools to the Canadian frontier.* Vancouver: Douglas and McIntyre.

Duncan, J., and N. Duncan. 2003. Can't live with them; can't landscape without them: Racism and the pastoral aesthetic in suburban New York. *Landscape Journal* 22(1): 88-98.

–. 2004. *Landscapes of privilege: The politics of the aesthetic in an American suburb.* New York: Routledge.

Dunk, T. 1991. *It's a working man's town.* Montreal/Kingston: McGill-Queen's University Press.

Dwyer, O.J., and J.P. Jones III. 2000. White socio-spatial epistemology. *Social and Cultural Geography* 1(2): 209-22.

Dyer, R. 1997. *White.* London: Routledge.

–. 2005. The matter of whiteness. In *White privilege,* ed. P.S. Rothenberg, 9-14. New York: Worth.

E. and S.W. 1908. John Green, guide. *Rod and Gun* 10(1): 10-14.

Eliot, C.W. 1902. *Charles Eliot: Landscape architect.* Boston: Houghton Mifflin.

Emerson, R.W. 1941. *The best of Ralph Waldo Emerson: Essays, poems, addresses.* Ed. G.S. Haight. Roslyn, NY: Walter J. Black. (Orig. pub. 1849.)

–. 1963. *Emerson's essays.* Introduction by Sherman Paul. London/ New York: Dent and Dutton. (Orig. pub. 1841.)

Environment Canada. 1987. *Management plan summary for Cape Breton Highlands National Park.* Ottawa: Ministry of the Environment.

Farish, M. 2006. Frontier engineering: From the globe to the body in the Cold War Arctic. *Canadian Geographer* 50(2): 177-96.

Farr, C.C. 1902. A trip to Matachuan. Part 2. *Rod and Gun* 3(8): 1-5.

Feaver, G. 1977. The Webbs in Canada: Fabian pilgrims on the Canadian frontier. *Canadian Historical Review* 58(3): 263-76.

Feder, G. 1993. The economics of land and titling in Thailand. In *The economics of rural organization,* ed. K. Hoff, A. Braverman, and J. Stiglitz, 259-68. Oxford: Oxford University Press.

Feder, G., and A. Nishio. 1998. The benefits of land titling and registration: Economic and social perspectives. *Land Policy Studies* 15: 25-43.

Feit, H. 1973. The ethno-ecology of the Waswanipi Cree; Or how hunters can manage their resources. In *Cultural ecology,* ed. B. Cox, 115-25. Toronto: McClelland and Stewart.

–. 1988. Self-management and state-management: Forms of knowing and managing northern wildlife. In *Traditional knowledge and renewable resource management in northern regions,* ed. M. Freeman and L. Carbyn, 72-91. Edmonton: IUCN/Boreal Institute.

Ferguson, J. 1990. *The anti-politics machine: "Development," depoliticization, and bureaucratic power in Lesotho.* Cambridge: Cambridge University Press.

Ferguson, M., R. Williamson, and F. Messier. 1998. Inuit knowledge of long-term changes in a population of Arctic tundra caribou. *Arctic* 51(3): 201-19.

Field, E., and M. Torero. 2002. Do property titles increase credit among the urban poor? Evidence from Peru. Mimeo. Princeton University.

Fine, R. 2008. Immigrant settlement in the Okanagan Valley. Paper presented at "Metropolis BC, Regionalization of Immigrant Settlement in Canada: The Attraction-Retention of New Immigrants," University of British Columbia, Okanagan, Kelowna, 15 May.

Fisher, R. 1977. *Contact and conflict: Indian-European relations in British Columbia, 1774-1890.* Vancouver: UBC Press.

Flanagan, T. 2007. A roadmap for Aboriginal self-reliance. *Fraser Forum* (September): 29-30.

Flanagan, T., and C. Alcantara. 2002. *Individual property rights on Canadian Indian reserves.* Fraser Institute Occasional Paper 60. Vancouver: Fraser Institute.

–. 2004. Individual property rights on Canadian Indian reserves. *Queen's Law Journal* 29: 489-532.

–. 2005. Individual property rights on Canadian Indian reserves: A review of the jurisprudence. *Alberta Law Review* 42(4): 1019-46.

Flanagan, T., C. Alcantara, and A. Le Dressay. 2010. *Beyond the Indian Act: Restoring Aboriginal property rights.* Montreal/Kingston: McGill-Queen's University Press.

Ford, G. 1909. The technical phases of city planning. In *An introduction to city planning: Democracy's challenge to the American city,* ed. B.C. Marsh, 123-36. New York: privately printed.

Forsyth, T. 2003. *Critical political ecology: The politics of environmental science.* London/New York: Routledge.

Foucault, M. 1972. *The archaeology of knowledge.* Trans. A.M. Sheridan. London: Tavistock.

–. 1979. *Discipline and punish: The birth of the prison.* New York: Vintage Books.

–. 1991. Governmentality. Trans. R. Braidotti and revised by C. Gordon. In *The Foucault effect: Studies in governmentality,* ed. G. Burchell, C. Gordon, and P. Miller, 87-104. Chicago: University of Chicago Press.

Francis, D. 1992. *The imaginary Indian: The image of the Indian in Canadian culture.* Vancouver: Arsenal Pulp Press.

–. 1997. *National dreams: Myth, memory, and Canadian history.* Vancouver: Arsenal Pulp Press.

Franklin, J. 1823. *Narrative of a journey to the shores of the Polar Sea: In the years 1819, 20, 21 and 22 ... with an appendix on various subjects relating to science and natural history.* London: John Murray.

Freeman, M. 1967. An ecological study of mobility and settlement patterns among the Belcher Island Eskimo. *Arctic* 20(3): 154-75.

–. 1979. Traditional land users as a legitimate source of environmental expertise. In *The Canadian national parks: Today and tomorrow,* ed. J.G. Nelson, R.D. Needham, S.H. Nelson, and R.C. Scace, vol. 1, 345-61. Waterloo: University of Waterloo, Faculty of Environmental Studies.

–. 1989. Graphs and gaffs: A cautionary tale in the common-property resources debate. In *Common property resources,* ed. F. Berkes, 92-109. London/New York: Belhaven Press.

–. 1992. Ethnoscience, prevailing science, and Arctic co-operation. *Canadian Papers in Peace Studies* 3: 79-93.

Freund, D. 2007. *Colored property: State policy and white racial politics in suburban America.* Chicago/London: University of Chicago Press.

Fung, R. 1991. *Out of the blue.* Toronto: Richard Fung.

Furniss, E. 1999. *The burden of history: Colonialism and the frontier myth in a rural Canadian community.* Vancouver: UBC Press.

Galabuzi, G.E. 2006. *Canada's economic apartheid: The social exclusion of racialized groups in the new century.* Toronto: Canadian Scholars' Press.

–. 2008. Social exclusion: Socio-economic and political implications of the racialized gap. In *Daily struggles: The deepening racialization and feminization of poverty in Canada,* ed. M.A. Wallis and Siu-ming Kwok, 235-51. Toronto: Canadian Scholars' Press.

Gandy, M. 2004. Rethinking urban metabolism: Water, space and the modern city. *City* 8(3): 363-79.

–. 2005a. Cyborg urbanization: Complexity and monstrosity in the contemporary city. *International Journal of Urban and Regional Research* 29: 26-49.

–. 2005b. Deadly alliances: Death, disease and the global politics of public health. *PLoS Medicine* 2(1): 9-11.

–. 2006. The bacteriological city and its discontents. *Historical Geography* 34(1): 14-25.

Garner, S. 2007. *Whiteness: An introduction.* London/New York: Routledge.

Gibson-Graham, J.K. 2002. Beyond global vs. local: Economic politics outside the binary frame. In *Geographies of power: Placing scale,* ed. A. Herod and M. Wright, 25-60. Malden, MA/Oxford: Blackwell.

–. 2008. Diverse economies: Performative practices for "other worlds." *Progress in Human Geography* 32(5): 613-32.

Gieryn, T. 1999. *Cultural boundaries of science.* Chicago/London: University of Chicago Press.

Giles, W. 2002. *Portuguese women in Toronto: Gender, immigration, and nationalism.* Toronto: University of Toronto Press.

Glassman, J. 2006. Primitive accumulation, accumulation by dispossession, accumulation by "extra-economic" means. *Progress in Human Geography* 30(5): 608-25.

Goheen, P. 1970. *Victorian Toronto: 1850-1900.* Research Paper 127. Chicago: Department of Geography, University of Chicago.

Goldberg, D.T. 1993. *Racist culture: Philosophy and the politics of meaning.* Oxford: Blackwell.

–. 1997. *Racial subjects: Writing on race in America.* London: Routledge.

–. 2002a. Racial rule. In *Relocating postcolonialism,* ed. D.T. Goldberg and A. Quayson, 82-102. Oxford: Blackwell.

–. 2002b. Racial states. In *A companion to racial and ethnic studies,* ed. D.T. Goldberg and J. Solomos, 233-58. Malden, MA/Oxford: Blackwell.

Goldie, T. 1987. Signs of the themes: The value of a politically grounded semiotics. In *Future indicative: Literary theory and Canadian literature,* ed. J. Moss, 85-94. Ottawa: University of Ottawa Press.

–. 1989. *Fear and temptation: The image of the indigene in Canadian, Australian, and New Zealand literatures.* Montreal/Kingston: McGill-Queen's University Press.

Goonewardena, K., and S. Kipfer. 2005. Spaces of difference: Reflections from Toronto on multiculturalism, bourgeois urbanism and the possibility of radical urban politics. *International Journal of Urban and Regional Research* 29: 670-78.

Gordon, A., and C. Newfield. 1994. White philosophy. *Critical Inquiry* 20: 737-57.

Gordon, C. 1991. Governmental rationality: An introduction. In *The Foucault effect: Studies in governmentality,* ed. G. Burchell, C. Gordon, and P. Miller, 1-51. Chicago: University of Chicago Press.

Gosine, A., and C. Teelucksingh. 2008. *Environmental justice and racism in Canada: An introduction.* Toronto: Emond Montgomery.

Grace, S. 2002. *Canada and the idea of the North.* Montreal/Kingston: McGill-Queen's University Press.

Grand Trunk Railway. 1908. *Temagami: A peerless region for the sportsman, canoeist, camper.* Montreal: Grand Trunk Railway.

Grant, J. 2006. *Planning the good community: New urbanism in theory and practice.* New York: Routledge.

Grant, S. 1988. *Sovereignty or security?* Vancouver: UBC Press.

Green, R. 1988. A tribe called wannabe: Playing Indian in America and Europe. *Folklore* 99(1): 30-55.

Greenfield, B. 1986-87. The idea of discovery as a source of narrative structure in Samuel Hearne's *Journey to the Northern Ocean. Early American Literature* 21: 189-208.

Gregory, D. 1997. Lacan and geography: The production of space revisited. In *Space and Social Theory: Interpreting Modernity and Postmodernity,* ed G. Benko and U. Strohmayer, 203-31. Oxford: Blackwell.

Grey Owl. 1931. *The men of the last frontier.* Toronto: Macmillan.

–. 1934. *Pilgrims of the wild.* Toronto: Macmillan.

–. 1935. *The adventures of Sajo and the beaver people.* Toronto: Macmillan.

Grillo, R. 1997. Discourses of development: The view from anthropology. In *Discourses of development,* ed. R. Grillo and R. Stirrat, 1-33. Oxford: Berg.

Grosser, H., A. Richardson, G. Wilson, J. Smith, and W. Joerns. 1905. Parks and public playgrounds: The record of a year's advance. *Annals of the American Academy of Political and Social Science* 26(3): 152-55.

Grove, R. 1995. *Green imperialism.* Cambridge/New York: Cambridge University Press.

Guha, R. 1997. The authoritarian biologist and the arrogance of anti-humanism: Wildlife conservation in the Third World. *Ecologist* 27(1): 14-20.

Guide, The. 1915. The lure of northern Ontario: A canoe trip in Temagami. *Rod and Gun* 16(12): 1207-8.

Gutteridge, D. 1973. *Coppermine: The quest for the North.* Ottawa: Oberon Press.

Gwich'in Renewable Resource Board. 1997. *Nành' Kak Geenjit Gwich'in Ginjik: Gwich'in words about the land.* Inuvik: Gwich'in Renewable Resource Board.

Hall, S. 1980. Race, articulation and societies structured in dominance. In *Sociological theories: Race and colonialism,* ed. M. O'Callaghan, 305-45. Paris: UNESCO.

–. 1996. For Allon White: Metaphors of translation. In *Stuart Hall: Critical dialogues in cultural studies,* ed. D. Morley and K.-H. Chen, 287-305. New York: Routledge.

Handa, H. 2003. *Of silk saris and mini-skirts: South Asian girls walk the tightrope of culture.* Toronto: Women's Press.

Haraway, D.J. 1989. *Primate visions: Gender, race, and nation in the world of modern science.* New York: Routledge.

–. 1992. The promises of monsters: A regenerative politics for inappropriate/d others. In *Cultural studies,* ed. L. Grossberg, C. Nelson, and P. Treichler, 295-337. London: Routledge.

–. 1994. A game of cat's cradle: Science studies, feminist theory, cultural studies. *Configurations* 2(1): 59-71.

–. 1997. *Modest_witness@second_millennium.FemaleMan©_meets_OncoMouse™.* New York: Routledge.

–. 2008. *When species meet.* Minneapolis: University of Minnesota Press.

Harder, J. 1898. The city's plan. *Municipal Affairs* 2(March): 25-45.

Hardesty, D. 1977. *Ecological anthropology.* New York: Wiley.

Hardt, M. 1999. Affective labor. *Boundary 2* 26(2): 90-100.

Hare, F.K. 1955. Mapping of physiography and vegetation in Labrador-Ungava: A review of reconnaissance methods. *Canadian Geographer* 2(5): 17-28.

Harris, C. 1993. Whiteness as property. *Harvard Law Review* 106(8): 1707-91.

–. 2002. *Making Native space: Colonialism, resistance, and reserves in British Columbia.* Vancouver: UBC Press.

–. 2004. How did colonialism dispossess? Comments from an edge of empire. *Annals of the Association of American Geographers* 94(1): 165-82.

Harrison, J. 2006. Re-reading the new regionalism: A sympathetic critique. *Space and Polity* 10(1): 21-46.

Harrison, J., and R. Darnell, eds. 2006. *Historicizing Canadian anthropology.* Vancouver: UBC Press.

Harrison, K. 1995. Samuel Hearne, Matonabbee, and the "Esquimaux Girl": Cultural subjects, cultural objects. *Canadian Review of Comparative Literature* 22(3-4): 647-57.

Harvey, D. 1989. *The condition of postmodernity.* Oxford/Cambridge, MA: Blackwell.

–. 2003. *The new imperialism.* Oxford: Oxford University Press.

–. 2005. *A brief history of neoliberalism.* Oxford: Oxford University Press.

Hayden, D. 1995. *The power of place: Urban landscapes as public history.* Cambridge, MA: MIT Press.

Hearne, S. C. 1791. A journal of observations made on a journey inland from Prince of Wales's Fort in Latitude 58"50 North to Lat. 72"00 beginning 7th December 1770 ending June 30th 1772 by Samuel Hearne. Stowe Manuscript. Transcription in Library and Archives Canada, Ottawa, MG21-StoweMSS.307.

–. 1795. *A journey from Prince of Wales's Fort in Hudson's Bay to the Northern Ocean 1769, 1770, 1771, 1772.* London: A. Strachan and T. Cadell.

–. 1958. *A journey from Prince of Wales's Fort in Hudson's Bay to the Northern Ocean, 1769, 1770, 1771, 1772.* Ed. with an Introduction by Richard Glover. Toronto: Macmillan. (Orig. pub. 1795.)

Hedican, E. 1995. *Applied anthropology in Canada.* Toronto: University of Toronto Press.

Helin, C. 2006. *Dances with dependency: Indigenous success through self-reliance.* Vancouver: Orca Spirit.

Hendrix, S. 1996. Testing the De Soto theory for property records modernization: An evaluation of the model and its applicability in El Salvador with lessons learned. *URISA Journal* 8: 63-74.

Henry, F., and C. Tator. 2010. *The colour of democracy.* Toronto: Nelson Education.

Herod, A., and L.L.M. Aguiar. 2006. Introduction: Cleaners and the dirty work of neoliberalism. *Antipode* 38(3): 425-34.

Hesse, B. 2002. Forgotten like a bad dream: Atlantic slavery and the ethics of post-colonial memory. In *Relocating postcolonialism,* ed. D.T. Goldberg and A. Quayson, 143-74. Oxford: Blackwell.

Heynen, N., J. McCarthy, S. Prudham, and P. Robbins. 2007. *Neoliberal environments: False promises and unnatural consequences.* New York: Routledge.

Hicks, J., and G. White. 2000. Nunavut: Inuit self-determination through a land claim and public government? In *Nunavut: Inuit regain control of their lands and their lives,* ed. J. Dahl, J. Hicks, and P. Jull, 30-115. Copenhagen: International Work Group for Indigenous Affairs.

Highway, T. 1989. *Dry Lips oughta move to Kapuskasing.* Saskatoon: Fifth House.

Hill, M. 1997. *Whiteness: A critical reader.* New York: New York University Press.

Hodge, J. 2007. *Triumph of the expert.* Athens: Ohio University Press.

Hodgins, B.W., and J. Benidickson. 1989. *The Temagami experience: Recreation, resources, and Aboriginal rights in the northern Ontario wilderness.* Toronto: University of Toronto Press.

Hookimaw-Witt, J. 1998. Any changes since residential school? *Canadian Journal of Native Education* 22(2): 159-70.

hooks, b. 1992. *Black looks: Race and representation.* Boston: South End Press.

Houston, C.S. 1984. *Arctic ordeal: The journal of John Richardson, surgeon-naturalist with John Franklin 1820-22.* Montreal/Kingston: McGill-Queen's University Press.

Hubbard, P., R. Kitchen, B. Bartley, and D. Fuller. 2002. *Thinking geographically: Space, theory, and contemporary human geography.* London: Continuum.

Hughes, C. 1984. History of ethnology after 1945. In *Handbook of North American Indians.* Vol. 5, *Arctic,* ed. D. Damas, 23-26. Washington, DC: Smithsonian Institution.

Huhndorf, S. 2001. *Going Native: Indians in the American cultural imagination.* Ithaca: Cornell University Press.

Hulan, R. 2002. *Northern experience and the myths of Canadian culture.* Montreal/Kingston: McGill-Queen's University Press.

Hulchanski, D. 2007. The three cities within Toronto: Income polarization among Toronto's neighbourhoods, 1970-2000. *Centre for Urban and Community Studies Research Bulletin* 40.

Hulme, P. 1990. The spontaneous hand of nature: Savagery, colonialism, and the Enlightenment. In *The Enlightenment and its shadows,* ed. P. Hulme and L. Jordanova, 15-34. New York: Routledge.

Hunter, J. 2007. How Campbell changed his view. *Globe and Mail,* 13 October. http://www.theglobeandmail.com/news/national/how-campbell-changed-his-view/article125472/.

Hutchings, K.D. 1997. Writing commerce and cultural progress in Samuel Hearne's *A Journey ... to the Northern Ocean. Review of International English Literature* 28(2): 49-78.

Iacovetta, F. 1992. *Such hardworking people: Italian immigrants in postwar Toronto.* Montreal/Kingston: McGill-Queen's University Press.

Ignatiev, N. 1995. *How the Irish became white.* New York: Routledge.

Ignatiev, N., and J. Garvey, eds. 1996. *Race traitor.* New York: Routledge.

Imperial Mineral Resources Bureau. 1922. *The mineral industry of the British Empire and foreign countries, war period, copper (1913-1919).* London: His Majesty's Stationery Office.

Inda, J.X. 2006. *Targeting immigrants: Government, technology, and ethics.* Malden, MA: Blackwell.

Indian-Eskimo Association of Canada. 1970. *Coppermine conference of Arctic Native people.* Coppermine, NWT: Indian-Eskimo Association of Canada.

Innis, H. 1954. *The cod fisheries: The history of an international economy.* Toronto: University of Toronto Press.

–. 1962. *The fur trade in Canada: An introduction to Canadian economic history.* Toronto: University of Toronto Press. (Orig. pub. 1930.)

Intercultural Society of the Central Okanagan. 2008. *The changing face of Kelowna: Are we ready? Summary report.* Kelowna: Intercultural Society of the Central Okanagan/Canadian Heritage.

Inuit Tapirisat of Canada. 1977. *Inuit Tapirisat of Canada: Speaking for the first citizens of the Canadian Arctic.* Ottawa: Inuit Tapirisat of Canada.

Ipellie, A. 1997. Thirsty for life: A nomad learns to write and draw. In *Echoing silence: Essays on Arctic narrative,* ed. J. Moss, 93-102. Ottawa: University of Ottawa Press.

IRRC/AINA (Inuvialuit Renewable Resource Committee/Arctic Institute of North America). 1996. *Circumpolar Aboriginal people and co-management practice.* Calgary: AINA.

Jackson, M. 2000. Grey Owl: Canada's voice for wilderness. *Paddler Magazine* 27(6): 34-36.

Jacobson, M.F. 1998. *Whiteness of a different color: European immigrants and the alchemy of race.* Cambridge, MA/London: Harvard University Press.

Jasen, P. 1995. *Wild things: Nature, culture, and tourism in Ontario, 1790-1914.* Toronto: University of Toronto Press.

Jenness, D. 1922. *Report of the Canadian Arctic Expedition 1913-1918.* Vol. 12, *The life of the Copper Eskimo.* Ottawa: F.A. Acland.

Jessup, L. 2002. The Group of Seven and the tourist landscape in Western Canada. *Journal of Canadian Studies* 37(1): 144-79.

Jhappan, R. 2007. The "New World": Legacies of European colonialism in North America. In *Politics in North America: Redefining continental relations,* ed. Y. Abu-Laban and F. Rocher, 27-50. Peterborough: Broadview Press.

Johnston, H.J.M. 1989. *The voyage of the Komagata Maru: The Sikh challenge to Canada's colour bar.* Vancouver: UBC Press.

Jones, W.M. 1899. *Sport and pleasure in the virgin wilds of Canada on Lakes Temiskaming, Temagaming.* Ottawa: Mortimer.

K.K.K. 1906. Spring's unrest. *Rod and Gun* 7(12): 1380-81.

Katz, C. 2001. Vagabond capitalism and the necessity of social reproduction. *Antipode* 33(4): 708-27.

Keil, R., and S.H. Ali. 2006. The avian flu: Some lessons learned from the 2003 SARS outbreak in Toronto. *Area* 38(1): 107-9.

–. 2007. Governing the sick city. *Antipode* 39(5): 953-55.

Kelm, M.-E. 1998. *Colonizing bodies: Aboriginal health and healing in British Columbia, 1900-50.* Vancouver: UBC Press.

Kelowna Capital News. 2006. British skilled workers interested in coming here: EDC. 25 October, A23.

Kelowna Daily Courier. 2008. Kamloops sawmill shuts down for good. 13 May, A2.

Kelsall, J. 1968. *The migratory barren-ground caribou of Canada.* Ottawa: Canadian Wildlife Service.

Kerr, J.B. 1890. *Biographical sketch of well-known British Columbians: With a historical sketch.* Vancouver: Kerr and Begg.

Keyes, D. 2007. Imaging Canada in the 1950s: Vincent Massey and Crown Imperial. Paper presented at the Canadian Communications Association annual meeting, Congress of the Humanities and Social Sciences, University of Saskatchewan, Saskatoon, 31 May.

King, T. 2003. You're not the Indian I had in mind. In T. King, *The truth about stories: A Native narrative,* 31-60. Toronto: House of Anansi.

Kobayashi, A. 1993. Multiculturalism: Representing a Canadian institution. In *Place/Culture/Representation,* ed. J. Duncan and D. Ley, 205-31. London: Routledge.

–. 2003. The construction of geographical knowledge: Racialization, spatialization. In *Handbook of cultural geography,* ed. K. Anderson, M. Domosh, S. Pile, and N. Thrift, 544-56. London: Sage.

Kobayashi, A., and P. Jackson. 1994. Japanese Canadians and the racialization of labour in the British Columbia sawmill industry. *BC Studies* 103: 33-58.

Kobayashi, A., and G.F. Johnson. 2007. Introduction. In *Race, racialisation and antiracism in Canada and beyond,* ed. G.F. Johnson and R. Enomoto, 3-16. Toronto: University of Toronto Press.

Kobayashi, A., and L. Peake. 2000. Racism out of place: Thoughts on whiteness and an antiracist geography in the new millennium. *Annals of the Association of American Geographers* 90(2): 392-403.

Koerner, L. 1999. *Linnaeus: Nature and nation.* Cambridge, MA: Harvard University Press.

Korneski, K. 2007. Britishness, Canadianness, class and race: Winnipeg and the British world, 1880s-1910s. *Journal of Canadian Studies* 41(2): 161-84.

Kosek, J. 2004. Purity and pollution. Racial degradation and environmental anxieties. In *Liberation ecologies: Environment, development, social movements.* 2nd ed., ed. R. Peet and M. Watts, 125-55. New York/London: Routledge.

Krech, S. 1999. *The ecological Indian.* New York: W.W. Norton.

Kulchyski, P., and F.J. Tester. 2007. *Kiumajut (talking back): Game management and Inuit rights, 1900-70.* Vancouver: UBC Press.

Kupsch, W., ed. 1968. *Proceedings of the First National Northern Research Conference.* Saskatoon: Institute for Northern Studies, University of Saskatchewan.

Lacan, J. 2002. *Écrits: A selection.* Trans. B. Fink. New York: Norton.

Lambert, D. 2001. Liminal figures: Poor whites, freedmen, and racial reinscription in colonial Barbados. *Environment and Planning D: Society and Space* 19: 335-50.

Larner, W., and W. Walters. 2004. Globalisation as governmentality. *Alternatives* 29(5): 495-514.

Latour, B. 1988. *The pasteurization of France.* Cambridge, MA: Harvard University Press.

–. 2005. *Reassembling the social.* Oxford: Oxford University Press.

Laut, A. 1918. *Pathfinders of the West: Being the thrilling story of the adventures of the men who discovered the great northwest.* New York: Macmillan.

Law, J. 1994. *Organizing modernity.* Oxford: Blackwell.

Lawley, D. 1994. *A nature and hiking guide to Cape Breton's Cabot Trail.* Grand Étang, NS: Nimbus.

Lawrence, B. 2002. Rewriting histories of the land: Colonization and Indigenous resistance in Eastern Canada. In *Race, space, and the law: Unmapping a white settler society,* ed. S.H. Razack, 21-46. Toronto: Between the Lines.

–. 2004. *"Real" Indians and others: Mixed-blood urban Native peoples and Indigenous nationhood.* Vancouver: UBC Press.

Lawrence, B., and E. Dua. 2005. Decolonizing antiracism. *Social Justice* 32(4): 120-43.

Lazzarato, M. N.d. Immaterial labour. http://www.generation-online.org/c/fcim-materiallabour3.htm.

Leacock, E. 1969. The Montagnais-Naskapi Band. In *Contributions to anthropology: Band societies.* National Museums of Canada Bulletin 228, ed. D. Damas, 1-17. Ottawa: Queen's Printer.

Lears, T. 1981. *No place of grace: The quest for alternatives to modern American culture, 1880-1920.* New York: Pantheon Books.

Lefebvre, H. 1991. *The production of space.* Trans. D. Nicholson-Smith. Cambridge: Blackwell.

Lethbridge, D. 1994. *SACAR second report: The danger is real.* Salmon Arm, BC: Salmon Arm Coalition against Racism.

Leung, C. 2004. *Yellow peril revisited: Impact of SARS on the Chinese and Southeast Asian Canadian communities.* Toronto: Chinese Canadian National Council.

Lévi-Strauss, C. 1966. The science of the concrete. In C. Lévi-Strauss, *The Savage Mind,* 1-33. London: Weidenfeld and Nicolson.

Lewis, H. 1977. Maskuta: The ecology of Indian fires in northern Alberta. *Western Canadian Journal of Anthropology* 7: 15-52.

Lewis, N. 1916. *The planning of the modern city: A review of the principles governing city planning.* New York: John Wiley and Sons.

Lewis, S. 1950. *Babbitt.* New York: Harcourt, Brace and World. (Orig. pub. 1922.)

Li, P.S. 2003. The place of immigrants: The politics of difference in territorial and social space. *Canadian Ethnic Studies* 35(2): 1-13.

Libin, K. 2008a. Rethinking the reserve. *National Post* (Toronto), 18 January, A1, A19-A21.

–. 2008b. Shackled by red tape. *National Post* (Toronto), 26 January, A1, A21.

Lipsitz, G. 1998. *The possessive investment in whiteness: How white people profit from identity politics.* Philadelphia: Temple University Press.

Loo, T. 2001. Of moose and men: Hunting for masculinities in British Columbia, 1880-1939. *Western Historical Quarterly* 32(3): 296-319.

–. 2006. *States of nature: Conserving Canada's wildlife in the twentieth century.* Vancouver: UBC Press.

Lozanski, K. 2007. Memory and the impossibility of whiteness in colonial Canada. *Feminist Theory* 8(2): 223-25.

Lucas, R. 2008. *Minetown, milltown, railtown.* Don Mills, ON: Oxford University Press.

Luke, T. 1995. On environmentality: Geo-power and eco-knowledge in the discourses of contemporary environmentalism. *Cultural Critique* 31: 57-79.

Luxton, M. 1980. *More than a labour of love.* Toronto: Women's Educational Press.

MacEachern, A. 2001. *Natural selections: National parks in Atlantic Canada, 1935-1970.* Montreal/Kingston: McGill-Queen's University Press.

MacHardy, C. 1999. An inquiry into the success of Tom Thomson's "The West Wind." *University of Toronto Quarterly* 68(3): 768-90.

Mackey, E. 2002. *The house of difference: Cultural politics and national identity in Canada.* London: Routledge.

Mackintosh, P.G. 2001. Imagination and the modern city: Reform and the urban geography of Toronto, 1890-1929. PhD diss., Queen's University.

–. 2005. "The development of higher urban life" and the geographic imagination: Beauty, art and moral environmentalism in Toronto, 1900-1920. *Journal of Historical Geography* 31(4): 688-722.

Mackintosh, P.G., and R. Anderson. 2009. The *Toronto Star* Fresh Air Fund: Transcendental rescue in a modern city, 1900-1915. *Geographical Review* 99(4): 539-62.

MacLaren, I.S. 1984. Samuel Hearne and the landscapes of discovery. *Canadian Literature* 103: 27-40.

–. 1993. Notes on Samuel Hearne's *Journey* from a bibliographical perspective. *Papers of the Bibliographical Society of Canada* 31(2): 21-45.

MacMillan, A.S. 1993. The Cabot Trail: A political story. *Cape Breton Magazine* 62: 66-70. (Orig. pub. 1952.)

MacNaull, S. 2002. The dragon transplanted: Chinatown the way it was. *Kelowna Daily Courier,* 1 December, A3.

–. 2006. Immigration seen as solution to labour crunch. *Kelowna Daily Courier,* 12 October, A3.

Mahtani, M. 2008. Discussant's comment: The "occult relation between man and the vegetable": Transcendentalism, race, city beautification and the park planning impulse in Toronto, circa 1900. Paper presented at "Rethinking the Great

White North: Race, Nature and the Historical Geographies of Whiteness in Canada," Queen's University, Kingston, 1-2 February.

Major, C. 2008. Affect work and infected bodies: Biosecurity in an age of emerging infectious disease. *Environment and Planning A* 40(7): 1633-46.

Manitoba Free Press (Winnipeg). 1894. The barren lands: They are not valueless as generally supposed. 15 June, n.p.

Manuel, A. 2005. Interview by Anna Maria Tremonti. *The Current*, CBC Radio, 24 November.

–. 2010. Review of Tom Flanagan's economic plan for Indian reserves. Mimeo. Indigenous Network on Economies and Trade.

Marcus, A. 1995. *Relocating Eden.* Hanover: University Press of New England.

Marrow, H. 2009. New destinations and the American colour line. *Ethnic and Racial Studies* 32(6): 1037-57.

Marsh, B. 1908. City planning injustice to the working population. *Charities and the Commons* 19(1) (1 February): 1514-18.

–. 1910. The economic aspects of city planning: Paper 57. *Municipal engineers of the city of New York, Proceedings:* 73-87.

Marston, S.A., J.P. Jones, and K. Woodward. 2005. Human geography without scale. *Transactions of the Institute of British Geographers* 30(4): 416-32.

Marten, T. 2009. The reconfiguration of downtown Kelowna, British Columbia, Canada, 1980-2006: A case study of Kelowna's neoliberal downtown transformation. Master's thesis, University of British Columbia Okanagan. http://circle.ubc.ca/handle/2429/11982.

Martin et al. v. British Columbia et al., [1985] 3 W.W.R. 577.

Mawani, R. 2005. Genealogies of the land: Aboriginality, law, and territory in Vancouver's Stanley Park. *Social and Legal Studies* 14(3): 315-39.

–. 2007. Legalities of nature: Law, empire, and wilderness landscapes in Canada. *Social Identities* 13(6): 715-34.

McCarthy, J., and E. Hague. 2004. Race, nation, and nature: The cultural politics of "Celtic" identification in the American West. *Annals of the Association of American Geographers* 94(2): 387-408.

McClintock, A. 1995. *Imperial leather: Race, gender and sexuality in the colonial contest.* New York: Routledge.

McCormack, P. 1992. The political ecology of bison management in Wood Buffalo National Park. *Arctic* 45(4): 367-80.

McCrank, N. 2008. *Road to improvement: The review of the regulatory systems across the North.* Ottawa: Ministry of Indian Affairs and Northern Development.

McDonald, M., L. Arragutainaq, and Z. Novalinga. 1997. *Voices from the bay.* Ottawa/Sanikiluaq: Canadian Arctic Resources Committee/Environmental Committee of Municipality of Sanikiluaq.

McGoogan, K. 2007. Foreword. In S. Hearne, *A journey to the Northern Ocean: The adventures of Samuel Hearne*, ix-xxiv. Surrey, BC: TouchWood Editions.

McGrath, R. 1993. Samuel Hearne and the Inuit oral tradition. *Studies in Canadian Literature* 18(2): 94-109.

–. 1998. *Escaped domestics.* St. John's: Killick Press.

McIntosh, P. 1995. White privilege: Unpacking the invisible knapsack. In *Women, images, and realities,* ed. A. Kesselman, D.L. McNair, and N. Schniedewind, 264-67. Mountain View, CA: Diane.

McKay, I. 1992. Tartanism triumphant: The construction of Scottishness in Nova Scotia, 1933-1954. *Acadiensis* 21(2): 5-47.

–. 2008. *Reasoning otherwise: Leftists and the people's enlightenment in Canada, 1890-1920.* Toronto: Between the Lines.

McKee, C. 2000. *Treaty talks in British Columbia: Negotiating a mutually beneficial future.* Vancouver: UBC Press.

McLaren, A.T., and I. Dyck. 2004. Mothering, human capital, and the "ideal immigrant." *Women's Studies International Forum* 27(1): 41-53.

McWhorter, L. 2005. Where do white people come from? A Foucaultian critique of whiteness studies. *Philosophy and Social Criticism* 31(5-6): 533-56.

Me. 1914. Biff and Hec and me. *Rod and Gun* 16(6): 569-77.

Métayer, M., ed. 1973. *Unipkat: Tradition esquimaude de Coppermine, Territoires-du-Nord-Ouest, Canada.* Quebec City: Université Laval.

Miller, L.K. 1904. *Children's gardens for home and school: A manual of cooperative gardening.* New York: D. Appleton.

–. 1909. School gardens for defective children. *Charities and the Commons* 21 (6 March): 107-9.

Mills, S. 1991. *Discourses of difference: An analysis of women's travel writings and colonialism.* London: Routledge.

Milton Freeman Research Limited. 1976. *Inuit land use and occupancy project.* Ottawa: Department of Indian Affairs and Northern Development.

Mitchell, David, and D. Duffy, eds. 1979. *Bright sunshine and a brand new country: Recollections of the Okanagan Valley, 1890-1914.* Sound Heritage Series 8(3). Victoria: Aural History Program, Ministry of Provincial Secretary and Government Services, Provincial Archives.

Mitchell, Don. 1996. *The lie of the land: Migrant workers and the California landscape.* Minneapolis: University of Minnesota Press.

Mitchell, T. 2005. The work of economics: How a discipline makes its world. *European Journal of Sociology* 46(2): 297-320.

–. 2007. The properties of markets. In *Do economists make markets?* ed. D. MacKenzie, F. Muniesa, and L. Siu, 244-75. Princeton: Princeton University Press.

Mitchell, W.J.T., ed. 1994. *Landscape and power.* Chicago: University of Chicago Press.

Mohanram, R. 1999. *Black body: Women, colonialism and space.* Minneapolis: University of Minnesota Press.

Mol, T., ed. 1986. *The Kristeva reader.* New York: Columbia University Press.

Mollett, S. 2006. Race and natural resource conflicts in Honduras: The Miskito and Garifuna struggle for Lasa Pulan. *Latin American Research Review* 41(1): 76-101.

Momer, B. 1998. The small town that grew and grew and ... *Salzburger Geographische Arbeiten* (Salzburg) (32): 65-80.

Monthly Review. 1796. Review of Samuel Hearne, *A journey from Prince of Wales's Fort in Hudson's Bay, to the Northern Ocean 1769, 1770, 1771, 1772.* 20: 246-51.

Moore, D.S., J. Kosek, and A. Pandian, eds. 2003. *Race, nature, and the politics of difference.* Durham/London: Duke University Press.

Moreton-Robinson, A. 2006. Towards a new research agenda? Foucault, whiteness and Indigenous sovereignty. *Journal of Sociology* 42(4): 383-95.

–. 2007. *Sovereign subjects: Indigenous sovereignty matters.* Crows Nest, NSW: Allen and Unwin.

Morris, P., and G. Fondahl. 2002. Negotiating the production of space in Tl'azt'en territory, northern British Columbia. *Canadian Geographer* 46(2): 108-25.

Morrison, D. 1987. Thule and historic copper use in the Copper Inuit area. *American Antiquity* 52(1): 3-12.

Morrison, T. 1992. *Playing in the dark: Whiteness and the literary imagination.* Cambridge, MA: Harvard University Press.

Mortimer-Sandilands, C. 2009. The cultural politics of ecological integrity: Nature and nation in Canada's national parks, 1885-2000. *International Journal of Canadian Studies* 39-40: 161-89.

Morton, J. 1974. *In the sea of sterile mountains: The Chinese in British Columbia.* Vancouver: J.J. Douglas.

Mowat, F. 1958. *Coppermine journey: An account of a great adventure – Selected from the journals of Samuel Hearne.* Toronto: McClelland and Stewart.

Murton, J.E. 2007. *Creating a modern countryside: Liberalism and land resettlement in British Columbia.* Vancouver: UBC Press.

Nadasdy, P. 2003. *Hunters and bureaucrats.* Vancouver: UBC Press.

Nash, L. 2006. *Inescapable ecologies: A history of environment, disease, and knowledge.* Berkeley: University of California Press.

Nazarea, V. 1999. *Ethnoecology: Situated knowledge/located lives.* Tucson: University of Arizona Press.

Nelson, R. 1969. *Hunters of the northern ice.* Chicago: University of Chicago Press.

Neumann, R. 2004. Nature-state-territory: Toward a critical theorization of conservation enclosures. In *Liberation ecologies: Environment, development, social movements.* 2nd ed., ed. R. Peet and M. Watts, 195-217. London/New York: Routledge.

New Liskeard Speaker. 1906. Oddfellows have glorious trip. 3 August, 1.

New Socialist. 2006. Special edition on Indigenous radicalism today. 58 (September-October). http://www.newsocialist.org/attachments/128_NewSocialist-Issue58.pdf.

Nicoll, F. 2004. Reconciliation in and out of perspective: White knowing, seeing, curating and being at home in and against Indigenous sovereignty. In *Whitening race: Essays in social and cultural criticism,* ed. A. Moreton-Robinson, 17-31. Canberra: Aboriginal Studies Press.

Nieoczym, A. 2007. No sex, no pot for workers. *Kelowna Capital News,* 23 September, 4.

Norris, J.M. 1909. Fishing in beautiful Temagami district: An earthly paradise. *Rod and Gun* 10(8): 696-703.

Nunavut Tunngavik Incorporated. 1997. *Mining policy, Oyagakheoktin Maligakhaen.* Cambridge Bay, NU: Nunavut Tunngavik Incorporated.

Okanagan College News. 2007. Jamaica connections will bring skilled workers, students to the Okanagan. 1 June. http://www.okanagan.bc.ca/administration/ publicaffairs/news.html?BlogEntryID=16972.

Okanagan Life Magazine. 2007. The future of our valley: A round table discussion. November, n.p.

Okanagan Partnership. N.d. *Two tomorrows.* http://www.okanaganpartnership.ca/ two_tomorrows.htm.

Olmsted, F.L., Jr. 1911. The city beautiful. *Builder* 101 (7 July): 1517.

Olund, E. 2002. From savage space to governable space: The extension of United States judicial sovereignty over Indian country in the nineteenth century. *Cultural Geographies* 9: 129-57.

O'Neill, J.J. 1924. *Report of the Canadian Arctic Expedition 1913-1918.* Vol. 11, *Geology and geography.* Ottawa: F.A. Acland.

Ontario. 1906. Department of Crown Lands. Commissioner to Lieutenant Governor of Ontario, recommendation. *Woods and Forests Branch report books,* 20 July. Archives of Ontario, RG 1-545-1-3.

Ontario (Attorney General) v. Bear Island Foundation (1984), 49 O.R. (2d) 353.

Ontario (Attorney General) v. Bear Island Foundation (1989), 68 O.R. (2d) 394.

Ontario (Attorney General) v. Bear Island Foundation (1991), 83 D.L.R. (4th) 381.

Ontario Ministry of Aboriginal Affairs. 2009. Temagami land claim. http://www. aboriginalaffairs.gov.on.ca/english/negotiate/temagami/temagami.htm.

Parkinson, M. 1914. Lake Timagami: A northern Ontario playground. *Canadian Magazine* 43(2): 167-72.

Peake, L., and B. Ray. 2001. Racializing the Canadian landscape: Whiteness, uneven geographies and social justice. *Canadian Geographer* 45(1): 180-86.

Peck, J. 1996. *Work-place: The social regulation of labor markets.* New York: Guilford Press.

–. 2008. Remaking laissez-faire. *Progress in Human Geography* 32(1): 3-43.

Peck, J., and A. Tickell. 2002. Neoliberalizing space. *Antipode* 34(3): 380-404.

Perry, A. 2001. *On the edge of empire: Gender, race and the making of British Columbia, 1849-1871.* Toronto: University of Toronto Press.

Peterson, J. 2003. *The birth of city planning in the United States, 1840-1917.* Baltimore/London: Johns Hopkins University Press.

Petitot, É. 1886. *Traditions indiennes du Canada Nord-Ouest.* Paris: Maisonneuve and C. Leclerc.

Pevere, G., and G. Dymont. 1996. *Mondo Canuck.* Scarborough, ON: Prentice-Hall.

Pile, S. 1994. Masculism, the use of epistemologies, and third spaces. *Antipode* 26(3): 255-77.

Piper, L. 2008. Making northern races out of northern places. Paper presented at "Common Ground, Converging Gazes – Integrating the Social and Environmental in History," Paris, 11-13 September.

Pipes, R. 1999. *Property and freedom.* New York: Alfred A. Knopf.

Pipkin, J. 2005. The moral high ground in Albany: Rhetorics and practices of an "Olmstedian" park, 1855-1875. *Journal of Historical Geography* 31: 666-87.

Polanyi, M., E. Tompa, and J. Foley. 2004. Labour market flexibility and worker insecurity. In *Social determinants of health: Canadian perspectives*, ed. D. Rafael, 67-77. Toronto: Canadian Scholars' Press.

Policy and Planning Department. 2009. *City of Kelowna. Heritage Driving Tour.* Kelowna: City of Kelowna.

Pollan, M. 2001. *The botany of desire: A plant's eye view of the world.* New York: Random House.

Powe, B.W. 1987. *The solitary outlaw.* Toronto: Lester and Orpen Dennys.

Pratt, G. 2005. Abandoned women and spaces of exception. *Antipode* 37(5): 1052-78.

–. 2009. Circulating sadness: Witnessing Filipina mothers' stories of family separation. *Gender, Place and Culture* 16(1): 3-22.

Pratt, M.L. 1992. *Imperial eyes: Studies in travel writing and transculturation.* London: Routledge.

Pringle, H. 1997. New respect for metal's role in ancient Arctic cultures. *Science* 277(5327): 766-67.

Pruitt, W. 1978. *Boreal ecology.* London: Edward Arnold.

Pulido, L. 2000. Rethinking environmental racism: White privilege and urban development in Southern California. *Annals of the Association of American Geographers* 90(1): 12-40.

Qoerhuk, J. 1973. Texte 80, told 11 March 1958. In Métayer 1973, 555-67.

R. v. Van der Peet, [1996] 2 S.C.R. 507.

R. v. White and Bob (1964), 50 D.L.R. (2d) 613.

Raffan, J. 1999. Being there: Bill Mason and the Canadian canoeing tradition. In *The canoe in Canadian cultures,* ed. J. Jennings, B.W. Hodgins, and D. Small, 15-27. Toronto: Natural Heritage/Natural History.

Rajan, R. 2006. *Modernizing nature: Forestry and imperial eco-development 1800-1950.* Oxford: Clarendon Press.

Raney, F. 1910. Canoe trips in Temagami. *Rod and Gun* 12(2): 186-93.

Ray, A. 1974. *Indians in the fur trade: Their role as trappers, hunters, and middlemen in the lands southwest of Hudson Bay, 1660-1870.* Toronto: University of Toronto Press.

Razack, S. 1998. *Looking white people in the eye: Gender, race, and culture in courtrooms and classrooms.* Toronto: University of Toronto Press.

–, ed. 2002a. *Race, space and the law: Unmapping a white settler society.* Toronto: Between the Lines.

–. 2002b. When place becomes race. In Razack 2002a, 1-20. Toronto: Between the Lines.

–. 2008. *Casting out: The eviction of Muslims from Western law and politics.* Toronto/Buffalo: University of Toronto Press.

–. 2011. The space of difference in law: Aboriginal deaths in custody. *Somatechnics* 1(1): 87-123.

Rettig, G. 1912. Civic improvement and beautification. In *Proceedings of the Canadian Club, Toronto, for the year 1911-1912,* vol. 9, 123-26. Toronto: Warwick Brothers and Rutter.

Richards, E. 1910. *Euthenics: The science of controllable environment.* Boston: Whitcomb and Barrows.

Richardson, J. 1823. Appendix 1: Geognostical observations. In Franklin 1823, 497-538.

Ridgeway, J. 1995. *Blood in the face.* New York: Thunder's Mouth Press.

Ridington, R. 1982. Technology, world view, and adaptive strategy in a northern hunting society. *Canadian Review of Sociology and Anthropology* 19(4): 469-81.

River Associates. 2003. BC Provincial Nominee Program: Strategic occupations. Draft evaluation report. August.

Robbins, P. 2004. *Political ecology: A critical introduction.* Malden: Blackwell.

Roberts, D.J., and M. Mahtani. 2010. Neoliberalizing race, racing neoliberalism: Placing "race" in neoliberal discourses. *Antipode* 42(2): 248-57.

Robinson, C.M. 1899. Improvement in city life: III. Aesthetic progress. *Atlantic Monthly* 83(500) (June): 771-85.

–. 1901. *The improvement of towns and cities or the practical basis of civic aesthetics.* New York: G.P. Putnam's Sons.

–. 1970. *Modern civic art or the city made beautiful.* 4th ed. New York: Arno Press. (Orig. pub. 1918.)

Rod and Gun. 1903. Our medicine bag. 4(11): 409, 411.

–. 1905. The "Bobs" on Temagami. 7(4): 424-25.

–. 1911. Why we take to the woods. 13(5): 560.

Roediger, D. 1991. *Wages of whiteness: Race and the making of the American working class.* New York: Verso.

Rose, C. 1994. *Property and persuasion: Essays on the history, theory and rhetoric of ownership.* Boulder: Westview Press.

Rose, N. 1996. *Inventing our selves: Psychology, power and personhood.* Cambridge: Cambridge University Press.

–. 1999. *Powers of freedom: Reframing political thought.* Cambridge: Cambridge University Press.

Rosenzweig, R., and E. Blackmar. 1992. *The park and the people: A history of Central Park.* Ithaca/London: Cornell University Press.

Ross, S., and A. Deveau. 1992. *The Acadians of Nova Scotia: Past and present.* Halifax: Nimbus.

Rosset, P.M., R. Patel, and M. Courville, eds. 2006. *Promised land: Competing visions of agrarian reform.* Oakland, CA: Food First.

Rossiter, D., and P.K. Wood. 2005. Fantastic topographies: Neo-liberal responses to Aboriginal land claims in British Columbia. *Canadian Geographer* 49(4): 352-66.

Rothenberg, P.S. 2005. *White privilege: Essential readings on the other side of racism.* New York: Worth.

Rousseau, P. 1972. Historical background. Seasonal report for Cape Breton High-lands National Park.

Roy, A. 2010. *Poverty capital.* New York: Routledge.

Roy, P.E. 1989. *A white man's province: British Columbia politicians and Chinese and Japanese immigrants, 1858-1914.* Vancouver: UBC Press.

Royal Commission on Aboriginal Peoples. 1996. *The report of the Royal Commission on Aboriginal Peoples.* 5 vols. Ottawa: Minister of Supply and Services Canada.

Ruffo, A.G. 1996. *Grey Owl: The mystery of Archie Belaney.* Regina: Coteau Books.

Russell, B. 1999. *More with less.* Toronto: University of Toronto Press.

Said, E.W. 1979. *Orientalism.* New York: Vintage.

–. 1993. *Culture and imperialism.* New York: Vintage.

Saldanha, A. 2006. Reontologizing race: The machinic geography of phenotype. *Environment and Planning D: Society and Space* 24: 9-24.

–. 2007. *Psychedelic white: Goa trance and the viscosity of race.* Minneapolis: University of Minnesota Press.

Sandilands, C. 2004. Where the mountain men meet the lesbian rangers: Gender, nation, and nature in the Rocky Mountain national parks. In *This elusive land: Women and the Canadian environment,* ed. M. Hessing, R. Raglon, and C. Sandilands, 142-62. Vancouver: UBC Press.

Sandlos, J. 2007. *Hunters at the margin: Native people and wildlife conservation in the Northwest Territories.* Vancouver: UBC Press.

Sangster, S.E. 1912. The woods Indian. *Busy Man's Magazine* 24(4): 122-28.

Sarasin, P. 2006. *Anthrax.* Cambridge, MA: Harvard University Press.

–. 2008. Vapours, viruses, resistance(s). The trace of infection in the work of Michel Foucault. In *Networked disease: Emerging infections in the global city,* ed. S.H. Ali and R. Keil, 267-303. Oxford: Wiley-Blackwell.

Satzewich, V., and N. Liodakis. 2007. *Race and ethnicity in Canada: A critical introduction.* Toronto: Oxford University Press.

Schick, C., and V. St. Denis. 2005. Troubling national discourses in anti-racist curricular planning. *Canadian Journal of Education* 28(3): 295-317.

Schmitt, P. 1969. *Back to nature: The Arcadian myth in urban America.* New York: Oxford University Press.

Schuyler, D. 1986. *The new urban landscape: The redefinition of city form in nineteenth-century America.* Baltimore/London: Johns Hopkins University Press.

Science News Letter. 1931. Airplanes enable geologists to survey Arctic copper. 20(546): 204.

Scott, J. 1998. *Seeing like a state.* New Haven: Yale University Press.

Sennett, R. 1998. *The corrosion of character: The personal consequences of work in the new capitalism.* New York: Norton.

–. 2006. *The culture of the new capitalism.* New Haven: Yale University Press.

Seshadri-Crooks, K. 2000. *Desiring whiteness: A Lacanian analysis of race.* New York: Routledge.

Sharma, N. 2006. *Home economics: Nationalism and the making of "migrant workers" in Canada.* Toronto: University of Toronto Press.

Sheridan, J. 2001. When first unto this country, a stranger I came: Grey Owl, Indigenous lessons of place, and post-colonial theory. In *Mapping the sacred: Religion, geography, and post-colonial literatures,* ed. J. Scott and P. Simpson-Housely, 419-39. Atlanta: Rodopi.

Shields, R. 1991. *Places on the margin: Alternative geographies of modernity.* London: Routledge.

Sibley, D. 1995. *Geographies of exclusion.* London: Routledge.

Sies, M.C., and C. Silver, eds. 1996. *Planning the twentieth-century American city.* Baltimore/London: Johns Hopkins University Press.

Sillitoe, P. 1998. The development of Indigenous knowledge: A new applied anthropology. *Current Anthropology* 39(2): 223-52.

Simmons, N., D. Heard, and G. Calef. 1979. Kaminuriak caribou herd: Inter-jurisdictional management problems. Paper presented at the 44th North American Wildlife and Natural Resources Conference, Washington, DC, 24-28 March.

Slotkin, R. 1973. *Regeneration through violence: The mythology of the American frontier, 1600-1860.* Norman: University of Oklahoma Press.

Smith, D. 1990. *From the land of the shadows: The making of Grey Owl.* Saskatoon: Western Producer Prairie Books.

Smith, L.T. 1999. *Decolonizing methodologies: Research and Indigenous peoples.* London: Zed Books.

Smith, N. 1984. *Uneven development: Nature, capital and the production of space.* Oxford: Blackwell.

Smith, T., and I. Stirling. 1975. The breeding habitat of the ringed seal *(Phoca hispida).* The birth lair and associated structures. *Canadian Journal of Zoology* 53: 1297-1305.

Smith-Rosenberg, C. 2004. Surrogate Americans: Masculinity, masquerade and the formation of a national identity. *PMLA* 119(5): 1325-35.

Sparke, M. 2000. Excavating the future in Cascadia: Geoeconomics and imagined geographies of a cross-border region. *BC Studies* 127: 5-44.

St. Croix. 1901. An exploration to the height of land. Part 3. *Rod and Gun* 3(7): 8-9, 11-13.

–. 1902. Second sight and the Indian. *Rod and Gun* 4(3): 103-4.

Statistics Canada. 2003. Longitudinal survey of immigrants to Canada: A regional perspective of the labour market experiences. http://www.statcan.ca/english/freepub/89-616-XIE/2006001/part5.htm.

–. 2008. 2006 census: Ethnic origin, visible minorities, place of work and mode of transportation. http://www.statcan.ca/Daily/English/080402/d080402a.htm.

Steeves, J. 2002. Kelowna's Chinatown brought back to life. *Capital News* (Kelowna), 3 November, A13.

–. 2005. Chinatown: Kelowna's community within. *Capital News* (Kelowna), 15 July, A3.

Stevenson, M.L. 2001. Visions of certainty: Challenging assumptions. In *Speaking truth to power: A treaty forum,* 113-33. Ottawa: Minister of Public Works and Government Services Canada.

Stolcke, V. 1995. Talking culture: New boundaries, new rhetorics of exclusion in Europe. *Current Anthropology* 36(1): 1-24.

Stoler, A.L. 2008. *Along the archival grain: Epistemic anxieties and colonial common sense.* Princeton: Princeton University Press.

Strahl, C. 2008. Kevin Libin: The lip service must end. *National Post* (Toronto), 22 February. http://network.nationalpost.com/np/blogs/fullcomment/archive/ 2008/02/22/kevin-libin-the-lip-service-must-end.aspx.

Stubben, J. 1885. Practical and aesthetic principles for the laying out of cities. Paper presented at the Deutschen Vereins fur offentliche Gesundheitspflege, Freiburg, Germany, September.

Studies in Political Economy. 1981. Rethinking Canadian political economy. Special issue, 6 (Autumn).

Sugrue, T. 1996. *The origins of the urban crisis: Race and inequality in post-war Detroit.* Princeton: Princeton University Press.

Sullivan, S. 2006. *Revealing whiteness: The unconscious habits of racial privilege.* Bloomington: Indiana University Press.

Sun Valley Window Cleaners. N.d. Jamaican employment and expansion. http://www. sunvalleywindowcleaners.com/Canada-Jamaica/jamaican_employment. asp?firstPlay=true.

Swyngedouw, E. 2004. Globalisation or glocalisation? Networks, territories and re-scaling. *Cambridge Review of International Affairs* 17(1): 25-48.

T.J.T. 1910. Two weeks in Temagami. *Outdoor Canada* 6(1): 18-20.

Taussig, M. 1980. *The devil and commodity fetishism in South America.* Chapel Hill: University of North Carolina Press.

Tennant, P. 1990. *Aboriginal peoples and politics: The Indian land question in British Columbia, 1849-1989.* Vancouver: UBC Press.

Tester, F., and P. Kulchyski. 1994. *Tammarniit (mistakes): Inuit relocation in the eastern Arctic, 1939-63.* Vancouver: UBC Press.

Theberge, J. 1981. Commentary: Conservation in the North: An ecological perspective. *Arctic* 34(4): 281-85.

Theriault, M.K. 1992. *Moose to moccasins: The story of Ka Kita Wa Pa No Kwe.* Toronto: Natural Heritage/Natural History.

Thobani, S. 2007. *Exalted subjects: Studies of the making of race and nation in Canada.* Toronto: University of Toronto Press.

Thomson, D. 1994. The response of Okanagan Indians to European settlement. *BC Studies* 101: 96-117.

Thorpe, J. 2008. Temagami's tangled wild: Race, gender and the making of Canadian nature. PhD diss., York University.

Tomic, P., R. Trumper, and L.L.M. Aguiar. 2010. Housing regulations and living conditions of Mexican migrant workers in the Okanagan Valley, BC. *Canadian Issues/Thèmes Canadiens* (Spring): 78-82.

Toronto City Council. 1911a. Appendix A, to the minutes of the city council for 1911. Report no. 1 Board of Control. In *City Council Minutes Toronto 1911,* vol. 1. City of Toronto Archives.

–. 1911b. Brock Avenue Supervised Playground. Appendix A, to the minutes of the city council for 1911. Report no. 5 of the Committee on Parks and Exhibitions. In *City Council Minutes Toronto 1911,* vol. 1. City of Toronto Archives.

Toronto City Directory. 1913. Vol. 38. Toronto: Might Directories.

Toronto Civic Guild. 1911. Population of the city of Toronto, from 1870. In *Letters, etc., 1911.* Civic Guild of Toronto Papers, S48, Baldwin Room, Metropolitan Toronto Reference Library.

–. 1913. Town planning and civic improvement. January. Civic Guild of Toronto Papers, S48, Baldwin Room, Metropolitan Toronto Reference Library.

Toronto Daily Mail and Empire. 1898. Park area and health. 3 January, 3.

Toronto Daily Star. 1901. Fresh air outings on the water. 13 July, 1.

–. 1902. The *Toronto Star* Fresh Air Fund. 14 July, 1.

–. 1904. One hundred miles in a canoe. 19 August, 5.

–. 1905a. The business relations of eastern and western Canada. 28 June, 1.

–. 1905b. Ontario: A field for the settler, the miner, the lumberman, and tourist. 23 June, 28.

–. 1905c. Temagami, mecca of sportsmen. 23 June, 29.

–. 1907. To regulate parks. 9 July, 8.

–. 1908. Toronto is not without slums. 26 June, 3.

–. 1911a. Funds for playground. 11 July, 2.

–. 1911b. Know thy city. 11 November, 9.

–. 1911c. Playground Assn. to get usual grant. 8 February, 7.

–. 1912a. Inspector Hughes wants vacant lots. 20 November, 9.

–. 1912b. Thrilling escape from burning home. 5 June, 2.

–. 1912c. Using the school plant. 25 March, 4.

–. 1915a. Freddie dreams of woods which he may never see. 5 June, 2.

–. 1915b. Summer heat brought misery to the Ward yesterday. 7 June, 4.

Toronto Globe. 1890a. Public playgrounds. 21 January, 6.

–. 1890b. U.C.C. grounds. 27 January, 4.

–. 1907. The wonderland of the dominion. 3 August, 4.

Toronto Guild of Civic Art. 1909. *Report on a comprehensive plan for systematic civic improvements in Toronto.* Civic Guild of Toronto Papers, S48, Baldwin Room, Metropolitan Toronto Reference Library.

Trails in Time. 2001. Traditional land use and resource management philosophies and practices of the Temagami Aboriginal people: Teme-Augama Anishnabai, Temagami First Nation, Ontario Native Affairs Secretariat joint project. Land Use and Resource Management Research Box 1, A-0. Temagami First Nation Band Office.

Tully, J. 2001. Reconsidering the B.C. treaty process. In *Speaking truth to power: A treaty forum,* 3-17. Ottawa: Minister of Public Works and Government Services Canada.

Turner, F.J. 1975. *The frontier in American history.* Huntington, NY: R.E. Krieger.

UBCIC (Union of BC Indian Chiefs). 2009. Joint statement of the Union of BC Indian Chiefs, BC AFN and the First Nations Summit. News release, 12 March. http://www.ubcic.bc.ca/News_Releases/UBCICNews03120901.htm.

UNESCO. 1956. *The race question in modern science.* Paris: UNESCO.

United Nations. 1948. *The universal declaration of human rights.* New York: United Nations.

Usher, P. 2000. Traditional ecological knowledge in environmental assessment and management. *Arctic* 53(2): 183-93.

–. 2004. Caribou crisis or administrative crisis? Wildlife and Aboriginal policies on the barren grounds of Canada, 1947-60. In *Cultivating Arctic landscapes,* ed. D. Anderson and M. Nuttall, 172-99. New York/Oxford: Berghahn Books.

Valverde, M. 1991. *The age of light, soap, and water: Moral reform in English Canada, 1885-1925.* Toronto: McClelland and Stewart.

Vanderbeck, R.M. 2006. Vermont and the imaginative geographies of whiteness. *Annals of the Association of American Geographers* 96(3): 641-59.

Veiller, L. 1907. The social value of playgrounds in crowded districts. *Charities and the Commons* 18 (3 August): 507-10.

Venema, K. 1998. Mapping culture onto geography: "Distance from the fort" in Samuel Hearne's journal. *Studies in Canadian Literature* 23(1): 9-31.

–. 2000. "Under the protection of a principal man": A white man, the hero, and his wives in Samuel Hearne's journey. *Essays on Canadian Writing* 70: 162-91.

Vernon, C.W. 1903. *Cape Breton, Canada, at the beginning of the twentieth century: A treatise of natural resources and development.* Toronto: National Publishing.

Vosko, L. 2000. *Temporary work.* Toronto: University of Toronto Press.

Wadsworth, W.R. 1899. With rifle and rod in the moose lands of northern Ontario. Part 1. *Canadian Magazine* 13(2): 149-57.

Wagner, J. 2008. Landscape aesthetics, water, and settler colonialism in the Okanagan Valley of British Columbia. *Journal of Ecological Anthropology* 12(1): 22-38.

Waiser, B. 1995. *Park prisoners: The untold story of Western Canada's national parks, 1915-1946.* Saskatoon: Fifth House.

Walcott, R. 2003. *Black like who? Writing black Canada.* Toronto: Insomniac.

Waldinger, R., and M.I. Lichter. 2003. *How the other half works: Immigration and the social organization of labor.* Berkeley: University of California Press.

Wall, S. 2005. Totem poles, teepees, and token traditions: "Playing Indian" at Ontario summer camps, 1920-1955. *Canadian Historical Review* 86(3): 513-44.

Walton, E. 1899. A woman's views on camping out. *Rod and Gun* 1(4): 72-74.

Walton-Roberts, M. 2004. Rescaling citizenship: Gendering Canadian immigration policy. *Political Geography* 23: 265-81.

–. 2005. Regional immigration and dispersal: Lessons from small- and medium-sized urban centres in British Columbia. *Canadian Ethnic Studies* 37(3): 12-34.

Walworth, A. 1948. *Cape Breton: Isle of romance.* Toronto: Longmans, Green.

Wang, M. 2004. Body politics in the SARS crisis. *Positions* 12(2): 587-96.

Ward, W.P. 1980. *White Canada forever: Popular attitudes and public policy toward Orientals in British Columbia.* Montreal/Kingston: McGill-Queen's University Press.

Waters, A. 2001. Kelowna's vanished Chinatown. *Kelowna Capital News,* 25 February, A3.

Watkins, M. 1977. The staple theory revisited. *Journal of Canadian Studies* 12(5): 83-95.

Weindling, P. 2000. *Epidemics and genocide in eastern Europe, 1890-1945.* Oxford: Oxford University Press.

Wenzel, G. 1991. *Animal rights, human rights.* Toronto: University of Toronto Press.

–. 1999. Traditional ecological knowledge and Inuit reflections of TEK research and ethics. *Arctic* 52(2): 113-24.

Whatmore, S. 2002. *Hybrid geographies: Natures, cultures, spaces.* London: Sage.

White, R. 1991. *The middle ground: Indians, empires and republics in the Great Lakes region, 1650-1815.* New York: Cambridge University Press.

Whiteley, R., L. Aguiar, and T. Marten. 2008. The neoliberal transnational university: The case of UBC Okanagan. *Capital and Class* 96: 115-44.

Wiegman, R. 1999. Whiteness studies and the paradox of particularity. *Boundary 2* 26(3): 115-50.

Wilder, C.S. 2000. *A covenant with color: Race and social power in Brooklyn.* New York: Columbia University Press.

Williams, G. 1970. The Hudson's Bay Company and its critics in the eighteenth century. *Transactions of the Royal Historical Society* 20: 149-71.

Williams, R., Jr. 2000. Documents of barbarism: The contemporary legacy of European racism and colonialism in the narrative traditions of federal Indian law. In *Critical race theory: The cutting edge,* ed. R. Delgado and J. Stafancic, 98-109. Philadelphia: Temple University Press.

Wilmot, S. 2005. *Taking responsibility, taking direction: White anti-racism in Canada.* Winnipeg: Arbeiter Ring.

Wilson, W. 1981. J. Horace McFarland and the City Beautiful movement. *Journal of Urban History* 7(3): 315-34.

–. 1989. *The City Beautiful movement.* Baltimore/London: Johns Hopkins University Press.

Winks, R. 1962. Foreword. In Innis 1962, vii-xv.

Winnubst, S. 2004. Is the mirror racist? Interrogating the space of whiteness. *Philosophy and Social Criticism* 30(1): 25-50.

–. 2006. *Queering freedom.* Bloomington: Indiana University Press.

Wolkowitz, C. 2006. *Bodies at work.* London: Sage.

Wong, L., and R. Trumper. 2007. Canada's guest workers: Racialized, gendered, and flexible. In *Race and racism in 21st century Canada: Continuity, complexity and change,* ed. S.P. Hier and B.S. Bolaria, 151-70. Peterborough: Broadview Press.

Wood, B. 1976. The growth of the soul: Coleridge's dialectical method and the strategy of Emerson's *Nature. PMLA* 91(3): 385-87.

Wood, P., and L. Gilbert. 2005. Multiculturalism in Canada: Accidental discourse, alternative vision, urban practice. *International Journal of Urban and Regional Research* 29: 679-91.

Woodsworth, J.S. 1972. *My neighbour.* Introduction by R. Allen. Toronto: University of Toronto Press. (Orig. pub. 1911.)

Woolford, A. 2005. *Between justice and certainty: Treaty making in British Columbia.* Vancouver: UBC Press.

World Commission on Environment and Development. 1987. *Our common future.* Oxford: Oxford University Press.

Wuest, D.Y. 2005. *Coldstream: The ranch where it all began.* Madeira Park, BC: Harbour.

Wylie, J. 2007. *Landscape.* London: Routledge.

Wynn, G. 2007. *Canada and Arctic North America: An environmental history.* Denver/Oxford: ABC-CLIO.

Yeigh, F. 1906. Touring in Temagami land. *Rod and Gun* 8(5): 324-27.

Young, T. 1996. Social reform through parks: The American Civic Association's program for a better America. *Journal of Historical Geography* 22(4): 460-72.

Zaslow, M. 1988. *The northward expansion of Canada, 1914-1967.* Toronto: McClelland and Stewart.

Žižek, S. 1989. *The sublime object of ideology.* New York: Verso.

Zoellner, D. 2004. Syndicates coaxed easterners to Kelowna. In *Our history, our heritage: One hundred stories celebrating one hundred years of Kelowna and district history,* ed. J. Ohs, 112-13. Kelowna: Okanagan Historical Society, Kelowna Branch.

Zucchi, J. 1988. *Italians in Toronto: Development of a national identity.* Montreal/Kingston: McGill-Queen's University Press.

Zueblin, C. 1905. *A decade of civic development.* Chicago: University of Chicago Press.

Contributors

Luis L.M. Aguiar is an associate professor of sociology and graduate co-ordinator for Unit 6 in the Irving Barber School of Arts and Sciences at the University of British Columbia. His research focuses on the racialization of the Okanagan Valley. He is co-editor of *White Fantasies: Whiteness in the hinterland of British Columbia* (forthcoming 2011) and of *The dirty work of neoliberalism* (2006). Currently, he is investigating the rise of global unions and their relevance for building cleaners across the globe.

Kay Anderson is a professor of cultural geography at the University of Western Sydney. The author of numerous works on race historiography, including *Race and the crisis of humanism* (2007), she also studied the historical geographies of racism in Canada, published in *Vancouver's Chinatown: Racial discourse in Canada 1875-1980* (2006). She has been editor of *Progress in human geography* and co-editor of the *Handbook of cultural geography* (2002).

Andrew Baldwin is a lecturer in human geography at Durham University. His current research focuses on environmental citizenship, environmental migration, race, and nature, and draws extensively from cultural and political theory.

Stephen Bocking is a professor of environmental history and policy, and chair of the Environmental and Resource Studies Program at Trent University in Peterborough, Ontario. His research interests include the environmental history of Arctic science and the political and social roles of science in environmental affairs. His most recent book is *Nature's experts: Science, politics, and the environment* (2004).

Emilie Cameron is an assistant professor in the Department of Geography and Environmental Studies at Carleton University. She is interested in relations between Indigenous and non-Indigenous peoples in Canada and the ways in which stories structure colonial and decolonizing geographies. Her current research examines the relationship between mineral exploration and mine development in the central Arctic and the settlement of comprehensive land claims.

Laura Cameron is a Canada research chair in historical geographies of nature at Queen's University in Kingston, Ontario, and her recent work addresses cultures of nature, art, and psychoanalysis. She heads the Transnational Ecologies subcluster of NiCHE (Network in Canadian History and Environment), which works to deepen communication concerning migrations of both species and environmental knowledge.

Jessica Dempsey is a doctoral candidate in the Department of Geography at the University of British Columbia. She is currently studying market-based biodiversity conservation.

Brian Egan is an assistant professor (adjunct) in the School of Environmental Studies at the University of Victoria, BC. His research focuses on historical and contemporary Indigenous struggles over land and natural resources in British Columbia.

Bruce Erickson is a post-doctoral fellow in environmental history at Nipissing University. His research interests include the cultural politics of the canoe in Canada and the relationship between wilderness politics and recreational activities. He is the co-editor (with Catriona Sandilands) of *Queer ecologies: Sex, nature, politics, desire* (2010).

Kevin Gould is an assistant professor in the Department of Geography, Planning and Environment at Concordia University in Montreal. He has broad research interests in economic geography and political ecology. His current work examines the politics of neo-liberal land policies in Guatemala.

Roger Keil is the director of the City Institute and a professor at the Faculty of Environmental Studies at York University, Toronto. His current research is on cities and infectious disease, urban and regional governance, global suburbanism, and urban infrastructures. His most recent publications are *Networked disease: Emerging infections in the global city* (co-edited with S. Harris Ali, 2008), *Leviathan undone? Towards a political economy of scale* (co-edited with Rianne Mahon, 2009), and *Changing Toronto: Governing urban neoliberalism* (co-authored with Julie-Anne Boudreau and Douglas Young, 2009).

Audrey Kobayashi is a professor and Queen's research chair in the Department of Geography at Queen's University. Her research is in anti-racism, immigration, citizenship, community participation, and critical disability studies.

Phillip Gordon Mackintosh is an associate professor in the Department of Geography at Brock University, St. Catharines, Ontario. He researches the social and cultural production of public spaces in the Victorian and Edwardian city.

Claire Major is a doctoral candidate at the Department of Geography, York University. Her dissertation is on the relationship between social class, social reproduction, and urban materiality in Fort McMurray, Alberta.

Tina I.L. Marten is an interdisciplinary PhD student (sociology and geography) in the Interdisciplinary Graduate Studies Department at the University of British Columbia – Okanagan. She studies neo-liberalism, immigration, and whiteness in Kelowna and the Okanagan Valley.

Tyler McCreary is a doctoral candidate in the Department of Geography at York University. His research interests include the geographies of whiteness and indigeneity, and the post-colonial politics of place. His current research explores the geographies of contemporary relationships between settlers and First Nations peoples in northern British Columbia.

Richard Milligan is a PhD student in the Department of Geography at the University of Georgia. His current research focuses on epistemic communities of nature, the performance of environmental knowledges, and the cultures and politics of conservation.

Sherene H. Razack is a professor in sociology and equity studies in education at the Ontario Institute for Studies in Education of the University of Toronto. Her interests lie in the area of race and gender issues in the law. Her most recent book is *Casting out: The eviction of Muslims from Western law and politics* (2008). She has also published *Dark threats and white knights: The Somalia affair, peacekeeping and the new imperialism* (2004), an edited collection *Race, space and the law: Unmapping a white settler society* (2002), and *Looking white people in the eye: Gender, race, and culture in courtrooms and classrooms* (2000).

Catriona Sandilands is Canada research chair in sustainability and culture in the Faculty of Environmental Studies at York University. Author of *The good-natured feminist: Ecofeminism and the quest for democracy* (1999), she is also co-editor of *This elusive land: Women and the Canadian environment* (2004) and (with Bruce Erickson) *Queer ecologies: Sex, nature, politics, desire* (2010). Her research has focused on the histories, cultures, and politics of Canadian national parks.

Juanita Sundberg is an assistant professor of geography at the University of British Columbia. She brings the insights of feminist geography and the sensibilities of an ethnographer to bear on the cultural politics of nature conservation. Her current research project examines how nature is enrolled in producing, negotiating, and contesting the US-Mexico border.

Jocelyn Thorpe is an assistant professor in the Department of Women's Studies at Memorial University of Newfoundland. She is the author of *Temagami's tangled wild: Race, gender, and the making of Canadian nature* (forthcoming), and her research examines how ideas about nature, race, gender, and nation shape our interactions with one another and with our environments.

Index

Notes: CBH stands for Cape Breton Highlands. Page numbers in italics indicate an illustration.

Aberdeen, Lord, 134
Aboriginal peoples. *See* Indigenous peoples, *and entry following*
Aborigines, Australian, 228-29, 261-62
Acadians, of Cap Rouge: expropriation of, 12, 62-82, 268; families of, 63-64, 67-68, 78-80; as figures of past, 63-65, 72-73, 74, 76-80, 82; ghosts of, 63-64, 76-80, 82; and history of previous expulsion, 73, 81-82; interpretive panels/materials on, 63-65, 76-80, 81, 276*nn*21-22, 276*n*24; ruined houses of, 63-64, 79-80. *See also* Cap Rouge, NS, expropriations at
actor-network theory, 13, 171, 188-90
African Americans, 5-6, 280*n*1
Agamben, Giorgio, and state of emergency/exception, 109, 110, 123
Alcantara, Christopher. *See* private property on reserves (Flanagan/ Alcantara)

Amis du Plein Air, Les, 65, 276*n*20; interpretive panels/materials by, 63-65, 76-80, 81, 276*nn*21-22, 276*n*24
Anahareo (Gertrude Bernard), 24, 25
anthrax threat, in US, 110
anthropologists, in northern Canada: ecological approaches by, 52-53, 56; and Indigenous knowledge, 49-51, 52-53, 56-57, 59, 269; and Indigenous land claims, 56-57; and studies of Inuit, 50, 181
"anti-conquest": in Hearne's *Journey*, 161-65; and Temagami tourism, 199, 207-8
anti-modernism: in CBH National Park, 64, 68-72, 267-68; in Grey Owl's world, 22-23, 26-30, 31, 34, 270, 273*nn*9-10; in Temagami, 204-5. *See also* modernity *entries;* past, historical
"anti-politics machine," 254-55

Arctic, Canadian. *See* North, Canadian,
    and entry following
Arctic Environmental Protection
    Strategy, 41
Arctic Institute of North America, 46
Asian Canadians: in British Columbia,
    122, 125, 131-32, 217-18, 279n5;
    and SARS outbreak in Toronto,
    107-26
Assembly of First Nations, 283n1, 284n6
Athabaska tar sands, 59
Athapaskan peoples, 50-51
Attenborough, Richard, 37
Atwood, Margaret, 22, 25, 37, 195, 269
Aurora Research Institute, 56
Australia: Aborigines of, 261-62;
    patriarchal white sovereignty in,
    228-29; Wide Brown Land of,
    259-63

Bakhtin, Mikhail, 108; carnival
    metaphor of, 107, 108-9, 117, 120,
    125-26
Banff National Park, 65
Basrur, Sheela, 278n2
beavers, Grey Owl and, 24-25, 30, 31,
    32, 37
Belaney, Archibald, 21-26; early life/
    relationships of, 23-25, 273n7;
    Indian surrogacy by, 11, 21-22,
    24-38, 270, 273nn8-10; pen name
    of, 25; as trapper/guide, 21-24.
    See also Grey Owl
Bengough, John, 103
Bennett, W.A.C., 279n3
Bennett, W.R. "Bill," 137, 279n3
Berger, Thomas, 40
Berkes, Fikret, 51, 56
Berton, Pierre, 10, 170, 267, 272n2
Beverly and Qamanirjuaq Caribou
    Management Board, and herds
    of, 56, 57
Bhabha, Homi, 150
biologists. *See* wildlife biologists, in
    northern Canada

bioterror, 110
Birney, Earle, 23
Bloody Falls, massacre at, 13, 154, 156,
    158-61, 170-72, 175-80, 184, 187,
    270; and absence of Matonabbee,
    158; differing opinions on, 156;
    and Hearne's neutrality, 159-61,
    171, 176, 270; and name of site,
    154, 171, 281n1; and questioning
    of Hearne's story, 281n5; and
    search for copper, 172, 175-80,
    186-87, 270; sexual overtones of,
    159-61, 171, 177, 270; and story
    as material ordering practice, 13,
    171-72; sublime/gothic treatment
    of, 153-54
Boudreau, Leo, 81-82
"boundary work," of scientists, 42, 43,
    48-49, 51, 59, 60
Boy Scouts, 26, 30
Brand, Dionne, 141-42
Brazeau, Patrick, 283n1
British Columbia: Asian immigrants in,
    122, 125, 131-32, 217-18, 279n5;
    Crown sovereignty in, 211-13,
    222-24, 228, 232, 282n1; early
    white-Indigenous interaction in,
    217; economy of, 128-30, 138;
    "Indian land question" of, 211-12,
    220; Indigenous land claims in,
    211-12, 213, 220-21, 233;
    Indigenous land title in, 212-13,
    218, 220-24, 225-27, 229-32;
    labour recruitment programs of,
    12, 130, 131, 132, 140-43, 144;
    racial rule in, 213-20, 227-32; rec-
    onciliation project of, 13, 211-32,
    267; reserves in, 128, 132-33, 211,
    212, 213, 218-20, 221, 225, 227-28,
    253-54; studies of Indigenous
    peoples in, 50-51; as white prov-
    ince, 13, 127-44, 211-32, 267. *See
    also* Kelowna, white hinterland
    of; Okanagan Valley, white hinter-
    land of

British Columbia, Indigenous land
claims cases of: *Calder,* 221;
Delgamuukw, 212, 233, 282*n*1 (Ch.
10); *Haida Nation,* 233; *Martin,*
282*n*3; *Ontario v. Bear Island
Foundation,* 282*n*1 (Ch. 9); *R. v.
Van der Peet,* 212; *R. v. White and
Bob,* 220-21; *Xeni Gwet'in,* 233
British Columbia, reconciliation project
in, 13, 211-32, 267; and Campbell's
"new relationship," 226-27, 234;
"cede/surrender/release" model
of, 222-23; conflicting understandings of, 224-27; and Crown
sovereignty, 211-13, 222-24, 228,
232, 282*n*1; Crown view of, 212-
13; and demarcation/segregation
vs mutual sharing, 224-25, 231;
and final settlement vs ongoing
process, 226; and "Indian land
question," 211-12, 220; and
Indigenous land claims, 211-12,
213, 220-21, 233; and Indigenous
land title, 212-13, 218, 220-24,
225-27, 229-32; and maintenance
of white province, 213, 216-20,
227-32, 267; "modify/release"
model of, 223-24; and natural
resources, 211-13, 220-22, 225,
226-27, 229-32, 254, 282*n*3,
283*n*5, 283*n*7; and racial rule,
213-20, 227-32; and reserves, 211,
212, 213, 218-20, 221, 225, 227-28;
shortcomings of, 229-32; and
treaty process, 212-13, 220-27,
228, 267, 283*n*5, 283*n*7, 283*n*12;
and treaty process referendum,
230-31, 254-55
British Columbia Claims Task Force,
221-23, 283*n*5
Brody, Hugh, 51, 57
Brooks, Van Wyck, 90-91
Buckland, F.M., 136
Buffon, Comte de, 36
Burke, Edmund, 153

Burnham, Daniel, 87

Cabot Trail, 63, 64, 66, 71, 73, 77, 79
Cadzow, Donald, 184
*Calder et al. v. Attorney-General of
British Columbia,* 221
Campbell, Gordon, and government of,
226-27, 230, 234
Canada First movement, 2, 31
Canadian Arctic Expedition, 181
Canadian Broadcasting Corporation
(CBC), 2
Canadian Forestry Association, 25
Canadian Museum of Civilization, 13,
147-48
Canadian Pacific Railway (CPR), 198
Canadian Parks and Wilderness Society,
38
Canadian Wildlife Service, 46-47
canoeing, 10, 33, 267; in Temagami, 196,
199, 206, 208
Cap Rouge, NS, expropriations at, 12,
62-82, 268; for aesthetic/scenic
purposes, 63, 64, 67-68, 72; of
large fishing families, 63-64, 67-
68, 78-80; as legitimate/inevitable,
65, 67, 76-80, 81-82; maps detail-
ing, 276*n*22; questioning of,
81-82, 274*n*4; as racialized, 64,
65, 66, 67, 68-73, 268; as second
Acadian expulsion, 73, 81-82; as
undiscussed/unexplained, 64-65,
74-75, 78-80, 276*n*21
Cape Breton Highlands National Park:
anti-modern Scottishness of, 64,
68-72, 267-68; boundaries of, 64,
66, 67; and Cap Rouge expropriations, 12, 62-82, 268; and coastal
driving experience, 66, 68, 71-72,
78; cooperating association of,
63-65, 76-80, 81, 276*n*20-22,
276*n*24; crofter's cottage in, 74,
275*n*10; ecologization of, 12, 65,
73-76; golf course in, 69; Keltic
Lodge in, 69-70, 274*n*7; landscape

of, 62-80; modernity of, 65, 72-80; name of, 69, 274*n*6; official creation of, 66; and Pleasant Bay, 64, 66, 67, 68; "sublime" aesthetics of, 63, 64, 65-66, 67-68; tourism in, 63, 64, 65, 68-69, 73, 75, 77-78, 80-81, 268; whiteness of, 12, 64-65, 68-81, 267-68; wild roses of, 62-63, 78, 82

capitalism, property: and disappearing wilderness, 26-27; and space as commodity, 33-34; and whiteness, 19-21

caribou, 44, 45, 46, 47, 56, 57-58, 169, 178, 186, 202

carnival, metaphor of, and SARS outbreak in Toronto, 107, 108-9, 117, 120, 125-26

Cascadia (Pacific Northwest), 136, 279*n*7

Castree, Noel, 173-74, 188-89

Cautley, R.W., 65-68, 274*n*3

Centre for Internationally Educated Nurses (CARE), 117, 278*n*6

Chéticamp, NS, 63, 66, 67-68, 71, 79, 274*n*5; as Acadians' new home, 67, 73, 78, 81-82

Chicago, 87, 91-92, 93

Chinese immigrants , 10, 111, 131-32, 277*n*9, 279*n*5; dangerous work given to, 114; head tax on, 112, 125, 131; and SARS outbreak in Toronto, 107, 108, 112, 121, 122, 124, 125; and "yellow peril," 122, 125, 132

Chinese Immigration Act (1923), 131

Chipewyan Dene. *See* Dene, Chipewyan

cities: and bacteriology, 110-11, 120-21, 122, 123; and hinterland, 128-29, 135-36; modernity/whiteness of, 34, 86, 104-6, 110-14, 121-22, 123-26, 266. *See also* Kelowna, white hinterland of; Toronto, *and entries following;* urban parks

City Beautiful movement, 85-86, 87-88, 90, 105

"civilization": and colonization, 128, 132-34, 136-37, 219, 228, 253-54, 266-67; and dispossession, 128, 133, 198, 203, 267; and healthy outdoor activities, 204-6, 208, 265-66; of Indigenous peoples, 156-58, 177, 184, 203-4; and "over-civilization," 27, 205; and scientific knowledge, 40-41, 44-45, 53-54, 267; and wilderness, 32, 34, 136, 200, 202, 204-6, 208, 265-66; and women's presence, 200

Clayoquot Sound, BC, 55

Cold War, 2, 237

colonialism: and conservation, 44-45, 267; and scientific knowledge, 40-41, 44-45, 53-54, 58-60, 267; and space, 21, 33-34; and travel writing, 198-99. *See also* white settler society and culture

colonization, 264-71; and "civilization," 128, 132-34, 136-37, 219, 228, 253-54, 266-67; and decolonization, 165-68; and displacement/ dispossession, 8, 13, 21, 211-32, 260-61, 265-70, 280*n*1; and domination, 59, 148, 217, 270-71; as fragile/unstable, 49, 261-62, 267, 269; and Indigenous assimilation, 45, 128, 163, 195, 216-20, 265-67; and North/national identity, 150-52; and search for copper, 175-76; violence of, 269-70; and whiteness, 10, 127, 131-32, 140-41, 148-49, 193-95, 216-18, 228, 264-71; and wilderness, 264-71. *See also* white settler society and culture

Columbian Exposition (Chicago, 1893), 87

Committee on Parks and Exhibitions (Toronto), 94, 97, 101-3

Conklin, Harold, 52

conservation, 37-38; and colonialism,
44-45, 267; and commodification,
33-34; Grey Owl and, 21, 22, 24-
25, 29, 31-34, 37-38, 270, 273*n*10;
by Indigenous peoples, 41, 44, 47,
267
Constitution Act, s. 35 of, 223, 231
contrapuntal music, 2-3
Cook, James, 216
Cooper, James Fenimore, 23
copper: and Bloody Falls massacre,
172, 175-80, 186-87, 270; Euro-
Canadian meanings/values assigned to, 181-84; Hearne's search
for, 12, 151, 160, 171, 175-80, 270;
Hudson's Bay Company search for,
151, 171, 176, 180, 184, 270; as important to Indigenous peoples,
178-84, 186; later exploration for,
180-81; mining of, 179, 184
Copper Indians. *See* Dene, Chipewyan
"Copper Inuit," 178, 181, 183, 184;
Bloody Falls massacre of, 154,
158-61, 170-72, 175-77, 184, 187,
270; and other conflicts with
Dene, 178, 181; and search for
copper, 172, 175-80, 186-87, 270;
"traditional" stories/culture of,
181-83, 184, 281*n*6. *See also*
Kugluktukmiut
copper stories, 175-90; of Bloody Falls
massacre, 172, 175-80, 186-87,
270; of Chipewyan Dene, 178-79;
Euro-Canadian translation/
summary of, 181-83, 281*n*6; of
Kugluktukmiut, 181-83, 184, 281*n*6
Coppermine River area: Hearne's journey to, 12, 151, 154, 160-61, 170-
71, 176; later exploration of,
180-81; Inuit claims to, 185-86;
mining in, 2, 169, 183, 184; "traditional" stories/culture of, 181-83,
184, 281*n*6. *See also* Bloody Falls,
massacre at; Hearne, Samuel, *and
entry following;* Kugluktuk, NU

Coulthard, Glen, 229-30, 233-34
court rulings, on Indigenous land
claims, 212, 220-21, 229, 233-34,
282*n*1 (Chs. 9 and 10), 282*n*3. *See
also* British Columbia, Indigenous
land claims cases of
Cowichan (people), 228, 245
Cree, 24, 57, 151; fishing by, 51, 56;
hunting by, 50
Creighton, Wilfred, 66-67, 274*n*4
critical race theory, 42, 260
Cruikshank, Julie, 50-51, 173, 178, 197
cultural ecology, 52-53, 56

David Suzuki Foundation, 38
decolonization, 165-68
Defence Research Board, 46
Delgamuukw v. British Columbia, 212,
233, 282*n*1 (Ch. 10)
Dene, Chipewyan, 12, 147, 151; and
Bloody Falls massacre, 13, 154,
156, 158-61, 170-72, 175-80, 184,
187, 270; ethnography of, 149,
156-61; importance of copper to,
178-80, 186; and Matonabbee,
156-58, 162, 163-64, 270; and
other conflicts with Copper Inuit,
178, 181; and search for copper,
172, 175-80, 186-87, 270
Dene, Sahtu, 187
Dennis, Clara, 71, 275*n*10
diamond mining, 2, 169, 175-76, 183, 184
Diefenbaker, John, 2
difference, race/whiteness as, 5, 29-30,
35-37; Seshadri-Crooks' work on,
34, 35-36, 72-73, 76, 265, 274*n*15,
275*n*11, 275*n*13
disaffiliation, 14-15. *See also* innocence
displacement, of Indigenous peoples,
8, 49, 203; and "anti-conquest"
narrative, 161-65; to reserves, 128,
132-33, 211, 212, 213, 218-20, 221,
225, 227-28, 253-54; and resettlement, 3, 44, 45; to residential
schools, 128

dispossession, of Indigenous peoples: in British Columbia, 13, 211-32, 267; and "civilization," 128, 133, 198, 203, 267; and colonization, 8, 21, 214, 218, 260-61, 265-70, 280n1; and construction of "white history," 148-52, 152-56, 216-18; and fiction of peaceful settlement, 1, 147-48, 216, 267; in Nova Scotia, 73; and past/pre-modern Indigenous society, 34, 160, 198, 202, 203-4, 216, 253-54; and private property on reserves, 235-36, 238-39, 240, 241, 251, 254, 268; and residential schools, 128; in Temagami, 13, 196-97, 198, 202, 203, 210; and *terra nullius* concept, 133, 149, 202, 217, 261, 266, 267, 280n1; violence of, 13, 128, 148, 156, 216, 240, 241

Douglas, James: and reserves, 218-19; treaties of, 132-33, 218, 228, 267

Du Bois, W.E.B., 5-6

Duncan, Dorothy, 70, 72

Echo Bay Mines, 184

ecology, and Indigenous knowledge, 52-53, 56

Egwuna, Angele, 23

Elizabeth Street playground (Toronto), 97-104, *102;* cost of, 101-2; location of, 86, 97-102, *98, 99, 100,* 277n9; and transcendentalism, 86, 94, 102, 103-4, 105; undesirable outcomes in, 103-4

Emerson, Ralph Waldo, transcendentalism of, 86, 87, 91; and City Beautiful movement, 85-86, 87-88, 90, 105; and "higher thought" associated with nature, 85, 86, 88, 90, 105. *See also* transcendentalism

entrepreneurial spirit, of white settler society, 136-37, 235, 239, 247-51, 268

environment, 41; of hinterland, 127; and Indigenous knowledge, 53, 54, 55, 59-60; of northern Canada, 169, 186; protests to protect, 195-96, 221, 282n3; and racism, 59-60

environmental formations, private property regimes as, 238-47, 248, 254-55, 284n2

Espaniel, Alex, 24

ethno-ecology, 52-53, 56

ethnography, Indigenous, 149, 156-61

eugenics, 8, 132

Feit, Harvey, 49, 50

Ferguson, Michael, 57

Fernow, Bernhard Eduard, 32, 34

Filipino Canadians, 107, 119, 122, 124

Fine, Robert, 140, 142-43

First Nations, 3; banned practices of, 29, 272n3; as "civilized," 156-58, 177, 184, 203-4; as depicted in travel writing, 199, 202-4, 206, 209; and disappearing wilderness, 11, 22-23, 26-30, 34, 37; as figures of past, 26-30, 31, 34, 41, 44-45, 74, 160, 198, 202, 203-4, 206, 209, 216, 219, 253-54, 260, 267, 270-71, 273n9, 275n15; Grey Owl's images of, 23, 24, 25; as guides, 12, 46, 149, 156-58, 162, 163-64, 170, 176, 197, 201, 202-4, 205, 209, 266, 270; and national parks rights/uses, 63, 75, 81, 275n16, 276n25; poverty of, 233-34, 236, 237-38, 241, 243, 245-47, 250-51, 252-55; and private property on reserves, 13-14, 233-55, 268; and reserves, 128, 132-33, 211, 212, 213, 218-20, 221, 225, 227-28, 253-54; and residential schools, 128; subjugation/annihilation of, 21, 27-30, 128, 131, 132-33; as term replacing "Indians," 282n4; "unused"/empty land of, 133, 149, 202, 217, 261, 266, 267, 280n1;

and white hinterland, 128, 131, 132-33, 137. *See also* Grey Owl; Indian surrogacy, *and entries following;* Indigenous peoples, *and entry following;* treaties/agreements, with Indigenous peoples; *specific First Nations*

First Nations Property Ownership Act (proposed), 234

First Nations Tax Commission, 234

Fisheries Research Board, 46

fishing: in Cap Rouge, 63-64, 67-68, 78-80; by Quebec Cree, 51, 56

Flanagan, Tom. *See* private property on reserves (Flanagan/Alcantara)

Ford, George, 92

Fordism, 115, 129, 279n3; and post-Fordism, 115, 129, 130, 138, 144

forest, Canadian boreal, 22-23, 25, 26-27, 30, 31-34

Forest Reserves and Parks Act, 63

Foster, Con, 24

Foucault, Michel, 172, 239, 261, 284n2

Franklin, Sir John: first expedition of, 180-81, 281n1

Freeman, Milton, 50, 57

Fung, Richard, 267

Frye, Northrop, 156

Game Acts, 44

Gandy, Matthew, 110

Geary, George, 103

ghosts: of Cap Rouge Acadians, 63-64, 76-80, 82; of disappearing wilderness, 22-23, 26-27, 30, 37; and relics of Grey Owl, 30, 37

global South, private property rights projects in, 237, 244-45, 246

globalization: and bioterror, 110; in hinterland, 129-30, 279n3; and SARS outbreak in Toronto, 278n1. *See also* neo-liberalism

Goldberg, David Theo, 86, 213, 215-16, 227

Gould, Glenn, 2-3, 10

governmentality, 239

Graham, R.H., 103

Grand Trunk Railway, 198, 202

Great White North, 1-4; extremity of, 259-63; Gould's approach to, 2-3; and immigration policy, 4, 112-14, 125, 131-32, 194; landscape of, 2-3, 43, 50, 59, 149, 152-56, 259, 280n2; and meanings of "white," 1; and multiculturalism, 3-4, 8-9, 107, 111, 112-14, 116, 120-21, 123-26, 147, 194; and national identity, 1, 2-3, 44, 150-52, 154-56, 259, 260; and race/racialization, 1-4, 10, 174-75; SCTV skit on, 128; and specificity of discourse, 172-73; Toronto and, 111. *See also* North, Canadian, *and entry following*

Grey Owl, 11, 19-38; admirers of, 22, 25, 28, 29, 32, 37, 269; and beavers, 24-25, 30, 31, 32, 37; biographies/ studies of, 273n5, 273n7; as conservationist, 21, 22, 24-25, 29, 31-34, 37-38, 270, 273n10; and disappearing wilderness, 11, 22-23, 26-27, 29, 34, 37; early life/ relationships of, 23-25, 273n7; film biography of, 37; as First Nations advocate, 28-29, 270; and forest, 22-23, 25, 26-27, 30, 31-32, 34; as ghost, 30, 37; and images of First Nations life/customs, 23, 24, 25; Indian surrogacy by, 11, 21-22, 24-38, 270, 273nn8-10; and national parks, 25, 32-33, 38; pen name of, 25; and "phantasy in white," 22-23, 26-27, 30; and production of wilderness as white space, 21-22, 25-26, 29-30, 31-38; and scientific discourse, 32-34; as trapper/guide, 21-24; and world of historical past, 22-23, 26-30, 31, 34, 270, 273nn9-10; writings by, 22-23, 25, 26, 28, 31

Group of Seven, 21, 31

Haida, 221, 233
Harcourt, Michael, 283*n*6
Hare, Kenneth, 46
Harkin, J.B., 65
Harper, Stephen, and government of, 234, 236
head tax, 112, 125, 131
Hearne, Samuel, 151; as anti-hero, 161-65; and Bloody Falls massacre, 13, 154, 156, 158-59, 170-72, 175-77, 184, 187, 270, 281*n*1, 281*n*5; Dene impressions of, 147; and failure of quest, 160, 171, 176; feminine persona of, 163-64; guides of, 12, 157, 163; and Hudson's Bay Company, 12, 151, 152, 170-71, 176, 184, 270; on landscape, 149, 152-56, 280*n*2; and Matonabbee, 156-58, 162, 163-64, 270; modern-day criticism of, 175-76, 180; narrative slippages by, 164-65; neutrality of, 159-61, 171, 176, 270; passivity/vulnerability of, 13, 148, 149, 150, 159-65, 166-67; racist ethnography of, 149, 156-61; and scientific writing/natural history, 149, 152-53, 161, 270; and search for copper, 12, 151, 160, 171, 175-80, 270; and search for Northwest Passage, 151, 152, 171
Hearne, Samuel, *A Journey to the Northern Ocean*, 12-13, 147-68, 169-90; and Canadian literature/narrative, 154-55, 156, 167; and colonialism, 148-49, 151, 152-53, 160-63; editions of, 167, 168, 181; ethnography in, 149, 156-61; innocent posture of, 13, 148, 149, 150, 159-65, 166-67; on landscape, 149, 152-56, 280*n*2; legacy of, 165-68; museum's interpretation of, 13, 147-48; and national identity, 150-52, 154-56; and nordicity, 153, 280*n*2; and resource speculation/extraction, 149, 169-90; as

scientific writing/natural history, 149, 152-53, 161, 270; and "sentimental" travel writing, 141-42; and socio-political landscape, 149-52; and "storying" of land, 149, 150-52, 152-56, 280*n*2; and sublime/gothic, 153-54; whiteness in, 13, 147-52, 167-68
Helin, Calvin: *Dances with Dependency*, 249, 283*n*1
hinterland, 127-31; cultural representations of, 128; economy of, 127, 128-30; environmental devastation in, 127; First Nations experiences in, 128, 131, 132-33, 137; Fordism and post-Fordism in, 129, 130, 138, 144, 279*n*3; globalization/neo-liberalism in, 129-30, 279*n*3; labour recruitment programs of, 12, 130, 131, 132; and metropolis, 128-29, 135-36; and nation building, 127; politics of, 129-30; racial exclusion in, 131-32; white privilege in, 127-31; white work ethic of, 127, 129-30, 141; and wilderness taming, 127-28, 129. *See also* Kelowna, white hinterland of; Okanagan Valley, white hinterland of
historical geography, of racism, 3, 6-7, 8
Holling, C.S., 53
hospitals, and SARS outbreak in Toronto, 109, 115, 117, 122; nurses in, 12, 108, 114, 116-17, 120, 123
hotel workers, and SARS outbreak in Toronto, 108, 114-16, 117-18, 120
Hudson's Bay Company (HBC), 24; Hearne's exploration work for, 12, 151, 152, 170-71, 176, 184, 270; and search for copper, 151, 171, 176, 180, 184, 270
Hughes, James L., 95
Human Genome Project, 36
hunting, by Indigenous peoples, 41, 44-45, 47, 49-55, 57-58, 267

hygiene, public: and SARS outbreak in Toronto, 113, 123; and urban parks, 87, 92-93

"Idea of North, The" (CBC radio documentary), 2-3
identity: American, 6, 26; immigrant, as stigmatized by SARS outbreak, 12, 107-26, 269; immigrant, as transformed/improved by parks, 12, 85-86, 90-94, 95-96, 102-6, 269; politics of, 260-61; of Scottish Nova Scotia, 64, 68-73, 267-68, 275*n*10. *See also* Indigenous identity; national identity; white identity
Ignatiev, Noel: *How the Irish Became White*, 6
immigrants: and bioterror, 110; as "garlic-eating," 135-36; as "hardworking," 112-13, 123; and infectious diseases, 110, 112, 122, 124, 269; in Kelowna/Okanagan Valley, 12, 130-31, 132, 135-36, 139-44, 268-69; as labourers, 132, 194; poverty of, 91, 97-104, 111; racist policies toward, 4, 12, 112-14, 125, 131-32, 194; and SARS outbreak in Toronto, 12, 107-26, 269; service work by, 12, 107-9, 111, 114-22, 123, 269; temporary/precarious work by, 109, 112-16, 138, 139-44, 268-69, 279*n*9, 280*n*11; in Toronto's Ward neighbourhood, 86, 98-99, 101-2, 277*n*9; as transformed/improved by urban parks, 12, 85-86, 90-94, 95-96, 102-6, 269; and white settler society, 110, 112-14, 131-32, 193-94, 265
immigration policy, Canadian: and Chinese, 112, 125, 131-32; and colonization, 10, 131-32, 140-41, 193-95; and labour recruitment, 113, 131-32, 194; and multiculturalism,

112-14, 194; racism of, 4, 12, 112-14, 125, 131-32, 194
India, refusal of immigrants from, 131
Indian Act, 128, 220, 228, 234, 248-49
Indian Affairs, Department of (DIA), 200-1, 206
Indian Affairs and Northern Development, Department of (DIAND), 55-56
Indian and Northern Affairs Canada, 236
Indian surrogacy, 22, 26, 29-30; and difference between cultures, 29-30; and difference of race, 36-37; and European annihilation/accommodation, 27-30; by Grey Owl, 11, 21-22, 24-38, 270, 273*nn*8-10; and nostalgia for past, 26-27; and "playing Indian," 22, 27, 29-30, 205-6, 270; and production of wilderness as white space, 21-22, 25-26, 29-30, 31-38; as sanitized savagery, 27, 205-6; and visible regime of whiteness, 34-38
Indigenous identity: as adopted by Grey Owl, 11, 21-22, 24-38, 270; as adopted by whites, 22, 27, 29-30, 205-6, 270; and colonial dispossession, 13-14; and residential schools, 128; and territorial land, 196, 223, 231
Indigenous knowledge in northern Canada: as accepted, 39-41, 46, 48-49, 50-51, 57-58, 269; assertion of, 55-58; and "boreal ecology," 48; and boundary work, 42, 43, 48-49, 51, 59, 60; and colonialism, 40-41, 44-45, 53-54, 58-60, 267; as dismissed/devalued, 39, 41, 42, 44-45, 46-48, 51, 53-54, 56, 57-58, 59, 267; ecological approaches to, 52-53, 56; and empirical results, 57-58, 60; environmental approaches to, 53, 54, 55, 59-60;

in global context, 42, 43, 51-55,
58-59; greater local control over,
55-56; and hunting practices, 41,
44-45, 47, 49-55, 57-58, 267; increased visibility/authority of, 60;
and natural history tradition, 149,
152-53; in Northern context, 43-
44, 51-52, 55-60; perceived marginalization of, 54-55; in political/
activist context, 55, 56-57; and
post-war wildlife research/
management, 41, 43-58, 267; and
pre-war research/expeditions, 41,
46; racial/geographical identity of,
11, 43-44, 48-49, 55, 58, 59; scientists' views of, 11, 39-60, 267, 269;
and "situated" nature of science,
42, 43, 49, 58; vs southern interventions, 40, 43-49; as "traditional ecological knowledge," 40,
276n25; and whiteness, 11, 42-43,
45, 46, 47, 48-49, 51, 53-54, 59-
60. *See also* anthropologists, in
northern Canada; Indigenous
peoples, of northern Canada; scientific knowledge, Western; wildlife biologists, in northern Canada
Indigenous land claims, 165, 195; and
blockades, 165, 221, 284n6; in
British Columbia, 13, 211-32, 267;
court rulings on, 212, 220-21, 229,
233-34, 282n1 (Chs. 9 and 10),
282n3; federal roadblocks to, 220;
and fiction of legal acquisition,
267; and Indigenous land title,
212-13, 218, 220-24, 225-27, 229-
32; limited success of, 229-32; and
natural resources, 21, 41, 185-86,
196, 211-13, 220-22, 225, 226-27,
229-32, 254, 282n3, 283n5,
283n7; in northern Canada, 55,
56-57, 185-86; and Nunavut
agreement, 169, 186, 282n7; and
private property on reserves, 235-
36; provincial task force on, 221-23,

283n5; as stalled in courts, 269; in
Temagami, 13, 195, 196-97, 200-1,
206, 266, 282n1. *See also* British
Columbia, Indigenous land claims
cases of; British Columbia, reconciliation project in
Indigenous peoples: colonization/
assimilation of, 45, 128, 163, 195,
216-20, 265-67; continued marginalization of, 8-9; and disappearing wilderness, 11, 22-23,
26-30, 34, 37; empowerment/
increased status of, 41, 42; as
figures of extremity, 260-62; and
Great White North myth, 1, 3;
land claims of, 55, 56-57, 165, 185-
86, 195, 266; as part of landscape,
128, 165, 260; as removed from
urban spaces, 266; subjugation/
annihilation of, 21, 27-30, 128, 131,
132-33; "unused"/empty land of,
133, 149, 202, 217, 261, 266, 267,
280n1; and white settler society,
44-45, 58-60, 110, 128, 194-95,
211, 218-20, 260, 265-67, 280n1.
See also displacement, of Indigenous peoples; dispossession, of
Indigenous peoples; First Nations;
Indian surrogacy; Inuit; modernity, Indigenous peoples and;
treaties/agreements, with
Indigenous peoples; *specific
Indigenous peoples*
Indigenous peoples, of northern Canada:
anthropologists' study of/work
with, 49-51, 52-53, 56-57, 59, 181,
269; and conservation, 41, 44, 47,
267; and environmental racism,
59-60; hunting practices of, 41,
44-45, 47, 49-55, 57-58, 267;
importance of copper to, 178-84,
186; and land claims/self-
determination, 55, 56-57, 165,
185-86; oral traditions of, 170,
178-79; and post-war wildlife

research/management, 41, 43-58, 267; and pre-war research/expeditions, 41, 46; resettlement of, 3, 44, 45; wildlife knowledge of, 41, 44-49, 50-51, 53-54, 55, 57-58, 267. *See also* Indigenous knowledge in northern Canada; Inuit

Innis, Harold, 128-29, 281*n*2

innocence: of liberal democracy, 8; of North/nature, 2, 7; of travel writing/tourism, 199, 207-8; and white disaffiliation, 14-15; and whiteness, 1, 13, 14-15, 20, 148, 149, 150, 159-65, 166-67

Institute for Liberty and Democracy (ILD), 244

Inuinnaqtun (language), 281*n*1, 281*n*4; copper story in, 181-83

Inuit, 3, 260; anthropological studies of, 50, 181; Bloody Falls massacre of, 154, 158-61, 170-72, 175-77, 184, 187, 270; and modern-day criticism of Hearne, 175-76, 180; and Nunavut, 169, 185-86, 282*n*7; oral traditions of, 170, 178-79; resettlement of, 3, 44, 45. *See also* "Copper Inuit"; Indigenous knowledge in northern Canada; Indigenous peoples, of northern Canada; Kugluktukmiut

Inuit Land Use and Occupancy Project, 57

Inuit Tapirisat of Canada (ITC), 186

Jamaican students/workers, in Kelowna, 141-43, 279*n*9

James Bay Agreement, on hydroelectric power, 57

Jasen, Patricia, 198, 200, 201-2, 206

Jenness, Diamond, 49, 181

John, Edward, 223, 224

Jules, Manny, 234

Kelowna, white hinterland of, 12, 127-44, 268-69; British

settlement/"civilizing" of, 132-34, 136-37; Chinese community in, 279*n*5; entrepreneurial spirit of, 137; First Nations experiences in, 128, 131, 132-33, 137; fruit growing in/around, 133-36; "gentleman farmers" of, 135-36, 268-69; immigrants in, 12, 130-31, 132, 135-36, 139-44, 268-69; Jamaican students/workers in, 141-43, 279*n*9; labour recruitment programs of, 12, 130, 131, 132, 140-43, 144; landscape of, 134-35, 143-44; politics of, 279*n*3; population/demographics of, 137-38; and privileging of western European immigrants/workers, 132-33, 140-41; promotion of, 134, 139, 143; reproducing whiteness in, 137-40; skilled white workers in, 130, 140-41; temporary non-white workers in, 130, 131, 132, 138, 139, 140, 141-43, 268-69. *See also* hinterland; Okanagan Valley, white hinterland of

Kelowna Accords, 234

Kelowna Economic Development Commission, 140, 142-43

Kelso, J.J., 92

knowledge, Indigenous vs scientific. *See* Indigenous knowledge in northern Canada; scientific knowledge, Western

Komagata Maru (ship), 131

Kugluktuk, NU, 281*n*4; mining in, 175-76; "traditional" copper stories/culture of, 181-83, 184, 281*n*6. *See also* Coppermine River area

Kugluktukmiut, 281*n*4; as "Copper Inuit," 178, 181, 183, 184; and criticism of Hearne, 175-76, 180; land/mineral claims of, 185-86; and mining economy, 175-76, 184-87; and reconciliation with Dene, 187; study of, 181; "traditional" copper

stories/culture of, 181-83, 184, 281*n*6. *See also* "Copper Inuit"
Kuliktana, Millie, 175-76

La Bloque (CBH National Park), 65, 67; interpretive panels at, 65, 76-77, 78-79, 276*n*22
labour, by immigrants, 132, 194; and "hard-working" stereotype, 112-13, 123; in Kelowna/Okanagan Valley, 12, 130-31, 132, 135-36, 139-44, 268-69; as service work, 12, 107-9, 111, 114-22, 123, 269; as temporary/precarious, 109, 112-16, 138, 139-44, 268-69, 279*n*9, 280*n*11
Lacan, Jacques, and theories of, 20, 35-37
landscape: of CBH National Park, 62-80; Indigenous peoples as part of, 128, 165, 260; of Kelowna, 134-35, 143-44; of national parks, 63, 65-66, 73-76, 265-69; of northern Canada, 2-3, 43, 50, 59, 149, 152-56, 259, 280*n*2; of urban parks, 266-67; white/European aesthetics of, 134-35, 265-69
Latour, Bruno, 172, 179, 188
Law, John, 170, 179, 180, 188
Le Buttereau trail (CBH National Park), 62-63, 82; interpretive panels at, 65, 76-77, 79-80, 276*nn*21-22
Leacock, Eleanor, 50
League of Indians of Western Canada, 28
Lefebvre, Henri, 6, 33-34
Lesotho, 254
Lewis, Henry, 50
Libin, Kevin, 252, 283*n*1
Linnaeus, Carolus, 152, 153, 161, 280*n*2
live-in caregivers, and SARS outbreak in Toronto, 12, 115, 118-19, 122
Locke, John, 240
logging, protests against, 195-96, 221, 282*n*3
Longfellow, Henry Wadsworth, 24

Louie, Clarence, 283*n*1

Macdonald, Angus, and "tartanization" of Nova Scotia, 68-71, 275*n*10
MacEachern, Alan, 63, 64, 65-66, 67, 68, 70, 71, 274*n*4, 274*n*6
Mackenzie, Bob and Doug (SCTV characters), 128
Mackenzie Valley Pipeline, 169; Berger inquiry into, 40
Manuel, Art, 235
Marsh, Benjamin, 93, 94
Marx, Karl, 33
"material ordering practice," 13, 170, 171-72, 180, 281*n*2
Matonabbee (guide), 156-58, 162, 163-64, 270
McFarland, Horace, 91-92
McGill University, 46, 56, 57
McGoogan, Ken, 167
McKay, Ian, 10-11, 64, 68, 69, 70, 71, 275*nn*8-10
McKim, Charles, 87
Meares Island, BC, logging protests on, 221, 282*n*3
Métayer, Maurice, and copper stories collected by, 181-83, 281*n*6
Mexican farm workers, in Okanagan Valley, 139, 141, 268-69, 279*n*9, 280*n*11
Mi'kmaq, 70, 73, 74, 274*n*6, 276*n*18
mining, in Nunavut, 184-87; copper, 179, 184; diamond, 2, 169, 175-76, 183, 184; and Inuit land/mineral rights, 185-86
modernity, Indigenous peoples and, 270-71; in CBH National Park, 74; and copper stories, 188; in Grey Owl's world, 22-23, 26-30, 31, 34, 270, 273*nn*9-10; and North/national identity, 150-52, 260; and private vs collective property, 242-43, 252, 268; and science/anthropology, 41, 44-45, 49-55, 58; in Temagami, 203-4, 205

modernity, and whiteness, 19, 34, 45, 74-76, 80-82, 266-67; in CBH National Park, 65, 72-80; in cities, 34, 86, 104-6, 110-14, 121-22, 123-26, 266; and colonization, 266-67

Montreal, 92

moose, 32, 50, 202, 204

Moreton-Robinson, Aileen, 228-29

Morrison, Toni, 150, 280*n*1

Mountain Equipment Co-op, 38

Mowat, Farley, 170

multiculturalism, 8; and immigration policy, 112-14, 194; and private property on reserves, 251-52; and racism, 3-4, 8-9, 112-14, 147, 194; and SARS outbreak in Toronto, 107, 111, 112-14, 116, 120-21, 123-26

national identity: of North, 1, 2-3, 44, 150-52, 154-56, 259, 260; as racialized, 3, 8-11; and sovereignty, 44; as white, 147, 166, 194-95, 280*n*1; and wilderness, 1, 2-3, 10, 14, 31-34, 37-38, 150-52, 154-56, 259, 260

National Northern Research Conference (1967), 46

national parks: ecologization of, 12, 65, 73-74; exclusionary aesthetics of, 63; expropriation and, 12, 62-82, 268; First Nations uses/rights in, 63, 75, 81, 275*n*16, 276*n*25; Grey Owl and, 25, 32-33, 38; landscape of, 63, 65-66, 73-76, 265-69; racialized uses/restrictions in, 38, 75-76, 80-81, 275*n*16, 276*n*17; recreational uses in, 38, 62-66, 69, 70, 75-76, 77-78, 80-81; whiteness of, 12, 38, 64-65, 68-77, 80-81, 266. *See also specific national parks*

National Parks Branch (later Parks Canada), 25, 65

National Post, "Rethinking the Reserve" (series), 236, 252, 284*n*3

natural resources: and Canadian sovereignty, 44; colonial extraction/exploitation of, 127, 170, 211; and Indigenous claims/rights, 21, 41, 185-86, 196, 211-13, 220-22, 225, 226-27, 229-32, 254, 282*n*3, 283*n*5, 283*n*7; mining of, 2, 169, 175-76, 179, 183-87; white management of, 41, 43-58, 267; white privilege and, 9-10

nature: and "higher thought," 85, 86, 88, 90, 105; and immigrant transformation/improvement, 12, 85-86, 90-94, 95-96, 102-6, 269; and race/racism, 1, 9-10, 153-54, 194-95, 260-61, 264-71; as social construction, 11, 13, 14-15, 194-95, 208-10. *See also* national parks; Temagami "wilderness"; Toronto, park planning in; urban parks; wilderness

n'Daki Menan ("our land"), Temagami as, 196-97, 199, 201, 202, 282*n*1

Nelson, Richard: *Hunters of the Northern Ice*, 50

neo-liberalism: flaws of, 242-43, 244-45, 246-47, 249-52, 254-55; and governmentality, 239; in hinterland, 129-30, 280*n*10; laissez-faire policies of, 238; multicultural, 251-52; in Okanagan Valley, 136-37, 138, 269, 280*n*10; and private property on reserves, 235, 236, 237-41, 244, 247-52, 254-55, 268; and "realm of abjection," 239-40; and service work, 114-15, 116, 118, 120. *See also* globalization

New Socialist (magazine), 284*n*6

Nisga'a Nation, Final Agreement with, 224, 231, 283*n*12

nordicity, aesthetics of, 153, 280*n*2; and landscape, 149, 152-56, 280*n*2; and sublime/gothic, 153-54

North, Canadian: climate change in, 169, 186; and colonialism through

conservation, 44-45, 267; Gould's
approach to, 2-3; innocence of, 2,
7; landscape of, 2-3, 43, 50, 59,
149, 152-56, 259, 280n2; mining
in, 2, 169, 175-76, 179, 183-87; and
national identity, 1, 2-3, 44, 150-
52, 154-56, 259, 260; post-war
wildlife research/management in,
41, 43-58, 267; scientists' view of,
43-44, 51-52; sovereignty of, 2,
44, 169; white control of, 21, 44-
45; winter as synonymous with,
155. *See also* Great White North;
Indigenous knowledge in northern Canada

North, Canadian, stories of, 169-90: and
actor-network theory, 13, 171, 188-
90; alternative, 13, 173, 187-90;
copper's significance to, 172, 175-
90, 270, 281n6; and emphasis on
racialization, 174-75; Indigenous
land claims in, 55, 56-57, 185-86;
and material ordering practice,
13, 170, 171-72, 180, 281n2; and
specific vs general, 172-74. *See
also* Bloody Falls, massacre at;
copper stories; Hearne, Samuel,
and entry following

North West Rebellion, 28

Northern Co-ordination and Research
Centre, 50

Northwest Passage, 2; Hearne's search
for, 151, 152, 171

Nova Scotia: early colonizers of, 73;
Mi'kmaq of, 70, 73, 74, 274n6,
276n18

Nova Scotia, and embrace of Scottish
heritage, 64, 68-73, 74; and
creation of "Highlands," 64, 68-72,
267-68; Macdonald's role in, 68-
71; and racial "dilution" concerns,
70-71, 72-73; as tourist-oriented,
68-69. *See also* Cap Rouge, NS,
expropriations at; Cape Breton
Highlands National Park

Nunavut, 185-86, 282n7. *See also*
Coppermine River area;
Kugluktuk, NU; Kugluktukmiut

Nunavut Land Claims Agreement
(NLCA), 169, 186, 282n7

Nunavut Tunngavik Incorporated, 186

nurses, and SARS outbreak in Toronto,
12, 108, 114, 116-17, 120, 123

Nuu-chah-nulth, 216, 276n25; logging
protest by, 221, 282n3

O'Brian, James, 95

Ojibway, 24

Okanagan College (Kelowna), 142

Okanagan Life Magazine, 139

Okanagan Partnership, 139, 280n10

Okanagan Valley, white hinterland
of, 12, 127-44, 268-69; British
settlement/"civilizing" of, 132-34,
136-37; cattle ranching in, 133;
economy of, 138; First Nations
experiences in, 132-33; First
Nations reserves in, 219; fruit
growing in, 133-36; gated communities in, 129, 136-37; "gentleman farmers" of, 135-36, 268-69;
globalization/neo-liberalism in,
136-37, 138, 269, 280n10; imagined future of, 139; immigrants
in, 12, 130-31, 132, 135-36, 139-44,
268-69; labour recruitment programs of, 12, 130, 131, 132, 140-43,
144; landscape of, 134-35; Mexican
farm workers in, 139, 141, 268-69,
279n9, 280n11; population/
demographics of, 137-38; reproducing whiteness in, 137-40. *See
also* hinterland; Kelowna, white
hinterland of

Olmsted, Frederick Law, 87

Olmsted, Frederick Law Jr., 90

O'Neill, J.J., 181

Ontario: early tourism in, 198, 199; and
Teme-Augama Anishnabai, 196,
200-1, 282n1 (Ch. 9)

Ontario (Attorney General) v. Bear Island Foundation, 282*n*1 (Ch. 9)
Oxford Paper Company, 66, 274*n*4

Pacific Rim National Park Reserve, 276*n*25
parks. *See* national parks; Toronto, park planning in; urban parks
Parks Canada (formerly National Parks Branch), 25, 63, 65, 77, 276*n*20, 276*n*25
past, historical: Acadians and, 63-65, 72-73, 74, 76-80, 82; in CBH National Park, 64, 68-72, 267-68; and fears of immigrant disease/ contamination, 110, 112, 122, 124, 269; as Grey Owl's world, 22-23, 26-30, 31, 34, 270, 273*nn*9-10; Indigenous peoples and, 26-30, 31, 34, 41, 44-45, 74, 160, 198, 202, 203-4, 206, 209, 216, 253-54, 260, 267, 270-71, 273*n*9, 275*n*15; "wild" Temagami as part of, 201-7, 209
Peary, Robert, 46
Pennant, Thomas: *Arctic Zoology,* 152
Penticton, BC, 132
personal support workers (PSWs), and SARS outbreak in Toronto, 108, 114, 115, 118-19, 278*n*5
Peru, 244
Petitot, Émile, 178
Phillip, Stewart, 283*n*9
Piikani (people), 245, 248
Pipes, Richard, 237
playgrounds, 102-3; in Toronto, 12, 86, 90, 94, 95, 97-104, 105. *See also* Elizabeth Street playground (Toronto)
Pleasant Bay, NS, 64, 66, 67-68, 71-72
Point, Steven, 227
Polar Continental Shelf Project, 46
poverty: on First Nations reserves, 233- 34, 236, 237-38, 241, 243, 245-47, 250-51, 252-55; of Toronto immigrants, 91, 97-104, 111
Pratt, Mary Louise, 161-62, 163-64, 166, 199, 200, 207
Prince Albert National Park, 25, 32-33, 38
Prince of Wales's Fort, 12, 151, 157, 170, 176. *See also* Hearne, Samuel, *and entry following*
private property on reserves (Flanagan/ Alcantara), 13-14, 233-55, 268; and "anti-politics machine," 254- 55; boundaries of, 235, 241-52; vs collective property system, 234, 237-38, 241-47, 248-49, 252, 268; as complete, 237-38, 248-49; and dependency on government, 236, 238, 249; development/ improvement through, 243-45, 248-51; and dispossession, 235- 36, 238-39, 240, 241, 251, 254, 268; and entrepreneurialism, 235, 239, 247-51, 268; as environmental formation, 238-47, 248, 254-55, 284*n*2; and "equality," 235-36, 251-52; and expanded state bureaucracy, 284*n*5; flaws of, 242-43, 244-45, 246-47, 249-52, 254-55; and global property rights projects, 237, 244-45, 246, 251; and governmentality, 239; and Indigenous land claims, 235-36; Indigenous views of, 234-35, 283*n*1; and inefficient use of land, 251, 252-54; legal argument for, 242-43; and mortgage defaults/ rent arrears, 245-47; and multiculturalism, 251-52; neo-liberalism of, 235, 236, 237-41, 244, 247-52, 254-55, 268; and poverty, 233-34, 236, 237-38, 241, 243, 245-47, 250-51, 252-55; and privatization/ investment, 238-39; and "realm of abjection," 239-40, 250-51; and

self-sufficiency, 14, 235, 236, 238; as white/colonial construct, 235, 236, 239-41, 247-52; and work of de Soto, 243-45
propinquity, 88, 90-94, 96-97, 105
Provincial Nominee Program (British Columbia), 140-41
Pruitt, William, 48

Qoerhuk, James, copper story told by, 181-83, 281*n*6

R. v. Van der Peet, 212
R. v. White and Bob, 220-21
race: colonialism and, 213-16; as differ-ence, 5, 29-30, 34, 35-37, 72-73, 76, 265, 274*n*15, 275*n*11, 275*n*13; and gender, in service work, 12, 107-9, 111, 114-22, 269; and geo-graphical location, 214; and Great White North myth, 1-4, 174-75; historicist and naturalist concep-tions of, 215-16, 219, 228; and Indigenous knowledge, 11, 39-60, 267, 269; and national identity, 3, 8-11, 147, 166, 194-95, 280*n*1; and nature/wilderness, 1, 9-10, 153-54, 194-95, 260-61, 264-71; purity of, 1, 35, 70-71, 153-54, 217, 265; and scientific knowledge, 11, 42-43, 45, 46, 47, 48-49, 51, 53-54, 58, 59-60; as social construction, 4, 11, 105, 121, 215; and urban infra-structure, 12, 85-86, 104-6; in US, 150, 280*n*1; as visual marker, 34-38; and whiteness as founding principle/master signifier of, 11, 20-21, 22, 35-37, 65, 72, 75-76
racial rule, 213-16; in British Columbia, 213-20, 227-32; historicist and naturalist conceptions of, 215-16, 219, 228
racism, 3, 4, 6-11; biological and cul-tural, 5; of Canadian immigration

policy, 4, 12, 112-14, 125, 131-32, 194; in cities, 112; disaffiliation from, 14-15; environmental, 59-60; as historical-geographic, 3, 6-7, 8; and multiculturalism, 3-4, 8-9, 112-14, 147, 194; and nation-state, 7, 30, 130; and nature/wilderness, 1, 9-10, 153-54, 194-95, 260-61, 264-71; and representation/ symbolism, 8-9; shame associated with, 125-26
racism, in Toronto: and labour market, 112-13; as latent, 107, 113, 114, 126; and park planning, 12, 86, 104-6, 269; and SARS outbreak, 12, 107-26, 269; and service work, 12, 107-9, 111, 114-22, 123, 269
Rae, Bob, 195
railways, 10-11; and Temagami region, 198, 199-200, 202, 207
Ray, Arthur, 281*n*2
recreational uses: in hinterland, 135; in national parks, 38, 62-66, 69, 70, 75-76, 77-78, 80-81; in Temagami "wilderness," 196, 198, 199, 202, 204-8, 265-66; in urban parks, 90, 91-92
Report on a Comprehensive Plan for Systematic Civic Improvements in Toronto (1909), 86, 87, 89, 90, 94-97, 104-6, 277*n*7; and propin-quity, 96-97, 105; Toronto Civic Guild and, 90, 94-95. *See also* Toronto, park planning in
reserves: agriculture on, 253-54; and band authorities, 248-49; in British Columbia, 128, 132-33, 211, 212, 213, 218-20, 221, 225, 227-28, 253-54; dependency of, 236, 238, 249; and disappearing/ dying culture, 27, 219; as equated with global South, 237, 244-45, 246; fight for greater freedoms on, 28; inefficient use of land on, 251,

252-54; mortgage defaults/rent arrears on, 245-47; poverty on, 233-34, 236, 237-38, 241, 243, 245-47, 250-51, 252-55; private property on, 13-14, 233-55, 268; small size of, 133, 196, 211, 212, 219, 228, 253-54; and Teme-Augama Anishnabai, 196, 200-1, 206. *See also* private property on reserves (Flanagan/Alcantara)
residential schools, 28, 128
Rettig, George, 94
Riding Mountain National Park, 25, 32-33, 38
Ridington, Robin, 51
Riel, Louis, 28, 29
Rio Tinto, 183
Robinson, Charles Mulford, 90, 91, 106
Roediger, David: *Wages of Whiteness*, 6
Roots, Fred, 58
Ruffo, Armand Garnet, 273*n*7

Said, Edward, 151, 214, 218, 261
Sami, 280*n*2
SARS outbreak in Toronto, 12, 107-26, 269; and bacteriological city, 110-11, 120-21, 122, 123; and bioterror/biophysical threat, 110-11; and carnival metaphor, 107, 108-9, 117, 120, 125-26; and Chinese Canadians, 107, 108, 112, 121, 122, 124, 125; and city responsibility, 123, 124; and Filipino Canadians, 107, 119, 122, 124; and hospitals, 109, 115, 117, 122; and hygiene, 113, 123; and multiculturalism, 107, 111, 112-14, 116, 120-21, 123-26; and pan-Asian solidarity, 124; and quarantine measures, 107, 118, 121; and racialized/gendered workforce, 12, 107-9, 111, 114-22, 269, 278*n*2; shame associated with, 124-26; and state of emergency/exception, 109, 110, 123; and white settler society, 107, 110, 112-14. *See*

also service work; service workers, as affected by SARS outbreak in Toronto
Scarborough Grace Hospital (Toronto), 117, 120
Science Institute of the Northwest Territories (now Aurora Research Institute), 56
scientific discourse: and colonization, 270-71; and Grey Owl as conservationist, 32-34, 270; and SARS paranoia, 110, 112, 122, 124; as used by Hearne, 149, 152-53, 161, 270
scientific knowledge, Western: authority of, 39, 40-41; and boundary work, 42, 43, 48-49, 51, 59, 60; critiques of, 41, 53; as imperialistic/"civilizing" presence, 40-41, 44-45, 53-54, 267; and Indigenous hunting practices, 41, 44-45, 47, 49-55, 57-58, 267; and negative attitudes toward government, 55-56; and post-war wildlife research/management, 41, 43-58, 267; "situated" nature of, 42, 43, 49, 58; southern interventions of, 40, 43-49; whiteness/unmarked status of, 11, 42-43, 45, 46, 47, 48-49, 51, 53-54, 58, 59-60. *See also* Indigenous knowledge in northern Canada
SCTV (television series), 128
service work: as affective labour, 115; credentialization of, 115-16, 117, 278*nn*4-5; and multiculturalism, 107, 111, 112-14, 116, 120-21, 123-26; and neo-liberalism, 114-15, 116, 118, 120; and performance/expectation context, 120-22; poor pay for, 115; poor protections for, 115, 116, 117-18, 119; as racialized/gendered, 12, 107-9, 111, 114-22, 123, 269; as risky, 114, 117, 118, 119, 122, 123, 125

service workers, as affected by SARS outbreak in Toronto: hotel staff, 108, 114-16, 117-18, 120; live-in caregivers, 12, 115, 118-19, 122; masks worn by, 108, 109, 117, 123, 125; monitoring of, 118-19; nurses, 12, 108, 114, 116-17, 120, 123; and performance/expectation context, 120-22; personal support workers, 108, 114, 115, 118-19, 278n5; risks taken by, 114, 117, 118, 119, 122, 123, 125; solidarity of, 124; termination of, 119

Seshadri-Crooks, Kalpana, on whiteness: and difference, 34, 35-36, 72-73, 76, 265, 274n15, 275n11, 275n13; as master signifier of race, 20, 36, 65, 72, 76

Seton, Ernest Thompson, 23, 26, 30

settlers, society and culture of. *See* colonization; white settler society and culture

severe acute respiratory syndrome (SARS). *See* SARS outbreak in Toronto

Sheridan, Joe, 28, 29, 32, 37

Skye, Isle of, 71, 72, 73

slavery, 5, 6, 265, 280n1

Smart, James, 274n6

Smith, Thomas, 48

Soto, Hernando de: *The Mystery of Capital*, 243-45

Speck, Frank, 49

St. John's Ward (Toronto). *See* The Ward (Toronto)

state of emergency/exception, 109, 110, 123

Stefansson, Vilhjalmur, 46

Steward, Julian, 52

Stirling, Ian, 48

Sto:lo Nation, 227

stories of northern Canada. *See* North, Canadian, stories of

Strahl, Chuck, 236, 252

sublime, aesthetics of: at CBH National Park, 63, 64, 65-66, 67-68; in Hearne's *Journey*, 153-54

Sullivan, Louis, 87

Suzuki, David, 195; foundation of, 38

Taylorism, 118

Temagami Forest Reserve, 201

Temagami region, 195-97; environmental protests in, 195-96; Grey Owl in, 23, 31; Indigenous dispossession in, 13, 196-97, 198, 202, 203, 210; as Indigenous land, 13, 196-98; Indigenous land claims to, 13, 195, 196-97, 200-1, 206, 266, 282n1; as n'Daki Menan, 196-97, 199, 201, 202, 282n1; and railways, 198, 199-200, 202, 207; recreational promotion of, 196, 198; tourism in, 197-201; as "wilderness," 13, 193-210, 266. *See also* tourism, in Temagami region

Temagami "wilderness," 13, 193-210, 266; being "savage" in, 204-6, 207-8; canoeing in, 196, 199, 206, 208; and early travel writing, 13, 193, 197, 198-99, 200, 201-10; as empty/unclaimed, 202; healthy outdoor activities in, 204-6, 208, 265-66; Indigenous guides/tourism workers in, 197, 200-1, 202-4, 205, 209; as part of historical past, 201-7, 209; and railways, 198, 199-200, 202, 207; as social construction, 13, 194-95, 208-10; as "sportsman's paradise," 198, 202, 205, 207-8; tourism in, 197-201; travel writing about, 13, 193, 197, 198-99, 200, 201-10; as "virgin" space, 31, 32, 201-2, 207; white-Indigenous encounters in, 199, 200-7, 209-10; white men and, 13, 193, 197, 200, 205-6, 207-9, 266; white women and, 199, 200, 208

Teme-Augama Anishnabai, 13, 266; colonial view of, 204-7; as depicted in travel writing, 199, 202-4, 206, 209; as figures of past, 198, 202, 203-4, 206, 209; Grey Owl's association with, 23; land claims of, 13, 195, 196-97, 200-1, 206, 266, 282*n*1; and Ontario government, 196, 200-1, 282*n*1; as primitive, 198, 202-6; and reserves, 196, 200-1, 206; in tourism industry, 197, 200-1, 202-4, 205, 209; tourists' dependence on, 202-4, 209; tourists' encounters with, 199, 200-7, 209-10; tourists' photographing of, 204, 209

Temiskaming and Northern Ontario Railway, 198

Temporary Worker Program (British Columbia), 140, 141

terra nullius, Indigenous land as, 133, 149, 202, 217, 261, 266, 267, 280*n*1

terrorism, biological, 110

Thailand, 245

Tootoosis, Johnny, 27-28

Toronto, 23, 199, 279*n*3; as bacteriological city, 110-11, 120-21, 122, 123; as "Episcopal city," 86; as global city, 111, 123-24, 125, 278*n*1; and Great White North, 111; immigrant poverty in, 91, 97-104, 111; as multicultural city, 107, 111, 112-14, 116, 120-21, 123-26; park planning in, 12, 85-106, 269; racism in, 12, 86, 104-6, 107-26, 269; SARS outbreak in, 12, 107-26, 269

Toronto, park planning in, 12, 85-106, 269; and children, 92, 94, 95-96, 97-104, 277*n*10; and City Beautiful movement, 87, 90; and immigrant poverty, 91, 97-104; and immigrant transformation/improvement, 12, 85-86, 90-94, 95-96, 102-6, 269; and park plan

(1909), 12, 86, 87, 89, 90, 94-97, 104-6, 277*n*7; and park/playground movement, 102-3; and persons per park acre, 93-94, 97; and playgrounds, 12, 86, 90, 94, 95, 97-104, 105; and propinquity, 92-94, 96-97, 105; racialization of, 12, 86, 104-6; and transcendentalism, 12, 86, 94-97, 105

Toronto, SARS outbreak in. *See* SARS outbreak in Toronto

Toronto City Council, 86, 105; Committee on Parks and Exhibitions, 94, 97, 101-3

Toronto Civic Guild (TCG), 90, 94-95

Toronto General Hospital, 122

Toronto Playgrounds Association (TPA), 103

Toronto Star Fresh Air Fund, 95-96

tourism, in Cape Breton Highlands National Park, 65, 68-69, 73, 75, 77-78, 80-81, 268

tourism, in Temagami region, 197-201; "anti-conquest" of, 199, 207-8; and colonialism, 198-99; evolution of, 199-200; Indigenous participation in, 197, 200-1, 202-4, 205, 209; innocence of, 199, 207-8; as middle-/upper-class activity, 199-200; and primitive, 198, 201-8; and railways, 198, 199-200, 202, 207; and romanticism, 198-99, 201-2, 203

"traditional ecological knowledge" (TEK), 40, 166, 276*n*25

transcendentalism, 87-88, 90; and City Beautiful movement, 85-86, 87-88, 90, 105; and Elizabeth Street playground (Toronto), 86, 94, 102, 103-4, 105; and "higher thought" associated with nature, 85, 86, 88, 90, 105; and immigrant transformation/improvement, 12, 85-86, 90-94, 95-96, 102-6, 269; and racialization of infrastructure, 12, 85-86,

104-6; and Toronto park plan (1909), 12, 86, 94-97, 105

travel writing, early, and promotion of Temagami region, 13, 193, 197, 198-99, 200, 201-10; and colonialism, 198-99; depiction of Indigenous peoples in, 199, 202-4, 206, 209; as male activity, 200; and tourism's "anti-conquest," 199, 207-8

treaties/agreements, with Indigenous peoples: and British Columbia process, 212-13, 220-27, 228, 230-31, 254-55, 267, 283*n*5, 283*n*7; federal, 282*n*2; on James Bay, 57; and Nisga'a, 224, 231, 283*n*12; on Nunavut, 169, 186, 282*n*7; and rejection of Kelowna Accords, 234; rights under, 3, 55, 245; as struck by Douglas, 132-33, 218, 228, 267; in Temagami, 282*n*1 (Ch. 9)

Trudeau, Pierre Elliott, 8, 33

Trutch, Joseph, 219

tuberculosis, 92, 122

Turner, Frederick Jackson, 26

Tyrrell, J.B., 181

Union of British Columbia Indian Chiefs (UBCIC), 234, 284*n*6

United Nations Development Index, 233

United Nations Educational, Scientific and Cultural Organization (UNESCO), 41

United Nations Office of the High Commission on Human Rights, Committee on Economic, Social and Cultural Rights (CESCR), 233

United States, 128, 193, 198, 282*n*1 (Ch. 10); identity in, 6, 26; Indian surrogacy in, 26, 27; Indigenous property reforms in, 248; park/playground planning in, 87-88,

90-94, 102-3; race/racialization in, 150, 280*n*1; transcendentalism/City Beautiful movement in, 85-86, 87-88, 90, 105; and "whiteness" of working class, 5-6

urban parks: and children, 92, 94, 95-96, 97-104, 277*n*10; and City Beautiful movement, 85-86, 87-88, 90, 105; and hygiene, 87, 92-93; and immigrant poverty, 91, 97-104; and immigrant transformation/improvement, 12, 85-86, 90-94, 95-96, 102-6, 269; and park/playground movement, 102-3; and propinquity, 88, 90-94, 96-97, 105; recreational uses in, 90, 91-92; and transcendentalism, 87-88, 90; as white settler landscapes, 266. *See also* Toronto, park planning in

urban spaces. *See* cities

Vancouver, George, 216

Walworth, Arthur, 71-72

The Ward (Toronto), 97-101, *100;* dangers of, 97, 103-4; Elizabeth Street in, 97, 99, 101-2, 277*n*9; housing in, *98, 99,* 99, 101; as immigrant neighbourhood, 86, 98-99, 101-2, 277*n*9; poor infrastructure of, *99. See also* Elizabeth Street playground (Toronto)

Webb, Sir Aston, 94

Wente, Margaret, 9-10

White City (Columbian Exposition, Chicago, 1893), 87

white identity: of British Columbia, 13, 127-44, 211-32, 267; of CBH National Park, 12, 64-65, 68-81, 267-68; disaffiliation from, 14-15; of Kelowna/Okanagan Valley, 12, 127-44, 268-69; and national identity, 147, 166, 194-95, 280*n*1. *See also* whiteness

white male, feminized/effeminate: as cured in Temagami, 205; Hearne as, 163-64

white male, privileging/hegemony of, 107, 113, 115, 129, 205; in Temagami, 13, 193, 197, 200, 205-6, 207-9, 266

white settler society and culture, 10-11, 21-22; and Australian Aborigines, 260-62; entrepreneurialism of, 136-37, 235, 239, 247-51, 268; and immigrants, 110, 112-14, 131-32, 193-94, 265; and Indigenous peoples, 44-45, 58-60, 110, 128, 194-95, 211, 218-20, 260, 265-67, 280*n*1; as intent of colonization, 10, 131-32, 140-41, 193-95; and SARS outbreak in Toronto, 107, 110, 112-14; and space, 21, 33-34; and urban parks, 266; work ethic of, 127, 129-30, 141. *See also* colonization

whiteness: of academy, 264, 268, 271; colonization and, 10, 127, 131-32, 148-49, 193-95, 216-18, 228, 264-71; as cultural/racial norm, 1-4, 5-7, 14, 42, 148-49, 150, 167-68, 215, 261-62; and difference, 5, 29-30, 34, 35-37, 72-73, 76, 265, 274*n*15, 275*n*11, 275*n*13; dis-affiliation from, 14-15; as founding principle/master signifier of race, 11, 20-21, 22, 35-37, 65, 72, 75-76; in Hearne's *Journey*, 13, 147-52; history/geography of, 6-7; and innocence, 1, 13, 14-15, 20, 148, 149, 150, 159-65, 166-67; invisibil-ity of, 11, 13, 35, 76, 143, 148-49, 207, 215; of Kelowna/Okanagan Valley, 12, 127-44, 268-69; of landscape, 134-35, 265-69; and modernity, 19, 34, 45, 74-76, 80-82, 266-67; and multiculturalism, 3-4, 8-9, 147; and national iden-tity, 147, 166, 194-95, 280*n*1; of national parks, 12, 38, 64-65, 68-77, 80-81, 266; as "natural," 36; "painless" privileging of, 129, 279*n*2; and property capitalism, 19-21; and racial purity, 1, 35, 70-71, 153-54, 217, 265; scholar-ship on, 4-11, 14-15, 260, 271; of scientific knowledge, 11, 42-43, 45, 46, 47, 48-49, 51, 53-54, 58, 59-60; as social construction, 11, 215; of space, 11, 21, 22, 25-26, 29, 31-34, 37-38; of Toronto, 12, 86, 104-6, 107-26, 269; of US working class, 5-6; visibility of, 34-38, 72, 143, 271; of wilderness, 1, 2, 3, 7, 9-11, 13, 21-22, 25-26, 29-30, 31-38, 153-54, 193, 197, 200, 205-6, 207-9, 217, 264-71. *See also specif-ic topics*

wilderness: and "civilization," 32, 34, 136, 200, 202, 204-6, 208, 265-66; colonization and, 264-71; canoe-ing in, 10, 33, 267; as commodity, 32-34; disappearing, 11, 22-23, 26-30, 34, 37; and dispossession/displacement, 265-67; extremity of, 259-63; ghosts of, 22-23, 26-27, 30, 37; Grey Owl's production of, 21-22, 25-26, 29-30, 31-38; as male preserve, 200; and national identity, 1, 2-3, 10, 14, 31-34, 37-38, 150-52, 154-56, 259, 260; and race/racism, 1, 9-10, 153-54, 194-95, 260-61, 264-71; racial purity of, 1, 153-54, 217, 265; recreation-al uses in, 196, 198, 199, 202, 204-8, 265-66; as social construction, 194-95, 208-10; as tamed in hin-terland, 127-28, 129; as "virgin" space, 31, 32, 201-2, 207; white-ness of, 1, 2, 3, 7, 9-11, 13, 21-22, 25-26, 29-30, 31-38, 153-54, 193, 197, 200, 205-6, 207-9, 217, 264-71. *See also* conservation; hinter-land; nature

wildlife, of northern Canada: human
qualities of, 50-51, 57-58; and
Indigenous hunting practices, 41,
44-45, 47, 49-55, 57-58, 267; and
scientific research/management,
41, 43-58, 267
wildlife biologists, in northern Canada,
46-49, 55, 56; aerial surveys used
by, 46, 47-48, 54; and caribou
herd "crisis," 57; and Indigenous
knowledge, 46-51, 53-54, 57-58,
269; and perceived Indigenous
wastefulness, 41, 44-45, 47, 267
Wisconsin Land Tenure Center, 244
Wood Buffalo National Park, 44
Woodsworth, J.S., 92, 104
World Bank, 244-45, 251
World Commission on Environment
and Development, 41

Zueblin, Charles, 87

Printed and bound in Canada by Friesens

Set in Futura Condensed and Warnock by Artegraphica Design Co. Ltd.

Copy editor: Deborah Kerr

Proofreader: Helen Godolphin

Indexer: Cheryl Lemmens